Hardip Singh Syan has a PhD in South Asian History from the School of Oriental and African Studies, University of London. He has taught and worked at the University of London, the British Museum and the Institute of Historical Research.

SIKH MILITANCY IN THE SEVENTEENTH CENTURY

Religious Violence in Mughal and Early Modern India

HARDIP SINGH SYAN

I.B. TAURIS

LONDON · NEW YORK

Published in 2013 by I.B.Tauris
6 Salem Road, London W2 4BU
175 Fifth Avenue, New York NY 10010
www.ibtauris.com

Distributed in the United States and Canada
Exclusively by Palgrave Macmillan
175 Fifth Avenue, New York NY 10010

Library of South Asian History and Culture, vol. 4

ISBN 978 1 78076 250 0

A full CIP record for this book is available from the British Library
A full CIP record for this book is available from the Library of Congress

Library of Congress Catalog Card Number: available

Typeset by Newgen Publishers, Chennai
Printed and bound by CPI Group (UK) Ltd, Croydon, CR0 4YY

CONTENTS

ABBREVIATIONS

AG Adi Granth, *Sri Guru Granth Sahib Ji,* Bhai Javahar Singh Kirpal Singh, Amritsar, n.d.

AR Miharvanu Sodhi, *Adi Ramayan,* ed., Prem Sagar Shastri, Bhasha Vibag, Patiala, 1989.

AS Piar Singh, ed., *Shanbhu Nath Vali Janam Patri Babe Nanak ji ki: Prasidh nan Adi Sakhian,* Loeir Mal, Patiala, 1969.

B40 Abrol, Daya Ram, *The B40 Janam-Sakhi,* ed., and trans., W.H. McLeod, Guru Nanak Dev University, Amritsar, 1980.

Bala Kirpal Singh, ed., *Janamsakhi Parampara,* Punjabi University Patiala, Patiala, 1969.

BN Chhibbar, Kesar Singh, *Bhai Kesar Singh Chhibbar krit Bansavalinama dasa patashahia ka,* ed., Piara Singh Padam, Singh Brothers, Amritsar, 1995.

Dabistan Grewal, J.S & Irfan Habib, eds., *Sikh History from Persian Sources,* Fiction House, Lahore, 2004 [1998].

DG Dasam Granth, *Sri Dasam Granth Sahib: Path-Sampadan ate Wiakhia, Vols.5,* eds., Rattan Singh Jaggi & Gursharan Kaur Jaggi, Gobind Sadan, New Delhi, 1999.

Harji Harji Sodhi, *Goshti Guru Miharivanu,* ed., Govindnath Rajguru, Panjab University, Publication Bureau, Chandigarh, 1974.

HN Ganda Singh, ed., *Hukumname: Guru Sahiban, Mata Sahiban, Banda Singh ate Khalsa ji de,* Punjabi University, Patiala, 1999.

JN   'Ashok', Shamsher Singh, ed., *Prachin Vara te Jangname,* Shiromani Gurdwara Prabandak Committee, Amritsar, 1971.

Miharvan   Miharban Ji Sodhi, *Janamsakhi Sri Guru Nanak Dev Ji, Vol.1,* ed., Kirpal Singh, Sikh History Research Department, Khalsa College, Amritsar, 1962.

Sainapati   Sainapati, *Kavi Sainapati rachit Sri Gur Sobha,* ed., Ganda Singh, Publication Bureau, Punjabi University, Patiala, 1996 [1967].

SDG   Dasam Granth, *Sri Dasam Granth Sahib: Text and Translation, Vol.2,* eds., and trans., Jodh Singh & Dharam Singh, Heritage Publications, Patiala, 1999.

VG   Gurdas Bhalla (Bhai Gurdas), *Varan Bhai Gurdas,* eds., Hazara Singh and Vir Singh, Bhai Vir Singh Sahit Sadan, New Delhi, 2005 [1911].

1

THE EARLY HISTORY OF THE SIKH COMMUNITY

What is Sikhism? This is, without doubt, a question that all Sikhs and observers of the Sikh tradition have attempted to answer at one time or another. It is especially pertinent when we consider the prominent role of violence and warfare in Sikh doctrines and civil codes in the light of increasing regulation by the state. Notions of 'lawful' or 'religious' violence have become far removed from the social, political and intellectual climate of early modern South Asia but, nevertheless, attempts to explore the ways in which the past can inform contemporary Sikh attitudes to violence, politics and sovereignty turn inevitably to the very beginnings of the community in the sixteenth and seventeenth centuries. Such 'authentic' visions of Sikh militancy, however, are often bereft of the lively debates and dissenting expressions that gripped the hearts and minds of early Sikhs.

This study is an intellectual history of seventeenth century Sikh society in Panjab and their discussions on 'militancy' and Sikhism. It will explore how the Sikh movement engaged with the topic of religious violence which culminated in certain sections of Sikh society rebelling against the Mughal state and explore how the Sikh literati justified and criticised the adoption of violence in Sikh thought, and how the Sikh community responded to these developments in Sikhism. It will examine the influence of the Mughal state in shaping these Sikh discourses on violence and interrogate existing grand historiographical narratives that depict seventeenth century Sikh society as placidly facing Mughal 'persecution' and then, eventually, reacting violently in self-defence. Instead, I will show that the Sikh community developed sophisticated ideas on violence, sovereignty and social order. Significantly these rationalisations caused the 'militant' Sikh movements to develop a specific political judgement of Mughal power: a variety of political responses to Mughal power gave way to one dominant critique, which eventually challenged Mughal authority in the Panjab. Unlike previous studies, I will attempt to examine 'militancy' as a concept in medieval South Asia and specifically within the Sikh community. I will try to illustrate how Sikh 'militancy' evolved from its genesis as a gentry (*zamindari*) movement to a movement dedicated to political sovereignty. In this narrative I will not engage in labelling groups in terms of *doxa*. Even as I contextualise Sikh society within a larger Mughal domain, my focus on heterogeneity within Sikh society will also bring out its complicated response to imperial formation in the Panjab region.

Introducing the Historical Context

The origins of Sikhism are present amidst the teachings of the medieval north Indian intellectual and mystic, Guru Nanak (1469–1539).[1] Guru Nanak was born in Talwandi, Panjab, to a middling Khatri family. Nanak's father was a local administrator (*patwari*) employed in the service of the village headman and his extended family were also widely engaged in administrative service. Accordingly Nanak received an education geared towards administrative service and he briefly worked as an administrator for the Lodi kingdom. But since childhood Guru Nanak was mystically inclined, a quality which did not wane in adulthood. Nanak grew into a charismatic saint and gifted theologian in medieval India. Guru Nanak's writings were entirely in verse: they oozed with divine love and philosophic insights wrapped in prosodic beauty. The mystical philosophy enunciated by Nanak is often said to be a part of the *Sant* tradition, yet at the same time he is seen as a unique thinker.[2] Nanak's uniqueness resulted in the creation of his own *Panth* (path) and *Sampraday* (system of teaching). Commonly

Guru Nanak's community of supporters was known as the *Nanakpanth* (the path of Nanak) and the individual supporters were known as *Sikh* (lit. disciple/student).[3] Guru Nanak established the foundation of Sikh teachings and created a permanent community of Sikhs at Kartarpur, Panjab, in the early fifteenth century. Prior to his demise, Guru Nanak appointed a successor, Guru Angad (r.1539–52).

Guru Nanak's four immediate successors expanded the early Nanakpanth both in the Panjab and more generally throughout the subcontinent.[4] Early Sikh community formation grew more distinct with the development of Sikh scriptures, Sikh rituals and Sikh sacred sites. In particular the community flourished in central Panjab which became the mainstay region of early Sikhism. Such success resulted in hostility from the Mughal state. In 1606 the fifth Sikh Guru, Guru Arjan Dev (r.1581–1606), was executed on the order of Emperor Jahangir (r.1605–27). The precise reasons for this are unclear, but many scholars have attributed it to Mughal religious discrimination.[5] Others have embedded the execution in wider changes in Mughal religious policy from the reign of Akbar (r.1556–1605) to Jahangir.[6] Nonetheless, the execution of Guru Arjan was deeply symbolic and significant to early Sikh society.[7]

The execution of Guru Arjan resulted in the creation of two rival Sikh Guru lineages: one lineage was led by Arjan's son, Guru Hargobind (r.1606–44), and the other by Arjan's elder brother, Prithi Chand (r.1606–18). The two lineages crucially differed in their respective views on Sikhism. Guru Hargobind famously adopted a militaristic stance which gave emphasis to both temporal power and spiritual power. In contrast, Prithi Chand rejected this militancy for the sake of 'peace' which, he argued, was 'original' to Sikh thought. Prithi Chand's son and spiritual successor, Miharvan (r.1618–40) continued his father's ideas in opposition to Guru Hargobind.

In the following decades the lineage of Guru Hargobind suffered from another execution of a Guru by the Mughal state. In 1675, Guru Tegh Bahadur (r.1663–75) was executed on the command of Emperor Aurangzeb (r.1656–1707); Aurangzeb's order was seen by many scholars as a bigoted act.[8] Aurangzeb is notorious in Mughal history because of his desire to associate the Mughal state with a distinct Islamic ideology which many have seen as being hostile towards 'non-Muslims'.[9] It has been argued that this hostile atmosphere caused Mughal decline and created profound problems for early Sikh society.[10] In 1699, Guru Tegh Bahadur's son and spiritual successor, Guru Gobind Singh (r.1675–1708), created a militant Sikh order known as the Khalsa. The Khalsa adopted a specific martial courtesy and in the early eighteenth century, Khalsa Sikhs fought against local Mughal power in the Panjab.[11] This resulted in Sikh state formation throughout the eighteenth and nineteenth centuries in North India. Several powerful Sikh kingdoms emerged, the most famous being led by Ranjit Singh (d.1839).[12] In the 1840s these Sikh kingdoms, located largely in the Panjab, were targeted by the ever-expanding East India Company. This conflict resulted in two Anglo-Sikh Wars (1845–49) and, in 1849, the East India Company annexed these defiant Sikh kingdoms. In the 1857 uprising the remnants of these Sikh kingdoms mainly backed the East India Company.[13] Under crown rule (post-1857) the Sikhs of the Panjab became pivotal to British military reforms.[14]

The history of pre-colonial Sikhism was violent in the dominant historical narratives. Sikhism emerged as a 'peaceful' religious movement but this 'peace' was disrupted by external violence primarily caused by the Mughal state. Consequently, Sikh 'peace' developed 'militancy' for self-protection after the execution of Guru Arjan. Thereafter, the hostility of Aurangzeb created the need for Sikh sovereignty. In the eighteenth and nineteenth centuries Sikh armies fought numerous wars to secure kingdoms, which were violently annexed by the East India Company in the mid-nineteenth century. In Sikh narratives, Sikh violence or 'militancy' was a necessity: it reflected the intolerable conditions of Mughal India so was centred upon 'righteousness'. Yet this conception of Sikh 'righteousness' is ambivalent and the contemporary historiography continues to perceive 'violence' romantically and simplistically.

In colonial India the Sikh community became categorised as a 'martial race'.[15] Through the works of colonial historians and anthropologists, Sikhism came to be seen as a 'militant' faith.[16] This 'militancy' was seen to be embedded in Sikh religious thought and Sikh social practices and throughout colonial India (post-1857) the Sikh community had a prestigious position in the armed forces, particularly the Khalsa Sikhs, who were baptised and had unshorn hair and carried arms.[17] For colonial anthropologists Sikhs who lacked these martial emblems lacked the Sikh 'martial' spirit and were thus unable to join the army as Sikhs. While Sikh military culture had existed since the seventeenth century, colonial notions of 'militant' Sikhism had further crystallised the modern Sikh identity as Khalsa Sikh; non-Khalsa Sikhs were considered to be on the peripheries of 'real' Sikhism.[18] In modern India and the global diaspora this image of 'militant' Sikhism has remained: 'genuine' Sikhs wear turbans and carry daggers.[19] Sikhism is often defined as a devotional faith which emphasises 'loving' 'God', yet it is juxtaposed with 'violent' attributes which reflect the tribulations of early Sikh history. Interestingly, these are largely seen as being external to the community rather than being caused by internal divisions.

Colonial and post-colonial Sikh thinkers have had to deal with the issue of 'militant' Sikhism without any actual knowledge of Sikh 'militancy'. By this I mean Sikh martial arts and the techniques of warfare, as well as the warrior mentality, the ethics and strategy of warfare, and the physicality of war. The process of colonial demilitarisation in the subcontinent has still to be fully explored, but I feel it is fair to suggest that the transition from pre-colonial to colonial rule significantly altered native attitudes and techniques of warfare.[20] By the time reformist Sikh movements emerged in the late nineteenth century the 'glory days' of Sikh kingdoms had long passed.[21] Sikhs only knew of military life in British barracks and had only experienced leadership under British officers. Colonial military life brought new changes to Panjabi Sikh habits and tastes such as tea drinking and wearing western dress.[22] Sikh 'militancy' was thus preserved by the colony and not by Sikhs in their practices and ambitions.

Despite this ignorance, Sikhs continue to possess a vision of Sikh 'militancy' in its heyday. This memory of their past was stored in the chronicles and accounts of early modern Sikh writers, and accompanying these historical sources were lively imaginations. Modern Sikh audiences were eager to hear the heroic tales of their ancestors and fearless martyrs and Sikh intellectuals were willing to entertain. The leading

Sikh theologian and litterateur, Bhai Vir Singh (1872–1957), pioneered the Panjabi novel in the late nineteenth century.[23] Vir Singh's novels were focused on eighteenth century Sikh men and women battling against the tyranny of Muslim politics.[24] These novels romanticised early modern Sikh 'militancy' as a glorious time; in that period Sikh men were brave and pious, and Sikh women were chaste, even though Sikhs were being oppressed by evil Muslims. The appeal of Vir Singh's novels has not diminished in post-colonial Sikh society and ideas of pre-colonial Sikh masculinity and femininity are still rooted in the idealism of Sikh 'militancy'.[25] Contemporary Sikh terrorists and the call for a Sikh state (*Khalistan*) have been constructed on a historical narrative which intertwines retrospective views of early modern Sikh 'militancy', state oppression committed by the Indian government and a belief that the Panjab is the Sikh homeland.[26] But for many post-modern Sikhs this romantic vision of the past has lost its relevance: Sikh martial traditions should be moderated.[27] Of course, the realities of Sikh attitudes towards ethno-nationalism and Khalistan are incredibly diverse and perfectly reflect the heterogeneity of the contemporary Sikh experience, and in general there seems to be a dislike for actual violence beyond the rhetoric.[28] Yet most Sikhs continue to view the early history of Sikhism with rose-tinted lenses. The gory reality of war and violence is forgotten in a narrative which accepts that early Sikh society *had to* react violently against Mughal 'persecution'.[29]

Sikh Historiography: Understanding Early Sikh Militancy

In the post-1947 historiography (after India's independence in 1947) there has been, when studying the development of seventeenth century Sikh 'militancy', a general failure to deal with concepts of 'peace', 'war' and 'violence', beyond simplistic and presentist readings. In these historical narratives there is a surprising lack of squeamishness at the presence and discussion of violence in Sikh doctrines, in part because these narratives never engage with the realities of warfare, that is, of human beings intentionally killing other human beings. Instead there is an acceptance that violence was an appropriate method employed by Sikhs in light of Mughal 'persecution'. But there is a deeper point to this prevalent historical narrative which is that violence was an acceptable method of social protest in medieval India because medieval India was a violent society. From a modernist perspective, violence in medieval India is apparent in the arbitrary nature of justice under the Mughal state: in this medieval context 'peace' and 'violence' were clearcut. Medieval Sikh *helplessness* required violence for independence from Mughal power in order to create 'peace' in Sikh kingdoms.

This historiography identifies two precise phases of Sikh 'militancy': firstly under Guru Hargobind who introduces 'mild militarisation', and secondly under Guru Gobind Singh who introduces 'full militarisation'.

The first phase was seen as a reaction to Guru Arjan's execution. Khushwant Singh vividly captures the romanticism of this moment by arguing: "Arjun's blood became the seed of the Sikh church as well as of the Punjabi nation" and it led "from a peaceful propagation of the faith to the forthright declaration of the right to defend that faith by force of arms".[30] While Singh's view is popular, McLeod and Grewal provided more nuanced approaches. McLeod wrote:

> The development which tradition ascribes to a decision by Guru Hargobind must have preceded, and in some measure prompted, the first Mughal efforts to curb the growing power of the community. The conflict with the Mughals certainly exercised a most important influence upon the subsequent development of the Panth, but not an influence of the kind attributed to it by Sikh tradition. The growth of militancy within the Panth must be traced primarily to the impact of Jat cultural patterns and to economic problems which prompted a militant response.[31]

Somewhat differently Grewal comments:

> The action of the state authorities was a stunning blow to the followers of Guru Arjan. Whether it was due to the intrigues of the slanderers of the Guru, or enmity of some local administrator, or the autocratic prejudice of the emperor, the injustice was patent enough. Guru Hargobind reacted to the event in proportion to

the enormity of the injustice. He girded two swords, as the Sikh tradition puts it, one symbolizing his spiritual authority and the other his temporal power. He encouraged his followers in martial activity. The Jat component of his followers needed only a little persuasion.[32]

All three historians accept Sikh 'militancy' as a common sense response. The emergence of violence is seen as 'natural': there is no qualification about what 'violence' means beyond 'self-defence'. However, McLeod and Grewal do raise the issue of audience; stating which Sikhs would have been receptive to 'militant' rhetoric.

The second phase is also seen as necessary and slightly spasmodic. Guru Gobind Singh reacts to the 'intolerant' milieu created by Aurangzeb. In Hari Ram Gupta's opinion: "Guru Gobind Singh reflected on the history of India as well as the history of the Sikhs... The greatest need of the time was to create a national army. Such an army was based on social justice... and... was to be inspired by feelings of patriotism and nationalism... This objective was achieved by his creation of the Khalsa".[33] The Khalsa were replacing the Rajputs: "the Rajputs were a valiant people, but they had failed in preserving India's independence".[34] Gupta's overt nationalism was not reiterated in other histories. For instance, McLeod argued that later Sikh 'militancy' was caused by Guru Gobind Singh's residency in the Panjabi hills and its *Shakti* (power) culture:

> The prolonged residence within the Sivaliks was that elements of the hill culture eventually penetrated the Jat Sikh culture of the plains and produced yet another stage in the evolution of the Panth. It is in the works of Guru Gobind Singh and in the developments which followed his death that we can observe this influence most plainly.[35]

There is still no discussion on the method of violence, rather it is assumed as an appropriate method for social protest. But what is subliminal even in these narratives is that Sikh 'militancy' was imbued with justice; Bhagat Singh comments on eighteenth-century Sikh chiefdoms:

The main springs of the ideals of the Sikh chiefs were the teachings of the *Gurus*. The Sikhs being dissociated from the ancient
past by many centuries and being not conversant with the Vedic
and other literature, they could not look back to the Hindu polity for guidance. The Mughal practices they had found to be very
irksome…[in response]. They brought into full play the great
qualities of service to humanity, clemency, forgiveness, humility, justice, equality, liberalism, respect and regard for women,
etc.[36]

There is no discussion by Bhagat Singh on the violence committed
by Sikh chiefs: Sikh violence was seen as 'good' violence as opposed to
'evil' violence committed by the likes of Aurangzeb.

In recent years this historical narrative has received critical attention from cultural historians who have tried to elaborate upon Sikh
military culture. In Deol's study of late seventeenth century Khalsa
culture he has argued that the Khalsa were embedded into a 'Puranic
metanarrative' of righteousness (*dharma*).[37] In addition, Deol argued
that early Sikh military culture was a product of a 'Rajput episteme':

What happened to the Khalsa at the end of the seventeenth-
century was far from a simple adoption of Rajput status: the
symbolic overtones of the discourses adopted by the Gurus
reflected in discourses about their followers, who became clas-
sicised *chhatri* warriors defending *dharma* and right. It appears
then that the Rajput episteme was used as a cultural referent for
high status, a discourse that contributed to a new metaphorical
and cultural position for the Guru and his Panth.[38]

Deol's thesis is useful because he attempts to understand Sikh military culture in the context of late seventeenth-century Mughal India.
Moreover, Deol's study articulates upon Sikh notions of 'courtesy' and
provides a possible understanding of Sikh ideas regarding violence.
Yet Deol's views are also problematic because he adopts a functionalist notion of a monolithic ahistorical 'Rajput' identity in Mughal
India without adequately considering the locality and local cultures.

Furthermore, Deol's thesis never directly engages with violence as a contested concept: Sikh 'militancy' continues to be seen as somehow 'natural' and chivalrous. In contrast, Dhavan's work on eighteenth-century Sikh chiefdoms provides greater focus on the locality and caste groups.[39] But Dhavan, too, never engages with the issue of violence: Sikhism by the eighteenth century is fully militarised and Sikh culture is inherently 'militant'.

The common feature found in these Sikh histories is the belief there is a shift from 'peace' to 'militancy'. All these histories have argued that Sikh society moved from being 'peaceful' to being 'violent', yet no historian has contextualised the notion of 'peace' and 'violence' in medieval India. No history has questioned whether 'militancy' was necessary in the seventeenth century. No history has considered early Sikh dialectics over 'militancy' and this is because they define Sikhism with narrow 'orthodoxy'.[40] Finally all these histories see violence as a tool of 'self-protection' but no history has linked religious/political violence to social order.

The history of early Sikh 'militancy' is seen to occur without any internal contestation. By comparison, Christian theologians debated the idea of 'just war' as opposed to the 'holy war' prescribed by Islamic theologians.[41] Yet medieval Sikh society has been portrayed as shifting from 'peace' to 'militancy' without any dialectics over the value of violence. For instance, there has been no discussion about Sikh distinctions between 'good' and 'bad' violence, nor has there been any discussion on Sikh social order.[42] The history of violence and its relationship to social order are well-established; acts of violence are typically embedded into discourses on social order and the conduct of war.[43] The fundamental problem with these current Sikh histories is they are viewing Sikh history with the romanticism fostered during the colonial period; and ultimately they adopt a modern Euro-American view (or Anglo-Saxon view) that there is firm difference between 'peace' and 'violence'.[44] This Euro-American dichotomy over 'peace' and 'violence' is linked to Enlightenment Christian 'love' and the history of violence and warfare in Western Europe.[45]

The reason why the history of seventeenth century Sikh 'militancy' has primarily been shown to lack contestation is due to the huge impact of *doxa* on Sikh history writing. Sikh history has thus far been written from [a relatively presentist] 'orthodox' angle and by this I mean that several principles are considered axiomatic to the Sikh 'tradition'. These principles include: a belief in ten Gurus from Guru Nanak to Guru Gobind Singh; the belief in the sacredness of the *Adi Granth* as an exclusive Sikh text or certain *Adi Granth* manuscript tradition; a belief in a 'legitimate' Sikh theology; and a belief in 'schismatic' Sikh movements. While Oberoi's study of colonial Sikh thought and praxis did raise some of these issues when defining 'Sikhism', his study primarily focused upon religious diversity in the Sikh tradition. Moreover, Oberoi's divide between 'Sanatan Sikh' and 'Singh Sabha Sikh' is analytically weak; it creates a simple binary model to understand the epistemic shift from colonial to post-colonial Sikhism. But what we are left with is another hegemonic divide where all precolonial Sikhs are described as 'Sanatan' and all colonial and post-colonial Sikhs as 'Singh Sabha'. I feel in recent postmodernist studies on Sikhism this tunnel-vision over 'Sanatan' opposed to 'Singh Sabha' continues to exercise a major influence but it displays a certain form of Sikhism which I would describe as 'elitist', because it sees religion as something which Sikhs live with independently from their communal identities (such as caste rank, kinship ties and socio-economic status). By contrast, anthropological studies on Sikh communities will underline how Sikhism is a lived experience: Sikh communities practice their faith along with their communal identities.[46] There is something we can label 'Sikhism', but these Sikh social markers operate alongside communal social markers. When we examine Sikh societies we have to examine Sikhism heterogeneously and not homogenously. It is imperative we abandon the belief in axiomatic Sikh principles and instead embrace a view in which Sikhism is a lived tradition. This is not to suggest that Sikhism is indefinable, rather these axiomatic principles must not be too exclusive.

The heterogeneous Sikh community can only be shown by writing Sikh history from new angles. Thus far early Sikh histories have been written without reference to the intellectual debates of ordinary Sikhs,[47] positing a completely coherent view of Sikhism in which Sikhs have no power to discourse on religion. This is because when any Sikh agent suggested ideas which were contrary to an emerging 'dominant' Sikh tradition they were labelled 'unorthodox' and instantly marginalised. Yet these internal disputes on early Sikhism show an angle of Sikh history which is variegated: Sikh communities were trying to fathom 'religion' in relation to their own lives. This allows us to trace the evolution of Sikhism not as a unified religion but from diverse communal perspectives. I disagree with the historiographical argument that there is a shift from a sixteenth century Sikh 'peace' to a seventeenth century Sikh 'militancy'. In order to understand seventeenth century Sikh dialectics on violence we must understand the nature of sixteenth century Sikh community formation and the manner in which they conceptualised religious violence. This is because I believe that firstly, the exclusive historiographical distinctions between religion – i.e., 'peace' – and violence are historically unjustified. By extension I also argue that, with more careful interrogation and historicisation, the supposedly novel experience of 'religious violence' in the seventeenth century may not, in fact, appear so unique. Secondly, the Sikh community has been depicted in terms of caste identities where some castes are intrinsically bellicose and others are passive. While I do agree that caste groups did have variant caste practices and identities, I am unwilling to ascribe homogenous typologies to specific sub-castes. Shared regional commonalities may too easily mask the various factors which influenced community formation so that the extent of their differences is not always clear.

The Compatibility of Religion and Violence

The problems that we face when examining the history of religious violence in South Asia, and elsewhere, stem from the history of religious violence in Western Europe and by extension North America. Such a history of religious violence is ultimately the story of religious toleration and multiculturalism: how do communities with different beliefs and backgrounds live together in harmony and mutual respect. Contemporary western societies are dealing directly with this issue in relation to Islam, immigration and diaspora communities. Often the polemics of these multicultural tensions dissolve into

polarised discussions about indigenous 'values' versus foreign 'values'
and whether they are compatible. It is obvious that no society has
so far found a perfect model for multiculturalism and that unfortunately intolerance for others seems to emerge in every age. That being
said, the intellectual history of the modern West does present itself
as being a history of growing tolerance. Typically the story of western
triumph starts in the 1650s; the intolerant 'wars of religion' culminated in the 1648 Peace of Westphalia. After that important truce
the Protestant and Catholic states of Europe had lost their hunger
to create Christendom: the 'wars of religions' had proved too costly.
While in the Middle Ages chivalrous societies had also attempted to
curb the dangers of unfettered violence through 'the Peace of God'
and 'the Truce of God', the following centuries had seen radical developments in Western Christianity.[48] The Enlightenment resulted in
the secularisation of society and the victory of empiricism over faith.
This created religious toleration by privatising faith. The removal of
religion from the public sphere caused major changes as Christian
piety became expressed through private worship dedicated to loving God and performing charity.[49] This change within Christianity
reflected political changes since the times of religious warfare, with
Christian states no longer fighting for God and Christ. In Western
eyes religious violence was undermined: 'true' religions could not
be violent because religion was about private worship and love. Of
course, this western triumphalism is a fantasy because Christian
warfare continued against fellow Christians and non-Christians
throughout the Enlightenment and beyond.[50] Kaplan has suggested
that the Enlightenment did not produce 'tolerance'; it produced a
distinctive 'code of civility' amongst European elites "according to
this code, the well-bred were supposed to be reasonable, moderate in
temper, refined in tastes, not given to passions and prejudices. They
were to be interested in the arts and sciences and devoted to the
improvement of humanity. Urbane, sociable, and always polite, they
were supposed to accept people's differences—including their varied
religious beliefs".[51] But this 'code of civility' produced 'intolerance'
for religious violence because only certain forms of religiosity were
'legitimate' in the eyes of the new elite. 'Reasonable' Christianity in

particular marginalised the fervour of militant Christianity that had once been its main expression.

This condescending European attitude about 'progression' and 'liberalism' never engaged with the Christian theory of 'just war'. Modern international law on the legitimacy of warfare has been constructed upon the 'just war' tradition without adequate consideration of violence and religion in other societies.[52] Contemporaneously, the West is unable to comprehend the violence in political Islam because they feel that Western violence does not invoke religious sentiments; they argue Islam per se is not 'bad', but there are certain *types* of Islam which are.[53] These forms of 'bad' Islam endorse religious violence and not the private worship of God: 'violent' Islam is a throwback to the militant fervour of Christian fundamentalism. However, the modern West has never tried to engage with the cultural and historical developments of other societies or with the 'intolerant' sections of its own societies. If the Enlightenment could not make all Europeans into 'tolerant' and 'civilised' human beings, then perhaps they should re-consider their both own intellectual heritage alongside that of other societies. As Kelsay has illuminated, Muslims do have a great tradition of 'just war' but the key to postmodernity is a universal dialogue on the rules of civility.[54] All societies have cultural and intellectual histories of violence and these histories must be explored.

Religious Violence in Medieval India

The cultural history of violence in South Asia has been profoundly shaped by its association with neo-Hinduism in modernity; and the relationship between Islam and Hinduism since the early medieval period. Gandhi's ideas on 'non-violence' and civil disobedience have been globalised, and through his influence Hinduism is often seen as a 'non-violent' and 'loving' faith. Yet such a perspective of religions in South Asia ignores the lengthy intellectual history of violence in South Asian religions, which often legitimised non-violence and violence.[55] Even Gandhian notions of non-violence were meant to coerce the 'victims' into changing their views by compelling them to be 'compassionate': Gandhi's 'non-violence' was a form of psychological violence.[56]

The history of communalism in South Asia has been dominated by the supposed conflict between the inherently 'aggressive' Islam and the naturally 'pacifist' Hinduism. This alleged conflict was particularly stressed by colonial scholars and the communal violence of the modern era further strengthened the existence of a conflict.[57] But to suggest this conflict was somehow rooted in the past and part-and-parcel of the South Asian mentality has been firmly dismissed by recent historical research.[58] Iconic events such as Hindu temple desecration by Muslim raiders in the medieval period have been contextualised within the political economy of India and have revealed the absence of communal conflict.[59] Significantly, historical research has demonstrated how neither 'Islam' nor 'Hinduism' was monolithic; instead Muslim and Hindu communities had immense internal diversities.[60] Pinch has further shown that South Asian religious violence does not share post-Enlightenment Christian binaries about religion and violence.[61] Examining ascetic warriors in early modern and modern South Asia, he demonstrates how they continued to believe in asceticism but also engaged in violence, politics and licentious behaviour.[62] These 'violent' yogis might appear contradictory and hypocritical because as ascetics they should have withdrawn from the world and not participated in politics and murder. But these ascetics openly and unashamedly acted like what we might today describe as organised crime gangs, albeit ones with strong ascetic principles. Pinch lucidly explains how it was due to their beliefs in *hatha-yoga* (violent yoga) which, through its austerities, confers immortality on earth.[63] With this immortality came god status and supernatural powers. The ascetic warrior was an ascetic because he had spiritually conquered death, and a warrior because immortality guaranteed him worldly power. Accordingly, there was no contradiction between being 'peaceful' ascetics and 'militant' warriors. This peculiar mix between violence and religion, and detachment and attachment, might seem curious to modern eyes. In medieval India, we also find this strange mix among Islamic groups: Digby informs us of roaming *Qalandars* who are frequently shown as being violent and threatening though at the same time they have opted out of 'life'.[64]

Unfortunately, in South Asian studies, there have not been many works on the cultural history of violence. In contrast, both the

Christian idea of just war and the Islamic idea of jihad have received much analysis.[65] In recent years, South Asian medievalists have begun to examine the 'civility' of medieval warfare, research which opens up new avenues for the history of violence.[66] The Sikh movement represents a fertile area for research because the Sikhs in Mughal India were essentially a religious group which adopted 'militancy' of a type which interweaved religious violence and courtly civility. But so far the history of Sikh 'militancy' has suffered from this modern dichotomy of 'peace' and 'militancy'.

The history of the early Sikh community is shown as having made a 'shift' from being 'peaceful' to 'militant'. The arguments of McLeod and Grewal were based on the premise that 'militancy' arrived in the Sikh community following the execution of Guru Arjan. But this implies that 'militancy' was absent from early Sikh thought and, taking into account the views of Pinch on ascetic warriors, it is necessary to explore just how fine this division between 'peace' and 'militancy' was in early Sikh thought.

Sikhism is said to have sprung from a belief in devotionalism (*Bhakti*) of the Sant tradition.[67] The Sants are portrayed as being solely interested in loving God with pious meditation. This is essentially correct, but it creates an image of *Sant Bhakti* as essentially 'peaceful'. However, if we look at three major Sant movements: the Sikhs, the Kabirpanth and the Dadupanth, we can see a common pattern by the late seventeenth century: all three began life as 'peaceful' devotional movements but by the late seventeenth century they all had military wings. The Sikhs created the Khalsa in Panjab; the Kabirpanth spearheaded the Satnami rebellion in 1672; and the Dadupanth had developed a wing of Rajput/ascetic warriors.[68] The question is, why did this change happen? And, more importantly, was this change simply one of 'peace' to 'militancy', or was it a reflection of 'original' Sant beliefs?

Medieval India had numerous theological schools that interacted with each other, often in competition. These competitions were not only about dialectics and eristics but about showing power, usually of a supernatural and miraculous nature; a display of grace and power beyond the intellect. The group most often depicted in medieval literature as possessing and demonstrating this miraculous power were *hatha-yoga* masters. These yogis appear in competition with Sufi masters and Bhakti saints.[69] The powers of these yogis were given a healthy respect but they themselves were unusual characters who lived on the edges of society, actually and morally; they could be pious or corrupt. As Pinch notes:

> *Bhakti* reformers were adamant in their disdain for *yogis* who claimed special powers by virtue of their hatha yogic and/or tantric prowess. The *bhakti* literature is rife with examples of puffed up *yogis* who are deflated and sent packing by humble, God-loving *sadhus*... From the *bhakti* perspective, a loving alliance between ascetic and sovereign, immersed together in loving devotion to Ram or Krishna, could be productive of great things. Wrongly constituted, however, it was susceptible to great mischief. If the sovereign was too easily taken in, or if the ascetic had an evil heart full of ulterior motives, civilization itself could be undermined.[70]

In early Sikh literature, too, the appearance of *hatha-yogis* was common. Many of Guru Nanak's hymns appear in contestation with such yogis.[71] In these anecdotes Guru Nanak rejects the lifestyle and asceticism of these yogis in favour of the householder's path. This distinction between 'householder' and 'renunciant' has not received adequate attention in the study of Sikh theology. But they comprise crucial choices for South Asian theologians when considering the 'purpose' of human life and 'militancy'.

A Medieval Debate: Householder versus Renunciant

In ancient and medieval South Asian theology and hermeneutics the issue of renunciation holds a central place.[72] The doctrines of the Upanishads created several axiomatic principles which can be seen as central to Indic religious traditions. Aside from these principles is the pivotal issue of how to live life. The Upanishadic framework argues the aim of life was to achieve liberation from the cycle of transmigration. This desire for salvation, more or less, dominated the spiritual aims of the Indic traditions. The question that remains is how to go about it and achieve this end? Renunciation became a popular option and is privileged in Brahmanical, Buddhist and Jain traditions. In order to curb the dangers of renunciation the Brahmanical tradition developed the well-known four stages of life (*ashrama*).[73] These saw renunciation as only the last phase in a man or woman's life, one in which they might understand that life was illusionary and thus achieve freedom from transmigration. But its dangers were the abandonment of all social/religious rituals and the potential disregard for the Vedic tradition. Thus the choice of being a householder or a renunciant was not an irrelevant aspect of Brahmanical and Indic theology but rather one which shapes its entire fabric. This is because if one believes in renunciation as being pivotal to human salvation it means life must be designed to include it.

In medieval India, discussions on the value of renunciation interested almost every thinker and intellectual circle. Its most famous proponent was the Advaita philosopher Shankra (788–820 C.E.) who established a popular monistic school of thought and reputedly founded the *Dasanami Naga* ascetic sect. As the Sanskrit literati were gradually replaced by the vernacular Bhakti tradition, the discourse of renunciation did not lose its relevance. In the medieval Bhakti tradition of the Sant strand its cardinality is largely rejected: Sants like Guru Nanak argue that loving God with true affection is enough to liberate the self from transmigration, so people may live as householders and never need to renounce the world. They would solve their inner conflict by being a renouncer within. This internal renunciation argues that man can only curb his senses by confronting them in the world and learning the ultimate reality. To show this belief in practice in early Sikh thought we can inspect several verses from the *Adi Granth*:

Many mendicants (*bhekh kari*) are lost in confusion (*bharmieiai*);
In their hearts (*hirda*) they practice deceit (*kapatu*).
In their heart they do not keep the Lord's form (*har ka mahalu*);
With death they are reabsorbed into the filth (*vista*) [of the womb]. (1)
Oh my mind, in the household (*grih*) remain in detachment (*udas*).

Performing genuine self-restraint (*sachu sanjamu*) [in the household];

In that Sikh (*gurmukhi*), who does so, shines forth (*pragat*) [discipleship]. (1) (Pause)[74]

In the fool (*manmukh*) attachment (*moh*) is ever-pervading (*viapia*);

[That fool] becomes an ascetic (*bairagu*) but never obtains separation (*udasi*) [from the world].

[The fool] never recognises the word (*shabadu*) [of God] and remains always in pain;

[The fool] even in the Lord's assembly [i.e. with the saints] remains oblivious to the Lord (*pati*).

The Sikh (*gurmukh*) has destroyed his ego (*haumai*);

[The Sikh] has adorned the Name [of God] and is now in bliss (*sukh*). (1)

My mind, day and night, those everyday hopes (*nit asa*) remain abundant [causing me pain].

Through service (*sevi*) to the True Master (*satgur*), attachment then burns [into nothingness];

In the household remain in detachment. (1) (Pause)[75]

The self (*mata*) wants to go west; [but the Lord] takes you north.

In an instant the constructor changes plans;

In our hands there is just intention. (1)

Our intelligence (*sianap*) does not [give us the ability to] fulfil our desires (*kami*);

Whatever my Lord (*thakur*) dictates (*anrupiu*) only that narrative (*bat*) happens. (1) (Pause)

[The individual really] desires obtaining land and wealth;

But within the body breath (*sas*) is disappearing.

In the end, armies (*lashkar*), commanders (*naib*), and servants (*khvas*) depart;

To the realm of death (*jam puri*) they travel. (2)

Becoming stubborn (*anani*) and self-centred, knowing only you as great.

[The saints] have left the world filled with falsehood (*nind*) and
joined a world of truth (*anind*);
In that realm they reside and eat. (3)
To whom the beneficent (*kirpala*) has given natural glory (*sahaj
sobha*) [i.e. spiritual truth];
That slave has also had the snares of death cut.
Says Nanak, those who have merged with the absolute Master;
Their blessing (*parwan*) is visible in the household and
renunciation.[76]

This viewpoint was in sharp contrast to those groups such as masters of *hatha-yoga* who argued that renunciation was fundamental to
achieving immortality. The Sants did not reject the idea of immortality – for them, it came from union with God and resulted in freedom
from death. The yogis argued this immortality would come through
mystical austerities which gave one freedom from death and power on
earth. This power allowed them to be bloodthirsty, violent, ascetic
warriors. Importantly, 'sin' or 'action' no longer applied to liberated
souls because the theory of cause and effect (*karma*) was applicable
only to souls in transmigration. Liberated souls achieved a position
of neutrality from 'virtue' and 'vice'; a freedom from 'action'. It was
here that 'violence' intermingled with 'religion': since 'violence' was
the power to bring death to others and carried with it karmic pun-
ishment, while an immortal could not be killed nor punished for
violence.

All these groups were searching for the nectar of immortality
(*amrit*). This nectar when drunk would undoubtedly result in some
sort of personal metamorphosis; an enlightenment and freedom from
death.[77] But where is it to be found? Guru Nanak's discourses with
the *yogis* centred upon debates over liberation and the value of asceticism in this objective. Nanak insisted that the 'name of God' is the
key to gaining *amrit* (immortality) and he flatly refuses to endorse the
power of renunciation. Instead he argued that the renunciant can only
exist within the world and has no need to renounce it, because he can
never escape it or life's needs.[78] In Guru Nanak's view, a householder
could achieve liberation by reciting the name and cleansing the self

without the need for any austerities. Importantly though, Guru Nanak does not refuse the *yogi's* point that there is such an end where there is immortality.

The major similarity, then, in medieval ascetic and devotional traditions is the belief in immortality. Both ascetics and devotional thinkers believe in the need for liberation, with which came divine union, metaphysical knowledge and supernatural powers. In the ascetic and devotional traditions the fully realised saint is considered to be a conqueror over death. The *hatha-yoga* masters literally believe in the immortality of their corporeal selves. The devotional thinkers accepted the mortality of the body but an immortality of the self; they refer to immortality with metaphors like 'crossing the ocean'.[79] Yet the end point was immortality and on earth a supernatural power and protection.

This supernatural power attached to immortality has what appears to the modern sensibility to be a 'strange' relationship to violence. This is because the warrior ascetics use their immortal charisma to be politically active. But the *yogi* was dually armed. On the one hand, he had actual weapons like swords and, eventually, guns. On the other hand, he had supernatural weapons to curse, maim and kill his opponents; these included the inability to die because the *yogi* had drunk the nectar of immortality by gaining the protection of gods/goddesses. These supernatural powers were religious powers obtained through austerities, yet they were also violent powers and made the *yogi* into an unstoppable force who inspired awe and fear. Bhakti devotees also possessed this peaceful/violent power. This is because once they obtained union with the divine they came under the protection of that divinity. Therefore they too became figures that could curse and/or kill, if human beings displeased them. In Guru Nanak's hagiographies he is portrayed not as a passive saint, but one capable of hurting those who do not respect him and acknowledge his grace.[80] While the image of the Sant saint is always of the 'peaceful' ascetic, one must not forget they inspired fear: that of offending the sacred and being cursed. This was ultimately a violent and militant fear.

The power of the 'curse' in Hindu traditions was frequently associated with *Rishis* (seers), Brahmans and ascetics. They were men who had supernatural powers, but no actual physical powers such as armies or even physical strength; their potency lay in their ascetic heat (*tapas*). In Ziegler's discussion of medieval Rajput traditions he remarks:

> It is often the Jogi (*sammi*-master) who has cast a curse (*sarap*) upon one ruler and presented the Raj to another Rajput as a boon (*var*), in return for his devoted service...Inherent within this system of ideas is the cultural conception that words, in particular the words of the Devi, the Brahman, the Caran, Jogi, and Pir (*Akalvamt*), etc., themselves have power. In very real sense, the potential for Rajput action and fulfilment of dharma are seen to be located in these "words". For it is through them that power is seen to be transferred. The words of the Jogi in the form of a curse (*sarap*) are seen to divest a ruler of power and cause him loss of his kingdom. The Jogi's words in the form of a blessing, just as those of the Rishi or Devi, etc., also give power and enable action. Thus power and action, both constituents of the code of conduct of the Rajput, reside in words as well as in the body of the Rajput himself.[81]

In sum the saint was never a passive figure; their 'words' were seen as critical to action. Therefore, apotheosised individuals were feared and respected because they could 'speak' and cause death. This is a militancy which even mighty kings feared and honoured in the medieval context.

The presence of verbal 'militancy' in 'peaceful' saints can be found in many compositions of the Sikh Gurus. An example which succinctly expresses this power of the protected saint was composed by Guru Arjan. This composition was specifically written with reference to a Khatri merchant, Marvahe, who attempted to slander Guru Amar Das:

> The petition (*mahajaru*) brought by you was full of falsehood (*jhuta*);
> On the sinner (*papi*) [who brought this petition] fell this grief (*santap*). (1)
> Whoever my Lord (*mera gobind*) wishes to protect (*sahiei*);

To them death (*jam*) does not come near. (1) (Pause)
[In the court of Akbar] you speak rubbish about the true court
[of Guru Amar Das];
The hands and head of the blind fool (*andha mur*) were seized. (2)
Doing such sin [against protected saints] results in illness (*rog*);
The Lord himself sits as the Just [*adali*] Judge. (3)
Acting alone, alone you are imprisoned;
Your fortune (*darb*) [disappears] when your companionship with
life [ends]. (4)
Nanak [Guru Amar Das] is protected in the court [of God];
Sent and protected by the Lord. (5)[82]

The slanderer was not given mercy for his crimes. Instead he had
challenged the protected saint and had incited the wrath of God.
For both faithful and sceptics, this showed a real power to inflict
violence on human beings. Theirs was a fear of impending furious
vengeance unleashed by the divine on those who attempted to harm
his friends.

The point which I want to emphasise is that the separation between
'peace' and 'militancy' seems to be blurred in medieval South Asian
theology. Saints might have been peaceful figures but their divine
aura is considered to be under the protection of higher authorities and
came with supernatural powers. These powers made them 'violent'
figures because they could curse and thereby harm and/or kill other
human beings. The reason why this is important in the Sikh case is
because I contend that it is not the case that militancy or violence is
something which emerges in early Sikh society. Militancy had always
existed in the immortality of the Guru and his divine presence. The
issue is, what type of militancy was it? Was it an overt physical violence like that practised by the warrior ascetics found in Pinch's history? Or was it a more subtle violence which surrounded the sanctity
of a saint?

The significance of this paradox over peace/militancy in medieval
South Asian theology and early Sikh thought might not seem immediately obvious. However, in the seventeenth century, when the Sikh
movement develops 'militancy', an argument will emerge regarding

the type of violence that Sikhs should practise. Should it be a peaceful inner violence or an overt political violence? The point I wish to make is that early Sikh society did not *shift* from peace to militancy; they changed the *type* of religious violence they practised. This shift was a contentious issue of debate throughout the seventeenth century and incorporated Vaishnava and Shakti ideas of righteousness and sovereignty.

Medieval Panjabi-Sikh Society: Cultures of Violence

The question of why human beings see violence as a legitimate means to achieve an end has hardly had a consensual resolution. At opposite ends of the spectrum, it has been argued that violence is driven by human biology and genetics, or arises from the social context.[83] Without getting into the merits, or not, of these interpretations, it would be hard to argue against the performative character of violence and its availability as a social and cultural resource. Violence is a socially available option, but it is one that is rationalised: human societies have an aversion to violence but see it as necessary when the circumstances call for it. It is a resource which controls 'unruly' elements in society; human societies, therefore, usually make distinctions between 'good' and 'bad' violence.

The development of 'militancy' in seventeenth century Sikhism has been associated with caste groups: the early history of the Sikh community is heavily influenced by inherent notions of caste in medieval Panjab. These divisions are between high and low statuses, purity and impurity, with social mobility being virtually non-existent. This notion of caste results in a static conception of society in which caste groups had inherent 'natures'. Notably two caste groups have been correctly identified as being the main supporters of the early Sikh community in Panjab: the Khatris and Jats. They are also two communities who have been depicted as the antitheses of each other. These contrasts include: urban/rural, mercantile/agricultural, literate/illiterate, high caste/low caste, non-violent/violent and so forth. These views were largely introduced by McLeod's revisionist analysis of early Sikh evolution:

All ten Gurus came from Khatri families and there are indica-
tions that the Khatris commanded a particular influence within
the Panth during its early years. From the very beginning, however, many Jats were attracted to the Guru's following . . . The origins of the Jat community are still disputed . . . with their strong
rural base, their martial traditions, their normally impressive
physique, and their considerable energy the Jats have for many
centuries constituted the elite of the Punjab villages . . . Why did
the Jats enter this new Panth in such large numbers? Their evident willingness to do so was presumably facilitated by the fact
that Khatris commonly served as teachers to the Jats. Khatris
could be expected to direct their teachings to Jats, and Jats could
be expected to respond.[84]

Indeed, McLeod's brief statement is self-evident in displaying the
apparent opposites in Khatri and Jat communities. He goes on to state
"the growth of militancy within the Panth must be traced primarily to the impact of Jat cultural patterns and to economic problems
which prompted a militant response".[85] Notwithstanding the merits
in McLeod's analysis, he takes a rather simplistic look into caste communities in medieval Panjab, making a major assumption in arguing
that these differences were as clear-cut as day and night. Instead these
caste communities had similarities with each other, but, even more
pertinently, within their internal caste structures they had differences
in how they viewed their endogamous and exogamous groups. So, for
instance, within the Khatri community two *gotra* (clans) groups could
be the direct opposite of one another: although they are, on the face
of it, Khatris, because of their differences in internal purity, matrimonial and kinship relations any other simlarities might be non-existent.
These complexities need proper attention – we must not reduce them
to stereotypes.

Nevertheless, stereotypical portrayals of caste groups are common.
Although Grewal's narrative of this period underlines the complexities of caste society, he sometimes provides a historically contingent
explanation for their social location and at other times he uses an
understanding of 'nature' to explain the attributes of their inherent

predispositions. Compare, for example, his treatment of the Khatris with the Jats. Regarding the former he states:

> All the Gurus, thus, were Khatris with a rural background. The subcastes to which they belonged were not among the important Khatri subcastes, not even the Bedi subcaste to which the founder of the Sikh Panth belonged. Their social position was rather low among the Khatris.[86]

Grewal notes that not all Khatris were the same; some enjoyed greater social prestige than other clans (*gotra*). However, when Grewal discusses Sikh militarisation in the seventeenth century he states the "the Jat component of his followers needed only a little persuasion".[87] The Jats are not differentiated; they are all 'militant' or embrace militancy. Both McLeod and Grewal are arguing that the Jats had a greater propensity for committing acts of violence and performing violent social roles than the Khatris. Significantly there is also a physiological element to this argument because McLeod states that the Jats had 'impressive physiques', implying the Khatris were physiologically weaker. Also, both assume that the Khatris have no martial traditions even though they held the warrior rank (*Kshatriya*).[88]

The idea that the Jats are 'violent' and the Khatris 'non-violent' is completely unqualified in the writings of the two historians. On the other hand, in medieval Panjab there seems to have developed a common 'Panjabi' culture which possessed a shared notion of 'elite' violence. By this I mean that Panjabis expressed their power of violence through certain common methods such as having a Kshatriya identity. Yet there were also separate cultures of 'caste' violence: for instance, Jat groups expressed their violent identities through tribal tales of honour and vendettas. By contrast, Khatris expressed their violent identities through codes of chivalry. The contrast between Jat and Khatri ideas of violence is significant when considering how seventeenth century Sikhism expresses its militancy. Sikh 'militancy' tapped into the culture of Panjabi violence and this affected its social appeal. Moreover, the problem with arguing that the Jats drove Sikh 'militancy' because they are naturally bellicose leads to questions about Sikh 'violence'. This is because Sikh violence implies religious violence but religious violence has to be driven by theological ideas. If the Jats are spasmodically violent simply because of their nature, then, is that Sikh violence even 'Sikh'? My point is that, for Sikhism to develop notions of religious violence, the Sikh literati had to have developed Sikh ideas of 'just war', otherwise Sikh militancy could not have emerged as coherently as it did. While caste groups and local cultures informed these Sikh ideas of 'just war', there had to be a specific appeal for caste groups to want to join a Sikh army. That is why it is crucial that we analyse violence in Panjabi culture; it allows us to understand how Sikh religious violence interacted with local ideas of violence.

Medieval Panjabi Kinship

It is difficult to conduct an ethnographical analysis of a medieval community because the thick description cannot be decoded with fieldwork. But we can work backwards by seeing the views of modern ethnographies and tracing the relevant nomenclature and systems in our historical literature. When examining such contemporary descriptions of Panjabi kinship we cannot be oblivious to the major difference which divides modern Panjab, caused by the partition of the subcontinent into India and Pakistan. This partition caused radical demographic changes in the Panjab region.

And yet, there is undoubtedly in modern Panjabi kinship systems a common cultural system of terminology which cuts across religious and social lines. A unique feature of this cultural system is the noun *Sak* (kinsman) and the adjective *Sakka* (real) and its plural *Sakke* (real as a collective) which plays a pivotal role in distinguishing the value of relatives and kindred. The relations that are known as *Sakke* (real) form the cardinal unit in Panjabi kinship because these 'real' relations are relationships that must be maintained and can (must) be called upon for aid in crises and social rituals. In Hershman's analysis of Indian Panjabi communities in the 1970s, he comments: "In Punjab I would argue that the *sakke* is socially a highly significant unit and organizes a significant proportion of Punjabi social behaviour".[89] In

Werbner's analysis of Pakistani Panjabi communities in the British diaspora during the 1970s and 1980s, she comments: "It must be stressed, therefore, that *biradari* does not simply imply a kin relationship. Consanguineous kinsmen are known as *rishtedar* and this term is extended to include their spouses as well. *Rishtedar* are either *nazdik* (close) or *dur* (far), and a distinction is made between 'real' (*sakke*) and classificatory kin".[90] So despite the differences in the two communities geographically, religiously and socially, there is a common kinship framework. The question, then, is when did such a cultural system emerge? For an answer we must look at the communities which reside in the region.

One of the earliest references to the term *Sak* can be found in the hymns of Guru Nanak, dating from sometime in the late fifteenth to the early sixteenth century. In a verse he says: "Bestowing your grace thereby placing truth; without the Name what other kinsman/ relation (*saku*) is there?" (*Nadri kare sach paeiaeh binu naveh kiaa saku*).[91] The image of the kinsman in early Sikh literature expresses the view that relations and kindred are merely transient relations, unlike divinity. In the poetic compositions (late sixteenth–early seventeenth century) of the Sikh thinker, Bhai Gurdas, the term *Sak* is used on several occasions to illustrate the illusion of worldly love for one's relatives. In a significant ballad he writes:

> The three houses which compose the family are in-laws (*sahur*), paternal (*piharu*) and maternal relations (*nanehala*). (1)
> In-laws consist of father (*sahura*) and mother (*sas*), sisters (*sali*) and brothers (*sala*). (2)
> Paternal relations consist of mother (*ma*), father (*piu*), sisters (*bhaina*), brothers (*bhaira*), and many more. (3)
> Maternal relations consist of grandfather (*nana*), grandmother (*nani*), aunts (*masian*), uncles (*mame*); such complexities (*janjala*). (4)
> To ensure such ties gold (*soina*), silver (*rupa*), diamonds (*hira*), food (*parvala*), are exchanged. (5)
> The affection (*pirhari*) between master (*piru*) and students (*muridan*), this kinship (*saku*) is always joyous (*sukhala*). (6)[92]

This verse is very important because Gurdas succinctly states the vast majority of kinship terms as found in modern Panjabi terminology.[93] Moreover, his direct discussion of exchange (*vartan*) as a means of maintaining 'real' relationships is reiterated in modern ethnographies on Indian and Pakistani Panjabi communities.[94] Aware of how these ties can become laborious and mundane since real affection is occasionally lacking, Gurdas again stresses that true kinship is with God and his saints. In other verses he mentions "all the kinsmen (*saku*), including friends (*mit*), sons (*put*), brothers (*bhaira*), look on angrily (*vihrani*)".[95] In addition, he also states that true kinship exists amongst genuine servants of God and Guru: "The kinship between brothers who serve the Guru is real; as the words of the Guru shine from their foreheads".[96] In another verse, after highlighting the fragility of actual kinship relations, he writes: "A Sikh (*gurbhai*) is a true kinsman (*sak sacha*) with fellow Sikhs (*gurbhaian*) because both acknowledge (*juhari*) the Guru's teachings (*gurvak*)".[97] Thus by the early seventeenth century there seems to be an accepted cultural system of 'Panjabi' kinship in which there is an accepted nomenclature and an accepted system of reciprocal exchange among 'real' (*sakke*) relations.

Another interesting example comes from another early seventeenth-century Sikh source, in Miharvan's *Janamsakhi* (biography) on Guru Nanak's life. Miharvan was related to the 'Guru's house' and would have been privileged with genealogical knowledge and a good understanding of the rites practised in his family and society. When discussing the episode of Guru Nanak's marriage when Nanak was fifteen or sixteen years of age, Miharvan provides us with information on the ceremonial exchanges that took place. Describing the splendour of Nanak's wedding day, he tells us of the order in which the wedding day food (*jevanvar*) was distributed amongst the guests:

> Firstly the local residents who had gathered in a crowd partook. Then the residents of Talwandi and their servants partook. Then the magnates of Talwandi partook. All the Khatris and Brahmans then partook. Finally all the 'real' (*sake*) relations who together composed the Bedi clan partook.[98]

There seems to be a very clear cultural system of ranking kinship within this system in Sikh sources of the medieval period. Equally intriguing is Miharvan's reference to the Khatris.

The Khatris in Mughal India achieved prominence as a scribal and administrative class and are comparable in this regard to the Kayasths.[99] They were also a successful mercantile group.[100] While the origin of the Khatris was in the Panjab, success in administrative service and commerce saw the settling of Khatri communities across northern India.[101] Despite this position in administration and commerce their caste status was *Kshatriya* (warrior caste) and they proudly believed in their martial roots as 'pure' Vedic warriors. When British ethnographers were engaging in research into the castes and tribes of colonial India, the Khatris began writing about their own history. Organisations such as the Khatri Hitkari Association (Khatri Improvement Association), based in Agra, began publishing studies on Khatri history.[102] A key concern on their agenda was to remove the view that they were not 'pure' Kshatriyas like the Rajputs. In Moti Lal Seth's *A Brief Ethnological Survey of the Khattris* (1905) he comments:

> It must be observed here, that what has been stated about the Rajputs in this book, should not be construed into a denial of the existence of martial spirit in them or of their claim to be classed as a military caste…But facts are facts after all and as such do not admit suppression, nor is it possible to be frank without speaking the truth. Whatever has been said about them is either supported by the authorities or warranted by circumstances that cannot be ignored even by an ordinary observer of the Indian people.[103]

Earlier in 1873 Kashi Nath wrote an article on the Khatris in *The Indian Antiquary*. Nath himself was Khatri and an official in the British civil service. He wrote:

> Judging from their physiognomy, they are of pure Aryan blood. Next to Kashmiris they are the fairest race in Hindustan; next

to the Brahmans they are the most religious class, reading much of the Hindu scriptures. As Guru Nanak belonged to this caste, he is regarded as the patron or national saint of the Khatris. His and his successors' compositions are looked upon with great reverence and respect, and generally read. The deistical doctrines and tenets inculcated by the great Khatri reformer have considerably influenced their morals, manners, and customs, weaning them to great degree from many superstitions still clung to by other Hindu tribes. This leads some to suspect their being genuine Hindus.[104]

Nath goes on to say "the Khatris are descendants of a warlike race. The name Khatri occurs in the Indian History since the time of Baber when he visited Guru Nanak. They were constantly employed by the Mughul emperors as soldiers".[105] There is a question here: if the Khatris were once warriors and kings, why did they become merchants and scribes?

Khatri sources provide us with an interesting explanation of why this change occurred. The most common claim is that they were soldiers in Ala al-Din Khalaji's (d.1316) army and had been warriors prior to 'Muslim' rule in North India. After some unknown battle they suffered mass casualties and Ala al-Din's wife was deeply moved by the cries of the widows. She described the image of these women in despair to Ala al-Din who decided to call his Khatri chieftains and demand they introduce widow re-marriage. The two Khatri chiefs, Lallu and Jagdhar, went home with this proposal, fully aware they could lose their position in the army if they did not adopt widow re-marriage.[106] The outrage of the Khatris made them reject the proposal and leave their martial professions for new pastures. In particular they chose trade and this is wonderfully summed up in a verse of the eighteenth-century Khatri poet, Anand Ram 'Mukhlis' (1699–1751): "O'friends, now that matters have come to arrows and swords (*shamsher-o-tir*) why should we stay here, for we are not soldiers? . . . why should we then not leave for the city to do business there?"[107]

This incident not only led the Khatris to change their professions, more significantly it resulted in the re-configuration of their endogamous and exogamous groups. The Khatris were divided into three major groups and were further divided into various endogamous sub-sections and numerous exogamous sections.[108] The first group was the *Bari* (twelfth) group which is divided into twelve exogamous clans and four endogamous groups known as the two-half houses, the four houses, the six houses and the twelve houses. This group has a high status since they are believed to have resisted the policy of widow re-marriage with the most vigour. The second group is known as the *Bunjahi* (fifty-two) group, consisting of fifty-two endogamous clans, who resisted the reforms with slightly less vigour than the *Bari* group. The third, largest, group is known as the *Sarin* which is derived from *Sharia-i Ain* (those who accept the regulations of Islamic law); this group is said to have been willing to accept the reforms on widow re-marriage.[109] Hence, the *Sarin* are often isolated from their *Bari* and *Bunjahi* counterparts especially regarding marriage alliances. This has caused the *Sarin* little problem since there exist over a hundred exogamous clans within the group. Each clan has their own genealogical link to the four great Kshatriya dynasties, with the solar dynasty being the most popular.

This new culture challenged the homogenous character of the Khatri community, making kinship a fraught issue. Regardless of the accuracy of these origins, the existence of such Khatri structures in sixteenth- and seventeenth century Panjab is unquestionable. This is because the Sikh thinker and Khatri, Bhai Gurdas, lucidly states its existence:

> There are many Khatris some are from the twelfth group
> (*barhi*), others fifty-two (*bavanjahi*). (1)
> There are the sub-groups of *pavadhe*, *pachadhia*, *falian*,
> *khokhrainu* and many more. (2)
> There are the groups of *churotari*, *sarin* and *vilahi*. (3)
> From them many incarnations (*avtar*) have arisen; all-conquering
> kings (*chakravarti raje*) residing in courts (*dargahi*). (4)
> Some claim descent from the solar (*surajvansi*), others the lunar
> (*saumvans*); claiming to be mighty warriors (*survir*) and soldiers
> (*sipahi*). (5)

But the true Lord (*dharamrai*) is the maintainer of order
(*dharamatma dharam*); he does not descend into frivolity
(*beparvahi*). (6)
The Khatris true virtues (*salahi*) are: charity (*dan*), warfare
(*kharg*), worship (*mant*), devotion (*bhagati*).[110]

The confirmation of these divisions in Khatri practices can be seen
in the relations of the Sikh Gurus, who were all from Khatri backgrounds. Importantly Guru Nanak's Bedi clan belong to the fifty-two
section, and all his successors to the *Sarin* section. Possibly this hostility explains why in an eighteenth century *Janamsakhi* Guru Nanak's
sons ask their father why he had appointed Guru Angad as his successor: "You have bestowed [your] royal authority upon an ignorant
Khatri. What will happen to us?"[111] This 'ignorance' was arguably
due to the lesser position of Angad in the Khatri hierarchy. The later
marriage of Guru Amar Das's daughter with Guru Ram Das was perfectly legitimate in the Khatri matrimonial system. An interesting
allusion to this acceptability within the Khatri kinship system is indicated by the eighteenth century source *Bansavlinama: Dasa Patshahia
ka* (Genealogy of the Ten Kings) by Kesar Singh Chhibbar:

The priest (*Purohit*) asked that mandatory question: 'son what is
your *jati?*'
Ram Das replied with gusto: 'Sodhi is my *jati*'.
The priest was pleased by this and went to meet his father,
Har Das.[112]

The question of having the correct rank was important in order for a
marriage to be conducted. The internal divisions within the Khatri kinship system illustrate how multifaceted this caste group was, and how
a one-dimensional view into the Khatris is potentially misleading.

Scholars have discussed how the Khatri community in medieval
India grew into an influential administrative and commercial class.[113]
However, this image is too homogenous when we consider the distinctions that existed within the Khatri kinship system. The Khatris
were divided over kinship rank and the region of the Panjab where

they lived. Variations over region cause immense problems because they potentially alter the value of kinship rank.[114] Despite having an elaborate kinship system the Khatris lack "any distinctive caste customs",[115] region can dictate these customs. Put simply, the Khatri matrimonial system narrows as the value of clan rank increases, so hypergamy is problematic among Khatris. These differences over clan rank seem to alter the occupational opportunities of medieval Khatri clans. High-ranking clans seem to enjoy better opportunities in administration and commerce, while low-ranking Khatri clans had limited access to education and such careers. For example, the Multani Khatris hold a very high rank in the Khatri kinship system: since the fourteenth century Hindu Multanis were identified in Sultanate sources as an influential merchant class.[116] Perhaps these early Hindu merchants develop a Khatri identity and assume a high ranking position because of their wealth. Cities such as Multan directly benefited from Mughal rule because the Mughals opened up international trade and gave Persianate Khatri Multanis a chance to become richer. In comparison, Khatri groups from central Panjab, excluding Lahore, were largely composed of low-ranking Khatri clans. These clans generally engaged in agriculture and local trade. For example, the first four Sikh Gurus were all native sons of central Panjab, but only Guru Nanak was a high-ranking Khatri – all the others were low ranking Khatris. While all the early Sikh Gurus were literate, Guru Nanak's family was well-to-do and his father (Kalu Bedi), father-in-law (Mula Chonha), and brother-in-law (Jai Ram), all worked as administrators in the Lodi kingdom. Nanak was sent to school to study Sanskrit and Persian along with subjects like accountancy.[117] Yet it seems unlikely that any of his immediate successors had these opportunities; they were employed in petty trade and agriculture. Indeed, the Gurmukhi script originated as an unsophisticated local administrative language in central Panjab.[118] These differences in education may have altered the vocabulary – such as Persian loanwords – used by early Sikh Gurus.[119] Moreover, these differences may indicate how social mobility varied among Khatris in medieval Panjab, rank and region playing a key role in determining success. So the Khatris were not simply a 'Munshi' class of intellectuals and businessmen, there were many Khatri clans who did not benefit from Mughal rule. Administration and commerce were not viable options for many low-ranking Khatri clans; instead gentrification and warfare might have provided better options.

Irrespective of individual ranking within the Khatri community the Panjabi Khatris never abandoned their caste rank of Kshatriya. Instead, as shown in colonial India, the Khatris believed they were of pure Vedic stock and they regarded the Rajputs as lesser Kshatriyas because they were not Vedic. Bhai Gurdas defined the Khatris as Kshatriyas and the Rajputs as Vaishyas.[120] While Khatri employment in warfare was waning, their ideas of violence were connected to a Kshatriya ideal. This social status of the Khatris as Kshatriyas seems to have been well established in the Panjab and this meant that the Khatris did not have social pressures to justify their rank. For Khatris the idea of becoming a Kshatriya was never used as a tactic for social mobility: all Khatris had martial genealogies. And they considered these martial genealogies as pure and must have connected violence to the court because only 'real' kings could use 'violence'. This may have encouraged the Khatris to seek government service because they did not want to severe their ties to royalty. For the Khatris, violence was connected to rank and social status.

Jat Panjabi groups also use the same kinship cultural system which is unique to the Panjab. However, unlike the Khatris, the Jats are typically viewed as 'low' caste and their origins are somewhat different. This resulted in variances in their genealogical visions of their roots, as well as differing internal structures which compose distinctly Jat cultural practices.

The origins of Jat communities in the Panjab emerge in the early medieval period with gradual migrations into the region from areas such as Sind.[121] Yet the Jats were not simply a single community; they are composed of numerous tribes. These divisions were further compounded by the areas in Panjab where migratory communities settled. Certain areas were more conducive to sedentarisation, while in other areas pastoralism remained strong. In Panjab certain sections of the Jat community experienced a process of gentrification and became *zamindars* of varying stations, while other sections of the community largely became agriculturalists. But as Chetan Singh notes, this process of sedentarisation was not complete and comprehensive in Mughal Punjab; especially so in 'tribal' areas like the Lakhi Jangal.[122] The settling of Jat communities in Panjab undoubtedly led to structural changes in the organisation of the community. Becoming incorporated into the culture and economy of the region has been described by some as a process of 'Sanskritisation'. Be this as it may, one vital element we find in the accounts of well-to-do Jat families and clans who become gentry groups is their claim to be Rajputs. Colonial ethnographers dealt thoroughly with this issue of distinguishing Jat from Rajput and the major distinction seems to be economic rather than social.[123] This is significant since Jat groups, more than Khatris, seem in this period to be seeking strategies to legitimate their status from being a 'low' caste group. Bhai Gurdas composed compositions on 'Rajput' and 'Jat' groups:

> There are many known as Vaishyas (vais); some are Rajputs who become local figureheads (ravat). (1)
> There are many divisions in their families such as Malan, Has, and Chauhan. (2)
> Some are Kachhawahas, others Rathors; becoming kings (rana rai) and ruling much land as landlords (bhumie bhari). (3)
> Innumerable claiming to be mighty warriors (balvand) like Bagh, Baghele, and Bundelas. (4)
> Many of them are courtiers in the courts of the gentry (bhurtie). (5)
> Many calculate profit (bhadurie) serving with great responsibility (itbari) in many lands (desi desi). (5)
> Wrapped up in pride (haumai) they kill each other; never eliminating their egoism (haumai). (6)[124]

> There are many called Shudras (sud); including many Kayasths (kaieth) employed as clerks. (1)
> Many shopkeepers (bania) are included, plus traffic officers (bhabharia), and many goldsmiths (sunare). (2)
> Vast quantities of Jats and well-known are the Calico printers (chhinbe). (3)
> Innumerable artisans like coppersmiths (thatheria) and blacksmiths (lohar). (4)

Many are identified as sellers of oil (*teli*) and caterers (*halwaie*)
hustling in the marketplace. (5)
Others are couriers (*pankhie*), barbers (*nai*), and itinerary
merchants (*vanjare*). (6)
In all four castes (*chahun varana*) there is a never-ending list of
surnames (*got*). (7)[125]

Bhai Gurdas seems to suggest the difference between Rajputs and
lower castes like the Jats is primarily an issue of land. Someone acquir-
ing land could easily claim Rajput status in the Panjab, but they could
not claim Khatri status. It is also interesting to note that Gurdas
makes a distinction between the Khatris and another fellow munshi
group, the Kayasths. Again, this underscores the Khatri belief that
they occupied a position of high rank in medieval Panjab.

In the genealogies of many Jat clans we find that they claim to
be Rajputs and explain how some action made them fall from grace.
Indeed, if we look at the genealogies of Jat families who become Sikhs
and then rose to the status of kings in the eighteenth and nineteenth
centuries we find this process of 'Rajputisation'.[126] Some claimed to
be 'Sikh' kings who were transformed by the mercy of their Guru and
God. Others claimed that they had been Rajputs who became lost in
the 'confusion' of the 'dark age' and were thus degraded as Jats.[127] In
Ziegler's study of middle-period Rajasthani Rajputs he discusses the
existence of these genealogical narratives which embed the fortunes of
Rajput groups within a universal framework.[128] In periods of 'confusion' (*vikhau*) Rajput clans lose their kingly status and often engage
in agriculture; when 'disorder' (*adharma*) ends they return to their
rightful status as kings. These Rajput narratives specifically depend
upon a cyclical narrative: order will follow disorder, victory will follow
defeat, and so forth, the cycle does not stop. Central to the Rajput's
success and failure is dependence upon his 'service' and his 'benefi-
cence'. Essentially the Rajput must maintain reciprocal relationships
with his gods, Brahmans, soldiers and subjects; the moment when this
reciprocity is broken the moral order breaks down. Importantly this
means the Rajput needs to have people with whom he can establish
reciprocal relationships. Without these people it is impossible for him

to break out of disorder and re-create order. Arguably the most vital relationship the Rajput could have was with divinity or, more precisely, Brahmans. The Rajput chief had to give the Brahmans gifts and receive their blessings. So when Jat groups claim Rajput status they must have these reciprocal relationships in order to explain the ending of 'confusion'. Jat Sikhs claiming Rajput status are saying that they possess these reciprocal relationships, not with Brahmans, but with Sikh religious authorities. It helps to explain why socially mobile Jat groups in central and western Panjab, while claiming Rajput status, also convert to Islam and Sikhism. This is because it might have been difficult for Jat groups to establish reciprocal relationships with Panjabi Brahmans because of their 'impurity'. However, Islamic and Sikh religious authorities with their egalitarianism would be open to Jat-Rajput patronage. Crucially Khatri groups had less need to convert because in the Panjab the Brahmanical authorities already saw them as 'pure' Kshatriyas. This made it impossible for Jat groups to claim Khatri status. In the Mughal period, the Bhattis are a group which are identified as being hostile to Mughal authority and carrying periodic raids into Mughal Panjab.[129] While the Bhattis were a Jat tribe, they still claimed to be Rajputs, and also Muslims. It can be suggested that in medieval Panjab the caste identities of 'Jat' and 'Rajput' were liminal identities. Rajput status in mainland Panjab was primarily based on being a member of the gentry and thus gaining a heroic martial identity. But the need to establish religious reciprocal relationships was fundamental to their Jat-Rajput status.

These liminal identities and the manner in which social mobility could alter these identities are important to consider. In particular the role of religion as a legitimising tool for Jat groups in the medieval period needs due attention. This is because claiming Rajput status was solely a matter of land and wealth, and not of customs and rites. For instance, Jat groups did not always adopt Rajput systems of kinship and honour as found in the Panjabi hills.[130] Religious conversion to Islam and perhaps Sikhism was driven as a tactic for social mobility by Jats and Rajputs. By contrast, high-ranking Khatri groups continue to maintain a Vedic Hindu identity. Jat-Rajput groups also converted to Islam to gain service and protection from Sufi shrines. The

Chishti shrine of Shaykh Farid had considerable prestige in western Panjab. The vast majority of Jat tribes in western Panjab claim they were converted to Islam by Shaykh Farid.[131] The early seventeenth-century source *Jawahir-i Faridi* speaks of an allegiance (*bai'at*) between the Chishti shrine of Shaykh Farid and local Jat-Rajput clans. This relationship was not only religious, it entailed political and military allegiance:

> And in the environs [Pakpattan] the Khokhars, Dhudhis, Jo'iyas, Bhattis, Wattus and other groups who became Muslim from the time of Baba Farid, until now are busy in prayer and fasting [i.e., they conform to the outward observances of Muslim law]. For they are the possessors of dignity in the environs of Pakpattan. They can place ten thousand cavalry and foot soldiers in his [Baba Farid's] service, and have complete faith in Baba Farid and his descendants, and are their *murids*.[132]

The mention of the nomadic Bhattis with their Jat/Rajput/Muslim identity suggests they may have seen in all these identities a ruse to be socially mobile; picking and choosing the best identity for the best circumstances. This is significant when we consider Jat conversions to Sikhism in later chapters; perhaps they converted in an effort to be socially mobile. This aspiration was lacking among Khatris of a certain rank who felt they were as high as can be.

It is important to note briefly the economic relationship between Khatris and Jats. McLeod asserted that the Khatris held a dominant position in the early Sikh community due to their literacy and high-caste status: they were the teachers of the Jats. "Khatris could be expected to direct their teachings to Jats, and Jats could be expected to respond".[133] This view has been widely reiterated in the historiography and the relationship has been seen as central to the recruitment of Jats into the Sikh community. But, as Mann has suggested, this might not have been the case: rather the Jat community may have been early adherents and the Khatris role as 'natural' teachers is misplaced.[134] Mann also notes the Jats had limited ties with the caste hierarchy of Panjabi society and that Sikhism may have offered the Jats an opportunity to construct social ties.[135] Importantly Mann highlights how in *Janamsakhi* anecdotes we find out that Guru Nanak's father-in-law, Mula Chonha, works as an administrator for the Jat landlord, Ajita Randawa.[136] If we expand this train of thought and examine other *Janamsakhi* figures we can detect an interesting pattern. Guru Nanak's father, Kalu Bedi, worked as an administrator for his village headman, Rai Bhoa, a high-caste Hindu. And Guru Nanak's brother-in-law, Jai Ram, worked as an administrator for the Lodi kingdom. All of Nanak's immediate relatives were professional administrators for local or regional lords, including Jat masters. From this we can infer that Khatris did seem to occupy a position as a professional class and some Jats held the position of being landlords. There was clearly a professional services relationship between high-ranking Khatris and high-ranking Jats, and this seems indicative of the wider socio-economic relationship between Khatris and Jats in medieval Panjab. While Mann may be correct in suggesting that the Jats were early adherents, McLeod, I feel, was not far off from the truth when suggesting that the Khatris held the position as a literate and influential class over Jats and others.

The Jat community viewed violence and the power of violence as pivotal to their social mobility. Rajputs had land and the status of warriors, and Jat groups aspired to become fully-fledged members of this military aristocracy. The cultural violence of Jats was centred upon a belief in clan honour. In comparison, the Khatris viewed violence in terms of purity and Vedic social order. The Khatris saw violence from an angle of chivalry; only good men fought for the good. In medieval Panjabi literature this image of the 'honourable' Jat versus the cultured 'civility' of the Khatri gentleman is apparent.

Violence and 'Good' Conduct: the Ideal Jat and Khatri

The most important genre in pre-modern Panjabi literature was the *qissa* (story); a 'long' narrative poem focusing on the exploits of two 'lovers'. Originating from the Perso-Islamic tradition of secular storytelling, this genre becomes rooted in the land and communities of medieval and early modern Panjab. As Shackle notes, "[F]ew genres show a more powerful attachment to the specificities of place than the Panjabi verse romance called qissa".[137] The genre is a vehicle for poets to express the realities of love (*ishaq majazi*) and as a metaphor to express the mysticism of spiritual love (*ishaq haqiqi*). The sharp contrast in flavours and moods allows these tales to highlight the limitations of love flourishing in the social and kinship structures which trap agents. And also to show how true lovers transcend such parameters in search of divine union.[138] While exported *qissas* such as *Laila-Majnun* and *Yusuf-Zulaikha* became popular, their fame was overshadowed by indigenous Panjabi *qissas*. These include: *Hir-Ranjha, Sohni-Mahival,* and *Mirza-Sahiban*. These *qissas* were all set in the Panjab and all the protagonists were from the region.

These *qissas* are fascinating because they centre upon a specific Panjabi world; it is the western Panjabi countryside, a Perso-Islamic literary style, and the clans involved are liminal Jat-Rajput clans who are always Muslims. While mystic themes have been inflected into these stories they are centrally stories of kinship and honour among these clans. The themes are of tragic love and mystical union represented by two lovers from opposing clans whose love cannot be socially accepted. Thus they are forced to hide their love and as the secret becomes public knowledge this results in clan conflicts over honour. These are stories are dealing with social etiquette: the conduct of these protagonists. While they only reflect a distinct part of Panjab these *qissas* grew immensely popular across the region. The most prominent Panjabi *qissa* to emerge was *Hir-Ranjha*, which has been popular in written and performed contexts from the sixteenth century until the present day. The story was based on two lovers, Hir and Ranjha, who were both members of Jat clans in the Sandal Bar in western Panjab. In the sixteenth and early seventeenth century this folk tale seems to be very prominent as numerous Panjabi poets either mention or compose their own version, including: Hari Das Haria, Shah Hussein, Gang Bhatt, Bhai Gurdas, Balki Kolabi, Damodar and Ahmed Gujar.[139] The emergence of this specific tale consolidates the view that there is a cultural system of Panjabi kinship by the sixteenth century, as it would be impossible to convey these conflicts of family loyalty if one's audience could not comprehend the intricacies.

These *qissas* also reveal the growing dominance of a Jat identity associated with the region. This Panjabi Jat identity brought ideas of Jat masculinity and honour which might have given them a sense of homogeneity. But this united identity is misleading, because many of the clans of the great *qissas* such as the Sial clan of the Sandal Bar region were liminal Jat-Rajput groups like the Bhattis.[140] In addition, clans such as the Sial claimed devotion to the Chishti saints in their west Panjab region.[141] This is in stark contrast with Jats in central or southern Panjab, many of whom were non-Muslims and were largely sedentary groups. It suggests that while an identity such as Jat was becoming dominant, this homogenous identity was in reality fragmented by regional differences.

The *qissa* tales placed emphasis on the Jat male involved in blood feuds seeking recompensation for injury to family honour and underscored the cultural importance of violence in medieval Jat culture. In the world of the *qissas* fathers and brothers had to be united and they had to protect their daughters and sisters from 'other' men.[142] Violence was never political and the greatest rivals to one's strength came from other Jat clans. The Jat depended upon the power of his physical strength and the supernatural power of local saints to help him defeat enemies. Jat violence was parochial in its means and aims: they never fought wars of religion, nor conquered great hordes, and they had no chivalric codes.

As with the making of a Jat identity in medieval Panjab, we can notice a similar process in the making of a Khatri identity. This notion of a Khatri *par excellence* emerges in Guru Nanak's hagiographies (*Janamsakhis*). Unlike many other Sant thinkers, Guru Nanak did not come from a lowly social position.[143] Instead, as we have seen, he was born to a literate and well-to-do Panjabi Khatri family near Lahore.[144] The Khatris were, generally speaking, a growing secretarial and mercantile caste in this era. In Guru Nanak's biographies the hagiographer presents an image of Guru Nanak as a Khatri. The image is not explicit since the author's intention is to focus on Guru Nanak's charisma, but the hagiographies contain many anecdotes about Guru Nanak's conflict with his otherworldliness and his worldly duties. This conflict aggravates his family, in particular his parents. The expressions of parental expectations reveal what they felt a Khatri young man ought to be in medieval Panjab. Their hopes are visible in the lifestyle they give their son and their laments when he frustrates their dreams.

An examination of Guru Nanak's childhood anecdotes reveal his father's initial desire was to educate his son. This begins with a primary education with a learned village Pundit. It seems to include studying Sanskrit, mathematics, accountancy and literacy. The Miharvan *Janamsakhi* tradition notes it was essentially that of a *patwari* (local accountant), meaning it was practical secular education designed for administrative service.[145] Thereafter he was sent to a local Mullah to study Arabic and Persian.[146] The acquirement of these literary and administrative languages was most probably sought by his father with the long-term prospect of having Guru Nanak find service with a master. While Guru Nanak hardly spent any time at school he does seem to have mastered these subjects.[147]

When Guru Nanak was a young married man with two sons he suddenly grew despondent. In the *Adi Sakhi* hagiography there is an intriguing scene:

> Baba Nanak did not do any worldly work. Neither his father nor his mother could say a thing to him. They could not give him any orders to work. And if Baba Nanak sat, he remained seated, and if he slept, he remained asleep. And with the saints Nanak had much love. Wherever the saints sat, he sat there too... Then Nanak's mother and father sat with him. They said: "If you are a beloved of God and remain seated all day, then how will your work happen? And why do you keep on giving to the renunciants and ascetics? When will you begin your earning of your daily subsistence? You have a family, sons, and a home, so earn your daily subsistence. Leave your ways, there is no benefit to them". Listening to every word Nanak became detached. Wrapping his face and head in cloth he lay down. Three or four days passed. He did not eat nor drink. Nor did he speak. Then his wife went to Nanak's mother's house and cried: "Mother-in-law your son just lies there, days have passed. He does not speak nor eat, or anything besides that". His mother came quickly over. She

spoke: "My son to lie does not befit you. Get up and tend your land. Earn your daily subsistence. Get up my child, bathe, eat, and drink" ... Then Kalu heard the news that Nanak only lies. He does not eat or drink. Father spoke: "My child for the son of a Khatri it is honourable to work. A Khatri invests the four or five pieces of wealth he has, with that he trades, earns his daily subsistence, and eats. Without earning his daily subsistence what worth is a man?[148]

This scene evokes the idea of Khatri conduct. A good Khatri has an established work ethic and sense of duty, something which Nanak is clearly violating here. His father speaks of *rojgar* (daily subsistence; employment). Following this, Guru Nanak does gain employment in the Lodi administration at Sultanpur, Panjab, through the personal recommendation of his brother-in-law, Jai Ram, a fellow Khatri, who was married to Guru Nanak's elder sister and must have been fluent in Persian and a trained administrator.

In later life Guru Nanak met many fellow Khatris in Panjab. A famous anecdote involves his old friend, known as Mula (lit. foolish).[149] The image of Mula is of a parsimonious merchant who wishes not to be involved with Guru Nanak. Guru Nanak is depicted as a fallen Khatri with his ascetic attire and lack of wealth and respectability:

Then Baba Nanak dressed in the style of a Hindu renunciant and a Muslim fakir. On one foot he wore a Muslim styled sandal, and on the other foot he wore a Hindu styled wooden sandal. On the lower half of his body he wore blue trousers, and on the upper half he wore a saffron blanket. On his head he donned a Muslim cap and on his forehead he applied a Hindu sacramental mark. To the Hindus they proclaimed him their leader and likewise the Muslims they proclaimed him their leader. To the entire world he appeared as one of unshakable faith in God. Whoever saw him felt delight. In this world he spread the way of enlightenment and discernment and made famous meditation on God. All over the world he constructed his place of Dharma. He firmly established the teachings of the name, charity, and cleanliness. He spoke if any child wishes to be my student then take up the trade of three wares of name, charity and cleanliness in this world, so Nanak recited. Then Baba Nanak proclaimed that Guru Angad is my one such child who is in union with me but still a separate form on earth. When I was [Guru Nanak] engaged in worldly work one Mula Khatri was my friend let us go and meet him. My desire is to meet him. Then Angad said very well let us meet him. Then Baba Nanak dressed in the manner of fakir with an ascetic loincloth and many others dressed in loincloths accompanied him. They arrived and stood over Mula Khatri's fears. Arriving with grace Baba Nanak met Mula's wife. She recognised Baba Nanak, after recognising him she went back inside her home. She told Mula your old friend has come in the condition of a socially dead and old ascetic. She went on he is in bad condition once he rode a horse, a rider, and happy too. Now his happiness is broken and he has come to beg something from you. Mula then ran and hid in his cellar. Baba Nanak asked Mula's wife where is Mula? She replied he is not at home. The Guru Baba replied he's not at home. She reiterated no he is not at home. Guru Baba then spoke you malicious merchant we came to meet you in friendship and you fled. The Guru Baba then spoke this verse: "Those who are friends with merchants their affection comes to nothing/ Foolish one, no one knows where and when death shall come". Saying this Guru Baba departed. When Baba Nanak had left the merchant came out of hiding and spoke and then his life disappeared. He cried shame has killed me.[150]

The image which is displayed in these medieval hagiographies is of a Khatri who is a part of the Persianate elite in Panjab. The Khatri has access to an education which includes studying Persian and Sanskrit, as well as important subjects like mathematics. He is expected to earn his living in service or commerce. His success is heavily dependent on his family: it is the family which ensures his education and finds him employment. The Khatri acts with etiquette befitting a gentleman and should not engage with disreputable characters. As the *qissas* reveal a

Jat *ideal* of clan honour and masculinity, so too the *Janamsakhis* reveal a Khatri *ideal*. But Guru Nanak's life is testimony that such ideals did not always translate into realities. The *qissas* also reveal how love violated the solid clan boundaries of Jat society. But they nevertheless reveal the development of such caste ideals in medieval Panjab.

The civility of the medieval Khatri gentleman arguably reveals an alternative culture of violence. The Khatris saw themselves as a Persianate elite and for them social mobility meant becoming more involved in courtly society. In this courtly world, violence was refined and expressed through chivalric codes. The vendetta-seeking Jat violence would appear uncouth in Khatri eyes because honour would have been connected to social rank; the Jat man would have appeared more like a hooligan and less like a Kshatriya. This Khatri culture of violence can be seen as an 'elite' culture of violence because socially mobile groups in medieval Panjab all sought to gain the power of violence by transforming their self-identities into Kshatriya or Rajput. But in medieval Panjab Kshatriya status could only come by gaining Persianate etiquette, while Jat groups were 'violent' they rarely adopted courtly civility. Hence, Jats who had Rajput status never expressed their honour through Rajput narratives of righteousness; rather they continued to act 'violently' in a distinctly Jat way. The Khatri culture of violence, however, was more pervasive and could develop into religious violence by utilising ideas of the Kshatriya, court and civility. Therefore, in medieval Panjab there existed a common culture of violence, but various social agents performed and used violence in different ways. Khatri society possessed a refined notion of violence connected to courtly civility, but Jats possessed a notion of violence which was connected to clan identity. When the Khatri used violence he would have been performing an act which reflected his Vedic social rank and he would have expressed this violence by showing his self-worth to chivalrous society. But when the Jat used violence he would have been performing an act which reflected his association with his clan and he would have expressed this violence by showing his self-worth to the clan.

When we look at how, in the seventeenth century, the Sikh movement develops militancy it is necessary that we understand these contrasting cultures of violence amongst Panjabi castes. Because Sikh violence was religious violence and the Sikhs had to develop a military culture, this military culture would have embedded itself within existing cultures of violence. Consequently, the social appeal of Sikh violence would have varied amongst the Sikh public.

2

THE EMERGENCE OF SIKH MILITANCY 1606-1644

In the aftermath of Guru Arjan's execution in 1606 by the Mughal state, the Sikh community saw the succession of a new Guru, an event which broke with past precedent: previously the Gurus had been nominated and appointed by their predecessor. These successions were largely conducted in an atmosphere of tranquillity. All the previous Gurus had departed this world in old age due to natural causes. Now, for the first time, the Guru had been cut down in the prime of his life due to an act of violence. For the Sikh community this was a point of profound transition. How would a successor Guru respond to the legacy of Guru Arjan's execution? Would there be a change in attitude and policies? Historical analysis, both pre-modern and modern, has given emphasis to this period as a major turning point in early Sikh evolution. This is because Guru Arjan's son and successor, Guru Hargobind, has been viewed as introducing significant reforms. These reforms saw the injection of militancy or a process of militarisation to the existing teachings of the Sikh Gurus.

The origins of these reforms began at the start of Guru Hargobind's Guruship. In June 1606 Guru Hargobind was initiated as the new Sikh Guru. The coronation began with the final rites for Guru Arjan and then the ceremony of succession. The eleven-year-old Guru Hargobind was clothed in the ritual dress and placed before him was the *seli topi* – a woollen turban which was worn by his predecessors.

Guru Hargobind asked the master of ceremonies, Bhai Budha, to place the *seli topi* in his treasury; he no longer required it. Instead, he adorned his head with a regally styled turban with a royal aigrette and tied a martial cummerbund around his waist. Taking out two swords he declared that one symbolised *miri* (temporal power) and the other, *piri* (spiritual power). Then he fastened both these swords to his waist. To the stunned congregation who came to witness the ceremony he announced that he would live in the manner of a king. He would practise martial arts, engage in the hunt, raise a standing army and construct a fort.[1] The exact reasons for this significant shift were not clear. Possibly this was an act of self-protection or impending retribution for his father's execution. These measures were not designed for the majority but only for the minority of the Sikh community. Nevertheless, the change was poignant as the Sikh Guru's persona dramatically altered.

Historians have endeavoured to explain the reasons behind Guru Hargobind's militant actions at this particular historical juncture.[2] Guru Hargobind himself provided no explicit reasons and thus the issue has been subjected to critical speculation. This has largely focused upon the impact of these militant reforms on Sikh community formation and early Sikh theology. However, historians have generally ignored the other major turning point which occurred with the his succession: the formation of a rival Guru lineage led by Guru Arjan's elder brother, Prithi Chand. The categorisation of Sikh history in terms of doxa and the presentist perspective which accompanies doxa has resulted in Prithi Chand's ostracism from Sikh histories.[3] Rather Prithi Chand is labelled as 'unorthodox' and Guru Hargobind as 'orthodox' and consequently Guru Hargobind's lineage has been enshrined and its history narrated. This teleological rendering of early Sikh history neglects the vital interaction between these two lineages and their intellectual contestation.[4] While in modern Sikhism Prithi Chand's ideas are deemed unorthodox, in early seventeenth century Sikh society the implications present in a label of this nature were unclear, suggesting also that early Sikh society did not respond to these developments along the juxtaposed binaries familiar to us today. In the hidden dialectics between Guru Hargobind and Prithi Chand

lies an untold history about early Sikh social formation and its interpretation of politics and religious violence.

Rival Guru lineages formed immediately after Guru Arjan's demise.
It is unclear how exactly both Gurus ascended to the Guruship and it
is unclear which lineage was nominated by Guru Arjan. Yet it seems
Guru Hargobind was the popular choice because he succeeded his
father in the symbolically important city of Amritsar; and even more
importantly Guru Hargobind was supported by Guru Arjan's chief
votaries, Bhai Gurdas and Bhai Budha. By contrast, Prithi Chand
seems to have appointed himself as the Sikh Guru, but his exact location is unclear; most probably he was living near Amritsar or possibly
in southern Panjab. Despite Prithi Chand being Guru Arjan's elder
brother and Guru Hargobind's eldest uncle, he seems to have been
the less favoured candidate. Prithi Chand had established a reputation amongst Guru Arjan's supporters as an envious and greedy man
and he and his supporters were known as the *minas* (hypocrites). This
ascription was popular amongst Guru Hargobind's supporters, hence
the negative connotations associated with this ascription still survive.[5]
The Prithi Chand sect is also known as the *chhota mel* (those who were
joined with the Gurus for a short time).[6] By contrast, Prithi Chand
and his supporters called themselves the *Bhagats* (God's devotees),
Nanakpanthis or simply the 'true' Sikhs.[7]

Prithi Chand's life has not been given sufficient historical scrutiny
and much we know of him comes from sources with an overt bias
against his spiritual claims.[8] While it is hard to determine whether
sources are deliberately attacking Prithi Chand out of dislike or genuine
grievance, it is nevertheless possible to construct a fairly detailed pic-
ture of his life and times. Prithi Chand was born in 1558 in Goindwal
to Guru Ram Das (r.1574–1581) and Bibi Bhani. At the time of his
birth, his maternal grandfather, Guru Amar Das (r.1552–1574), was
the Sikh Guru. The young Prithi Chand grew up under the tutelage
of his father and grandfather and received an education geared towards
the service of the Sikh community. This would have entailed studying Sikh and devotional literature, classical Indian music, languages
including Sanskrit and Persian, and general temple administration.
In 1560 his second brother, Mahadev, was born – he would become

an ascetic. In 1563 his youngest brother, Guru Arjan, was born, and would succeed their father, Guru Ram Das, in 1581. Prithi Chand developed into an accomplished administrator and diligently served his father and grandfather. As to be expected given his status as the eldest son, he expected to succeed his father as the Sikh Guru. But Guru Arjan was deemed the most worthy candidate: Arjan had been publically blessed by Guru Amar Das when he was a young boy. This conferral of blessing was sign that Arjan was destined to be the Guru. And so, when the moment came to choose a successor, Guru Ram Das had no doubt that Arjan would be the next Guru. Prithi Chand felt rejected, yet he seems to have accepted Guru Ram Das's reasons for being overlooked. But Guru Arjan's supporters viewed this moment as the start of a bitter rivalry directed by Prithi Chand towards Guru Arjan. While in Prithi Chand sources he is shown as a devout servant to Guru Arjan and deeply attached to his younger brother. In rival sources Prithi is depicted as a man who coveted the Guruship more than anything else and who was intent upon ensuring he and his off-spring inherited that glittering jewel.[9] These sources highlight how he used to taunt Guru Arjan about his wife's inability to produce an heir. But in 1595 Guru Hargobind was born and Prithi Chand's jeal-ousy grew ever greater because he feared his own chances and those of his sons in obtaining Guruship were disappearing, so much so that, according to these sources, Prithi Chand attempted to poison Guru Hargobind with the aid of a servant, but the plot failed.

After the birth of Guru Hargobind, Prithi Chand decided to leave Amritsar and moved to his in-laws' village of Hehar, near Lahore. It is possible that his desire to leave Amritsar was a reflection of his growing isolation and the frustration of living with Guru Arjan. The fact that he left Guru Arjan's service does cast serious doubts over the Prithi Chand sources that argue he was sincerely devoted to his brother. It is likely that Prithi moved to Hehar in about 1596, and then in latter half of his life (post-1606) he moved to the vil-lage of Kotha Guru in southern Panjab. Despite leaving Amritsar, Prithi Chand apparently did not give up on his dreams and he sought to eliminate Guru Arjan. In rival sources he is depicted as making friendships with local Mughal agents such as a courtier named Sulahi

Khan and a wealthy Khatri revenue official named Chandu Shah.[10] These companionships were designed to create enmity for Guru Arjan in the hearts of local officials. It has even been suggested that Prithi's endeavours were partly responsible for Guru Arjan's arrest and execution. Following the execution Prithi Chand declared he was the legitimate successor; he was either in Hehar or Kotha Guru when he made his position clear and his decision must have been based on either sheer opportunism or sincere belief.

Prithi Chand was a devotional poet in the style of the early Sikh Gurus.[11] While he did not produce a huge corpus of literary works, his pen-name of 'Nanak', 'Jan Nanak' (the slave Nanak) and 'Nanak Das' (the slave Nanak) reflects his desire and belief in his spiritual lineage. Only appointed Sikh Gurus ever wrote compositions with the name Nanak, showing their unity of being with Guru Nanak. In comparison to Guru Arjan, who wrote a vast array of poetry and the compiled the *Adi Granth,* Prithi Chand's literary achievements were far from stellar. But some have suggested that a key reason for producing a Sikh canon by Guru Arjan was driven by the desire to limit interpolations by wannabe gurus like Prithi Chand.[12]

Prithi Chand passed away in April 1618 in the village of Kotha Guru. He had been unable to establish a sizable support base and had not disturbed Guru Hargobind one iota since his accession. But with his death Prithi Chand was not about to fade away into obscurity; he had four sons: Manohar Das (1581–1640), Lal Chand, Nihal Chand and Chandarsen. While his three younger sons seem to disappear without a trace, his eldest son, Manohar Das, achieved the opposite.

Manohar Das, better known as Miharvan, succeeded Prithi Chand in April 1618.[13] He was an individual of considerable intellectual substance and he proceeded to provide a textual pedigree to his lineage's claims to Guruship. Miharvan was born to Prithi Chand and Mata Bhagvano on 9 January 1581 and he spent his entire childhood and adolescence in Amritsar. He had trained under the tutelage of Prithi Chand and Guru Arjan; he was educated in Sanskrit, Persian, Hindi, Sikh scriptures (*Gurmukhi*), poetics and classical Indian music.[14] He developed into a fluent thinker with great proficiency in Sikh teachings, exegesis and classical music.[15] Moreover, he was a literary talent and a luminary amongst medieval Sikh and Panjabi litterateurs. Throughout his adulthood he composed a vast number of poetic compositions under the same pen names used by Prithi Chand. He wrote a substantial corpus of prose and verse works on Sikh, Hindu and Islamic traditions: this array of traditions illuminates his diverse education and religious interests. This corpus includes: *The Discourses of Kabir, The Prophet Muhammad's Counsel, The Discourses of Muslim Saints, The Discourses of the Devotees, The Discourses of Hindu Saints and Ascetics, The Discourses of Guru Nanak* and *The Discourses of Guru Amar Das*.[16] The repetition of 'discourse' (*gosht*) in these titles shows how Miharvan's primary aim as a writer was to explain complex philosophical issues. There is some doubt whether all these works are entirely Miharvan's or whether they are composite works, but there is no such doubt in the votaries of the Miharvan tradition.[17]

Despite being closely attached to Guru Arjan as a boy and young man, Miharvan always acknowledged the leadership of his father above any other. Miharvan would have been about fifteen years old when Prithi Chand left Amritsar for Hehar in 1596. This means that Miharvan would have witnessed the birth of his cousin-brother, Guru Hargobind, but probably only saw him last when Hargobind was a year old. Miharvan remained with his father throughout his stays in Hehar and Kotha Guru, and undoubtedly would have witnessed Prithi Chand's coronation. In Prithi Chand's mind there was no question that Miharvan would succeed him and Miharvan's brothers do not seem have challenged his appointment. Miharvan would have been about thirty-seven when he became the new Guru. Immediately, he moved from Hehar to Kotha Guru, then spent several years in the Panjabi hills, before finally returning to central Panjab where he settled in the village of Muhammadipur, near Lahore.

Although his succession was disputed, the eventful early period of Hargobind's Guruship is the subject of interest in the Sikh literary canon, which recounts the ways in which he began implementing his ideas of '*piri*' and '*miri*'. Immediately on his accession in 1606 Guru Hargobind began recruiting an army known as the *Akal Sena* (Army of the Immortal) and also the *Budha Dal* (Army of Bhai Budha). Opposite his father's Harmandir Sahib temple he constructed a fort called the *Akal Takht* (Throne of the Immortal). True to his word, he recruited many martial artists, warriors, bards and musicians into his service. The adolescent Guru began participating in hunting and other martial pursuits. Thereafter his hunting and an unpaid fine levied on his father resulted in his imprisonment on imperial orders in Gwalior fort. The length of this imprisonment is unknown; Sikh scholars have estimated the time period from two months up to twelve years. It is certainly known that Guru Hargobind was originally detained in 1611 and released by at least 1620. This imprisonment was most probably served with several family members, including his wives and children.[18]

Guru Hargobind and Miharvan were two rival Sikh Gurus: the cousins were two contrasting figures with alternative visions of Sikhism in the early seventeenth century. The conflict between the cousins was centred on their claims that they represented the previous Sikh Gurus and had spiritual authority over the Sikh community. This conflict becomes evident sometime during 1615–1620, especially by the early 1620s.

Their conflict was different from that of their fathers. While the animosity between Guru Arjan and Prithi Chand was mainly over the terms of succession to their father's Guruship, in the second generation, Miharvan challenged the intellectual foundations of Guru Hargobind's Sikhism. They clashed over issues such as lifestyle and appearance of a Sikh Guru; Sikh community formation; Guru Nanak's personality and teachings; and ultimately over militancy and courtly decorum as spiritually enabling lifestyle choices for the Sikh community. These debates are significant because they reflect the fissures within Sikhism, wide-ranging contradictions that were later resolved into pacifist and militant binaries which had the potential of leading the community into divergent directions.

In discussing the conflict between Guru Hargobind and Miharvan, I will examine how the Sikh literati developed two opposing visions of Sikhism which were profoundly centred upon the role of Sikh militancy. These energetic discussions were attached to debates over the legitimacy of Sikh Guruship. These were not recondite intellectual discussions; lay followers were the targets of these public debates.

It is here that we can see the beginnings of an enlarging public debate attempting to fathom Sikhism; questioning, disputing and choosing their leaders and beliefs. Furthermore, these debates were not 'merely' intellectual; they were intrinsically related to the socio-economic cleavages within the community of Sikhs, reflected in arguments by rival claimants to the status of Guruship. These rival arguments also reflected different cultures of violence as found in the Sikh community.

The sources that referred to here are largely early seventeenth-century Sikh sources. They include Sikh scriptures as contained in the *Adi Granth;* the ballads of the Sikh thinker Bhai Gurdas; the hagiographies (*Janamsakhis*) of Guru Nanak; and the works of Harji. I have consulted Persian sources such as the *Dabistan*. It is necessary to see these sources dialogically, meaning they were not written in isolation, but with reference to each other. As a result, I have been able to construct a history in which sources are discussing the nature of Sikhism with each other. I have attempted to identify these topics of discussion by tracing persistent themes and ideas in various works and then comparing and contrasting those themes with each other.

Code of Conduct of a Guru: Lifestyle and Appearance

The most tangible difference between Guru Hargobind and Miharvan concerned their respective opinions on dress and ways of living. Guru Hargobind's militant reforms came with an explicit change in his dress and mannerisms. Recall the rejection of the *seli topi* for a crown more accustomed to kings and noblemen than saintly figures. This change in apparel was significant because it radically changed what was visually expected from a Sikh Guru. To this new dress was added 'strange' (because it was so unexpected and new) behaviour such as going hunting, riding, rearing falcons, eating meat, and engaging with all sorts of new servants like soldiers. This became a source of discord amongst the Sikh community. They began enquiring whether such an aristocratic comportment was befitting for a saint and especially for a successor to Guru Nanak's legacy. The Sikh literati were widely involved in the articulation of these anxieties, discoursing on these reforms, criticising or justifying these measures according to their respective sentiments.

There are two sources which foreground these polemics. The first source is a collection of ballads composed by Guru Hargobind's devout servant, Bhai Gurdas. Gurdas was a maternal uncle to both Guru Hargobind and Miharvan. His works were primarily focused on Sikh mysticism, but he also made insightful comments on his social and religious milieu. Moreover, Gurdas had served Guru Amar Das (r.1552–1574), Guru Ram Das (r.1574–1581) and Guru Arjan before serving Guru Hargobind. He was Guru Arjan's amanuensis for the *Sri Guru Granth Sahib* and was himself a skilled litterateur of Sikh philosophy.[19] In his lifetime he composed a series of poetic compositions in Punjabi and Braj. I will focus on his ballads (*varan*) which are widely available in print.[20] Gurdas' ballads are difficult to date precisely, proving contentious amongst Sikh scholars. While scholars are in agreement that the works are those of Bhai Gurdas, and without any interpolations, it is more problematic to identify when exactly specific ballads were composed. This is because while some ballads make clear historical references, others do not. For the historian the task in using Bhai Gurdas' writings for an early history of the Sikh community depends upon determining approximately when a ballad would have been written.[21] That being said, I have tried to use ballads which I believe clearly reflect early seventeenth century Sikh literary style.[22]

The second source is by Guru Harji who was Miharvan's eldest son and spiritual successor. Harji composed a biography on his father titled *The Discourses of Guru Miharvan (Goshti Guru Miharvanu)*. Harji was from the next generation of savants to intellectualise the position of the Miharvan School to a larger reading and listening public. Like his father, he too possessed a sizable corpus of literary works.[23] Harji's biography of his father sheds important information on Miharvan's thought and self-image. The hagiography was written by Harji, probably with the assistance of other scribes in the 1640s or 1650s.[24] While the actual text has no date, we know it is a work by Harji because firstly, after Harji no Sikh writer produced any works on Miharvan's life; secondly, the text only discusses the spiritual lineage up to Harji;

and lastly, the text displays the literary style of early seventeenth-century Sikh literature.

The works of Bhai Gurdas and Harji were staunchly opposed to each other and this makes their texts significant when read in contrast to each other. This cross-referencing of both sources helps identify potential intellectual contests between the thinkers and their rival lineages.

Bhai Gurdas in a revealing and well-known ballad highlights the controversies that had flared up due to Guru Hargobind's militaristic behaviour. In this ballad he writes of the questions that were being posed to him by certain Sikhs:

The previous Gurus used to sit at one temple (*dharmsal*);
But this Guru [Hargobind] roams from place to place.
Kings (*Patisah*) used to visit the homes of the previous Gurus;
But this Guru was imprisoned in the Emperor's fort.
The previous Gurus used to make congregations flourish;
But this Guru roams the land without any fear.
The previous Gurus used to sit on their beds and bestow
contentment;
But this Guru keeps dogs for the hunt.
The previous Guru's used to listen, sing and explain;
But this Guru he neither listens, sings or explains.
This Guru does not keep close to his servants (*sewak*);
Rather he gives favour to liars and evildoers.
[Gurdas' reply] The inherent truth (*sach*) cannot be concealed;
The disciples (*Sikh*) [knowing this] like bees adore the lotus feet.
The impatient are unknowingly being made to endure [these
reforms].[25]

The complaints against Guru Hargobind must have been widespread, otherwise it seems unlikely that Gurdas would have brought up the issue with such contemplation and self-assurance. The criticism was voiced from the position of Sikhs who had obviously accepted the order prior to Guru Hargobind's reign. It shows a clear attachment to the earlier principles of Sikhism and reflects alarm at the new changes.

Since Gurdas' criticism contrasts the old with the new, it is worth speculating how the new order might have impacted on old elites within the community; was Gurdas' criticism touched by a fear of both being marginalised in the [new] community and great concern about the direction that spirituality was taking in Sikhism? Guru Hargobind is accused of associating with disreputable characters: this could be a reference to his army and the new social groups who became inclined towards Sikhism owing to its militancy. Moreover, the juxtaposition deployed by Bhai Gurdas is telling – it is the conduct of the renouncer and the sovereign that are contrasted. The easy recourse to this binarism suggests that in the early seventeenth century, certain sections of the Sikh community expected the Sikh Guru to behave in a specific way; that some did expect the Sikh Guru to shun temporal authority. The tenor of his ballad also suggests a desire amongst some to abide by hallowed traditions, that Sikhism should not be transformed by its successors. Yet Bhai Gurdas acknowledges that change is a matter for the Guru to decide, even though the devotion of the Sikhs has not changed. The telling sentiment is carried in the conclusion: Sikhs are still like bees enamoured with the lotus, but the lotus has the power to change its hue and scent.

In direct contrast to Bhai Gurdas' ambivalence with Guru Hargobind's ideas, Harji eulogises Miharvan as the epitome of sainthood in his dress and conduct. He argues insistently that Miharvan is the perfect successor to Guru Nanak. While Miharvan sources in this early period are largely quiet over the precise circumstances of Guru Arjan's demise and the existence of Guru Hargobind's claims to Guruship, Harji deliberately focuses on Miharvan's inheritance of the Guruship from his father. He goes on to recount the perfection of Guru Nanak's and Prithi Chand's conduct and a description of Miharvan's daily activities:

> After the pervious Gurus, Lord (*Padshah*) Miharvan, sat [on the throne of Guruship]. He began earning his devotional wealth (*bhagati*) [i.e. he started his reign as the Guru]. In what way did he earn his devotion? The Lord (*satgur*) Miharvan arose with a strong body (*baltan*) and primordial awakening (*adi laikari*), [this

is how] his fame (*parkrit*) remains in the world. When the last watch of night emerges; then for two watches (*dui gharia*) he meditated with a rosary (*mala*). He caressed the ego (literally 'mouth' *mumh*) that dwells inside.

Then after this period was over he arose. Then laying down in prostration at the feet of the *Adi Granth* (*pothi* – could refer to other scriptures as well) for two watches and he caressed his rosary. When this was finished his house servants (*mahiai sewak*) came close with his dishes and were successful [i.e. they served him]. Washing his mouth becoming pure he continued lying down in prostration at the feet of the *Adi Granth* (*pothi*) with his rosary. Then the congregation of his Sikhs and family members came close and prostrated at his feet. They came for his sight (*darsanu*).

Then in this good natured (*subhau*) atmosphere, to the new (*niti nai*) congregants Miharvan asked about their happiness (*kusalu*) 'Brother, are you happy (*sukh*)?' Then all the people replied 'yes, your grace is our happiness' (*tera prasadi sukhu heh*). Then Miharvan related to the congregation the anecdotes of the saints (*bhagatan kian sakhian*) and the anecdotes of the Sikh Gurus (*guru kian sakhian*), as well as discourses (*katha charca*) on the incarnations (*auru* – incarnations?) and God's mysteries (*nimati aan*). All heard Guru Miharvan's explanations (*bachni*) and they felt tranquillity (*mahasitalu*). Then all the Sikhs touched his feet and headed home.

Then after that he massaged his body with oil and bathed. He then applied the sacral mark (*tilak*) on his forehead. He worshipped the *Adi Granth* (*pothi*) and then did all his everyday duties. Then he distributed charity (*dan*). Then for a long period in Yogic postures (*lambe asani hoi kari dandutu*) he meditated. Throughout the day, day or night, he recited the *Japji* twenty-one times…

In order to get a glance of the divine (*parmesur ke bhekh*) many came to see him such as guests, fakirs, yogis, renunciants, Pandits, detached ones, monks, and so forth…

When he sat to perform devotional music (*kirtan*), his performance was so imbued with love that among the listeners not even
a drop of compassion (*dhiraju*) was left in them. The time was
such that all those who participated in the performance all their
desires came to fruition. Then all their minds focused upon God.
There no burden of illusion or ego (*maiaa moh*) remained. Then
after the performance the congregation of Sikhs departed.[26]

Harji's portrayal of Miharvan's dress shows that he visually looked very
similar to previous Gurus. On his forehead he applied the sacral mark;
his clothes were undoubtedly saintly in guise; he wrote compositions;
engaged in preaching and devotional singing. His daily life was dedicated to meditation and earning devotional wealth. He venerated the
sacred scriptures of the *Adi Granth* and possessed a *pothi* (manuscript)
of the *Adi Granth* which played a central role in his court. Despite
his spiritual practices he continued to perform his household chores.
Importantly his day was partially dedicated in entertaining and edu-
cating his congregation. The importance of Harji's representation of
Miharvan in contrast to Guru Hargobind is the power and routine of
the Sikh court. The complaints directed to Gurdas about Hargobind
were over his misbehaviour in giving favour to new Sikhs over votaries.
This notion of gaining the Guru's 'grace' or 'favour' would have been
well established by the early seventeenth century in the Sikh court:
Sikhs would have desired the Guru's grace in the court. In turn this
meant the Guru would judiciously bestow his favour on the worthy;
this favour was unlikely to be monetary, but something spiritual. But
Guru Hargobind was accused of breaking this arrangement because
he never stayed at one court nor did he give gifts to the worthy.
However, Miharvan made no such *faux pas* in his conduct, rather he
was readily available in his court and he offered his grace to the 'worthy'. Therefore, Miharvan continued the expected court mechanism
of service (*sewa*) and grace (*prasad*).[27] It seems Harji was asserting the
image of Miharvan as the maintainer of the 'true' court.

In Harji's description of Miharvan's court the emphasis placed on
his exegetical skills is very important. This is because it shows how
Miharvan was using his skills as a rhetorician to talk with Sikhs. His

literary works were not composed for a mystical fraternity or private consumption, they were designed to interact with Sikhs and their personal dilemmas. Harji tells us that Miharvan related to Sikhs the anecdotes of saints, Sikh Gurus, incarnations and then God. It is possible that the ordering of these subjects was not random but reflects how Miharvan delivered his sermons by focusing first on the worldly symbols of divinity as reflected in the lives of the saints. Thereafter Miharvan have sought to use saintly allegories to explain the mysteries of an unknowable God.

Harji's also attempts to associate Miharvan with Sikh devotional music (*kirtan*). The practice of *kirtan* was central to Guru Nanak's philosophy and the majority of the hymns in the *Adi Granth* were composed using the classical Indian music system of *rag*.[28] Guru Nanak's aesthetics wholeheartedly embraced music and poetry, but rejected devotional dancing as found in some Hindu and Sufi devotional circles.[29] Miharvan's expertise as a musician was constantly highlighted by Harji as a perfect reflection of the divinity dwelt within him. For example, Harji informs us of how Miharvan performed *kirtan* with immense passion and skill when entertaining the congregation of Ganjhal, central Panjab:

> Then the master's (*sri satguru*) heart (*manu*) became focused (*tiki*) on Ganjhal. Then day and night *kirtan* was performed. Many string players (*rababia*) were gathered. When Guru Miharvan sat to perform *kirtan*, then many musical instruments were played including the *rabab, panchvaj, bheri, sankh, dolak, murali, tal, nad, ransing, sirande, dutare, bina, kathtal,* and *hudka*. The sound was like the natural sound of rain (*indar*). In the *kirtan* new scripture (*bani*) was also revealed. It is known that Guru Miharvan's *kirtan* was identical to the previous Gurus and the successor Gurus.[30]

It is telling that Harji says that Miharvan's performance was identical to his predecessors. It is also important to note that Miharvan is composing new scriptures even after the *Adi Granth* has been canonised. His skill as a musician was arguably more significant than his literary feats because ordinary congregants would have had no access to his

manuscripts and may have found his intellectual sermons too sophisticated. But his musical performances may have been more powerful in
conveying his spiritual aura. The music would of course have enticed
listeners, but even the sight of all these musicians would have been
impressive. In the same manner Guru Hargobind would have seemed
equally impressive with his physical prowess, mighty army and strong
steeds.

There is an interesting contrast between Harji's images of Miharvan
and Gurdas's comments on the complaints against Guru Hargobind. It
seems Miharvan was actively trying to show continuity with his predecessors by emphasising the point that his dress and conduct were what
was to be expected of a Sikh Guru. This issue of expectation was vehemently expressed in the complaints against Guru Hargobind. Guru
Hargobind was participating in activities which were uncharacteristic
of his predecessors and for certain Sikhs he seemed to be abandoning his duties as a Guru. The Miharvan School were unquestionably
making a critique of Guru Hargobind's demeanour and authority
as a Guru. There was perhaps an attempt by the Miharvan camp to
appease the clamours of unrest found among Guru Hargobind's supporters by suggesting Miharvan was the 'true' Guru since he fulfilled
the needs of Sikhs in a manner identical to previous Sikh Gurus. Guru
Hargobind was accused of not having a permanent base, but Miharvan
has. Guru Hargobind was accused of being hostile to royal patronage,
but Miharvan has no hostility towards royal gifts. Guru Hargobind
was accused of roaming and not helping congregations, but Miharvan
made it a primary duty to help his flock. Guru Hargobind hunted and
ate meat, while Miharvan was a vegetarian and 'non-violent'. Guru
Hargobind did not explain, write, listen or sing, but Miharvan excelled
in all these skills. Guru Hargobind kept company with bad people at
the expense of his existing servants, but Miharvan had no such companions, only loyal Sikhs. Bhai Gurdas attempted to curb any unrest
by arguing the essence of devotion is unwavering loyalty to one's lord
regardless of their conduct. For the Sikh community this must have
been a period of great confusion. There were two vastly contrasting
Guru lineages and Sikhism was a religious system which required only
one Guru. Hence, to remain neutral on this issue was untenable: Sikhs

had to choose one of the two. This decision would have been based on who they felt most represented Sikhism and the reasons for how they formulated their vision on Sikhism must have been related to their own lives and social backgrounds.

The situation was particularly significant because the early seventeenth century saw major developments in Sikh community formation in three broad spheres: theologically, geographically, and socially. These innovations fundamentally informed the contrast between Guru Hargobind and Miharvan and their appeals amongst the Sikh community.

Theologically, the Sikh community had, in the last few years, seen the making of Sikh scriptures with Guru Arjan's compilation of the *Adi Granth* in 1604. The *Adi Granth,* also known as the *Sri Guru Granth Sahib,* was the first authoritative book of Sikh scriptures which contained the writings of all the previous Sikh Gurus and several mystics from Hindu and Islamic traditions.[31] The text was composed by Guru Arjan, and Bhai Gurdas acted as his amanuensis. Significantly it contained no works from any Miharvan authorities.[32] The *Adi Granth* marked a decisive point in Sikh community formation because it gave them a scriptural cannon comparable to the Vedas and the Qur'an. Although some have suggested that the plurality of hymns in the *Adi Granth* undercut its exclusivity as a Sikh text, the assumption that a religious text had to be *de novo* had, in a different context, also led to hostile remarks about the Qur'an and its Biblical moorings. More importantly, among the Sikh community the text became a focal point for 'orthodoxy' and 'tradition'. This can be vividly seen from the attitudes of the Sikh literati towards the text. For example, the works of Bhai Gurdas and Miharvan can be seen in many respects as works of exegesis on the *Adi Granth.*[33] Furthermore, the possession of an *Adi Granth* manuscript became a source of prestige and spiritual power within the Sikh community. Numerous Sikh families of note used their possession of a *pothi* (manuscript) of the *Adi Granth* to highlight their religiosity. The Miharvan School reiterate this point in their early literature: their possession of a manuscript warranted respect and prestige.[34] Guru Hargobind's family possessed the original manuscript written by Guru Arjan known as the *Kartarpur Bir,* a manuscript that was stolen by Guru Hargobind's errant grandson for his propagandising.[35]

The presence of an authoritative text provided a source for the dissemination of knowledge and the *Adi Granth* transformed Sikh exegesis and devotional music. It also limited interpolations and sparked a significant hermeneutical divide, one which further complicated the contest between the Guru Hargobind and Miharvan camps.

The emergence of the *Adi Granth* as an 'authoritative text' has provoked recent analysis into its textual history.[36] There has been some confusion within academic ranks regarding the 'truth validity' of an authoritative text that has multiple manuscripts and its resolution has led textual historians into an unending search for an 'ur' manuscript. Predictably all that this search has confirmed is the presence of several manuscripts which differ from one another. These variant *Adi Granth* traditions lucidly indicate the existence of differing Sikh intellectual traditions from the early seventeenth century. The precise reasons for these variations are not clear; they range from scribal errors to intellectual disagreements. But these variant manuscripts and the differing traditions which they sustained undermine the argument for a fixed and eternal *Adi Granth* which was universally recognised by Sikhs from its inception. More significantly, at least for my argument: the existence of these variant traditions shows how the Sikh literati were attempting to canonise *Gurbani* (the Guru's utterances) from the early seventeenth century onwards. The symbols of the 'book' and 'sacred speech' were becoming pivotal to Sikh identity in the early seventeenth century.

Geographically the Sikh community saw the growth of sacred sites and clear regional divides of supporters. Bhai Gurdas discusses the presence of Sikh congregations across South Asia in his ballads.[37] Patna seems to have had a particularly strong Sikh community because we possess several letters written by Guru Hargobind to his Patna followers.[38] But it was in the Panjab that the main Sikh congregation resided and Guru Hargobind and Miharvan mainly lived there. We see the growth of Sikh temple towns under Guru Arjan in central Panjab known in the Panjabi idiom as Majha and officially attached to the Mughal province of Lahore. The previous Sikh Gurus had built hospices (*dharamsala*) in the areas of their residence; for example Guru Angad at Khadur and Guru Amar Das at Goindwal, both in the Lahore province. But Guru Arjan constructed *dharamsalas* in areas other than his place of residency. These temples included Kartarpur (1594), Taran Taran (1590), and Sri Hargobindpur (1595). Significantly Guru Arjan expanded his father's town of Ramdaspur into Amritsar. These *dharamsala* emerged to provide pilgrimage sites and distinctly sacred Sikh spots, gradually growing into commercial centres as the temples drew in pilgrims and began bustling with enterprise.[39] Certainly the concentration of temple towns in the Majha region indicates increasing support in the region for Sikhism. The Panjabi plains or *doabs* (land between two rivers) emerged as a region with strong Sikh support. This was contrasted with western Panjab and the Panjabi hills which had no major Sikh sites. In addition, southern Panjab known as Malwa had limited Sikh presence. The importance of these variations in geographical support altered the manner in which Sikhism developed in the Panjab as a whole. Despite inter-regional similarities in caste and ethnic groups, regional location changed their attitudes towards Sikhism.

The social composition of the Sikh community was definitely in a process of transformation. Early Sikh literature seems to suggest that the main caste group that formed the Sikh community were the Khatris.[40] All the Sikh Gurus were from Khatri backgrounds and this partly explains the appeal. Moreover, Sikh teachings did not castigate the Khatri community's mercantile pursuits; they only moralised on the right conduct of a merchant. The Khatris were high-caste Hindus belonging to the Kshatriya rank and continued to observe many Hindu customs such as wearing the sacred thread. The growth in 'temple towns' in central Panjab during Guru Arjan's reign in particular suggests the emergence of greater diversity within the Sikh community. Increasing numbers of low-caste groups from artisan and agricultural backgrounds joined the Sikh community. This appeal was probably heightened due to the egalitarian principles of Sikhism. It has been argued that this period saw a rapid rise in ordinary Jat followers.[41] Several Jat Sikhs had been prominent in the Sikh movement prior to Guru Arjan such as Bhai Budha. In stark contrast to the Khatris, the Jat community were a low caste, agricultural, and in many ways non-Hindu group. Furthermore, the Jat community had a larger population than the Khatris in Panjab. But beyond numbers, some Jat families had become landlords (*zamindars*) in the region and landlordism often came with claims of Rajput status which reflected the martial aspects of Jat culture.[42] The Sikh movement gave the Jats an opportunity to gain an education and salvation; it provided social mobility. Many artisanal groups probably felt the same and saw Sikhism as a means for helping their social rank. The Khatris in many respects did not see Sikhism in this way, as they were already an elite group in the region; they probably saw Sikhism more as an aid to their mercantile pursuits. Of course, among the Khatris there were immense internal disparities, and some Khatri groups would indeed have seen Sikhism as a religion of social mobilisation. But the early seventeenth century saw the growth in non-Khatri Sikh leaders, usually at the expense of Khatris. This was largely a gradual process as non-Khatris, particularly Jats, became literate and began occupying positions of authority. Throughout Hargobind's Guruship this shift in the social composition of Sikh community saw greater tensions and cracks along caste lines.

The expansion of the Sikh community was accompanied by the emergence of Sikh literary genres.[43] These ranged from erudite, scholastic literary traditions to more vernacular forms. The *Adi Granth* formed the nucleus of all these works; its hymns inspired the need to contextualise and explain the inner meanings of their sacred verses. Scholastic traditions included the poetic works of Bhai Gurdas and Miharvan. These works were a mixture of high intellectualism and occasional plain language designed for the average person. More explicit folk literature emerged with the *Janamsakhis* (lit. birth anecdotes) surrounding Guru Nanak's cult of personality.[44] These anecdotes, written in a clear prose style, were rich with ethnographical details of rural Panjab reflective of their intended audiences. Their emergence shows how in this period there was a growing interest among Sikhs to understand the life and teachings of Guru Nanak. The anecdotes created a distinct image of Guru Nanak which ultimately revealed their discursive stance on what they believed was 'real' Sikhism.

The importance of these developments in the early seventeenth century Sikh community underscores the tensions present in its early community formation. While there was a notion of 'Sikhism', the Sikh community were divided by their communal identities which caused them to have alternative visions of Sikhism. Moreover, neither Guru Hargobind nor Miharvan were exact opposites. Both claimed legitimacy from Guru Arjan and ultimately Guru Nanak. Hence they both revered the Adi Granth; they believed in performing devotional music (*kirtan*); they stressed the power of meditation (*simran*); they believed in exegesis (*katha*); they continued the practice of congregation (*sangat*) and Sikh temples; and they placed emphasis on Guru Nanak's three tenets of charity, meditation and cleanliness (*dan, nam, ishnan*). The major difference was their conduct: for his detractors, Guru Hargobind only seemed to advocate these ideals, but Miharvan lived them. From a different perspective, Guru Hargobind's unusual appearance offered Sikhs a Sikhism which balanced the 'spiritual' and 'temporal', but Miharvan only offered Sikh 'spiritualism'. The rival camps were asking the Sikh community to seriously consider their beliefs and choose the real Guru.

The differing positions that members of the Sikh community took on the issue of militancy, for example, was strongly influenced by their caste and social backgrounds. Caste boundaries played a major role in the early Sikh community and the diversity in castes resulted in multiple interests even though they were embedded in a common Panjabi cultural system. This schism over Guruship allowed caste groups to choose a Guru on the basis of their own needs and interests. The contrast between Guru Hargobind and Miharvan was intellectual but their appeals among the Sikh community saw a divide in terms of supporters along caste and social backgrounds. The Jat community of central Panjab largely sided with Guru Hargobind as did the artisan caste groups.[45] Generally lower caste groups sought Guru Hargobind as their Guru.[46] The Khatris, on the other hand, seem to have been more divided in their choice of Guru, the community having kinship links to both Guru Hargobind and Miharvan. It is unclear whether the families of Guru Hargobind and Miharvan were conflicted over the 'rightful' Guru. It seems that their choices were based largely on personal evaluations of spirituality and not proximate kin ties. For example, Bhai Gurdas was the maternal uncle of both Hargobind and Miharvan, but he rejected Miharvan's candidature, it seems, for religious reasons. Both Guru lineages therefore had a unique appeal amongst Khatri supporters along the lines of kinship and cultural traditions. It is important to keep in mind that there were wide social and economic disparities amongst the Khatris and there are anecdotes of Khatri merchants whose wealth forced them to shun the Sikh Gurus, and another of a poor Khatri man begging Guru Nanak to help him pay for his daughter's wedding.[47] Sikh tradition records Miharvan's close connection with wealthy Khatri families such as Chandu Shah's family,[48] but Guru Hargobind seems to appeal to Khatri groups from lower social positions as shown by his Khatri soldiers. Military professions seem to have declined in respectability among Khatri mercantile elites from the early medieval period onwards.[49] The grey divisions we seem to be faced with in the early years of Sikh community formation suggest that Guru Hargobind had a broad social appeal, specifically among lower caste groups. Miharvan's appeal, on the other hand, was mainly amongst elite Khatri groups.

The differences in support bases for Guru Hargobind and Miharvan also had implications on the subject of social mobility. Early Sikh teachings were especially opposed to caste barriers. They rejected the idea that human beings were destined to live in prosperity or degradation on the grounds of birth. They advocated that all human beings, irrespective of birth, had the ability and right to liberation. Caste barriers were rejected in Sikh temples and religious rituals. Nevertheless, radical policies such as cross-caste marriage were never proposed and the Sikh community continued to operate on clear caste divisions.[50] The desire for cross-caste marriages was probably a non-issue for many Sikhs. Early Sikh teachings based on egalitarian principles encouraged and uplifted low social groups. However, Guru Hargobind's militant reforms were not simply religious in nature: they promoted social mobility. Previous Gurus had hired servants because of their religious commitment to Sikhism. Guru Hargobind was the first to hire servants from the ranks of soldiers, people who were elevated not on the merit of their religious devotion to Sikhism. We should see these

developments as a moment when Guru Hargobind transformed himself into a landlord (*zamindar*), a process analogous to the one described
elsewhere by Perlin as gentrification.[51] Guru Hargobind was not only a
spiritual guide but also a temporal guide who could aid his Sikhs as a
ruler, in temporal matters. He possessed land, wealth and an army; he
could offer job opportunities and provide actual physical protection.
For some members of the Sikh congregation, this change in the status of the Guru undermined his spiritual sanctity since Gurus should
concern their thoughts only with the metaphysical. But for others the
change in status of Guru Hargobind had genuine benefits; he could be
a spiritual guide and a temporal patron. By contrast, Miharvan, who
attempted to maintain a firm distinction between the 'empirical' and
'spiritual', offered no such incentives to the votaries in his service. He
was a spiritual guide unaffected by worldly pursuits and wealth. And
yet the contest between Guru Hargobind and Miharvan was linked to
greater social changes in the Sikh community, including changes in
both Gurus and Sikhs.

Court of Man and Court of God

Religious groups in medieval South Asia often made a distinction
between the 'court of man' and the 'court of God'. They would argue
that their leaders were a manifestation of divinity on earth. They were
real kings honoured by God and their metaphysical power impinged
upon the temporal power of actual kings.[52] This type of thought was
found in diverse religious traditions, in theological literature and popular anecdotes. Only occasionally did these ideas go so far as to turn
into episodes of political conflict between religious fraternities and
kings. Commonly, the belief in the spiritual power of the saint over
the king existed harmoniously with state patronage. A good example
is the patronage Sufi shrines received from kings.[53]

   The Sikh tradition was unexceptional in this case and also
stressed the Guru's kingship in God's court and consequently over
actual kings. In early Sikh literature the notion that the Guru was a
king and the earth was his kingdom is constantly restated.[54] Almost
always the Guru's authority was metaphysical but this exoteric

sphere was nonetheless very real. The first Gurus were bereft of
wealth and armies yet were still described in terms associated with
worldly kings. They were titled as *Chakravartin, Raja* and *Padshah.*
Popularly they were known as *Din Duni Padshah* (king of spirituality and temporality) and *Sacha Padshah* (true king).[55] Before Guru
Hargobind these regal images were purely metaphysical: the Guru's
power was not tangible in the eyes of non-believers and their conduct
was far from kingly courtesy. However, Guru Hargobind's power
was real, with his army and other visible signs of sovereignty. This
created a problem for the Sikh literati: was the construction of temporal authority an 'illusion' in the spiritual sense? The *Adi Granth*
hymns had portrayed kings as divine agents capable of giving justice
and injustice to their subjects. But kings were arrogant and foolish, failing to recognise God's power and his unconquerable agent
of death. Since all temporal power succumbs to death, so too would
Guru Hargobind's construction of his authority – this too would face
death. Did not Guru Hargobind's egotistical ambitions burden the
self with illusion? For example, kingly power was described in the
Adi Granth in the following ways:

> Kings, lords and noblemen won't remain;
> Their commands cease over shops, cities and markets.
> The fool believes his beautiful home will remain his;
> The wealth that fills the chest swiftly empties.
> Horse drawn chariots and canopied chariots pulled by camels
> and elephants;
> Leopards that make up the estate: when can you own those
> items?
> The luxury tent with its laced bed and silken tent-walls;
> Nanak, there is only the True Giver: the wise recognise
> nature.[56]

> Constructing beautiful gates, homes and palaces;
> Manifold wonderful castles.
> Quilt draped elephants and horses;
> Having a large army:
> No one will depart with these things;

These futile possessions are only murdered.
Many are known as emperors, kings, lords and noblemen.
One is known as a gentry lord, another a local chief; burning to
death due to their pride.
The fool forgetting the Name, burns like stalk in a forest fire.[57]

Reading scriptures becoming lost in the text: so many guises
rife with pride.
Bathing at the sacred spots, so what? In your heart there's only
dirt and delusion.
Bereft of the teacher, how will you comprehend? The intellect
becomes the emperor.[58]

The last stanza of the composition shows a complicated idea of kingship, in which the mind becomes king even though one engages in
'pious' activities like studying scriptures and going to sacred spots.
This was indeed a tricky issue: Guru Hargobind might appear like
a king but his mind might be like a Guru's mind and, equally,
Miharvan might appear like a Guru, but his mind might be like a
king's mind.

The Sikh literati could either justify or criticise Guru Hargobind's
militancy by turning to the *Adi Granth*. The supporters of Guru
Hargobind and Miharvan did not begin their contestation on opposite
planes but instead shared a common base. They both agreed that Sikh
teachings maintained a view that the householder's path was more
favourable than renunciation. Only in old age or extreme cases would
renunciation be appropriate. The vast majority should practise the
householder's way and cleanse the self by renouncing their illusionary senses through the aide of meditation in private and within the
congregation. This meant Sikhs should participate in life and earn
an honest living. They should cultivate civic virtues such as charity
and equality by living in congregation. Undoubtedly the Sikhs would
encounter illusion in their daily lives since the world was not the ultimate end and can distract man from his spiritual duties. However, the
renunciant may also be deluded because he fails to see that the illusion
is not external but internal. The Guru is the guide who helps his Sikhs
learn and secures their freedom by leading them along the path. This

was the baseline on which both camps agreed. For example, the *Adi Granth* notes:

> The fool feeling despondent, leaves his home becoming wicked, viewing only other's homes.
> Abandoning the householder's duties; never meeting the Lord; travelling in a circle of dubiety.
> Going to distant lands; constantly studying scriptures; thirst is always growing.
> A raw intellect which never recognises the word: filling their stomachs like cattle.
> Friend, in this manner lives the true renunciant.
> [He who learning] the Guru's teachings, applies with devotion the One:
> To who your Name is bejewelled is in satiety. (Pause)[59]

The question that was asked was: what if Sikhs were prevented from following their path due to cruelty and injustice caused by external agents such as kings? Two responses emerged.[60] The Miharvan School argued that all actions are caused by God's will and if one suffers pain, it must be endured. This endurance was faith in God and acceptance of his commands. The pain suffered was illusionary so the believer should not be overcome by it. While the followers of Guru Hargobind agreed that all actions were the result of God's will and pain must be endured, they further explained that God was also righteous and removed evil agents in his divine game. The Guru, when participating in temporal affairs, was not engaging in illusion but rather breaking it; he was protecting those who have earned divine protection. The Miharvan School responded by arguing that the Guru could not meddle in temporal affairs; his was a metaphysical kingship. He must guide his Sikhs by teaching them and thus protecting them from their baser senses. The followers of Guru Hargobind responded by stressing that some types of pain that were caused by other human agents, such as cruelty, was simply not spiritual. One could overcome such cruelty with power (*Shakti*) and the Guru must teach his Sikhs this lesson. These opposing opinions had alternative visions of Sikh life: Miharvan, in the end, saw his Sikhs becoming physical renouncers, while Hargobind saw renunciation within the household.

In early seventeenth century Sikh literature we see these debates appearing in occasionally obscure ways. The arguments were constructed on opposing intellectual frameworks of Sikhism which appealed to certain audiences. Significantly, these debates become integrated with Vaishnava and Shakti philosophy in later decades.[61]

These debates on popular and intellectual levels are articulated in the *Janamsakhis*. The Miharvan and Hargobind traditions appear to have opposing images of Guru Nanak's life and teachings in certain important anecdotes which reveal alternative images on the role of the Sikh Guru. In Miharvan's image of Guru Nanak, Nanak is depicted as a 'renouncer' who overcomes external evil through his supernatural powers and wisdom. In Hargobind's image of Guru Nanak, Nanak is displayed more like a 'householder' who actively engages with temporal authorities.

Remembering Guru Nanak

The early seventeenth century sees the emergence of a significant Sikh genre, the *Janamsakhis* (lit. birth anecdotes).[62] These were essentially biographies of Guru Nanak, similar to Islamic *Hadiths* and Buddhist *Jatakas*. This genre was largely exclusive to the Panjab and written in early Panjabi dialects. Stylistically the anecdotes were in prose with occasional verses quoted from the *Adi Granth* in order to contextualise and verify an anecdote. Designed for mass circulation, this literature appealed to both preachers and laymen. On a basic level, the anecdotes were easily comprehensible to the average reader or listener but they could also be expanded into sophisticated sermons by converting the anecdote into a parable.

It is widely agreed among scholars that the origin of the *Janamsakhis* was in an oral tradition emerging from the times of Guru Nanak's life.[63] Undoubtedly Guru Nanak was a known saint who inspired anecdotes regarding his life and teachings. Oral transmission of *Janamsakhis* was the main mode of communicating the wonder of the saint. However, from the late sixteenth and early seventeenth centuries onwards, written texts of *Janamsakhis* began appearing as authentic biographies of Guru Nanak. This conversion of oral into written tradition resulted in the production of several *Janamsakhi* texts composed by differing Sikh groups. Unfortunately there exists no 'original' *Janamsakhi* from which we can construct a neat textual history. Instead the diverse traditions evolved together, a shared evolution which is reflected in their external similarities. But, internally, these various traditions differed in their ideological visions of Sikhism. Thus while the inner core of all these traditions glorified Guru Nanak, the myths and miracles ascribed to Guru Nanak were employed by the authors in different ways to show a particular image of Guru Nanak and Sikhism. Essentially the *Janamsakhis* were sophisticated texts which established a specific framework of Sikhism.

Textual analyses of the *Janamsakhis* are complicated because they lack a point of origin and follow multiple traditions. However, Mann has recently suggested the need for greater study of the *Janamsakhi* manuscripts, thereby "developing a clearer understanding of their dates of origin and the context of their production".[64] One way we can achieve this is by moving away from a chronological inquiry, analysing instead specific anecdotes across various traditions. Such study can enlighten us on particular discourses and the controversies which concerned the authors and, by extension, touched the lives of their audiences. McLeod asserted this point when noting early controversies over ritual bathing:

> Elsewhere a narrator or commentator emphasizes an issue so deliberately that one must assume a background of contemporary controversy. The stress laid upon the importance of the daily bath suggests that the doctrine affirming it was either disputed or widely neglected during the seventeenth century.

> Although references to the ritual bathing obligation appear in several of the *janam-sakhis* all do not treat the controversy with the same concern. In this, as with so many issues, it is the *Miharban* tradition which betrays the strongest interest. This underlines the necessity of distinguishing the different

janam-sakhi traditions and, wherever, possible, of determining
their particular interests, the date of their composition, and
the dates of individual manuscripts...The historical value of
a *janam-sakhi* is greatly enhanced when its distinctive point of
view and period of composition can be identified.[65]

Indeed, *Janamsakhis* were not simply texts to express panegyrics: they
had distinctive views on Sikh teachings and the community. Analysing
the similarities and differences of an anecdote found in many traditions allows us the potential to see the discourse and dialectic amongst
the Sikh literati.

The importance of the *Janamsakhis* in revealing the intellectual
contest between Guru Hargobind and Miharvan is due to the different traditions we possess from the seventeenth century.[66] It is important to keep in mind that Miharvan composed his own *Janamsakhi*
on Guru Nanak and it is likely his sons expanded his biography by
adding two more volumes to his. Thus the distinctly Miharvan tradition of the *Janamsakhi* is traceable to that period. This work was
not only a biography but an exegetical work highlighting Miharvan's
allegorical skills. In contrast, Bhai Gurdas' ballads had biographical compositions on Guru Nanak's life but they lack the style to be
classed as *Janamsakhi* literature. And yet, given Bhai Gurdas' prominence in the Sikh community, he had a huge influence over supposedly 'orthodox' *Janamsakhi* traditions. These orthodox traditions
include the *Adi Sakhi* (original anecdotes) tradition and the *Puratan*
(ancient) tradition. These two *Janamsakhi* traditions differ from one
another in terms of their anecdotes, and the *Puratan* tradition has
two slightly differing manuscripts. The labelling of these two traditions as 'orthodox' is because they do not contradict or challenge the
orthodox biography established by Bhai Gurdas, whereas the (unorthodox) Miharvan tradition does. Finally we have another unorthodox tradition known as the *Bala* (Bhai Bala) tradition, attributed
to Bhai Bala but originally written by a Sikh group known as the
Hindalis and composed during Guru Hargobind's reign. Compared
to the others, the Hindalis were a smaller and less influential group
and this *Janamsakhi* was their major contribution. In its narrative

they stress the subordination of Guru Nanak to their leader Baba Hindal.[67]

By cross-examining the anecdotes from the Miharvan and the Bhai Gurdas traditions we can elucidate the alternative images of Guru Nanak and Sikhism that had currency in the seventeenth century.

The first anecdote I will examine is the discourse between Guru Nanak and the Mughal ruler, Babur. This anecdote is present in the earliest *Janamsakhis* and there are interesting variations in their narratives.[68] It is likely that the *Janamsakhi* tradition picked up the exchange between the two protagonists from Guru Nanak's hymns known as the *Baburvani* (utterances concerning Babur) in the *Adi Granth*.[69] Guru Nanak and Babur were contemporaries and it is possible that they may have met.[70] Whether they did or not, the *Baburvani* was composed by Guru Nanak with definite reference to Babur's raids into northern India. Guru Nanak was well situated to have witnessed these raids: he worked as an administrator for the Lodis and he contextualised Babur's raids in his more general discourse on the transience of politics. In Sikh anecdotes Guru Nanak is described as witnessing Babur's devastating raids in Saidpur (Eminabad). Some anecdotes then developed into narratives in which Guru Nanak and Babur discourse on religion and politics. In early modern interpretations of this anecdote Sikh authors used it as a template to explain Mughal moral decline and Sikh political triumph. In these narratives, early Mughal history was embedded in a Sikh narrative of sovereignty and state formation.[71]

From the different versions of this anecdote in the early seventeenth century we can infer Sikh understandings of their contemporary political circumstances. Later Sikh communities saw this anecdote in a political sense. However, its significance is not the assertion that Guru Nanak's authority is greater than Babur's: this is often expressed in other hagiographical literature of this era such as the Vallabha anecdote of Surdas meeting Akbar or Dadu Dyal discoursing with Akbar.[72] Its significance becomes discernible if we contextualise these varying anecdotes in the reign of Guru Hargobind and the polemics concerning militancy. In this particular anecdote spiritual and temporal authorities are meeting and seventeenth century

Sikh authors used it to either support or reject Guru Hargobind's reforms by ascribing alternative ideas on spirituality and temporality in Guru Nanak's life and teachings. It must be remembered that both Guru Hargobind and Miharvan camps were claiming continuity from Guru Nanak. They each claimed to be a new lamp lit with Guru Nanak's flame (*jot*), meaning they were literally an animated form of Guru Nanak. We have three varying versions of this anecdote: the Miharvan tradition, the Bala tradition, and the 'orthodox' traditions.

All our narratives have several common features. They all place the anecdote in Saidpur and its sack by Babur. They all agree that this incident occurred roughly in the early sixteenth century, probably sometime around 1520. They all assign the *Baburvani* to this anecdote. They all include a story of Guru Nanak along with other fakirs encountering an Afghan wedding party which refused to give them alms in celebration. This wedding party was slaughtered by Babur, and a Brahman and his family were spared by heeding Guru Nanak's advice to leave the targeted area. Therefore, this anecdote had an established narrative frame to which the various *Janamsakhi* traditions could add detail and colour.

The Miharvan tradition records that Guru Nanak neither met nor discoursed with Babur. Instead Guru Nanak's *Baburvani* was composed in relation to the Afghan wedding party and in particular to a band of powerful ascetics. The parable of this anecdote was to show the futility of supernatural powers and the pervasive presence of death:

When Guru Baba was in Saidpur he went to a ground where powerful ascetics resided. The powerful yogis there asked "Nanak you are most able in dialectics, but we are unconvinced with your thoughts. But we will be convinced if you show us a miracle". Guru Nanak replied "yes, but I am just a householder Khatri born in the Dark Age and a carrier of shit and piss. You are instead yogis aged hundreds of years and mighty ascetics who have seen many miracles, so what can I display to you?" They responded "Nanak, you are indeed powerful, give us this boon of showing us a miracle". From Guru Baba Nanak's mouth these words came out "How can this poor Khatri show you a miracle, I am not of your strength. Here in this location Mir Babur will arrive and to him who will demonstrate a miracle, we are not of your power. Early tomorrow when Mir Babur arrives go and show him your miraculous powers". Saying this Guru Baba Nanak departed, fully aware that behind him Mir Babur has arrived at the yogis' ground, and is getting ready to massacre them. Seizing the yogis, he began hacking their ears off and looting all their possessions. Even if some yogis resisted by using their steel discs to fight they were eventually killed. They all died with the prophecy of Baba Nanak. Neither was any Mughal horse killed nor any Mughal soldier blinded. None of the yogis' miraculous powers of turning death on its heels came to any avail. These master ascetics ability to turn death had no substance in the end. Say Waheguru. Then Guru Baba Nanak said "Mardana, who bought the heads of the yogis?" Mardana replied "you were the trader, you killed them". Then Guru Baba Nanak said "Mardana, men are naturally beings which live and die, in one's hands there is nothing". Recite brother Sri Ram Krishna Waheguru Sacha.[73]

Miharvan's anecdote focuses on Guru Nanak as the spiritual guide. Guru Nanak does not engage with kings like Babur but guides foolish ascetics to the truth. Significantly, Miharvan stresses Guru Nanak's humbleness by repeating his identity as a simple Khatri householder. Moreover, Nanak appears like a renouncer with 'inactive' militancy, because he knew the ascetics would be murdered by Babur. Despite the claims of the ascetics about their miraculous powers, they could not foresee their impending doom and due to his occult powers, Nanak did not need any temporal powers.

The anecdotes of Bhai Gurdas show Guru Nanak directly involved with Babur. Not all tell of a discourse between Guru Nanak and Babur but all include Guru Nanak being captured as a prisoner during Babur's sack of Saidpur.[74] A convenient starting point is with Bhai Gurdas' ballad on this episode:

Discussing (*goshti*) with the saints (*sidh*), masters (*nath*), and incarnations (*avatar*) Nanak showed his wonder (*kan pharaiea*). (1)

Babur humbly submitted (*mil niv niv*) to Nanak (*babe*), as did all the lords (*nawabs*). (2)

Leaving temporal kings (*patisaha*) aside, abandoning union (*jog*) and pleasure (*bhog*), he became dedicated to helping the masses (*chalitu rachaiea*). (3)

Becoming the carefree (*bemohtaju*) king of divinity and temporality (*din dunia da patshahu*), he entered the house of rule (*raj ghar*) [i.e. he entered the metaphysical realms]. (4)

Like the Creator is existent in all creation (*kudrat*), so Nanak is one with creation (*kudrat*). (5)

Uniting the separated and merging those who are continually being separated. (6)

In the holy congregation (*sadh sangat*) the unknowable (*alakh*) is known (*lakhaiea*). (7)[75]

Bhai Gurdas' ballad discusses an actual submission by Babur to Guru Nanak when they met. Guru Nanak is referred to as king of both spiritual and temporal realms, a reference which differs from the Miharvan tradition where Guru Nanak's dual authority is not elaborated. Significantly, of the two literary traditions, it is Bhai Gurdas' narrative that is expanded upon in the *Janamsakhis*. While the Colebrooke manuscript of the *Puratan* tradition only discusses Guru Nanak's capture by Babur during the Saidpur sack, both the Hafizabad manuscript of the same tradition and the *Adi Sakhis* record a discourse between Guru Nanak and Babur. The following passage is from the *Adi Sakhis:*

Then Babur became the king. The power of the Afghans was made null and void. In the land his presence became manifested. Babur the king held rule from Khurasan. Guru Baba entered into Babur's military camp. There he discoursed with the king. It was known that Babur was a Qalandar (mystic). He remained in the world and his rule was of divinity. In the first quarter watch at night he engaged in dancing and listening to music. In the

following watch he caressed his rosary. In the final quarter watch
of night he tied an iron chain around his feet and fried his head.
In all the four watches of the night he remained in servitude
to the Lord. He perpetually remained in servitude to the Lord.
Rising early he did his ablutions, did the morning prayer, and
read the thirty sections of the *Qur'an* and then ate several ounces
of cannabis. He daily consumed several ounces of cannabis, some
grown others from safflower. In this manner was Babur's nature.
When Baba Nanak entered the military camp and saw the many
slaves that had been captured. The many female and male prisoners whose necks and feet were cuffed and the tyranny they
suffered. The Baba came with grace. The Baba became overawed
with a mystical intoxication and the Baba spoke these verses:
"Khurasan was saved and Hindustan was terrorised...Nanak
dying in this world is futile one does not live unless they speak
of the Name". When these words were spoken then in Mir
Babur's ears the words were heard and he asked "which fakir is
speaking these words, bring him to me". Then a servant went
to the Baba and spoke the king has called for you. Baba said
"fine let us proceed". When he arrived in Babur's presence then
Babur spoke "the composition you just spoke please recite it for
me again". The Baba then recited it. He then explained to Babur
the hidden meaning and to Babur came contemplative relief.
Babur spoke "friend seeing you is pleasing" and conversed with
the fakir. Then arrived Babur's time for intoxication and then
came the king's cannabis in the court. Babur said "fakir you
also should partake in the cannabis" and Baba replied "I have
already eaten the drug". Babur asked "do you eat it every day?"
The Baba replied "my lord I have only eaten once and since then
I have remained drunk all day and night". He then displayed
his drunkenness and the joy of intoxication. The king became
shocked at such a sight and he then spoke "what type of cannabis is that which if eaten on one day continually remains?" Baba
spoke: "Your terror is the cannabis which intoxicates me and my
thought is constantly on the leather pouch...Nanak, Lord give
me the alms like those at the gate". Hearing these words Babur

became delighted. He said "Baba give me your company as I travel and remain my companion". Guru Baba replied "not for long only one day I'll be your companion". The king said make it three days and the Baba agreed three days. The Baba looked at the many slaves and vast quantities were dying. They were starving and naked, some in dire hunger. Glory to Afghan rule which will remain until the seventeenth and not even a morsel for the miserable masses remains. Those who take over the administration of the land they won't even have a tattered rag covering them. When Baba arrived with grace he did so in a mood of great intoxication. He stood without any emotion and came. He then fainted and fell and was out for a while. Coming to his senses he spoke: "On whose head are gorgeous plaits and on the parting a vermillion mark... Nanak whatever You wish so that is what is a human's fate". Speaking these words the Baba became intoxicated and losing heart he fell. He became wrapped in the vision of absorption. Seeing the souls the fearful fakir became grateful and fell. Some remain and never leave. When the Baba's condition became like this news was given to the king. The king came with humility he bowed his head and stood waiting. He enquired "what's going on with this fakir?" The people spoke "my lord looking at these slaves this fakir's condition has become such, he has become fearful". The king spoke "truthfulness and wisdom this fakir has, truly he is close to God". The king spoke "O' God give this fakir the power to rise and sit and give me this happiness. I am hungry for his vision and his words comfort my heart". Then the Baba arose in good condition and went to the court. They proclaimed Nanak is coming. Then Baba made the request "you act righteously and know all". The order was made to please Nanak and to remove his fear all the slaves will be released. This request was made directly to the king. The awakening of Nanak allowed the king the company and sight of the Baba. This sight brought tears to the king's eyes. The Lord Baba's lordship cannot be fathomed. The king became in awe and clasping his hands he stood up attentively. Then Guru Baba spoke "Mir you are in bliss" and Babur then kissed his feet and became most grateful. The Guru Baba spoke "to you there is this order if you wish for God's beneficences then free all the slaves". King replied "but gives onto me one boon" and Guru Baba said "ask what you desire and in God's court your boon will be granted". The king requested that his dynasty will continue from throne to throne and that it cannot be snatched away. Guru Baba spoke "that the Lord will do this" and after saying this, the king freed all the slaves. Bringing the slaves in the presence of the Baba they were clothed and set free. Once all had been freed the king prostrated at the Baba's feet and hands and received blessing. Then he left the Baba's presence and the Baba continued to roam.[76]

The *Adi Sakhis* show a Guru Nanak as a 'Guru Baba' who has the power to grant and take away kingship. This power highlights Guru Nanak as a spiritual guide, with interest and ability to alter the temporal world; his intervention helped free the slaves in Babur's possession. In a continuation of the theme, Sikh tradition records that Guru Hargobind did not leave the Mughal jail in the Gwalior fort until all of his fellow prisoners, also unlawfully imprisoned, were released with him. This is why Guru Hargobind is known as *bandi chhor* (liberator of captives).[77] There is a considerable shift in the depiction of the Guru in this narrative from Miharvan's.

The *Bala* anecdote relates a slightly different version of events. The *Bala* tradition developed into a mainstream Sikh *Janamsakhi* from the nineteenth century onwards.[78] But its roots are in the teachings of the Hindali sect. We know nothing of their teachings apart from the Hindali desire to subvert the Sikh tradition by making Guru Nanak subservient to Baba Hindal's authority. Thus they had little time for Guru Hargobind or Miharvan. They too record a discourse between Guru Nanak and Babur, where the former is portrayed in unflattering terms. Following Guru Nanak's capture he is brought to Babur because his officers say that he is a saint. The conversation between the two is full of disrespect towards Guru Nanak; for instance, Babur accuses him of being a liar when Nanak speaks of his intoxication. The anecdote also attributes hymns to Guru Nanak which are not found in the *Adi Granth*. The last paragraph of the discourse is translated below:

> Then Babur spoke "Listen Nanak dervish. You are a follower of Kabir". Then Guru Nanak replied "Listen Babur Qalandar to be a follower of Kabir one must play for the Lord. With Kabir or God I have no relation. I know of Kabir's and God's form so I am only a slave of the Lord, it is true I wear his tunic. Some go with the tunic and others go without it. Great saints and prophets there have been. What can be said even I must go. Then Babur replied "Nanak dervish you have come with purpose, take this gift from me, you are a fine fakir". Nanak replied "One arrives and God gives. With this gift all partake". Babar said "Go Nanak dervish whichever direction you wish to go that route is open to you".[79]

In the *Bala* tradition Guru Nanak is shown as Babur's inferior in many ways and, ultimately, the inferior of Baba Hindal. This Hindali supremacy is shown in the discussion of Kabir who occupies a position of spiritual authority in the Hindali pantheon of saints. Babur authorises Guru Nanak to be a preacher immune from Mughal persecution largely because of his spiritual descent from Kabir.

The three anecdotal traditions we possess show alternative images of Guru Nanak and his encounter with Babur. The significance of these variations lies in their portrayal of Guru Nanak and how this depiction would be used by a preacher/listener to explain Sikh teachings in the early seventeenth century. The Hindalis were the most unusual since they actually wanted to undermine Guru Nanak's authority. In contrast, the Miharvan and the Bhai Gurdas derived traditions wanted to show Guru Nanak's spiritual authority. Clearly these two traditions did not only want to show Guru Nanak's greatness; they also wanted to underscore how their respective, contemporary Sikh Gurus embodied those foundational ideals. From these variations we can glean the manner in which the debates in the organisation of the Sikh community, its ideologies and the shift towards militancy had become a subject of great importance to the fraternity.

The Miharvan tradition portrayed Guru Nanak as unconcerned with Babur and his temporal power, depicting him instead as a non-violent spiritual guide who was more comfortable in the company of ascetics. This was consistent with Miharvan's own conduct and his position that a Sikh Guru needs to function as a guide who is not engaged in worldly pursuits. The Bhai Gurdas tradition shows a Guru Nanak who discourses with Babur and prevails upon him to release the captured slaves. It created the memory of an ancestor whose conduct was in harmony with Guru Hargobind's; like Guru Nanak, Guru Hargobind discoursed with kings and freed slaves in the spiritual as well as the material world. In suggesting that Guru Hargobind's conduct was not antithetical to Guru Nanak's, the criticism of the Miharvan followers was neutralised.

Another important anecdote concerns Guru Nanak's birth and mission. This question of what Guru Nanak's purpose was is crucially important in establishing the path his successors might take because his life was seen as being pre-destined and ordained on a divine mission. This belief was found in both the Miharvan and Guru Hargobind lineages. Both believed Guru Nanak was appointed by God and sent specifically in the Dark Age (kal yug) to create his way (panth) dedicated to the worship of God. This mission portrayed Islam and Hinduism as two civilisations opposed to each other but woven together on a common thread of divinity. Guru Nanak's Sikhs were at times a third distinct or common path which was embedded into a Hindu framework.[80] For the Sikh literati a detailed explanation of Guru Nanak's mission allowed them to explain both his past lives and their contemporary Gurus.

The Miharvan tradition clearly stated that Guru Nanak was Raja Janak in his previous life.[81] In Hindu classical traditions Raja Janak of Videha was considered to be of supreme eminence. Janak's name appears in the *Ramayana* and the *Upanishads* as a perfect king, both spiritually and temporally.[82] The Miharvan Janamsakhi recounts how Raja Janak was called into the court of God and told of his imminent birth in the Dark Age as Guru Nanak in order to free the sinners from hell. The story went that Janak, while residing in the heavens, felt mercy for the dwellers of hell. Through his piety he gained their release into the heavens. When in heaven Janak asked those former sinners how they were feeling. They replied they were happy but starving. Janak then asked God why they were starving in heaven. God explained they had only achieved heaven through Janak's merits and so could not feed off their own virtues. In order to nourish them God decided to send the sinners back to earth, with Janak as Guru Nanak to teach them the path towards liberation. The Miharvan tradition acknowledges Guru Nanak's past as a king. It stressed, however, that Guru Nanak's role in life was to teach and instruct human beings the path to liberation. The anecdote stated Guru Nanak's teachings will focus on: "truth and contemplation, compassion and righteousness, name and charity and cleanliness, gentleness and self-restraint, good works and discernment".[83] Guru Nanak was meant to be an exemplary teacher and not a king. Guru Nanak's kingship was of a metaphysical nature. The *Dabistan* observes these beliefs were popular among early seventeenth century Sikhs: "in the view of Nanak's followers, Guru Nanak in one of the past worlds was Raja Janak, and, along with temporal sovereignty, had performed righteous spiritual deeds and called upon people to turn to God ... Today, the people from hell are those who have become his followers".[84]

In contrast, the texts associated with Guru Hargobind's followers make no explicit references to Guru Nanak as Raja Janak. They may still have held this opinion but Bhai Gurdas attempted to stress the role of Guru Nanak as a divine incarnation (*avatar*) in the Dark Age. He wrote:

Hearing the cry [for righteousness] the Bountiful (*datar*) sent
Guru Nanak to the world (*jag*). (1)
Making the washing of his feet (*charan dhoie*) a practice (*rahrasi*)
he gave his Sikhs a drink of that nectar (*charanmrit*). (2)
The omnipotent and omnipresent Lord, in the Dark Age (*kal yug*) he showed the one (*ik*). (3)
He firmly established the four feet of order (*char pair dharam de*) and made the four ranks into one (*chari varn ik varnu*). (4)
He made prince and pauper (*rana rank*) equals and spread the feet of wind (*pavna*) across the earth. (5)
He changed God's game (*khel*) and turned the body upside down. (6)

> In the Dark Age Baba Nanak teaches us to swim and he taught
> the formula of True Name (*satinamu*). (7)
> To sail across the Darkness Guru Nanak arrived. (8)[85]

The important emphasis on Guru Nanak as an incarnation of God
gave Bhai Gurdas the opportunity to discuss previous incarnations.
Prominent in this emphasis was a discussion of Vishnu's role in maintaining the universal order (*dharma*). Gurdas frequently discussed the
righteousness of Vishnu's incarnations while also stressing their arrogance. In Bhai Gurdas' view Vishnu was not the ultimate end but
was a divine god. Vishnu and other *devtas* (gods) such as the goddess
Durga were important spiritually and temporally. In Hindu thought
these gods were not only metaphysical but capable of taking birth in
human form and ridding humankind of evil. These gods were associated with militant, regal, and violent imagery and were active agents
who would be summoned in times of necessity. Bhai Gurdas commented on Vishnu's incarnations:

> Vishnu (*bisan*) took ten famous forms and with furious anger
> (*vair virodh*) destroyed (*saghare*) the mighty warriors (*jodh*). (1)
> They are the fish (*machh*), tortoise (*kachh*), boar (*vairah*), lion-
> man (*narsingh*), dwarf (*bavan*), and the Buddha (*budhare*). (2)
> The others were Parasram, Ram, Krishna, and to come Kalki,
> they became arrogant (*ahankare*). (3)
> Parasram annihilated all the Kshatriyas in one sweep; the
> Ramayana records the epic battle. (4)
> Lust and anger (*kam krodh*) was not brought under control
> and greed (*lobh*), attachment (*moh*), and ego (*ahankar*) were not
> killed. (5)
> They made no offering (*bhetia*) to the True Lord (*satigur*) and
> did not join (*sahlang*) the blessed congregation (*sadh sangat*). (6)
> In the ego (*haumai*) there are many vices (*vikare*). (7)[86]

Bhai Gurdas' point was that Vishnu's incarnations were true and just
in their initial actions. However they became intoxicated with their
successes and failed to establish a path of devotion to God. Ultimately

Bhai Gurdas was arguing that Guru Nanak was an incarnation like Vishnu but who did not fall prey to his baser instincts. Instead he spread order and established a path of true devotion.

The fascinating aspect of Bhai Gurdas' argument was his readiness to debate the role and purpose of an *avatar*. Gurdas argues all *avatars* are active figures in temporal affairs and overtly possess the inclination for energetic intervention in the material world to aid their missions. Ram kills Ravana and Narasingha (lion-man) saves Prahlad, examples which are repeated in many other episodes of *avatars* battling against the demons. Through divine figures, righteous action was engaged in an everlasting battle with the illusion of life. In this discourse, however, it is this illusion which is eventually triumphant; it eventually seeps into their conduct. The pleasures of life overtake their senses and they forget death and God. Nevertheless, they are real and righteous. Furthermore, they take on strange and unassuming forms like animals, pillars, dwarfs, men, and so forth. Vishnu's forms contradict the power of his opponent by sometimes appearing in a weaker form; for example, the Ramayana is a tale of men and monkeys challenging demonic gods.[87] Guru Nanak is also an incarnation in Bhai Gurdas' view but one whose flame is lit in Guru Hargobind's life. Unlike the other *avatars* before him, Guru Nanak was incarnated with full control over his senses when he planted the name of God on earth. Bhai Gurdas suggested that Guru Hargobind's ferocious demeanour may appear strange to the laity but that was because he was an incarnation and incarnations often have an extraordinary visage. Bhai Gurdas countered the criticism present in Miharvan's writings by arguing that the Guru should participate in temporal affairs because *avatars* do so with a purpose to fulfil God's plans; the assumption of a temporal attribute by Guru Hargobind was, in the final analysis, an emanation of God – the ultimate spiritual lord.

These Vaishnava and later Shakti frameworks would become cardinal to Sikh discourses on militancy and political sovereignty in later decades. But in these early discussions they centred on the role and manifestation of the Guru. Miharvan's Guru was only a spiritual teacher. Bhai Gurdas' Guru was an *avatar* on a divine mission affecting the spiritual and temporal realms. Miharvan's Guru was more like a renouncer with his 'inactive' militancy and power to curse. Bhai Gurdas' Guru was more like a householder with his 'active' militancy and ability to kill enemies through the force of arms.

The intellectual opposition between the Guru Hargobind and Miharvan lineages was firmly entrenched by the 1640s. But like all intellectual discourses these debates also had their material and social dimensions. Publically Guru Hargobind and Miharvan attempted to establish independent bases of authority in the Sikh community. The Sikh literati disseminated these anecdotes and explanations among the Sikh public. These discourses certainly influenced Sikhs but other social changes were also dictating their choice of Guru.

Seventeenth-Century Developments Within the Sikh Community

In the final year of Guru Hargobind's reign (1643–44) the author of the *Dabistan-i Mazahib* claims to have met with the Guru. The *Dabistan's* authorship is still unclear with the only firm identity being his pen-name Mobad (Parsi priest).[88] Nevertheless, the author made several detailed observations on the Sikh community he encountered in the Panjab. The author claims to have conversed with many Sikhs including Guru Hargobind and his successor Guru Har Rai. In addition, he met Guru Harji, Miharvan's successor, in Amritsar. Succinctly, he noted the contesting seats of Guruship:

> After Arjan Mal his brother Pritha, whom his followers call "Guru Miharban" [the kind Guru] sat in his place; and today, when it is 1055 Hijri [A.D. 1645–46], Guru Harji is his successor. They call themselves the "Bhagats" or Devotees of God; but the followers of Guru Hargobind, the son of Arjan Mal, call them "Mina", which name is regarded as derogatory among them.

> After Arjan Mal, Hargobind also made a claim to succession and sat in his father's seat...He encountered many difficulties. One was [i.e. arose from the fact] that he adopted the style of soldiers, and, contrary to his father's practice, girded the sword, employed servants and took to hunting.[89]

Mobad inaccurately reported Prithi Chand's epithet as Miharban. Instead Miharban referred to Prithi Chand's successor. But the passage otherwise sums up the tension between Guru Hargobind and Miharvan in the early seventeenth century quite accurately. Interestingly, his account also describes Guru Hargobind with qualities associated with a member of the landed gentry. And Miharvan appears in the image of a *Bhagat*, i.e., a 'renouncer', an ascetic saint in the more conventional sense.

The *Dabistan* also comments on the changing social composition of the Sikh community. It identifies the growing influence of the Jat community to the detriment of the Khatris within the Sikh fraternity. Mobad remarks: "they have made Khatris subordinate to the Jatts, who are the lowest caste of the *Bais* [Vaishyas]. Thus most of the leading *masands* (commanders/officers) of the Guru are Jatts, and the Brahmans and Khatris [comprise the] . . . disciples and followers of the Guru".[90] This disparity in the social distribution of *masands* seems to have resulted in hostility. The *Dabistan* records how a Khatri named Pratap Mal insulted a Jat *masand* named Dwara by saying: "O fool, my foot is always washed by Jatts like you, I never let my hands touch my feet".[91]

The changing social composition of the Sikh community was arguably reflected in Sikh literature and in the debates that raged over its new militant disposition. The literary works of the Miharvan tradition, especially their *Janamsakhi,* have a clear bias towards the interests of the Khatri community.[92] The Khatris seem to have been unenthusiastic at the prospect of militancy and the new bent given to Sikh teachings. By contrast, the literary works of Guru Hargobind's supporters seem to have had wider support, especially amongst the lowest castes such as the Jats and artisans, who seem to have stuck with Guru Hargobind: the *Dabistan* testifies to this. The *masands* also stayed with Guru Hargobind and did not defect to Miharvan's lineage.

It needs to be explained why Guru Hargobind's militancy had a greater appeal amongst Sikhs than Miharvan's non-militant stance. If Sikhs sincerely wanted an 'original' Sikhism they could have turned to the eloquent Miharvan. But largely they opted for Guru Hargobind. This can partly be explained by the efforts of the Sikh literati; perhaps

Guru Hargobind's supporters did a better job at proselytising. But from the 1640s onwards, the Miharvan tradition controlled Amritsar and thus ran the most sacred temple in the Sikh community. Mobad saw Guru Harji in Amritsar since he was running the Harmandir Sahib temple.[93] Even then the Miharvan School did not gain more supporters than Guru Hargobind. The reason for Guru Hargobind's success was also due to the changing social position of the Sikh Guru in relation to his Sikhs.

Guru Hargobind became gentrified in the early seventeenth century.[94] Hargobind clearly possessed significant wealth and land, and to an extent his predecessors never had. Without this financial support it would have been impossible for Hargobind to facilitate his reforms. There seems to be only one explanation for why Hargobind was so wealthy: unlike his predecessors he had inherited considerable assets from Guru Arjan who had an extensive property portfolio. Guru Arjan owned the rights to Amritsar, Taran Taran, Sri Hargobindpur, and Kartarpur; all these properties were located in central Panjab. Previous Gurus had been unable to claim the property of their predecessor because prior to the succession of Guru Arjan no son had inherited the seat of Guruship from their father. Instead successions had occurred on a master-student basis: for example, Guru Nanak appointed his student, Guru Angad, over his two sons. However, inheritance of Guruship did not mean inheritance of property rights over their predecessors' home/temple or any assets from their estate. They only gained the rank of Guru. The previous Guru's sons inherited their father's entire estate. As a result, the succession of a Guru often led to tensions between the chosen Guru and their predecessor's sons. These tensions are alluded to by Bhai Gurdas:

> Sri Chand [Guru Nanak's son] became an ascetic (*bal jati*);
> He built a temple in honour of Guru Nanak (*babana dahura*). (1)
> Lakhmi Das [Guru Nanak's son] and his [Nanak's] grandson Dharamchand;
> Became lost in their personal worth (*aapu ganeiaa*). (2)
> Dasu [Guru Angad's son] sat on a bed [i.e. spiritual seat] and Datu [Angad's son] sat like a saint;

In an effort to bring Sikhs to them. (3)
Mohan [Guru Amar Das's son] became infatuated (*kamala*);
He spent his days meditating in his attic (*chubara*). (4)
Prithi Chand [Guru Ram Das's son] became a charlatan (*mina*);
He established a path of crooked madness (*tedhak baral*). (5)
Mahadev [Guru Ram Das's son] became too proud (*ahanmeo*);
Becoming defiant he began barking like a dog (*kuta*). (6)
Though immersed in the sensuality of sandalwood (*chandan*)
[i.e. being the Guru's sons];
They never became perfumed by that wondrous fragrance. (7)[95]

Gurdas explains how every Sikh Guru had sons that were envious of their father's position and felt it right that they should inherit the Guruship. But their fathers chose merit over blood and this left some of their sons out in the cold because they feared they would lose their status and the wealth that came with being the Guru's son. As a result, these sons staunchly protected their properties and felt hostility towards the student who had been appointed Guru. But new Gurus never coveted the properties of their masters, and usually attempted to appease the angry sons by reassuring them that their property still belonged to them. The new Guru would simply leave the headquarters of their master and establish a new base. Guru Angad left Kartarpur and established his base in his hometown of Khadur. Guru Amar Das left Khadur for Goindwal. Guru Ram Das, although Guru Amar Das's son-in-law, established his base in Ramdaspur. It was relatively easy for a chosen Guru to set up a new headquarters because they simply returned to their hometowns.

Guru Arjan, however, was the first Sikh Guru appointed by his father. Consequently Arjan inherited his father's property and it is for this reason that he developed Amritsar and was not forced to leave the region. Nevertheless, Guru Arjan was the youngest of three sons and had to share his inheritance equally with his brothers. But the Amritsar Arjan inherited was much smaller than the Amritsar he created. So while Prithi Chand and Mahadev would have had partial ownership of Guru Ram Das's Amritsar, everything that Guru Arjan built afterwards, including the central temple, was solely his property.

Moreover, Guru Hargobind was Guru Arjan's sole heir, inheriting his father's property and wealth without any complications. Prithi Chand claimed to be Guru Arjan's successor but he could not claim any of his estate. Also Prithi Chand had left Amritsar in 1596 and moved to Hehar. Therefore, Guru Hargobind inherited a substantial financial base, far greater than the possessions of Prithi Chand or Miharvan.

Guru Hargobind's wealth provided him with financial independence which allowed him to implement his policies. The properties he owned were temple towns and lucrative pilgrimage sites. These towns thrived and became commercial centres with bustling marketplaces. As mentioned earlier, some scholars have argued that Bhakti religions like Sikhism were conducive to capitalist enterprises.[96] The seventeenth century saw growing commercialisation and monetisation in Panjab and these temple towns would have greatly benefited from these developments.[97] Moreover, Guru Hargobind would have received donations from Sikhs and regular tribute through the system of *masands*. This ready wealth explains why he was able to introduce militant reforms so successfully at the start of his reign. Importantly, like any gentry lord in this era he was able to offer service (*naukari*) and hire a staff.[98] This recruitment drive is best illustrated in his creation of an army. Guru Hargobind most probably dabbled in the military labour market as shown in his recruitment of peasants and others amenable to military service. Sikh tradition records that one of Guru Hargobind's most prized warriors and his training partner was an Afghan named Painda Khan. This man, famed for his great strength, was an orphan whose uncle enrolled him in service to Guru Hargobind's retinue.[99] In the *Dabistan* the author mentions being friends with a Sikh Khatri merchant who procured horses for Guru Hargobind from Kabul and central Asia,[100] so it seems Guru Hargobind was also fully attuned to the intricacies of the horse trade and used the trading expertise of his Khatri followers.

This process of gentrification experienced by Guru Hargobind must have changed his image amongst the Sikh community. He would no longer only be a spiritual guide; his ability to provide service would have made him a valuable source of employment. Sikh tradition records that when Guru Hargobind announced his reforms, soldiers predominated amongst those who came to him seeking service.[101] Besides Jats, other groups joined his army which seems to have been composed of a diverse mix of caste and ethnic groups such as Jats, Khatris, Tarkhans, Rajputs, Afghans and Indian Muslims. The existence of a considerable Muslim contingent is testified to by Guru Hargobind's construction of a mosque for his Muslim troops in Sri Hargobindpur. The *Dabistan* remarks that Guru Hargobind "had seven hundred horses in his stable. Three hundred battle-tested horsemen and sixty musketeers were always in his service".[102] This was not a large war band for this era, comparatively speaking, but still considerable especially for a commander recently mobilising forces. Other professions such as bards and musicians specialising in heroic music were also recruited.[103] Beyond these martial professions the assembly of soldiers, administrators and servicemen would have profited local merchants and artisans. Guru Hargobind was creating an important market for supplies and emerging as a source of local financial prosperity.[104] He must also have been purchasing horses and, we may assume, other military supplies such as swords, matchlocks, armour and gunpowder. As Amritsar grew in stature as the Sikhs premier pilgrimage site, reflecting Hargobind's increasing popularity, the greater consumption of food at Amritsar's free kitchen (*langar*) would have benefited local food producers and sellers. Amritsar's expansion would also have been good for the local real estate market. But Guru Hargobind's consumption was not confined to the bare necessities – like other gentry lords of the era, he had an aristocratic demand for luxury goods.[105] In a letter to his Patna congregation Guru Hargobind asked to be sent: a thick bag full of woven silk and cotton cloth known as cardamom because of its colour; a pair of young cuckoos who have started to talk, presented in a birdcage; and a pair of luxury pigeons.[106] Because he requested these goods from Bihar they must have been unique to the region. Against this background, it is reasonable to suggest that trade and commerce in and around Amritsar must have experienced a period of growth in the early seventeenth century. And given Amritsar's close proximity to Lahore, it too must have benefited from this development. The expansion of Amritsar could only have added to Guru Hargobind's prestige and wealth as more traders and people flocked to his temples. It should not miss our scrutiny that Guru Hargobind appealed directly to a method of social mobility preferred by Jats and other lower caste Panjabis, which required developing a Rajput identity. Guru Hargobind was a Kshatriya lord and by serving him his staff would have gained a certain civility associated with chivalry.

In stark contrast, Miharvan lacked financial independence and actively sought patronage.[107] In this respect he was no different from his father and had probably learnt how to engineer a support base and raise funds. Prithi Chand had bequeathed to his successor a partial claim to Amritsar and property in the Panjabi villages of Hehar, near Lahore, and Kotha Guru in southern Panjab (Malwa). It appears that Miharvan was in Hehar when Prithi Chand died and he immediately set off for Kotha Guru. In Kotha Guru he began touring the Malwa region and preaching to the masses.[108] This need to tour and perform music must have been a necessity for Miharvan in order to raise his public profile and increase the wealth of his treasury. The Malwa region was an ideal location because the Sikh population was sparse, but Miharvan did not seem to feel content with his progress in the region. He needed wealthy patrons, ideally including a king, to raise his profile and appeal to a level comparable with that of Guru Hargobind.

Miharvan's search for patronage and new proselytising areas led him to the Panjabi Hill States, in particular to the Rajput principality of Kangra, around the Suket region, where he stayed from approximately 1627 to 1630.[109] Kangra was a relatively autonomous region with limited Mughal influence. Famed for its impregnable fortress and mountainous terrain, the region was conquered in 1621 by Mughal forces.[110] This conquest did not lead to the region being fully integrated into the Mughal Empire; it was simply made a Mughal feudatory state. The political elites of the region were largely Rajput clans and culturally the region was distinct from the Panjabi plains. However, Kangra's history in the 1620s "is very confused and uncertain" because the process of Mughal conquest was not straightforward.[111] The conquest of Kangra resulted in a guerrilla movement led by Hari Chand and Chander Bhan Chand.[112] There is very little detail regarding Miharvan's stay in the region but his main companions seem to have been Rajput elites.

The Miharvan sources do not convey the political instability of the period,[113] and the success of his search is unclear because sometime after 1630 he returned to the Panjabi plains and never returned to the hills. It is possible that the political situation of the region prevented him from establishing a permanent support base, but a nineteenth-century treaty between the state of Kangra and Ranjit Singh does mention an oath sworn to God and a list of Sikh Gurus from the ruler of Kangra. That list significantly includes a mixture of 'orthodox' and Miharvan Sikh Gurus, including Miharvan's son Harji, along with Guru Gobind Singh and others.[114] So perhaps Miharvan and his successors continued to exert some degree of influence in the region, even if they did not achieve an exclusive religious monopoly. Importantly, Miharvan seems to have had no contact with Sikh communities outside of Panjab and his migration into the hills can be seen as a part of a strategy to gain patrons and strongholds of support in peripheral areas of Sikh support.

Prithi Chand was allegedly an associate of the Lahore-based Mughal courtiers Sulahi Khan and Chandu Shah. It is incredibly difficult to verify these claims and individuals because neither figure was of any significance in the Mughal system. That of course does not mean they did not exist, but it may mean that their roles have been overblown by chroniclers desperate to tell a complete story. Chandu Shah is a particularly notorious character in Sikh sources because he a wealthy Khatri merchant based in Lahore and worked as a Mughal revenue official. His position and wealth apparently gave him access to the great and the good of Mughal society, including even Emperor Jahangir. Chandu Shah had come into conflict with Guru Arjan after Arjan refused to accept Chandu Shah's offer of marriage between his daughter and Guru Hargobind. This infuriated Shah and he became desperate for vengeance; some have even argued Shah was instrumental in Guru Arjan's execution, but Mughal sources do not support this view.[115] Anti-Miharvan sources have argued that Miharvan continued to build alliances with Chandu Shah and his family.[116] According to Max Arthur Macauliffe: "Mihrban exchanged turbans with Karam Chand, Chandu's son, in token of life-long friendship, and took counsel with him to effect the Guru's ruin. They proceeded to Prince

Khuram, afterwards the Emperor Shah Jahan, and poisoned his mind against the Guru".[117] Again this easy access of the Shah family to the Mughal Emperors is questionable. But regardless of the veracity of these claims, it is possible to suggest that the Miharvan camp was purposefully attempting to gain Khatri benefactors by pandering to Khatri interests. The main support base of the Miharvan tradition in central Panjab, where the bulk of Sikh supporters resided, was largely from Khatri groups. It may be that Miharvan realised that his ideas had little appeal to groups seeking social mobility because he could not offer service. Moreover, he had a greater need for groups who would give him financial stability. This arguably led to greater conservatism in Miharvan's ideas since he did not want to alienate high-caste and wealthy groups by advocating militancy, unlike Guru Hargobind, who would have been a threat to established gentry groups in the region. In addition, the late nineteenth century chronicler, Giani Gian Singh, claimed that Miharvan had become an associate of Sulahi Khan's son, Jamal Khan, and with his help, in 1628, he made an unsuccessful petition to Emperor Shah Jahan to expand his ownership of Amritsar.[118] These claims are unsupported, but do still reflect Miharvan's need to gain external patronage in order to compete with Guru Hargobind.

The sharp difference in the financial and support bases of Guru Hargobind and Miharvan have been largely under-studied. Guru Hargobind's capacity to outmanoeuvre Miharvan was not only due to the greater appeal of his ideological stance. It is important to pay attention to his emergence as a member of the gentry with a resource base which did not require any external patronage. This transformation in Guru Hargobind's social status gave his Sikh movement the ability to encourage social mobility. Guru Hargobind was no longer a spiritual authority: he was an actual patron of local goods and services. This must have given him the impetus to drive his policies of militarisation and temporal lordship. For the Sikh community in central Panjab the militant Sikh movement arguably provided greater financial and social benefits than ever before.

The final periods of Guru Hargobind's and Miharvan's reigns were an antithesis. Miharvan returned to the Panjabi plains from Kangra by 1630 and eventually settled near Amritsar in Muhammadipur. He spent the last ten years of his life (1630–40) doing what he had done since his succession in 1618: travelling, writing and preaching. His travels were largely local and he never left the Panjab region. In 1640 he died and nominated his eldest son, Guru Harji, to be his successor. The Miharvan movement would continue under Harji, who like his father was a literary talent and intellectual.

Guru Hargobind, after his release from Gwalior fort during the period 1611–1620, returned to Amritsar to assemble his retinue and community. His fondness of hunting brought him into the nominal service of Shah Jahan. This service, according to the *Dabistan*, was simply a show of respect and not enrolment into any administrative service; it stated that Guru Hargobind was a friend of the local commander (*faujdar*), Yar Khan.[119] This relationship with Shah Jahan and Yar Khan eventually soured and led to several battles.[120] It is possible that the relationship deteriorated because of Miharvan's companionship with Chandu Shah's family and Jamal Khan. The first battle occurred at Jallo in 1628 and, significantly, in 1634 there was an imperial assault on Amritsar. Having repulsed this assault Guru Hargobind moved to his other property of Kartarpur. He left Amritsar never to return in order to spare the region any problems. This resulted in Amritsar falling into the hands of his family members and eventually, by the 1640s, the Miharvan tradition. Another battle at Kartarpur in 1635 saw Guru Hargobind move to the southern Panjabi Hill State of Bilaspur; he settled in a town known as Kiratpur.[121] Mobad met Guru Hargobind in Kiratpur and remarked:

After the battle of Kartarpur he went to Phagwara. From there, since it was difficult for him to stay in any place near Lahore, he proceeded to Karaitpur [Kiratpur] which is situated in the Punjab hills. That area belonged to Raja Tarachand, who did not pursue the path to allegiance and obedience to King Shah Jahan. The people of that area worshiped images... Today most people from amongst the masses (*ri'aya*) of that territory are the *Guru's* followers.[122]

Mobad laconically commented that it was difficult for Guru Hargobind to remain in Lahore; he meant the Lahore province of the Mughal Empire which occupied central Panjab, including Amritsar. Guru Hargobind did not choose to retreat to the Punjabi Hills in search of patronage. Instead the region's lack of Mughal authority gave him and his followers' greater peace and avoided expensive military engagements. This changing social status of Guru Hargobind can be seen in similar discussions of social mobility by Kolff on Rajputs, Alam on Awadh's religious gentry, and Wink's analysis of the Marathas.[123] He remained in the region for the rest of his life. It seems he established a successful community and continued to maintain his retinue. Importantly, he did not lose contact with the Panjabi plains or his *masands* and continued to maintain control over his property and community. In the final months of his reign, in 1644, he nominated and appointed his grandson, Guru Har Rai, as his successor.

Mughal Power

By the late seventeenth century, the Sikh movement would develop a hostile attitude towards Mughal power. This can be traced to the execution of Guru Arjan. Nevertheless, there are no overt signs of genuine hatred. For instance, Guru Hargobind is said to have nominally accepted Emperor Shah Jahan's authority although his relationship with the Mughal state turned unpleasant as his gentrification brought him into direct conflict with the Mughals. Lurking in the background is the presence of Miharvan and his supporters who are shown as being well-connected with Mughal elites and who may have weakened Guru Hargobind's relationship with the imperial centre. Hargobind was unable to remain in the Lahore province and felt it safer to leave the heartlands of his dominion. We have no information about whether Guru Hargobind was blatantly critical of Mughal power. This is mainly because he did not compose any works and we only possess a few letters which shed no light on this matter. However, we can assume that Sikhs of central Panjab would have resented Guru Hargobind's reasons for departure and the consequent loss of social and economic opportunities.

There are embers of dissent in the works of Bhai Gurdas. Gurdas had witnessed Guru Arjan's execution and Guru Hargobind's diplomatic migration. He critically commented on Mughal symbols of authority. This critique might be simple poetic license expressing the glory of the Sikh Gurus opposed to mighty kings but in the context of Sikh gentrification these comments develop greater steel: they were not empty words but potential threats. Gurdas wrote:

[The wealthy] construct tall palaces (*mahal*) that they
then lavishly decorate with moats (*vichhavane*) and other
adornments. (1)
Becoming great magnates (*vade duniadar*) they take on many
titles (*nau*). (2)
Building forts (*ghar*) and thousands of castles (*kot*), they then
work as rulers (*raj kamavane*). (3)
Retaining innumerable *Mansabdars* (Mughal imperial officers)
and paying them great salaries (*vajah*). (4)
They are filled with complete and utter pride (*ahankar*);
constantly being born and re-born. (5)
In the true court (*sacha dargah*) [of God] they stand terrified.
(6)[124]

Another cogent criticism can be found:

The temporal kings (*duniava patisahu*) die bequeathing
kingship to their sons. (1)
Their sons make their commands (*hukmi*) to their slaves (*bande*)
and soldiers (*sipahi*). (2)
They go and have their *khutbah* (public prayer) read and the
Qazi (Muslim jurist) and *Mullahs* (Muslim jurist) bear witness.
In the imperial mint (*taksalai*) his coins (*sikka*) are struck, and
the affairs of white and black [justice] fall under his commands
(*hukmai*). (3)
Seizing all wealth and territory (*mal mulku*) in his dominions,
he sits on his throne of fortune (*takht bakhti*), without any
concerns (*beparvahi*). (4)

On the throne of the Guru's house (*babane ghari*) the cart-road
(*gadi rahu*) is followed by looking towards the previous Guru.
(5)
There is one proclamation (*dohi*), one mint (*taksal*), one *khutbah*
(public prayer), and one throne (*takht*) in the true court (*sacha
dargahi*). (6)
The Sikh (*gurmukhi*) finds the blissful fruit (*sukh phalu*) of
divine justice (*dadi ilahi*) in the Guru's court. (7)[125]

Bhai Gurdas has other general criticisms on kings and the vanity of
their powers.[126] These ballads are specifically directed at Mughal kings
and reveal an attitude of dissatisfaction within certain sections of the
Sikh community towards the Mughals. They contain a clear statement
regarding the divine authority of kings and their need to be just. The
Sikh Guru is seen as the real king whose royalty is imbued with justice.
And if we recall, in Bhai Gurdas' writings the lineage of Gurus from
Guru Nanak threads its way to Guru Hargobind. Significantly from
these literary and socio-political roots a more articulated Sikh cry for
political sovereignty would emerge against the Mughal state over time.

By contrast it can be suggested that the Miharvan tradition and
other Sikh groups had a more favourable attitude towards the Mughals.
This is because they did not flee from the Lahore province but continued to preach in the region. Guru Hargobind had been forced by
Mughal hostility to find solace in the Panjabi hills. It is likely that
local authorities would have been cautious of all Sikh groups in the
region and their potential allegiance to Guru Hargobind. It is probable that they would have enquired, as Mobad had done, about the reasons for the divisions in the Sikh community. For example, now that
Guru Hargobind had left Amritsar, was this Guru Harji, who now
controlled Amritsar, an ally or enemy of Guru Hargobind? Of course,
we know that Harji was an enemy, and it seems the local authorities
understood this too. In Pashaura Singh's analysis of early seventeenth-
century *Adi Granth* manuscripts he discusses a manuscript known as
the Lahore recension.[127] This manuscript is dated 1610 and is thus
probably an early seventeenth century work composed in Lahore,
either the city or the province. Importantly, it is completely without

the *dhunis* (heroic tunes) as found in the Kartarpur recension attributed to Guru Arjan. These heroic tunes are associated with Guru Hargobind's martial ethos, although Singh argues they existed prior to Guru Hargobind's reign. Be that as it may, it is likely that they would have enjoyed particular popularity under Guru Hargobind. The omission of these heroic tunes from the Lahore recension may have been an act to neutralise any perceived notions of Sikh militancy. While there is no evidence to suggest that this was the work of Miharvan or any other Sikh group it does suggest that the Sikh literati were perfectly aware of local Mughal concerns and reactions against any threats to their local power. Perhaps Harji and the Miharvan tradition continued to place emphasis on their non-violent stance by omitting or downplaying the role of the heroic elements found in the *Adi Granth* in an effort to appease local authorities. Guru Hargobind made no such exertions.

The issue of Mughal patronage also highlights growing divisions over Mughal power among the two contesting lineages. The gentrification of Guru Hargobind delimited his need for external patronage. His predecessors did receive land grants and revenue remittances from local lords and the Mughal state; for instance, Sikh sources claim Akbar gave the Panjab a revenue remittance on Guru Arjan's request.[128] Other Sikh groups such as the Miharvan Sikhs seem to have continued to seek patronage, as shown by Miharvan's trip to Kangra, meetings with Chandu Shah and friendship with Jamal Khan. This gave them an alternative perspective on Mughal power where it appeared less of a threat and more of a benefactor. Prithi Chand and Miharvan are shown to be closely connected to local Mughal officials and Khatri families enrolled in Mughal service. This was arguably to maintain their sources of finance. Consequently, this is likely to have limited their enthusiasm for militancy since many of the local groups that supported them were dependent on the prosperity of the Mughal Empire. As I will discuss later on, Sikh groups opposed to the Guru Hargobind lineage are recorded in Sikh tradition to have gained Mughal patronage. Guru Hargobind's grandson, Dhir Mal, received a land grant from Shah Jahan, and his great-grandson, Ram Rai, a land grant from Aurangzeb. However, what these issues do highlight is the ways in which the Mughal state impinged upon Sikh sectarian divisions over Guruship. All rival lineages had to contend with Guru Hargobind's gentrified power; they therefore needed funds and the Mughal state was universally regarded as a great source of funding. While the Mughals probably had very little interest in Sikh schisms and the authority of the Guru, they would have bestowed grants, mindful of their great interest in the local circumstances and their own status as the paramount authority in the region. From the Sikh point of view, however, the Mughals were an entity with the potential to shape their lives. Thus the Mughal state would have grown in importance as a talking point for the Sikh literati in the early seventeenth century. They would be asking whether the Mughals were just or unjust, questions which were ultimately linked to their beliefs in the nature of Sikhism and the credibility of its shift towards temporal lordship and militarisation.

Conclusion

In this chapter I have attempted to show how Guru Hargobind's militarisation was contested by Miharvan's ideas of Sikhism. The contrast between Hargobind and Miharvan focused upon the direction of the Sikh movement after Guru Arjan's demise. While Guru Hargobind chose a path which fused the spiritual and temporal, Miharvan chose a path which was mainly spiritual. This debate was manifest in early seventeenth century Sikh literature and dealt with many issues, such as the Guru's code of conduct and Guru Nanak's life and teachings. However, this intellectual contest was centred upon the Guru's purpose in the world and his duties towards his Sikhs. Miharvan and his supporters argued that the Guru was a spiritual guide and not a temporal king; the Guru's job was to unfetter Sikhs from worldly illusion, a goal which could only be achieved by the Guru living an exemplary life and disassociating himself from illusion. Miharvan's ideal Guru was that of a renouncer, who possessed 'inactive' militancy. Guru Hargobind and his supporters accepted the role of the Guru as a spiritual guide, but they also argued the Guru had a temporal role. The Guru could change the world for the better and could protect his Sikhs from evil; the Guru was like Vishnu, an 'active' temporal and spiritual agent. Hargobind's ideal Guru was more like a householder and king, one who possessed 'active' militancy.

The intellectual contest between Guru Hargobind and Miharvan had established a contrast between householder and renouncer and active and inactive militancy. In the coming decades these would shape the debates of their successors and crucially influence the role of militancy in Sikhism.

It is important to keep in mind that the intellectual stance of Guru Hargobind and Miharvan was influenced by their socio-economic positions. Guru Hargobind had experienced a process of gentrification as a consequence of his inheritance from Guru Arjan, becoming a local squire with the wealth and power to allow him to develop his army and support base. In comparison, Miharvan remained relatively impoverished and was unable to compete financially with Guru Hargobind. As a result, Miharvan seems to have sought patronage from local elites, while Guru Hargobind was self-sufficient. In the 1640s the Miharvan tradition gained control of Amritsar, yet Guru Hargobind had managed to establish a successful estate in the Panjabi hills.

The contrasting philosophies and financial capabilities of Guru Hargobind and Miharvan impacted upon their support base. Guru Hargobind had gained considerable support amongst Jat and other lower-caste groups in the Panjab, but Miharvan had a much narrower base largely made up of high-caste Khatris. Guru Hargobind's appeal must have stemmed from his charisma, lineage and, significantly, his gentrification. He offered service to numerous professions and became both a spiritual guide and temporal patron and, importantly, provided lower caste groups a popular method of social mobility by offering them the opportunity to gain a chivalric civility. For many Jat peasants this type of martial identity was what they desired. However, Miharvan seems to have offered little to his servants apart from the well-established court mechanism of 'grace' and 'favour'. For Khatri groups which had little to gain from Guru Hargobind's courtly service, the traditional relationship of 'grace' offered by Miharvan would have been welcomed. These contrasting needs from the Sikh community underscore how early seventeenth century Sikh society was deeply divided by their communal identities.

3

DEBATING THE
HOUSEHOLDER'S PATH
1644–1675

The mid-to-late seventeenth century (1644–75) is typically regarded as an unimportant phase in the development of late seventeenth century Sikh 'militancy'.[1] Two major events start and end this thirty-year period: the demise of Guru Hargobind in 1644 and the execution of Guru Tegh Bahadur in 1675 by the Mughal state. These two events sandwiched the period and are often seen as being indicative of the wider socio-political milieu of Mughal India. In 1658, Aurangzeb (r.1658–1707) became the Mughal Emperor after a war of succession with his elder brother, Dara Shukoh (d.1658) and other siblings. Aurangzeb's reign is enveloped in historiographical notoriety: one group of historians underlines his attempts to associate the Mughal state with a distinct Islamic ideology, while another emphasises the systemic crisis that contributed to its long-term decline.[2] In the contemporary historiography late seventeenth century Sikh 'militancy' is seen as a product of Aurangzeb's India: the Emperor's religious stance and subsequent political policies created an atmosphere of 'intolerance'.[3] This resulted in a 'Hindu/nativist' reaction to overthrow Mughal power. The execution of Guru Tegh Bahadur on Aurangzeb's command is usually seen as an example of growing Mughal 'bigotry'. The Sikh community was forced to adopt full militarisation in the late seventeenth century in order to protect themselves from Mughal 'tyranny' inspired by Aurangzeb.

This grand narrative of late seventeenth century Sikh history is problematic because it implies there was a single Sikh experience of Mughal domination. This vision creates a communitarian reading of the past, allowing Sikhs to trace their history as a monolithic community. If in the seventeenth century there was a homogenous Sikhism, it should not be read to mean much more that the presence of distinct Sikh social markers and religious practices. Sikhism did not replace existent communal ties (such as caste rank, kinship ties and socioeconomic status) nor did it eradicate communal identities; instead communal groups embedded Sikhism into their lives. As a result, there was no single Sikh experience in the late seventeenth century and not all Sikhs viewed this era as 'tyrannical', or shared the same experience of Mughal 'tyranny'. As a general context to the period it is important to keep in mind that Sikh groups at the time had differing opinions on both the milieu of Mughal India and on Sikhism itself.

The mid-to-late seventeenth century (1644–75) was an important period of debate and engagement amongst Sikh intellectuals and their gradually expanding audience, largely provoked, as we have already seen, by the divergent positions taken by contrasting lineages. Prior to this, early Sikh thought had advocated a philosophy which rejected extreme asceticism and accepted the householder-renunciant ideal. This view argued that spiritual liberation did not require the literal abandonment of 'worldly' duties and rituals. Early Sikhism proposed that one could achieve liberation by living as a householder and renouncing the world. These doctrines were captured in Guru Nanak's famous maxim *dan, nam, ishnan* (charity, meditation, cleanliness).[4] An example of early Sikh conduct is found in Guru Nanak's anecdotes with merchants. In the *Janamsakhis* Guru Nanak frequently discoursed with merchants and more often than not the merchant is portrayed as being intoxicated by wealth; Guru Nanak taught the merchant about the transience of wealth, but never forbade mercantile pursuits.[5] Sikhs were meant to live 'good lives' and curb their senses, but there was no elaborate discussion over the value of this 'goodness'. For example, if the Sikh merchant wanted to become a powerful temporal figure like a king, was this desire inappropriate for the householder-renunciant? In early Sikhism it appears that problematic questions over social mobility and social change were not prominent in discourse. However, Guru Hargobind radically changed this early Sikh dynamic by introducing the concept of 'active' militancy. In contrast, Miharvan explicitly rejected Guru Hargobind's temporality and violence by undermining the renunciatory aspects in the philosophy of 'real' Sikhism. These contrasting viewpoints on Sikhism impacted upon the householder-renunciant ideal because 'active' militancy expanded the potential lifestyle of the householder into a larger public arena as a political agent. But the inherent issue which emerged was: if the householder-renunciant becomes embroiled with politics can he ever renounce his/her more carnal senses? The question became centred on human necessity versus human desire. For the Sikh community this issue became teleological; what is the aim of a Sikh life? Is the aim of life to achieve a state of personal renunciation or is it to achieve spiritual liberation? What actions must the Sikh perform in order to achieve their aim of life? Quite clearly these intellectual debates had important material repercussions and, as they circulated, their votaries referred to them to explain their communal lifestyle choices in very creative ways.

Following the demise of Guru Hargobind and Miharvan Sikh public philosophy became focused on this relationship between 'militancy' and the householder-renunciant. This is because the successors of Guru Hargobind and Miharvan neither rebuked nor rebutted the views of their predecessors, rather they crystallised their respective intellectual positions.[6] The earlier issue of whether Vishnu had a role in the Sikh world was largely resolved: it had been established that Vishnu does plays some sort of a role, so in this era the Sikh literati began considering what exactly that role was and how it related to ordinary Sikh lives. Even as the Sikh literati debated these issues, the responses of the heterogeneous Sikh community was mediated by social developments, some local and endogenous, others exogamous and conditioned by the larger Mughal world.

In this chapter I will utilise two major Sikh sources: the writings of Guru Harji and the writings of Guru Tegh Bahadur. Unfortunately this period is not teeming with an abundance of Sikh sources but these writings may be very useful if we view them dialogically: they were written for specific Sikh audiences and reflect seventeenth century Sikh debates. It is within this dialogic universe that one can locate an emerging Sikh public philosophy. Persian chronicles from the seventeenth and eighteenth centuries also contain occasional glimpses into Sikh society and I refer to several Persian chronicles from nineteenth century Panjab when discussing the life and execution of Guru Tegh Bahadur. Of course, nineteenth century chronicles are not contemporary, but they do provide interesting explanations for why Guru Tegh Bahadur was executed and reflect pre-colonial historical understandings of this pivotal incident.

Crystallising the Sikh 'Tradition'

In 1644 there were three claimants to Sikh Guruship. Guru Har Rai succeeded Guru Hargobind and his base was in the Panjabi hills. Guru Harji succeeded Guru Miharvan and he established his headquarters in Amritsar. The third claimant was Guru Har Rai's elder brother, Dhir Mal (1627–77) who established his base in Kartarpur in central Panjab, a property he inherited from Guru Hargobind.[7] All three were from the same familial and spiritual genealogy and each controlled at least one sacred Sikh temple. Significantly, all three disregarded each other's spiritual claims and actively sought to disseminate their ideologies to the Sikh public. Unlike Guru Har Rai or Guru Harji, Dhir Mal was a maverick; he never established an ideological school and had a hostile relationship with Guru Hargobind. By contrast, Guru Har Rai and Guru Harji had been legitimately and publically nominated by their predecessors. One major difference between Guru Har Rai and Guru Harji was their ages: Har Rai was only a teenager but Harji was a mature adult when he inherited the Guruship. Another important difference was Harji's high literary output compared to Har Rai's complete lack of literary production.[8] Nonetheless, throughout the 1640s and 1650s Guru Har Rai and Guru Harji continued to engage in an ideological battle to win the hearts and minds of Sikhs on the issue of 'militancy'.

Guru Har Rai was born in 1630 to Guru Hargobind's eldest son, Gurditta. Gurditta had already passed away, as had Hargobind's son Atal Rai. Hargobind's remaining three sons, Suraj Mal, Ani Rai and Tegh Bahadur were overlooked for the Guruship. Har Rai was only fourteen at the time of his succession and his older brother was the defiant Dhir Mal. Hargobind had frequently attempted to make peace with his eldest grandson, but Dhir Mal was unable to curb his own ambitions for power. Consequently Har Rai was chosen ahead of Dhir Mal. He spent his entire reign in the Panjabi hills in Kiratpur and Nahan. By contrast, Harji would have been about thirty-five when he succeeded Miharvan in 1640.[9] Harji had been raised in Hehar and, after Miharvan's coronation in 1618, he served his father wherever he travelled. It appears that Harji eventually moved from Muhammadipur to Amritsar in about 1635 and remained there until his death in 1696. He was appointed Guru ahead of his brothers Karan Mal and Chaturbhuj. Like his father, Harji developed into an accomplished litterateur specialising in exegetical and anecdotal literature.[10]

Neither Guru Har Rai nor Guru Harji rebutted or disputed the views of their predecessors but sought to support and develop their respective ideologies on militancy. In dress and mannerisms, Har Rai wore regal clothes and engaged in noble pursuits such as hunting, horse riding and rearing falcons.[11] Moreover, he continued to offer service and maintained Guru Hargobind's army.[12] But he never returned to the Panjabi plains and remained a resident of the southern Panjabi hills. Harji, on the other hand, dressed like his father in the expected guise of a saint and became a skilled litterateur and preacher. He spent his entire tenure in Amritsar and it is quite possible that neither he nor Guru Har Rai ever met in person; they certainly did not meet after becoming Gurus. Despite this lack of personal contact, their viewpoints on Sikhism were irreconcilable and individually and collectively their supporters began a war of words.

The contest between Har Rai and Harji was centred upon Amritsar and central Panjab. Central Panjab had been the mainstay headquarters of the early Sikh Gurus who had all established temples in the region and were native sons. Yet when Guru Hargobind chose to leave central Panjab for the Panjabi hills it marked a significant change: Sikh congregations no longer had easy access to Hargobind and his successors. Earlier Miharvan had found it difficult to penetrate Guru Hargobind's support base in central Panjab and was forced to seek patrons in places such as Kangra. But when Guru Hargobind departed from central Panjab it opened up a potential gap in the region. Miharvan was unable to fill this vacuum because he was growing old and possibly lacked the energy to proselytise. But when Harji succeeded Miharvan in 1640 he took control of the symbolically important city of Amritsar.[13] He had a distant claim to the property because he was the great-grandson of Guru Ram Das and he was Guru Hargobind's nephew. Since no other relations seemed to dispute Harji's claims to take over the city's administration, he seems to have ruled it in relative peace.

Harji's possession of Amritsar gave him a unique opportunity to proselytise and to establish the dominance of the Miharvan lineage. He had access to a wide audience of Sikhs and a new source of funds. Miharvan had struggled to compete financially with Guru Hargobind, but Harji would have collected the revenue generated by the Golden Temple. Considering that Amritsar was a growing commercial centre in the seventeenth century it is likely that these offerings generated a substantial turnover.[14] Harji was equipped with money and an audience and he attempted to harness his skills as an exegete to convince the masses of his legitimacy. This objective could only be achieved by denouncing Guru Har Rai's and Dhir Mal's claims to Guruship. However, Harji did not have Guru Har Rai's existing wealth, reputation and infrastructure of missionaries. These missionaries (*masand*) were closely attached to the region and had profound local knowledge. The *Dabistan* remarks: "most of the leading *masands* of the *Guru* are Jats".[15] These Jat missionaries would have had an affinity with the Sikh masses in central Panjab because they were from the same ethnic and cultural background. The *Dabistan* also mentions several of Guru Hargobind's missionaries who were Sikh celebrities famed for their piety, such as Ramdas Chanda and Bidhi Chand.[16] Guru Har Rai probably had many such celebrities as his missionaries, so while he might have been far away from the everyday realities of central Panjab, his missionaries gave him an important edge in the region.

Later Sikh chronicles also state that Dhir Mal hired missionaries and sent them across Panjab.[17] In mid-seventeenth century Panjab a debate over Guruship was taking place among Sikh missionaries from rival camps, but what were they saying?

The *Goshti Guru Miharivanu* (the Discourses of Guru Miharvan) is a combination of biography, hagiography and exegesis.[18] The work details Miharvan's life and forty-five discourses he delivered during his reign and has remarkable similarities in style to Miharvan's hagiography of Guru Nanak, but is devoid of ethnographical context or entertaining episodes as found in the *Janamsakhis*. Instead the aim of the text is to show the profundity of Miharvan's thought and to establish the legitimacy of his Guruship. The text is not sermonising but interactive – the discourses are centred upon questions by ordinary Sikhs to Miharvan on everyday spiritual concerns. Questions focus on ethical and moral conduct and often deal with salvation and why human beings are unable to achieve freedom from life. It can be inferred from the nature of this text that Harji used these discourses when preaching to the Sikh masses. The emphasis on ordinary people and their problems was possibly Harji's way of saying 'I feel your pain' and, more importantly, Miharvan 'feels your pain'. Harji was trying to gain supporters from a broad social spectrum with a populist rhetoric and high intellectualism.

Not only is the *Goshti Guru Miharivanu* a significant text, it is an unusual one in the context of seventeenth century Sikhism. No successor of a Sikh Guru had ever written a hagiography of their predecessor.[19] Through the text Harji created a personality cult around Miharvan and challenged Guru Hargobind's legitimacy. Harji had little to gain by directly attacking Guru Har Rai because his opposition was towards Guru Hargobind and his claims to be Guru Arjan's successor. Harji attempted to create continuity and affinity between the previous Sikh Gurus and Miharvan, which would, in turn, foreground Harji's genealogical and spiritual rights over Guru Har Rai. Perhaps Harji purposefully sets these discourses in central Panjab, and largely in the town of Muhammadipur near Lahore, in order to appeal to the local population.[20] He was a native of central Panjab and wanted to emphasise his local roots.

The *Goshti Guru Miharivanu* is philosophically intriguing and represents an early example of medieval Sikh exegesis. It is a mixture of Sikh, Vaishnavite and Vedantic thought; it is not possible to say whether this philosophic mixture reflects general Sikh beliefs in medieval India.[21] But the manner in which Harji merges these various philosophies results in creating a devotional faith which stresses 'tradition' and 'social order'. The world is depicted as phenomenal and man's life is to realise his union with God. This perspective suggests that the best life is lived in devotion and renunciation from temporal illusion. In this view the Guru offers his Sikhs transcendence over materialism, a role as a householder that does not seek to alter the status quo through ambitious endeavour.

Harji is unequivocal in emphasising Miharvan's claims to Guruship and the veracity of his teachings. He expresses these views thus:

> The discourses of the True Master (*Satiguru*) Miharvan, if one reads or studies or listens [to this text] with love along with focus with a pure soul and with devotion, then [the text] will cut their transmigration. Here [in this text] one can attain the entire treasury of joys [in this mortal life]. Thereafter [this mortal life] one will join the form of God and one will merge [with God]. They shall go through comings and goings (life and death). If one in this manner naturally reads or studies or listens then they shall have their noose of death cut.

> Brother, please recite wonderful lord Nanak; True Master Angad; True Master Amar Das; True Master Ram Das; True Master Arjan; True Master Sahib [and] True Master Miharvan. It is they who have described the dalliance of the Lord.[22]

By focusing on the spiritual legitimacy of Miharvan and Miharvan's father Prithi Chand in the genealogy of Sikh Gurus, Harji tacitly defends his claims to the exalted position. Notably, in this entire text there is no discussion of Guru Hargobind nor of his successors: they simply do not exist! Rather than attacking Guru Hargobind and giving him (even) a negative creditability, Harji apotheosises Miharvan and tries to promote loyalty to that spiritual lineage.

As already mentioned, Miharvan's discourses in the *Goshti Guru Miharivanu* were largely directed to ordinary Sikhs who were curious about Sikhism and theology. Interestingly, in the discursive strategy of the text these Sikh characters were never identified by their communal identities; they were only generically referred to as Sikhs. Harji was creating a broad social appeal by forming an inclusive philosophy which gave greater emphasis to being Sikh over other identities and engaging Sikh audiences on issues concerning 'Sikh life' and the householder-renunciant ideal.

Creating the Legends of Guru Miharvan

Harji's attempts to make Miharvan seem like the 'real' Sikh Guru meant placing his protagonist within a Sikh metanarrative of sainthood. The text begins by identifying the qualities of a Sikh Guru, and identifies the possession of the *shabad* (sacred word) or *bani* (divine word) as the fundamental hallmark.[23] Guru Nanak gave Guru Angad "the foundations of the sacred word" (*shabad ki thapna*)[24] and in turn this gift was given to each succeeding Guru. But Miharvan was special because he had the eloquence to explain (*arth*) the revealed word (*bani*) of God. In an opening anecdote about Guru Nanak and Guru Angad, Harji establishes the power of *bani* and the divinity of Miharvan:

> When Guru Baba Nanak was living (*salamati*) in this world (*sehnsar*). Then one day Guru Angad came to Guru Baba and made this supplication (*benti*). "O Guru Baba, eternal lord (*patsah salamati*), this word (*bani*) of yours. [This word] God (*parmesur*) himself has spoken and the language is esoteric (*siddhi bhashia*) [i.e. divine revelation]. And in order to understand the meaning (*arthu*) [of this word] is very hard. There are only few with the intellect (*giani*) to understand this. And without knowing the meaning [of the word] one's heart (*manu*) does not become drenched [with devotion]. Moreover, without knowing the meaning liberation (*mukti*) cannot occur. Teacher (*gurudev*) explain this matter."

Then Guru Baba Nanak spoke "My fellow (*purkha*) Angada, this is God's (*parmesur*) word (*bani*). When I was travelling (*udasi*), then from my mouth this divine word was revealed. That is why in the world [this word] is hidden. Only a few that know of this and even they do not know. Now I have made you my heir. In your mouth the divine word will sprout. Furthermore, after you, those men who will inherit the word (*shabad ki thapna*). That divine word will become manifest in their mouths. And the seventh Guru after me [i.e. Guru Miharvan]. He [Miharvan] will have God's blessing (*parmesur ki agiaa*) enabling him to make famous the meaning (*arth*) of my divine word. Also he will make famous the meaning of all the words of all the devotees (*bhagata*)."[25]

Miharvan was not only a carrier of the revealed word but also an exe-gete par excellence. He had a unique blessing that gave him the ability to explain eruditely the deeper meanings of the Guru's utterances to all people. Indeed Miharvan's works were primarily works of discourse (*gostht*): he was always trying to explain the meaning of the divine word. This opening anecdote established the significance of Miharvan in the lineage of Sikh Gurus and underscored his greatest talent as an interpreter of *Gurbani* (the Guru's word).

Next Harji establishes the core principles of Guru Nanak's teach-ings: the name, charity, cleanliness, gentleness, self-restraint, compas-sion, devotion, poverty, selflessness, exertion, wakefulness, truthfulness and thoughtfulness.[26] After establishing this general framework of piety he discusses Miharvan's birth which, interestingly, is identical to the birth of Guru Nanak as found in the *Janamsakhis*.[27] When Guru Nanak was born many metaphysical beings come to greet his arrival on earth and the same beings come to greet Miharvan:

Along with the birth of Guru Miharvan three and thirty million gods greeted him and from the sky rained flowers . . . and eighty-four *Siddhas*, fifty-two *Virs*, sixty-four *Yoginis*, and nine *Naths*, all came to greet him. Furthermore all the previous masters of my spiritual school came [greeted him]. All the saints and prophets

and a multitude of theological schools gave their greetings to
Guru Miharvan. They offered prayers [to him].[28]

Miharvan is obviously identified as a great saint because of his auspicious birth and he crucially gains the blessings of Guru Ram Das and
all the previous Sikh Gurus.[29] Continuing on from the opening anecdote, Harji informs us that Guru Ram Das named his eldest grandson
Manohar (heart stealing; delightful; charming) because all those who
heard and/or read Manohar's works would be delighted.[30]

Harji next deals with the relationship between Guru Arjan and his
elder brother Prithi Chand.[31] He states that both Prithi Chand and
Miharvan were loyal and dedicated servants to Guru Arjan and it was
because of this service that Prithi Chand inherited the Guruship. Harji
fails to discuss Guru Arjan's execution or that he had a son; in this
narrative it is clear Prithi Chand and eventually Miharvan will inherit
the Guruship. Harji is very deliberate in communicating the special
love between Guru Arjan and Miharvan, an affection that distin-
guished him from his peers. He says: "When Miharvan turned sixteen
years old. When (Guru Arjan) saw the extent of Miharvan's devotional
service and intellect, Guru Arjan with great affection bestowed his
grace on him. When the entire family and Sikh congregation saw this
bestowal of grace by Guru Arjan they felt love".[32] This act of public
blessing by Guru Arjan legitimises Miharvan because such acts of public devotion were only reserved for saints and their possible successors.
Through this tactic Harji is trying to dispel the idea that Miharvan
and Prithi Chand were enemies of Guru Arjan – instead they were the
most sincere votaries Guru Arjan possessed. Significantly, individuals
such as Bhai Gurdas are completely absent from this narrative because
Bhai Gurdas had stated outright that Prithi Chand was a charlatan,
literally a *mina* (hypocrite).[33] Yet Harji cleverly invokes the dynastic
knowledge of the 'Guru's family' who were present when Guru Arjan
blesses Miharvan and later states that Miharvan is a 'clan devotee' (*kul
bhagat*)[34] and speaks continually of his 'hereditary tradition' (*posti*).[35]
As a 'real' (*sakke*) relation to Guru Arjan, Harji could argue against the
dynastic knowledge of other Sikh missionaries who were only servants
to the Sikh Gurus and not family members. After Miharvan serves

Guru Arjan, Miharvan then serves Prithi Chand and then Miharvan is declared the next Sikh Guru.

In this narrative Harji is determined to prove why Miharvan was the Sikh Guru. This is slightly unusual in medieval Indian hagiographies in which authors tend not to directly offer evidence of divinity.[36] Instead hagiographers tend to illustrate the power of the saint only through his anecdotes. But Harji feels it necessary to qualify the precise reasons why Miharvan is the Guru and this pursuit shows how much Harji is trying to make Miharvan stand out in a crowded marketplace. He identifies four reasons:

> Listen good brothers, about what type of man Miharvan was. Firstly, he was a clan devotee (*kul bhagat*). The meaning of being a *kul bhagat* is the due to the following reasons. He was the incarnation (*avatar*) of Sukdeo [Sukhdev – a famous Vedic seer]. He was the son of a devotee [Prithi Chand's son]. He was the nephew of a devotee [Guru Arjan's nephew]. He was the grandson of a devotee [Guru Ram Das's grandson]. He was also a devotee due to his own devotion.

> Secondly he was a devotee of sight (*darshan*). He appeared with the sacral mark on his forehead (*tilak*), rosary (*mala*), *Adi Granth* (*pothi*), stringed instrument (*rabab*) and he was a performer of *kirtan*. If anyone saw him he appeared like a proper devotee (*sanpuran bhagatu*).

> Thirdly he was a devotee of speech (*vachna*). When discussing knowledge (*gianu*) he was the speaker of sweet speech (i.e. a great rhetorician).

> Fourthly he was a devotee of tradition and custom (*rahit*). He was filled with great love (*maha prem ras*).[37]

These four reasons reveal the conservative position of both Harji and Miharvan: Miharvan was a Guru because he had pedigree, he appeared in appropriate dress, he was an intellectual and he was a preserver of traditional values. His rivals could, of course, also claim the same pedigree, but Harji would argue that even if they looked like 'real' Gurus, they did not talk like 'real' Gurus nor have policies like 'real' Gurus. If you wanted to know the mysteries of Guru Nanak's teachings then only Miharvan could teach you.

Interestingly, Harji presents Miharvan as a physically powerful man with the physical signs (*lakshna*) of a warrior.[38] He describes Miharvan's body:

> Guru Miharvan's navel (*nabhu*) appeared as if a lotus flower was shining forth [i.e. it appeared like a lotus] and it gleamed twenty-four hours a day. Guru Miharvan's heart was as pure as the sky (*arsi*) [or heaven]. In which the Lord always dwelt with virility. Guru Miharvan's chest was very beautiful and it was so broad that within in it the power of the three worlds resided (*tin lok ka bal*). Guru Miharvan's arms were also long and reached his knees. In his arms he had power of the three worlds.[39]

Miharvan is described has having power of the three worlds in his arms and chest. His arms are described as reaching his knees: this is not a curious thing to remark upon, instead it was the sign of being an archer. A master archer would ideally have long arms and a powerful chest, physical traits which would allow him to fire arrows with speed and accuracy. This was a comment about Miharvan's 'inactive' militancy: Miharvan might not look like a warrior nor play the role of one, but he was a perfect physical specimen with the body of a warrior.

Harji provides a hyperbolic description of Miharvan's life as a Sikh to produce awe and wonder in his audience. But his anecdotes also showed how Miharvan was a conservative Guru who had a strong attachment to the teachings and conduct of his predecessors. Moreover, Miharvan's anecdotes and teachings are shown to have a clear Vaishnavite imprint and, in particular, a belief in Krishna. This Vaishnavite influence undoubtedly reflected a genuine religious and philosophic belief, but it would have added to Miharvan's image as a preserve of 'Hindu' tradition. That being said, his actions were distinctively Sikh. For instance, Harji states that Miharvan conducted building works at sacred Sikh sites such as Guru Amar Das' Goindwal temple.[40] Miharvan becomes an accomplished Sikh 'Guru' specialising in exegesis, devotional music and writing devotional works. In his devotional works he also "introduces new compositions (bani)".[41] This is significant because after Guru Arjan no successor until Guru Tegh Bahadur would write any devotional works. Harji is trying to show how Miharvan is continuing Guru Arjan's legacy while the other so-called 'Sikh Gurus', like Guru Har Rai and Dhir Mal, do not perform their duties. Harji's desire to show Miharvan's connection to the early Sikh Gurus is reiterated when he discusses Miharvan's death; when Miharvan enters the heavens he is greeted by every Sikh Guru and every saint found in the *Adi Granth*.[42]

The *Goshti Guru Miharivanu's* first objective of apotheosising Miharvan is achieved by showing Miharvan as Guru Arjan's true successor. Little attention is given to Miharvan's father and his activities: Prithi Chand is shown as a votary of Guru Arjan, but Miharvan is something special. Harji wants to establish him in the mode of his predecessors, yet at the same time he wants to show how Miharvan is the greatest Sikh Guru. Miharvan is charismatic, intellectual and humble: Miharvan is the epitome of saintliness. Since Harji never admits the existence of Guru Hargobind it is difficult to know exactly what he feels about him but we can see he is making a veiled point on the temporality of Guru Hargobind and Guru Har Rai. Harji creates a series of dichotomies between Miharvan and Guru Hargobind which are then measured against the 'original' Sikh teachings as taught by the early Sikh Gurus. Miharvan's life, actions and teachings are shown to be in-line with 'original' Sikhism, but Guru Hargobind's temporality is depicted as being starkly opposed to 'original' Sikhism. Harji is asking his Sikh audience to contemplate 'original' Sikhism and then to think which Sikh Guru embodies that 'originality'. The manner in which Harji tries to gain adherents leads him to ask Sikhs what they feel is the relationship between the Guru and their lives. This type of questioning returns to the issue of the householder-renunciant – what is the 'ideal' Sikh life? Harji's public philosophy is centred upon understanding the role of religion (*Bhakti*) in Sikh lives.

Devotion and Life: Sikh Public Philosophy

The *Goshti Guru Miharivanu* was composed dialogically; the partici-pants in this dialogue were Harji's immediate followers and, even more ambitiously, a more widespread Panjabi Sikh community. Through this innovative narrative medium, Harji was directly talking to all Sikhs about Sikhism and its role in their lives. Apart from canonis-ing Miharvan, Harji's discourses between Miharvan and various Sikhs focused upon the householder-renunciant ideal. He attempted to explain the aim of Sikh life by constructing a metaphysical metanarrative of human existence and thereby explaining the role of saints in the world. He did this by creating a coherent conversation between Miharvan and certain Sikhs on questions which affected ordinary believers such as 'how does one effectively worship God'. Consequently he was able to dismiss the validity of Guru Hargobind and establish Miharvan as the 'true' Sikh Guru by arguing implicitly that Guru Hargobind neither provides the correct means nor ends for Sikh emancipation.

The first example I have of Harji's public philosophy is when he discusses the role of Vishnu in the current Dark Age (*kal yug*). Vishnu's incarnation had been cardinal to Bhai Gurdas's justification for Guru Hargobind's 'militancy'. Yet Harji unequivocally rejects this view of Vishnu as an 'active' force in the Dark Age and his perspective on Vishnu clarifies his view on the householder-renunciant path:

> Then looking towards the throne (*mahalu*) a servant (*sewak*) peti-tioned: 'Lord (*patishah*), in each age Krishna emerges as an incar-nation in many forms. And Krishna takes on many different names. In each age in what way does one do his worship (*pujita*)? Bless me with an explanation'.

> Then Guru Miharvan spoke: 'Listen son, in the Age of Truth (*sat jug*) Krishna took the form that was pure white (*setu varnu*), the four armed form (*chaturbhuj*), and his aim was to create the world; in his hands he held the staff (*danda*) and earthen ves-sel (*kamandal*) for libations (*dhare*). Men (*manushu*) in the time of the Age of Truth were peaceful (*shanti rupu*), well-mannered (*aruni ravaik*), good hearted (*suhiradu*) and with objective view

(*samdrishti*) and control over their senses (*indria*) and they used to worship (*bhajte*) the Lord [because of their virtuous dispositions]...this was the manner (*rahit*) of the people of *sat jug*.

In the Age of *Treta* was an age in which the Lord was a protector (*rakti*) [the epic form] and the four armed form (*chaturbhuj*). He carried the trident (*trimeshala*). He had three qualities and with hair (*kes*) glittering like the sun (*suaran?*)...In the Age of *Treta* gods and men they used to worship God by following the injunctions of the three Vedas...

In the *Duvapar* Age the Lord came in the form of Syam (Krishna) in the hue of linseed flowers (*alsi ke puhp*). He wore the yellow robe (*pitambari*)...In the Age of *Duvapar* gods and men used to worship Lord Krishna by prostrating to his kingship...

In this Dark Age those great saints that shall come they'll come with *Nam Kirtan* (devotional worship) and God will send them...Listen son, these souls roaming in confusion in this life, they only need to learn the value of *Nam Kirtan,* there is no other profit. Those who do this their transmigration will be cut...

Son, in the Dark Age there will be many great saints (*bare bhagati*). Son, the path of [ritual] actions (*karman ka marg*) alone is suitable to some castes and not other castes. But the path of devotion at the feet of Lord Krishna is not limited to any caste.[43]

Harji is making a pertinent point on 'militancy' by discussing the various incarnations. He argues that Vishnu has come in many forms and each one was directly related to the time period. Each time period varies not only due to the challenges human beings face, but in each age human morality and spirituality degenerates into 'confusion'.[44] So in each age the mode of worship must change. Significantly, in each age prior to the present Dark Age, Vishnu actually appears on earth with 'active' militancy. In previous ages Vishnu violently uproots any evildoers but in the Dark Age he will not take such an 'active' role. Instead he appears in the devotion of his saints and within Vishnu's saints one can find the path of salvation. Harji is coherently arguing that Guru

Hargobind's 'active' militancy is deluded because he has failed to understand this important conception of time and its relationship to Vishnu. For Harji, in the Dark Age only proper saints like Miharvan can save his Sikhs, while people such as Guru Hargobind are 'false' saints who lead people astray. Furthermore, Harji's manner of argument stresses the idea of 'perfect order' and 'renunciation' because human beings can only improve their lives by becoming 'devoted' to God. Consequently human beings become confined in a universe in which non-religious acts have little merit because human beings cannot externally eliminate 'evil' – so they should seek transcendence, not materialism. Harji states 'true' saints possess *Nam Kirtan* (devotional worship), which refers to the ability to meditate on God and perform devotional music. He has already established that Miharvan possesses *Nam Kirtan* because Miharvan is only a devotee of God and not a temporal figure. This implies 'saints' like Guru Hargobind with their temporality have no tangible signs of *Nam Kirtan* and thus it is possible to doubt their saintliness. Harji is telling his audience, find the Guru who has *Nam Kirtan,* and this can only mean Miharvan and not Guru Hargobind.

Harji further emphasises this notion of transcendence over materialism when discussing the 'ideal' human life. This discussion is centred upon the Brahmanical traditions of renunciation and the four stages of life:

Then in that servant's thought the fact arose that the Master's [Miharvan] mind is both worldly (*chit sansar*) and in detachment (*udas*). [Then the servant thought] who knows of my enquiry [into detachment]. To fulfil this desire to know [he went to] the Master and whatever one wants to ask so ask that, after what can be learnt? At those moments put forward or don't put forward your queries. Then this servant supplicated: 'Yes my Lord in this world how does one perform devotion (*bhagati*) without abandoning the world (*bina sansar ke taiga*)?'

Then Lord Miharvan spoke: 'Listen son (*bachcha*), what Krishna told Gosai Narad on the tenets of devotion (*bhakti ke dharam*) I'll relate that to you. What your personal duty (*Dharma*) is, is known as *Varna* (rank/caste) and *Ashrama* (stage of life). *Varna* is known as Brahman, Kshatriya, Vaishya, and Shudra, and he who maintains that rank. And the meaning of *Ashrama* – well he who abandons the four *Varnas* and is beyond the fourth stages then he has fully completed the duties of *Varna* and *Ashrama*. What are those four *Ashramas?* From the beginning disciple- ship (*brahmacarya*); secondly householder (*grahsatu*); thirdly forest dweller (*baniprastu*); and fourthly renunciant (*saniasu*).

Also listen to the duties of these stages of life. Discipleship which is the first stage: [one should] go under the protection of a teacher and study knowledge of wisdom. Remain away from the fla- vours and tastes (*rasan te bhogan*) until the education is finished. Moreover, one should be adept in living by the duties of a house- holder. Getting the command from your teacher and bestow a gift (*dakshina*) to your teacher. Discoursing with your teacher, taking his blessings, and then enter into the householder's stage.

When one's grandchildren (*santan balka*) are born then the third stage arrives which is the forest dweller. As a result, one goes and dwells in the forest. When one lives in the forest and then blooms forth knowledge and one takes renunciation. But if your wife hasn't achieved enlightenment then become divorced (*bida kare*) from her.

And then transcending and completing the duties of the four *Varnas* and the four stages of life. But if one is unsuccessful it is because one vice (*bancha*) in the mind was not removed'.

Then this servant petitioned: 'Yes my Lord but why in the duties of *Varna* and *Ashrama* does one continue to be unsuccessful? That action, which to my mind needs companionship, why is that purpose not achieved? That action hasn't been practised. To move from failure and succeed, how exactly does one abandon friendship with the world?'

Then Miharvan replied: 'Listen son, how a man works (*kirti*) in the waking state (*jagata*). In his dreaming state (*supna*) those actions [committed in the waking state] become manifest (*drishti*). All that appears in the dream state is fruitless (*niphal*). In this way even the entire *Varna* and *Ashrama* system is mythical (*mithia*). And the rewards (*phal bhog*) also seem mythical (*mithia*). Because the rewards [of life] appear and then disappear. He who knows this practises the actions of removing birth. They separate (*tiagi dur*) from prohibited actions (*nishidhi karmu*). Rather they practice daily pious (*nit nimati*) actions such as bathing (*ishnan*), charity (*dan*), evening prayers (*san-dhia*), ancestor worship (*tarpanu*), reciting the Vedic verses (*gayatri*), breathing exercises (*pranyamu*) that give one strength (*bal baisudeu*). Also they practice those actions such as going to sacred spots and grounds. If they do this then sin (*bhirstu*) will not affect them. This is God's blessing (*agiaa*). Keep doing these actions, but do not expect reward (*phalu*) from these actions'.[45]

The discourse continues at length. It is fascinating because the servant's questions are focused upon liberation and transcendence. Miharvan answers the questions by arguing there is an ideal system of life but then admits that this ideal system does not always work out and may even be a myth. Miharvan is entering into a problematic paradox in which life becomes illusion and illusion becomes life. But Miharvan's answer to this issue is to reinforce the need to perform devotional duties and, importantly, to separate any desire for reward from one's devotional acts. Failure to achieve liberation means one should work harder and be more devoted, without any expectation of pleasure in return for toil and effort. In addition, Harji creates a universe in which 'social order' is paramount. This is because if life is an illusion then so too is social mobility and social justice: humans should just accept the structures and systems embedded into their lives. They become unable to change the structures and systems around them. This view-point allows the dominance of elite social groups over non-elite social groups; questions over materialism and differences in social status are seen as unimportant in the masterplan of liberation.

Overall, Harji's public philosophy gives greater weight to the renunciant than to the householder. While he never rejects the vital-ity of the householder stage, it is clear he sees the end of human life (and the end of transmigration) as renunciation. Therefore, Sikhs should live morally good lives which are geared towards the fourth stage of asceticism. In Harji's view, saints like Miharvan are there to guide humankind and these saints are the form of Vishnu in the Dark Age. Because the nature of the Dark Age is distinct from previous ages, 'active' militancy is illogical: only devotion in its strictest definition gives one salvation. The aim of Harji's message to Sikhs is to show that he is the bearer of 'tradition' and this emphasis on 'tradition' subverts any message for 'change' or even 'reality'. In Harji's portrayal of the world there are never any incidents of prejudice or inequality, rather life is contained in a perfect functionalist universe where human beings only have spiritual needs: there are no questions in the *Goshti Guru Miharivanu* dealing with social and material problems. Harji's conservative thought seems geared to appeal to socially elevated Sikh groups, such as elite Khatri and Jat societies, with limited attraction to the poorer classes. It is possible that Harji was trying to gain a stranglehold over elite Sikh society by appealing to their desire to preserve 'traditional' society. His desire to maintain 'traditional institutions' is clear when he discusses 'the four stages of life' (*Ashrama*) which favour Brahmanical society and exclude lower social groups who are unable to participate in Vedic rituals. But Harji does not address this issue of social exclusion and this is partly done by limiting ethnographical details: his Sikh characters have no social identities. His philosophy is also heavily Vaishnavite, perhaps in an attempt to balance Sikhism with existing social rituals. Sikhism does challenge several 'Hindu' social rituals and Harji's conservative discourse limits this challenge to the 'Hindu social order'.[46]

But how did Guru Har Rai respond to Harji's arguments? He did not produce any written works nor commission any known written works. Therefore, it is very difficult to know exactly how he responded to Harji's 'social order' with its emphasis on tradition and social stability. But the late seventeenth century Persian chronicle, *Khulasatu't Tawarikh* by Sujan Rai Bhandari, makes a revealing statement about Guru Har Rai's conduct during the war of succession between Aurangzeb and Dara Shukoh:

Although Dara Shukoh put an appearance of preparations for a fight, at heart he was a prey to demoralization and fear. He thought it to be beyond his power to face the Imperial Army [of Aurangzeb] in battle, and entertained the design of proceeding to Multan and Qandahar. This he indicated to his close courtiers and confidants through hints and allusions. People intuitively realised that once [Aurangzeb's] glorious camp moved in this direction, he [Dara Shukoh] would take flight without daring to enter battle. As a result, they decided to separate from him. Thus Raja Rajrup departed with the excuse that he needed to go to his native territory (*watan*) to gather troops and conciliate local chiefs (*zamindars*) of the [Punjab] Hills. From expediency, he left his son as his agent at Lahore; but after some days, his son also departed one night. So too Guru Har Rai, the successor of Baba Nanak, who had come with a large force, left on the excuse of collecting [more] troops. Thus most people separated themselves from Dara Shukoh...[47]

If this statement is accurate it shows that Guru Har Rai was an active political agent in the 1650s and was willing to get involved in the succession struggle. He had an army and the ability to recruit more soldiers. His actions suggest that he continued Guru Hargobind's tradition of 'active' militancy by getting involved in political matters including war. This lifestyle would have provided Harji with the perfect image for lampoon. Nevertheless, Guru Har Rai was rejecting the intellectual position of Harji which favours transcendence over materialism and arguing that Sikh Gurus can change their societies: if Guru Har Rai was involved in the succession struggle he was actively involved in the socio-political developments of Mughal India.

As already noted, it is difficult to know precisely the position of Guru Har Rai and his supporters, because of the lack of primary sources. Nevertheless, in Sikh legends associated with Guru Har Rai, he often got involved with local political disputes. For example, when he was travelling in southern Panjab two brothers, Kala and Karam Chand of the Marhaj tribe, approached him for assistance.[48] The brothers complained that "people of the Kaura tribe would not allow them to live among them". Guru Har Rai agreed to petition the Kaura chief, Jait Pirana, and asked him to give the brothers adequate land. Jait Pirana replied, "give a morsel to eat, but not land to live upon". Interestingly, this legend was specifically about land and landlordism, and may reflect how socially mobile cultivators were unable to purchase land from existing *zamindars* in the mid-seventeenth century. It also shows how local groups might have looked upon affable squires such as Guru Har Rai to give them assistance in local matters. In this report, Guru Har Rai had no objections about getting involved in these temporal affairs. The episode also shows how Guru Har Rai was not interested in maintaining the status quo but was perfectly willing to encourage social mobility. Guru Har Rai was willing to give his Sikhs sustainable livelihoods *and* spiritual liberation.

Guru Har Rai's public philosophy expanded the potential of the householder. In his Sikhism, householders could, and even should, engage with all temporal and transient affairs including politics and warfare. This is because human beings required hospitable societies and social structures in order to live good moral lives. This may be why Guru Har Rai felt inclined towards Dara Shukoh and considered it necessary to get involved in the war of succession. Yet Guru Har Rai's public philosophy was similar to Guru Hargobind's 'active' militancy in the sense that it did not give direct agency to Sikhs to become politically involved. Instead, the Guru was still the major political agent. Nonetheless, there was the potential from this incipient temporality that Guru Har Rai's successors could give ordinary Sikhs political agency.

In the 1640s and 1650s Guru Har Rai and Guru Harji crystallised their respective ideological positions. While Harji campaigned on a platform which argued for 'tradition' and 'social order'; Guru Har Rai campaigned on a platform which allowed for 'social change' and active involvement in political affairs. This era established the directions which both Guru lineages would take in the coming decades.

Growing Mughal Influence (1658–1663)

According to Sikh tradition after Aurangzeb was enthroned he began to take a lively interest in the Sikh community.[49] While this interest is often seen as an example of Aurangzeb's religious views, it is possible that he was more interested in the Sikhs because of Guru Har Rai's apparent alliance with Dara Shukoh. Sikh tradition alleges that Aurangzeb invited Guru Har Rai to the Mughal court in Delhi during the period 1658–60.[50] Guru Har Rai sent his eldest son, Ram Rai, to Delhi as his envoy. In the Mughal court Ram Rai allegedly pandered to Aurangzeb's religious views – some Sikh traditions even suggest that Ram Rai was made a hostage. It is difficult to ascertain the precise nature of the transactions at the Mughal court and certainly no contemporary source sheds any light on this meeting. But we do know for certain that Ram Rai was excommunicated by Guru Har Rai for some grievous error, and this prompted Ram Rai to establish his own Sikh 'tradition' although he did not establish an ideological position. But the Sikh tradition associated with Guru Har Rai argues that Ram Rai became a Mughal stooge and received patronage from the Mughal state. It is alleged that Ram Rai was given imperial grants for Chandraval Khera near Delhi and for Dehra Dun in Uttar Pradesh, but there is not sufficient evidence to unequivocally support these claims.[51] Despite any confirmation at this level, Ram Rai's alienation was quite apparent. He went on to become a close ally of his uncle, Dhir Mal, who challenged Guru Har Rai's legitimacy. Dhir Mal's family tradition claims he received Mughal patronage under Shah Jahan, but this too is unclear.[52] However, in 1677 Dhir Mal died in the Mughal fort of Ranthambhor and we may assume that he was a Mughal prisoner prior to his death.[53] It is not known why Dhir Mal fell foul of Mughal authority, but it is interesting because two years earlier, in 1675, Guru Tegh Bahadur had been executed by the Mughal state. Nothing definite is known about how Harji was faring in his relations with the Mughal state through this period.

Before Guru Har Rai's demise in 1661, he appointed his youngest son, Har Krishan, as his successor. Guru Har Krishan was only five years old and apparently was the object of great enmity from his older brother, Ram Rai. Sikh tradition claims that Ram Rai incited Aurangzeb to call Guru Har Krishan to the Mughal court and to remove him through some nefarious method. Guru Har Krishan did travel to Delhi but he never met Aurangzeb; he instead organised several charities in Delhi. In particular he dedicated his time to small-pox eradication and contracted the disease himself. Before Guru Har Krishan passed away he appointed his uncle Guru Tegh Bahadur as his successor.[54]

During this five-year period (1658–1663), the Guru Hargobind Sikh tradition argues there is growing Mughal hostility towards the Sikhs, spearheaded by Aurangzeb.[55] The Sikh community was indeed attracting greater interest from the Mughal centre, but it is unclear why this might be the case. It appears that the Guru Har Rai line-age bore the brunt of this attention, while Harji's activities seem to have gone unnoticed. In addition, both Ram Rai and Dhir Mal were engaged in courting the Mughal state and asking for royal patronage in return for their loyalty. In the political context of the period, we do know that both had personal vendettas against Guru Har Rai and that they pandered to local Mughal agents and even Aurangzeb himself. It is unlikely that the Mughal state was concerned by Sikhism in its narrowest sense, but Guru Har Rai's type of Sikhism, with its abil-ity to spark political dissent, was potentially dangerous. This concern would have been exacerbated because Guru Har Rai's headquarters was based in the semi-autonomous Panjabi hills, which were not fully integrated into the Mughal system.[56] Moreover, Guru Har Rai had supporters across the Panjab and, crucially, his main support base was in the Lahore province, which was economically and militarily pivotal to Mughal authority.[57] Although it is difficult to detail the chronology of 'distrust' between the Mughals and the Sikhs during this period, in the structure of relationships between the two realms, the carefully balanced world could easily be destabilised, leading to hostility. Not surprisingly, retrospective readings could easily link events that led to a worsening relationship, even if the unfolding developments seemed a great deal more contingent to participants at the time.

All Along the Watchtower: Guru Tegh Bahadur's Missions (1663–75)

When Guru Har Krishan appointed Guru Tegh Bahadur as his succes-sor he apparently did so by cryptically saying 'Baba Bakala' (the father lives in the village of Bakala).[58] 'Baba Bakala' was obscure because the term *Baba* could either mean 'father' (especially grandfather) or 'spiritual master', or even both 'father' and 'spiritual master' but it was clear Guru Har Krishan had appointed an elder male relative to succeed him and with this information Guru Har Krishan's votaries travelled to Bakala in Panjab. When they arrived in Bakala they found several would-be Sikh Gurus claiming that they were Guru Har Krishan's legitimate successor, including Guru Har Krishan's uncle, Dhir Mal, who attempted to assert his legitimacy. However, with some ingenuity, Guru Tegh Bahadur was appointed as Guru Har Krishan's successor; Tegh Bahadur was Guru Hargobind's youngest son and had been a resident of Bakala since 1644. Dhir Mal was annoyed with the appointment and made an unsuccessful attempt to assassinate him.

On accession, Guru Tegh Bahadur immediately began touring Sikh congregations across North India and symbolically began his travels by going to his hometown of Amritsar where he attempted to confront Guru Harji. Sikh tradition varies in its description of the meeting. One narrative suggests that Harji locked the gates of the Golden Temple, another tells how he met Guru Tegh Bahadur and pandered to him.[59] Regardless of the outcome of this alleged meeting between them, it was a bold move by Guru Tegh Bahadur to confront Harji, who was startled by his directness. Thereafter for several months Guru Tegh Bahadur continued to tour central and southern Panjab. These tours into the Panjabi heartlands were significant because no Sikh Guru from the Guru Hargobind lineage had travelled to the region in nearly thirty years. By 1665, Guru Tegh Bahadur reached Bilaspur in the southern Panjabi hills where the rulers bestowed a land grant in the region of Makhowal upon him. Guru Tegh Bahadur decided to establish his headquarters in Makhowal, but he did not choose a sedentary lifestyle and continued to travel and preach.

In 1665 Guru Tegh Bahadur began his five-year tour of central and north-eastern India. He travelled to many major cities and visited Patna, Benares, Dacca and Assam. These tours were usually to see Sikh congregations and other sacred sites to preach and perform charitable works. It is unclear whether Guru Tegh Bahadur had inherited Guru Har Rai's army and whether it accompanied him on his travels.[60]

Nonetheless, he was an accomplished soldier and swordsman and hence he was called 'Tegh Bahadur' (brave swordsman). Interestingly the Sikh tradition associated with Guru Tegh Bahadur states that, in 1668, he accompanied the powerful Mughal *mansabdar,* Raja Ram Singh Kachhawaha, to Assam; Ram Singh was sent by Aurangzeb to bring the region into peace.[61] Guru Tegh Bahadur's letters do mention that he was travelling to Assam with a Raja and this must be Raja Ram Singh Kachhawaha.[62] By approximately 1670, Guru Tegh Bahadur returned to Makhowal.

In 1672–73, Guru Tegh Bahadur began another tour into southern Panjab. He had previously visited the region in 1664. After this tour he returned to Makhowal and travelled to Delhi the next year. In Delhi, he and his travelling companions were imprisoned and executed by the Mughal state in November 1675.

Why was Guru Tegh Bahadur executed? The popular historiography attributes his execution to Aurangzeb's 'intolerant' religious stance. In John F. Richards' general history of the Mughal Empire he comments:

By the early 1670s the Sikhs ran foul of Aurangzeb's iconoclastic policies. Imperial officers received orders to demolish Sikh Gurdwaras as well as Hindu temples. At the same time several instances of Muslims being converted to Sikhism by the Guru were reported to Aurangzeb who ordered Tegh Bahadur's arrest. In Agra, the Guru and five companions were captured, arrested and taken to Delhi. There the qazi's court tried and convicted the Sikh leader for blasphemy, sentenced him to death and carried out the execution in November, 1675. After this second martyrdom the annual spring Baisakhi congregation of Sikhs in the hills acclaimed Gobind Singh, the young son of the slain leader, as the new Guru. At one stroke Aurangzeb earned the bitter hatred of thousands of Jat and Khatri Sikhs living in the North Indian plain.[63]

Sikh accounts further garnish this narrative by arguing that a deputation of Kashmiri Pundits arrived at Makhowal in a bid to gain Guru

Tegh Bahadur's assistance in combating Aurangzeb's prejudices.[64] These Kashmiri Pundits were allegedly being forcibly converted to Islam by Aurangzeb and his local agents in Kashmir. They wanted Guru Tegh Bahadur to go and meet Aurangzeb and attempt to end Aurangzeb's intolerant policies. Guru Tegh Bahadur agreed to the request and was executed because Aurangzeb was apparently incensed at his presumptuous intercession on behalf of the Kashmiri Pundits. Aurangzeb offered Guru Tegh Bahadur the option of conversion to Islam or death: Guru Tegh Bahadur chose death. This Sikh narrative originated from post-Aurangzeb Sikh chronicles and accounts and there are no contemporary Sikh sources from the seventeenth century which unequivocally support this early modern Sikh narrative.

The major issue with this contemporary explanation of Guru Tegh Bahadur's execution is the predominance given to the personal religious motivation of the Mughal Emperor and the equally simplistic homogenisation of the Sikhs within the Hargobind lineage. Aurangzeb is shown as being brutish, bigoted and motivated by a personal vendetta against the Sikhs. But Guru Tegh Bahadur was not the only Sikh 'Guru' in this period; other 'Gurus' included Guru Harji, Guru Dhir Mal, Guru Ram Rai and possibly many other minor figures. Given this complex state of affairs it seems unlikely that Aurangzeb would have targeted a specific Sikh Guru on purely personal grounds. It is somewhat unrealistic to suggest that Aurangzeb believed in the authority of one Sikh Guru over another. However, Guru Tegh Bahadur was a successor to the Guru Har Rai lineage and, as already discussed, Guru Har Rai had attracted greater Mughal interest. While neither Aurangzeb nor the Mughal state executed Guru Tegh Bahadur simply because he was a 'non-Muslim', the Mughal state had far more reason to be anxious of Guru Tegh Bahadur's interpretation of Sikhism. Because of the nature of our sources it is difficult to identify the specific 'crime' Guru Tegh Bahadur committed which resulted in his execution. But through a careful examination of the sources we have, it is possible to infer how Guru Tegh Bahadur's leadership was perceived by Sikhs and non-Sikhs, and the problems that it could have held for the Mughals.

In early modern Sikh chronicles Guru Tegh Bahadur was willing to meet Aurangzeb in order to assist several Kashmiri Pundits.

In these narratives, Guru Tegh Bahadur's help was sought by the Pundits who begged for Guru Tegh Bahadur's protection. The Guru had agreed to their request and petitioned Aurangzeb. But the narratives also suggest the futility of his mission, because Aurangzeb is deliberately portrayed as a dogmatic puritan who was too far from divinity to accede to Guru Tegh Bahadur's request. In Delhi, he was arrested and executed by Aurangzeb because he refused to convert to Islam and refused to perform a miracle. Yet when Guru Tegh Bahadur is beheaded he leaves a note saying 'not the secret but the head was given up': this was Guru Tegh Bahadur's miracle.[65] Sikh narratives of this event fail to highlight the complex networks of power in Mughal India and the wider socio-economic influences affecting Sikh society. Muzaffar Alam perfectly captures the reason for this anti-Mughal bias: "to the Sikhs the Mughal state was the source of all tyranny, since the state not only had the largest share in the social surplus but it also legitimatized and sustained the existing power-structure in the locality".[66] Thus, in early modern Sikh narratives the exploitative, hegemonic Mughal state is contrasted with the unified and righteous Sikh community.

If we compare these accounts with nineteenth century Persian chronicles about Guru Tegh Bahadur's execution, some of these homogenised binaries vanish and are replaced with a retrospective teleology of events which is rather interesting.[67] These nineteenth century chronicles were all produced in the Panjab by groups interested in the Sikhs; these included Sikh kingdoms and the East India Company. Among the chronicles is a fascinating account of Guru Tegh Bahadur's execution written by Sohan Lal Suri, titled *Umdat ut-Tawarikh*. Sohan Lal Suri was a chronicler employed by Ranjit Singh to write a history of the Sikhs.[68] Despite Suri's employment in a major Sikh kingdom his explanation of Guru Tegh Bahadur's execution is unlike the explanations found in the Sikh tradition. Instead Suri's discussion of the execution centred upon Mughal political control:

> Guru Tegh Bahadur went to the country of Malwa [southern Panjab] and stayed there to give instruction to his followers in a befitting manner.

With the passage of time thousands of soldiers and horsemen used to be with him; camels and goods of all kinds remained at his disposal. Furthermore, those who were refractory towards the *amils*, the *zamindars*, the *ijaradars*, the *diwans* and the officials in general used to take refuge with Guru Tegh Bahadur. Regardless of the number of people present with the Guru, they were all fed by him.

Pain inevitably follows comfort. Some degraded persons reported to Emperor Alamgir (Aurangzeb) that Guru Tegh Bahadur was staying in the country of Malwa with thousands of soldiers and horsemen; whosoever was refractory towards the officials took refuge with him. They warned the Emperor that if no notice of the Guru was taken he would be an incitement to insurrection; if he was allowed to continue his activities for a long time, it would be extremely difficult to deal with him...

Upon this, the Emperor sent towards Guru Tegh Bahadur experienced soldiers, instructing them to bring the Guru to Shahjahanabad. They hastened to deliver the Emperor's message: the Emperor desired a miracle from the Guru; he should lose no time in presenting himself to the Emperor so that the manifestation of his spiritual powers should make him famous everywhere. The Guru replied that he was a *faqir* who had renounced worldly ambition and was contented with obscure existence; he did not wish to associate himself with *amirs*. The messengers of the Emperor insisted that Guru Tegh Bahadur should accompany them to Shahjahanabad and, eventually, succeeded in taking him to the imperial court.

The Emperor was extremely anxious to witness a miracle. He asked Guru Tegh Bahadur to present himself. During the meeting the Emperor asked Guru Tegh Bahadur why the name *'tegh bahadur'* (brave swordsman) had been adopted by him. The Guru replied that his name was actually *'degh bahadur'* (brave with the cauldron), but the common people wrongly pronounced it Tegh Bahadur. The significance of the words *degh bahadur*, he further amplified, was that his followers derived comfort from the open kitchen maintained by him...

The Emperor...insisted that Guru Tegh Bahadur should work a miracle, but the Guru persisted in refusing. The Emperor ordered the Guru to be placed in confinement until he worked a miracle.

In the eyes of godly men, a prison is no different from any other place...

Then Guru Tegh Bahadur received the news that his son [Guru Gobind Singh] had ascended the *gaddi* (seat) of Guruship in his place. He was very happy over this and he now prophesied that the destruction of Emperor would take place before long...

The Emperor's men became more and more insistent on the performance of a miracle and, at last, Guru Tegh Bahadur suggested that he would write something on a piece of paper for them so that if a person tied it on his neck, he would be proof against all kinds of weapons. He suggested further that he would tie this piece on his own neck and then an experienced soldier could then try his sword on it so that the truth of his claim is established. And then, he tied the piece of paper on his neck and challenged them to try a sword on him. When the sword was struck his head was severed from his body. The bright day of comfort turned into the dark night of pain...

Afterwards, he [Aurangzeb] ordered his men to remove the piece of paper from Guru Tegh Bahadur's neck in order to see what was written on that. What was written on the piece of paper was: 'Not the secret but the head was given up'.[69]

Suri's palpably retrospective account argues that Guru Tegh Bahadur was specifically targeted and executed by the Mughal state because he was attracting refractory groups in southern Panjab. Guru Tegh Bahadur was not just gaining supporters: these supporters were armed and disgruntled with local Mughal power. Furthermore, Guru

Tegh Bahadur was attracting supporters by his charisma and his free kitchen: he made it a personal duty to ensure all those who came to him were well-fed. And yet, if you read this late account alongside the earlier ones, there are some interesting connections.

The common theme found in early modern Sikh and Persian histories on Guru Tegh Bahadur is the characterisation of him as a Guru who also abided by the norms of a patrimonial feudal lord. Guru Tegh Bahadur was an attractive leader because he was considered a respected saint; he was charismatic; he was well-educated; he was a highly-skilled warrior and he maintained a large free kitchen. This kitchen would have been open twenty-four hours a day and seven days a week and it would have had no caste or social barriers. His policies were focused upon giving material assistance to depressed social groups. Unlike his contemporary rivals, Guru Tegh Bahadur did not only offer spiritual guidance; he worked hard to create a community and provided them with material sustenance. In Sikh narratives, Guru Tegh Bahadur's sense of welfare to his subjects went beyond his immediate community; he was willing to sacrifice his life on behalf of Kashmiri Pundits irrespective of the fact that these Kashmiri Pundits were not Sikhs. In Persian narratives, Guru Tegh Bahadur is shown as a local political leader whose strength is constructed upon his willingness to help depressed social classes. Thus, it appears from these accounts that Guru Tegh Bahadur was enlarging the Guru Hargobind lineage from its immediate, local context, to one that was more inclusive and trans-regional. Or, to look at it from another perspective, Guru Tegh Bahadur was ambitiously moving from his earlier gentry-*zamindari* foundation to that of a Raja who provided sustenance, social services and protection to a more diverse constituency. While Sikh temples and previous Sikh Gurus had provided for some of these facilities, the nature of Guru Tegh Bahadur's charisma together with the conjuncture of other political and economic transformations in the Panjab gave him a social appeal which outstripped any of his predecessors or rivals.

It is difficult to ascertain the precise content of Guru Tegh Bahadur's teachings, especially in the context of his promise of material assistance. However we do posses several brief letters written by him to Sikh congregations based in Patna, Delhi, Benares, Mirzapur and Dacca.[70] Through the examination of these letters we can unearth the substance of Guru Tegh Bahadur's public philosophy.

Sikh Public Philosophy (1663–75)

Throughout Guru Tegh Bahadur's tenure as Guru he regularly sent letters to congregations outside Panjab. These letters or *Hukumnama* (letter of command) were usually brief and addressed to the leaders of specific congregations: they sometimes held direct commands and sometimes acknowledged the congregations' activities.[71] But the letters always contained a personal promise from the Guru to his congregation that their faith would be rewarded.

The tradition of writing letters to various congregations seems to have been an early activity of the Sikh Gurus. The earliest example we have of this *Hukumnama* tradition is with Guru Hargobind. After Guru Hargobind, both Guru Har Rai and Guru Har Krishan continued to send letters, but Guru Tegh Bahadur sent more than any of his predecessors. Significantly, Guru Tegh Bahadur's letters continued to follow the style of writing present in earlier letters by Guru Hargobind and Guru Har Krishan; if they differ, they do so in their tone and sentiments. These changes in Guru Tegh Bahadur's letters show why he was such an attractive hero to refractory groups.

First, let us examine the letters of Guru Hargobind and Guru Har Krishan. Guru Hargobind sent the following letter to his congregations in Patna, Alamgir, Bina and Manger:

I greet you with *'Kartar, Kartar'* (Creator, Creator). The Guru shall protect your honour. [If you] recite 'Guru, Guru' your life will improve: the Guru shall fully fulfil the congregation's aspiration and the Guru shall fully fulfil the congregation's daily needs (*rozgaru*). Keep this injunction: do not go near meat or fish. Receiving the congregation's letter, I'm completely aware [of the congregation's condition]; the congregation's wishes shall be achieved.[72]

In another letter to Patna, Guru Hargobind said:

[If you] recite 'Guru, Guru' your life will improve: the congregation's aspiration will be fulfilled, the congregation's daily needs will be met, to those who will take on the congregation's labour. The Guru's orders are: to perform devotional music [and] keep this injunction with dexterity, do not go near meat or fish. The congregation of Eastern India is verily the Guru's Khalsa (pure/ crown lands).[73]

In the early 1660s, Guru Har Krishan sent a letter to Patna in which he remarked:

The Guru shall assist the congregation; the Guru of the congregation shall fulfil its daily needs, and [the Guru] shall satisfy everyone's desire.[74]

Both, Guru Hargobind's and Guru Har Krishan's letters reiterate the point that the Guru will sustain and satisfy their congregations. They promise to fulfil the congregation's *rojgar:* their daily needs and employment. The Guru in the Guru Hargobind tradition is depicted as the bringer of material and spiritual solace.

Guru Tegh Bahadur's first letter to Patna is identical to Guru Har Krishan's letter to that congregation:

The Guru shall assist the congregation; the Guru of the congregation shall fulfil its daily needs, and [the Guru] shall satisfy everyone's desire. On the Diwali celebration day to the entire congregation my sight will arrive, whichever Sikh will come for my sight, he shall feel bliss.[75]

But in later letters Guru Tegh Bahadur begins using a new phrase centred upon 'devotional service' (*sewa*). He continually remarks 'it is the time of service' (*sewa ki vela/ sewa ka vaqat*). He says in a letter to Patna:

The Guru shall protect the entire congregation belonging to the province of Patna. That Sikh who meditates upon *Waheguru* (wonderful Lord), to him the Guru shall fulfil all his desires. We have gone further afield with the company of the king [Raja Ram Singh Kachhawaha]. I have left my family in Patna. That Sikh who does *Waheguru* (devotion) perform his service [as a consequence] the congregation shall easily obtain wealth (copper and gold coins?). It is the time of service; whichever Sikh shall perform service, to him I shall bless him with his daily needs. It is the time of service.[76]

In a later letter to Patna he stresses the importance of '*sewa*' (service):

For the sons of Sikhs it is the time for service: those who yearn [to perform service] then they shall increase the congregation's sustenance. It is the ardent joy of the Guru [to see] the entire Guru's congregation in happiness and plentifulness.[77]

In letters to Sikhs in Benares Guru Tegh Bahadur says their 'trade/business dealings' (*karbar*) will improve with devotion:

The Guru shall protect the entire congregation belonging to the province of Benares: your trade shall prosper.[78]

Guru Tegh Bahadur's public philosophy continued to accept the householder-renunciant ideal and he gave precedence to the householder over the renunciant. Unlike Guru Hargobind and Guru Har Rai, he clarified the role of the householder-renunciant, discussing the ideal householder-renunciant in his poetic compositions where, for instance, he wrote:

That man who in pain, who does not feel his pain.
He who has no love with joy and to others gives no fear;
He who considers gold and earth equally. (1) (Pause)
To whom neither does slander nor does praise matter;
To whom greed, attachment, and arrogance are not present. (1)
He who is indifferent in laughter and hurt;
He who is indifferent in honour and shame. (1)

To whom the intellect's hopes are separate;
He who lives in the world without desire.
The touches of lust and anger are not found in him;
In his heart resides the Lord. (2)
The Guru's grace has been given to that man;
[As a result] this world becomes perceivable.
Nanak, he merges with the Lord; as water merges with
water. (3)[79]

Guru Tegh Bahadur's householder-renunciant had no visible signs of renunciation; rather the renouncer simply dwelt within the mind. The Sikh could externally wear the garbs of temporality, yet this did not reflect his soul. Guru Tegh Bahadur was arguably moving further away from Harji's model of Sikhism by suggesting that Harji spent too much time focusing on the aesthetic and not enough time on the essence. In Guru Tegh Bahadur's supposed interview with Aurangzeb this point is reiterated, and Aurangzeb is accused of seeing religion externally and never from an angle of compassion and virtue.

The manner in which Guru Tegh Bahadur expressed the householder-renunciant ideal further bound the householder to temporality. This is because Guru Tegh Bahadur chose charity as the means to help people irrespective of their social rank and would travel to different locations solely to provide welfare. He was also willing to help groups who were dissatisfied with local government and who were armed, though there is no evidence to suggest Guru Tegh Bahadur encouraged violence. But he did not deter lobbying and his own intervention with the Kashmiri Pundits is an example of his own lobbying activities. Significantly, Guru Tegh Bahadur connected the duties of the householder to social change and this meant greater involvement in political and social enterprises. In his letters he emphasised the relationship between service (sewa) and material subsistence (rojgar), advising Sikhs that their lives will improve if they do service. But this service could mean anything from acts of charity to fighting injustice and Guru Tegh Bahadur's own life was an example of perfect service.

While his predecessors had encouraged political involvement through the Guru, Tegh Bahadur was beginning to provide Sikhs with independent political agency through the aegis of the Guru. Sikhs were being encouraged to gather resources and to distribute those resources fairly. This idea of justice as the fair distribution of resources by virtuous Sikhs also served the important discursive need of juxtaposing the 'ideal' that the Sikhs were seeking to actualise, against the needs of the world they inhabited.

Guru Tegh Bahadur's householder-sovereign ideal allowed for social mobilisation. His charity and protection was inclusive and he became a figure who combined spiritual liberation with material success. He undermined Harji's perspective that one should follow the four stages of life which ended with asceticism and which favoured elite social groups who were able to participate in Vedic rituals. Guru Tegh Bahadur provided a public philosophy which opposed renunciation as a necessary stage in life. Moreover, he became a spiritual and temporal king: he gave his Sikhs freedom from hell and worldly tyranny. In sum, Guru Tegh Bahadur became an 'active' Vishnu figure.

It seems that Guru Tegh Bahadur did gather a loyal support base. Following his demise, the *Maasir-i Alamgiri* mentions that, on 27 October 1676, two bricks were hurled at Emperor Aurangzeb as he was returning home from the *jami masjid;* the brick thrower was identified as a follower of 'Guru Tegh Singh'.[80] Sikh legend also records that after Guru Tegh Bahadur's execution his body was secretly recovered by a few Sikhs and transported to Makhowal.[81] In Makhowal his body was cremated by his nine-year-old son and successor, Guru Gobind Singh. By comparison, after Guru Arjan was executed in 1606 there are no records of any Sikh protest against the Mughal state. The execution of Guru Tegh Bahadur seems to have left a bitter taste in the mouths of his supporters and there seems to have been growing resentment towards Mughal power. Guru Tegh Bahadur's public philosophy had created a Sikh community which was politically active and politically ambitious; he had connected religion with sovereignty more lucidly than of his predecessors or competitors.

As Guru Tegh Bahadur's popularity grew, Harji became increasingly marginalised. His public philosophy failed to gain supporters from a broad social spectrum, possibly because he offered very little to the ordinary believer. Despite Harji's attempts to present his ideas in an erudite manner, he lacked succinctness and usually wrote esoterically. His gnostic inclinations were also found in the works of rivals, but they did not place emphasis on a mystical lifestyle, being instead willing to discuss the bread and butter of life. Harji's mysticism was not completely unsuccessful; the Miharvan lineage spawned a mystical sub-sect, the *Divanas* (the possessed), who flourished in late seventeenth century southern Panjab.[82] The *Divanas* disappeared in the early twentieth century and it is difficult to assess their real origins but they were a popular mystical fraternity which claimed discipleship from Miharvan and would have acknowledged Harji's leadership as well. The emblems of the *Divanas* seem to have included shaving their hair, blackening their faces, carrying rosaries and other standard symbols, dancing and eating cannabis.[83] They were largely non-celibates and seem to have lived as householders and ascetics. Harji's public philosophy may have created this extreme version of the householder-ascetic. Therefore, even though Harji's ideas might have appeared conservative, it is possible his insistence on renunciation was seen as dangerous to conservative society since asceticism was always considered to carry a danger for Brahmanical society because it required the suspension of social rituals; for many such rituals were pivotal to their self-identity.[84] Interestingly, in the early eighteenth century Ram Rai's lineage also seemed to develop into a Sikh mystical fraternity.[85]

Conclusion

In the 1670s, it appears there were two dominant Sikh public philosophies on the ideal Sikh life: the householder-sovereign versus the householder-ascetic. These contrasting visions on Sikhism reflected competing visions of temporality. Guru Tegh Bahadur's householder-sovereign allowed Sikhs to become agents for social change; they should live good moral lives and create hospitable societies. Meanwhile, Harji's householder-ascetic saw life as an illusion which required renunciation as a means to gain emancipation. Harji's ideas contained a conservative vision of 'social order' and 'tradition', but seemed to descend further into an ascetic-based mysticism.

The contrasting stances taken by Guru Tegh Bahadur and Harji impacted upon their support base. Guru Tegh Bahadur gathered supporters from a wide social spectrum and this was largely due to his householder-renunciant ideal. For instance, he gathered support from Jat and peasant cultivators as mentioned in Suri's account of the Guru's mission in southern Panjab. Khatri support also seems strong, as can be inferred from Guru Tegh Bahadur's letters to cities such as Benares in which he specifically comments upon trade (*karbar*); Benares had a large Khatri mercantile class.[86] Also Sikh tradition records that the companions who were executed along with Guru Tegh Bahadur were Brahmin Sikhs.[87] But Harji's attempts at establishing the dominance of the Miharvan lineage were wholly unsuccessful. It seems Harji had some supporters amongst elite Khatri society, but evidence for this support gets to be increasingly nuanced and dispersed. Harji's name, for example, was mentioned in a nineteenth-century Kangra treaty as a 'Sikh Guru', an unusual reference at a late date.[88] But Harji appealed only to the peripheries of society while Guru Tegh Bahadur had a central appeal. The basic premise that Guru Tegh Bahadur's Sikhism had greater social utility than Harji's Sikhism seems acceptable.

In the public debates that gripped the heterogeneous Sikh community during these thirty years, Guru Tegh Bahadur seems to nudge ahead as the popular choice. The Sikh community did have different communal needs but during this period Sikhism does not seem to challenge them. However, Guru Tegh Bahadur had created a public philosophy which began to envisage wholesale political change; this also meant challenging the existing Mughal structure. The prospect of eliminating the Mughal state created tensions as social groups began considering the relationship between Sikhism, communal needs and Mughal power. In the following chapters I will examine how late seventeenth century Sikh public philosophy created variegated visions of sovereignty and Mughal 'tyranny' along communal lines.

4

SOVEREIGNTY AND SOCIAL
ORDER 1675–1699

The execution of Guru Tegh Bahadur marked a significant point in early Sikh history and this event has often been seen as the catalyst which propelled late seventeenth century Sikh 'militancy'. Unlike Guru Arjan's execution in 1606, sectors of the Sikh community were already militarised, and Guru Tegh Bahadur's execution created a supposedly 'intolerable' milieu. In the case of Guru Arjan's execution, Jahangir and other 'bigoted' Islamic agents in the Mughal court were held responsible, but this was a narrow section of elite Mughal society and 'persecution' of the Sikhs was limited. However, in the case of Guru Tegh Bahadur's execution, Aurangzeb and the entire Mughal state were seen as culpable. This is because of the more widespread perception that Aurangzeb fervently wished to transform the Mughal Empire into an Islamic theocracy in which 'non-Muslims' would be not be tolerated. The execution marked the genesis of a sustained persecution of the Sikh community and, more generally, 'non-Muslims'. This perspective subscribes to the opinion that the evolution of the Mughal Empire was primarily based upon 'religion': the Mughal state evolved from being a 'tolerant' polity under Akbar into an increasingly intolerant one under his successors. The Sikhs and other 'Hindu' groups such as the Marathas, Jats and Rajputs, reacted violently to Aurangzeb's policies and, in the late seventeenth century, they each attempted to overthrow the Mughal state. In this reading, the 'militant' Sikh movement was led by Guru Tegh Bahadur's only child and successor, Guru Gobind Singh (r.1675–1708), who created the Khalsa in 1699.

While this irredentist viewpoint on Mughal history has proved popular, it is quite misleading. Recent research has shown that different 'Hindu' groups had no common bond of unity, but instead each group reacted differently in accordance to their locality, culture and political thought.[1] In addition, these 'Hindu' groups did not have a unified dislike for Islam and did not perceive Aurangzeb's reign in identical ways. In medieval texts from the late seventeenth century we often come across the contrast of the 'Hindu' and the 'Turk', as well as a hatred for Aurangzeb by 'Hindu' groups[2] but these 'contrasts' and 'hatred' seem to be largely political and do not reflect the reality of Hindu-Muslim political relationships. For example, early modern Dadupanthi texts from the kingdom of Amber have strong anti-Muslim sentiments, but Amber was politically dependent upon the Mughal state.[3] Similarly the Sikh movement has been labelled as 'anti-Islamic' because of their militancy in the late seventeenth century which was directed against the 'Muslim' Mughals.[4] The notion that 'Hindu' groups needed to attack 'Islam' in order to assert their own political authority undermines medieval discourses on sovereignty. In seventeenth century South Asia, 'Hindu' and 'Muslim' groups did not homogenously view sovereignty and political thought but had differing ideas on the 'ideal' political system. Of course, religion seems to play a major role in these political discourses but, more importantly, religion was not seen as exclusive from politics. Instead these discourses on sovereignty considered the role of religion within politics: South Asia was not simply entrenched in the mire of 'oriental despotism'.[5]

The execution of Guru Tegh Bahadur did anger his supporters and the manner of his demise resulted in the formation of a Sikh martyrdom culture.[6] While Guru Arjan's demise was seen more as a mystical sacrifice (*kurbani*), Guru Tegh Bahadur was seen as a martyr's (*shahid*) fight against tyranny. And yet, other than Guru Gobind Singh's brief biographical passage on Guru Tegh Bahadur's life there are no detailed late seventeenth century narratives describing his martyrdom. Guru Gobind Singh noted:

> The Lord kept safe their [Kashmiri Pundits] sectarian mark and sacred thread;
> In the Dark Age he [Tegh Bahadur] performed self-sacrifice to prevent great evil.
> The motive behind the act was the protection of the virtuous.
> He gave his head but didn't utter any cries of pain. (13)
> He offers this self-sacrifice for the purpose of righteousness.
> He gave his head but never disclosed his secret.
> They perform plays and magic to achieve their misdeeds.
> The people of God feel ashamed at witnessing such deceits. (14).
> By breaking the body-pitcher upon the head of the king of Delhi [Aurangzeb];
> He then journeyed to God's realm.
> Tegh Bahadur alone done this deed, no other has done this. (15)
> When Tegh Bahadur departed, the world felt sorrow.
> In the world there were cries of distress,
> In the heavens there were cries of joy.[7]

Guru Gobind Singh's passage communicates his own and, presumably, the sentiments of his followers at Guru Tegh Bahadur's execution. The Guru is depicted as a righteous hero who fought for justice. Although Guru Tegh Bahadur challenged Aurangzeb, the Mughal Emperor is not directly referred to in this passage. Instead it is the world over which he presided that is described as bringing 'great evil'. As mentioned in the last chapter, in 1676 a Sikh allegedly attempted to attack and/ or assassinate Aurangzeb for his role in the execution.[8] Undoubtedly Guru Tegh Bahadur's execution was blamed on Aurangzeb and for the Sikh community it created bitter feelings of resentment towards the entirety of the Mughal political system. But despite this, it is impor- tant to remember that Guru Tegh Bahadur's execution did not cause outright revolution. Instead it shifted the attention of Sikh discourse towards sovereignty and the recreation of an ideal social order. If the Sikh community wanted to replace or to reform the Mughal state, it had to possess an alternative vision of political power.

In the last quarter of the seventeenth century there is a growth in Sikh literature dealing with sovereignty and social order. The major Sikh writer in this era was Guru Gobind Singh, who wrote a substantial corpus of poetic works which were compiled in an anthology known today as the *Dasam Granth* (Book of the Tenth King).[9] Since the turn of the twentieth century the authorship of the *Dasam Granth* has come under the critical gaze of the Sikh community over its veracity as a Sikh scripture (*Gurbani*). Because the *Dasam Granth* mainly contains the poetic re-telling of classical 'Hindu' mythic literature such as the legends of Vishnu and Durga, as well as erotic poetry, the legitimacy of the *Dasam Granth* became embroiled with colonial Sikh identity politics.[10] Some Sikhs argued that the anthology was in part composed by Guru Gobind Singh's courtiers and did not reflect his views; others that the text had been interpolated by hostile 'Hindu' intellectuals; yet others argued the text was Sikh scripture.[11] Neither in colonial nor post-colonial Sikhism has the issue of the *Dasam Granth's* authorship been satisfactorily resolved. What is germane, however, is that pre-colonial Sikh society wholeheartedly accepted the *Dasam Granth* as the work of Guru Gobind Singh.[12] There is no evidence whatsoever to suggest that they questioned the its authorship and it played a central role in shaping pre-colonial Sikhism and Sikh identity. Since my concern is to reflect on the place and authority occupied by the *Dasam Granth* in pre-colonial Sikhism, the universal ascription of its authorship to Guru Gobind Singh is of greater relevance than the debate over its 'actual' author. In the late seventeenth century, Sikhs regarded Harji as the other major Sikh writer of the era. Despite his growing political marginalisation, Harji continued to write theological works. Interestingly, Harji also composed a corpus of poetic works based entirely upon a re-telling of classical 'Hindu' mythic literature in an anthology known as the *Sukhmani Sahasranama* (Innumerable names which bring bliss).[13] Thus far no scholar has attempted to make a comparative study of the *Dasam Granth* and the *Sukhmani Sahasranama*, which is unfortunate since it serves to foreground the differences in Guru Gobind Singh's and Guru Harji's public philosophy on sovereignty and social order.

In recent years there has been greater research on the late seventeenth century discourses conducted by Guru Gobind Singh and his Sikhs.[14] Specifically, scholars have attempted to contextualise Guru Gobind Singh's courtly culture inside the variant expressions of medieval civility.[15] These studies are valuable in contextualising Sikh intellectualism within Mughal culture, but, generally speaking, they have failed to examine Sikh political thought. An exception amongst these studies has been Jeevan Deol's work on Sikh sovereignty, community formation and military culture.[16] I agree with the direction of Deol's revisionism, but I disagree with his conclusions. Deol argues that late seventeenth century Sikh notions of sovereignty and social order were culturally 'Rajput' and that in seventeenth century India there existed a 'Rajput episteme'.[17] Deol conceptualises 'Rajput' identity by depending entirely on the works of Ziegler and Kolff and he fails to note the differences or critique the functionalism inherent in each scholar's works.[18] Moreover, Ziegler's and Kolff's research was conducted on Marwari and central Indian Rajput groups, but Deol essentialises from these local studies to conceptualise a universal 'Rajput culture' across the subcontinent without any further historical and ethnographical research. Nor does he question Kolff's distinction between the 'Rajput Great Tradition' and the 'spurious' Rajput tradition, which Kolff argues emerged in Mughal India and was fundamentally based upon 'genealogical orthodoxy'.[19] Deol summarises the meaning of 'Rajput' in the seventeenth century thus:

> It should by now be clear in the seventeenth century, Rajput status had come to be associated with power and dominance. To be a Rajput, whether within the Rajasthani high tradition or 'spurious Rajput' traditions described by Kolff, was to control men and land and thereby to enjoy high status within society. In the 'high' Rajput tradition, the identity implied rank and status within the imperial system as well as the local level. The imperial system accorded a relatively high status to the Rajput,

which in this context most probably meant a Rajput who ruled or controlled clients... In the context of early Sikh history, then, both levels of Rajput identity would have operated as influential paradigms. 'Spurious Rajput' constructions of identity provided a convenient and prestigious rubric under which to assemble the military service groups which seem to have been entering the Sikh Panth from the time of Guru Hargobind onward, and a Rajput identity may have been the logical one for such classes to adopt when they were actually in military service. At the same time, its associations with valour, self-sacrifice and high social standing would have granted it an added cachet. At another level, the status and reputation provided by 'high Rajput' constructions of identity would have constituted an important model for the Gurus' projection of themselves as rulers at the same time as it would arguably formed the basis of the cultural expectations of their followers.[20]

Deol continues by illustrating how Guru Gobind Singh's court attempted to create 'genealogical orthodoxy' which, with military culture, was embedded into the mythic tales found in the *Dasam Granth*. Yet he concludes that Sikh narratives were somewhat unique:

Unlike the Rajput rulers of Rajasthan whose claims to rulership extended to specific territorial regions, the Sikh Gurus combined soteriological status with a following that extended across north India and beyond. It is not surprising, then, that the reinterpretation of Rajput narratives that occurred at the court of Guru Gobind Singh had a wider remit than the original Rajasthani paradigms. Where other Rajput rulers adduced mythological origins and inserted their lineages into narratives of the decline and reconstitution of society in order to justify their claims to land and status, the narratives refashioned at the Guru's court had wider cosmological implications. In this new context, Rajput narratives of exalted descent and the protection of values associated with *dharma* were embedded in texts that renarrated the eternal battles of the gods and the demons, thus creating a metanarrative that involved the Guru and his Khalsa in a cosmic battle between good and evil.[21]

Deol argues that late seventeenth century Sikh sovereignty was essentially 'Rajput' in its origins and expression, but these 'Rajput' narratives were embedded within Sikh metaphysics.

Deol's thesis is questionable in several respects. Most obviously he has overstressed the conception of a 'Rajput episteme'. While it is plausible to argue that 'Rajput' status carried with it a certain martial prestige in medieval India, this was largely symbolic. For instance, in respect to the Marathas and their claims of being Rajputs, Wink notes that Rajput status "provided the Marathas with a model and might be seen as the first stage of gentrification of Indo-Muslim sovereignty".[22] In 1674, when Shivaji was consecrated as a Kshatriya king and it was proclaimed that he was a descendent of Rajputs, it did not alter Maratha political thought. It seems Shivaji chose to perform the consecration ceremony because he was persuaded by his ministers that his conversion from Shudra to Kshatriya would give him greater political legitimacy amongst non-Maratha groups.[23] The Marathas could then portray themselves as 'Hindu' kings and protectors of Hindu *dharma*. Irrespective of this genealogical myth, the Marathas continued to believe in a distinctly Maratha form of sovereignty known as *svarajya* (self-rule). Wink argues that *svarajya* was a form of "zamindari sovereignty"; consequently *svarajya* did not exclusively refer to Maratha sovereignty, but also referred to complex local relationships.[24] The belief in *svarajya* was accompanied by Maratha political theories where *dharma* referred to a 'perfect' social order, one which was conceivable only with the extension of their political dominion.[25] The Maratha example illustrates that medieval 'Hindu' military groups might have adopted a [martial] Rajput personae, but this did not subsume their divergent social and political identities or their locally contextualised military strategies.

Furthermore, Deol's episteme does not consider the dialectics that could be sparked with the process of becoming a 'Rajput'. When Shivaji decided to become a Rajput the issue was not straightforward, but instead resulted in a debate amongst the Marathi and Banaras

Pundits about whether in the Dark Age *Kshatriyas* even existed.[26] For the Marathi Brahmin intelligentsia Shivaji's consecration made a profound point about caste and *dharma* (universal order) in an age of increasing disorder (*adharma*). But these local tensions reflected more complex histories of migration and settlement in the Maratha region; and the political relationships between Brahmins and rulers in the region. The forming of a sovereign identity in early modern India did not simply occur due to the sheer will of an individual, there was always the issue of recognition in the locality. If Guru Gobind Singh created a distinctly 'Rajput' identity it would be necessary to contextualise this identity within the Panjabi milieu. It would be important to determine what exactly the Panjabi Brahmin literati actually felt about Sikhism and if they communicated their ideas to the Sanskrit literati in the region and across India.[27]

In the late seventeenth century, Sikh litterateurs began discussing the issue of sovereignty and social order. These Sikh dialectics did not merely deliberate over 'Rajput' traditions; rather these Sikh dialectics developed from Guru Tegh Bahadur's notion of the 'householder-sovereign'. By the early 1670s Guru Tegh Bahadur's householder-sovereign and Harji's householder-ascetic represented two opposing visions of Sikhism. The contrast was not only theological; it also affected Sikh involvement in the medieval world. Guru Tegh Bahadur had developed Guru Hargobind's 'active' militancy and argued that Sikhs should actively get involved in their material world. Harji, meanwhile, continued to insist that Sikhs should abandon temporal involvement beyond the bare necessities. The execution of Guru Tegh Bahadur (and perhaps even Dhir Mal's death in a Mughal fort, a subject which has gained less attention) created Sikh anxiety towards the Mughal state, even if it did not immediately lead to Sikh hostility.

Late seventeenth century Sikh public philosophy debated the nature of sovereignty and social order, asking such questions as: what are the characteristics of a righteous monarch; what society is perfect; and what role should Sikhs play in creating a better society? There was no single answer to these questions and the various Sikh lineages responded differently. However, these answers were important in giving Sikhs political agency. The politicisation of Sikhism might very well result in a clash with the Mughal state, and while Sikhs might have felt aggrieved at Mughal mistreatment, not all wanted to challenge Mughal authority or believed that Mughal power was detrimental to their lives. Previously, Sikh public philosophy had influenced the quotidian by discoursing on spiritual liberation; now it began to influence the quotidian by discoursing on politics and power.

These Sikh dialectics over sovereignty and social order mainly occurred through re-telling of 'Hindu' mythic tales. The works of the *Dasam Granth* and the *Sukhmani Sahasranama* were focused upon the myths of Vishnu. The *Dasam Granth* also gave considerable attention to the myths of Durga. Via these Vaishnavite and Shakti frameworks on kingship, militancy and temporality, Sikh intellectuals debated politics and power. As we have seen in previous chapters, the role of Vishnu in the world had been a vital issue for the Sikh literati but during this era we see the development of sustained analysis on his role as a political agent. That this was a sustained analysis on Vishnu and temporal authority can be seen through the fact that Guru Gobind Singh and Harji each wrote a version of the *Ramayana*. This enduring narrative has often been used in South Asia to express political views and it seems the Sikh literati also used this method. Similarly, the myths of Durga had greater temporal than metaphysical relevance because Durga was an active temporal agent. The Sikh literati attempted to understand sovereignty by examining 'saviour' gods and their battles with 'arrogant' demons.

In this chapter I will examine the ways in which late seventeenth century Sikh public philosophy evolved, showing this evolution by analysing the writings of Guru Gobind Singh and Harji. My literary analysis will mainly focus on the themes of sovereignty and social order. Furthermore, I will try to tie Guru Gobind Singh's and Harji's writings to wider socio-political developments. This contextualisation will help us understand why Guru Gobind Singh and Harji had such opposing visions on 'militancy' and temporality. It will also help explain why they created polarised Sikh social institutions. Lastly, I will try to illustrate how the heterogeneous Sikh community reacted to the changes introduced by Guru Gobind Singh and Harji. This will offer a more comprehensive vision of Sikh society just prior to the eighteenth century, and will enable us to identify Sikh attitudes towards the Mughals and the creation of the Khalsa.

As I have already mentioned, my main sources for this chapter are the *Dasam Granth* and the *Sukhmani Sahasranama*. Both were intended to be Sikh 'scripture', for the Sikh community and, inevitably, they were aimed at rival Sikh Gurus. As a result, it is possible to see the *Dasam Granth*, the *Sukhmani Sahasranama* and the Sikh community in dialogue with one another on the meaning of 'Sikhism'. There are uncertainties regarding the 'veracity' of the texts, especially if read from the angle of canonical 'authority' but I have tried to view them in their 'performative context' and their meaning to historical Sikh communities. The idea that all Sikh communities, throughout history, have viewed and understood scripture identically is obviously erroneous. For our purpose, it is more relevant to consider that pre-colonial Sikhs believed that Guru Gobind Singh or Harji authored these texts. Similarly, it is unimportant whether gods like Vishnu were symbolic or real from the modernist perspective; what matters is what our historical agents believed. Here, therefore, I have analysed the *Dasam Granth* and the *Sukhmani Sahasranama* as being in 'conversation' with one another on Sikhism in the late seventeenth century. In particular, I have focused on the themes related to sovereignty, violence and social order.

Sikh Public Philosophy: Being a Sikh Guru (1675–99)

After Guru Tegh Bahadur's execution in November 1675, there were four claimants to Sikh Guruship. In Amritsar, Guru Harji continued to preach, but he had become an unpopular and isolated mystic figure. Despite this marginalisation, he was still in control of Amritsar and probably believed in his potential to expand his congregation. Whether or not Harji would be able to proselytise successfully was another matter, but Harji certainly believed in his own charisma and continued to write theological works. He notably produced the *Sukhmani Sahasranam*, a work dedicated to classical Hindu myths and especially those of Vishnu. In contrast, Ram Rai and Dhir Mal continued to propagandise their spiritual authority, but neither produced any writings. In 1677 Dhir Mal died in a Mughal fort, probably having been a prisoner for an unknown period prior to his death; it is unclear why Dhir Mal was imprisoned. Ram Rai had at best a peripheral influence and his community largely descended into a mystical fraternity. Unlike Harji, Ram Rai lacked a prime location to preach from and mainly travelled around the Panjabi hills and southern Panjab, without establishing widespread support. The final claimant was Guru Tegh Bahadur's only child, Guru Gobind Singh, who resided in Makhowal.[28] He had been born in Bihar and had spent the last few years in Makhowal. Guru Gobind Singh was only nine years old at the time of succession and his maternal uncle, Kirpal, acted as his guardian. He was raised in the Panjabi Hill State of Bilaspur-Kahlur where he received a princely education which included the study of martial arts, Persian, Sanskrit, Braj, music and religious studies. Excelling in these subjects, Guru Gobind Singh developed into a skilled warrior and poet. In his Sikh court he employed an army and a retinue of litterateurs.[29] An accomplished Braj poet, Guru Gobind Singh wrote vast quantities of work dealing with Sikh devotionalism, the myths of Vishnu, the myths of Durga and 'mirror-for-princes' texts, which have been compiled in the *Dasam Granth*. He was undoubtedly the most popular Sikh Guru and financially very powerful. His court could be favourably compared, for instance, with the courts of Jodhpur and Amber with their Persianate-Braj culture.[30]

By the 1680s, three major Sikh Gurus and several Sikh fraternities were operating in the Panjab. But Guru Gobind Singh was most unusual because he appeared like a Mughal nobleman in his dress, lifestyle and wealth. In comparison, Harji and Ram Rai appeared in the guise of Sikh mystics and their support bases were mainly mystically inclined Sikhs such as the *Divanas* (the possessed) and possibly the *Udasis* (detached ones). Sikh tradition argues that there was widespread corruption amongst Guru Gobind Singh's missionaries (*masands*); this missionary service had been first established by Guru Amar Das and had been crucial to the administration of previous Gurus.[31] But these missionaries were accused of defrauding Sikhs by claiming they were doing the Guru's work and several petitions for reform to the missionary system were made to Guru Gobind Singh and even to Guru Tegh Bahadur. Early on Guru Gobind Singh had promised he would reform the missionary system at the right time. While Guru Gobind Singh spent his entire reign in the Panjabi hills, the southern-half of central Panjab, southern Panjab and, later, travelling to the Deccan, he continued to have widespread support across Panjab and the subcontinent[32] mainly amongst the Jats and Khatris. He established two courts: firstly, at Makhowal (renamed Anandpur) in 1675–1704; secondly, at Paonta between 1685 and 1688. During the period 1704–1708, Guru Gobind Singh had a peripatetic court.[33]

There was a stark contrast in the lifestyles and political involvement of Guru Gobind Singh and his rivals. Harji seems to have lived a relatively peaceful life with no involvement with the Mughal state. His possession of Amritsar meant he had little financial dependence upon the Mughals and he does not seem to have been greedy for patronage. Yet Harji seems to have become unpopular amongst the Sikh masses in Amritsar, who mostly supported Guru Gobind Singh. Sikh tradition records that after Harji died in 1696, his son and successor, Har Narayan (also known as Niranjan Rai) was so despised that Amritsar's Sikhs asked Guru Gobind Singh to evict him.[34] In the early eighteenth century Amritsar was under the command of Guru Gobind Singh's votary, Bhai Mani Singh, and so it is probable that Amritsar's Sikhs were pivotal in ending Niranjan Rai's tenure.[35] Harji himself seems to have been popular amongst the wealthy Khatri community in the locality – for example, in the early eighteenth century a Khatri supporter of Niranjan Rai, Chuhar Mal Ohri, used his Mughal connections to order a reprisal against some Khalsa Sikhs over mistreatment in commercial dealings.[36] On the other hand, Ram Rai seems to have been eager for Mughal patronage and this is possibly because he lacked any resources and did not inherit anything from Guru Har Rai's estate. Ram Rai did not manage to establish any substantial support and became a mystic figure. Nonetheless, Ram Rai possessed symbolic importance because he was Guru Har Rai's son and Guru Har Krishan's elder brother. His family connections entitled him both to portions of the Guru's estate and to widespread respect. But Guru Gobind Singh had the wealth, accrued from Guru Hargobind's gentrification in the early seventeenth century, to be completely self-sufficient. His lifestyle made him an active figure in the Panjabi hills.

Guru Gobind Singh grew up in the Panjabi hills where he was surrounded by numerous Rajput chiefs and Mughal officials.[37] His courtly etiquette, military skill and religious charisma brought him both the friendship and enmity of local chiefs. Certain local chiefs were concerned at his armed camp; in particular, the ruler of Bilaspur, Bhim Chand (1667–1712), felt the Guru was a menace. In 1682, a local battle occurred between Bhim Chand and Guru Gobind Singh which resulted in the Sikhs repulsing Bhim Chand's attack. From 1685–88 Guru Gobind Singh moved his court further south to the Sirmur region of Paonta and, in October 1688, fought the battle of Bhangani (near Paonta) against local hill chiefs. After his victory, he still feared further battles, so he returned to Makhowal and spent the period 1688–90 fortifying it. In 1690 Guru Gobind Singh and his army fought the battle of Nadaun, mainly against the kingdom of Kangra. Having suffered defeat, the principality of Kangra felt Guru Gobind Singh was a growing danger and enlisted the help of the Mughal *faujdar* (local military commander). In the period 1694–99, Guru Gobind Singh had several skirmishes with hill chiefs and local Mughal agents. Although this period of warfare was significant for Guru Gobind Singh and for politics in the Panjabi hills, these battles did not spill over into the Lahore province and thus did not directly affect the entire Panjabi Sikh community. Nevertheless, towards the end of the seventeenth century Guru Gobind Singh was attracting more intense military and political pressure from the Mughal state. Initially these conflicts had been confined to the semi-autonomous hill region, but local Mughal officials were worried about local Sikh influence.[38] Considering that in late seventeenth century Mughal India several regional insurrections had threatened Mughal security, it is likely the state wanted to stamp out any nascent threats, but these Sikh–Mughal conflicts happened after 1700.

In the late seventeenth century there was a plain disparity between the political involvements of the Sikh Gurus. Harji and Ram Rai largely disengaged from political activity and became dependent upon the Mughal state for protection and patronage. Guru Gobind Singh increased his independence by developing a powerful regional army and court. The eighteenth century account,

Ibratnama (1723) by Muhammad Qasim, commented upon Guru Gobind Singh's power:

> This young man [Guru Gobind Singh], in comparison with his precursors, had more abundant resources for comfort and material for entertainment. The magnificence of his state grew to such an extent he was not behind the nobles of 5,000 [*zat*] or even the rulers of the principalities in anything concerned with greatness of splendour or accumulation of resources... After some time, the inclination to serve him on the part of all kinds of people exceeded every limit and there was no month or year when the roads were not filled by the caravans of people carrying offerings to him. In the meanwhile, some *zamindars* adopted discipleship sold to them by him, and, by reason of the large number of retainers and abundant resources, and upon incitement and spells by him, became contumacious in the matter of paying the money [in tax and tribute] due to the Emperor, and began to establish unprecedented innovations in cities and villages.[39]

Guru Gobind Singh had transformed his estate into something more sizable and converted himself into a local monarch. He became an attractive patron to disadvantaged local groups. He had the power and influence to make an indelible mark on regional politics and it seems that this frightened local political agents. He was unable to appease local agents through diplomatic methods which forced him to militarise further, and this in turn caused both his power and fear factor to grow. Unlike previous Sikh Gurus, Guru Gobind Singh's power was profoundly political and, given the heightened geo-political sensitivities of late-seventeenth century Mughal India, it was seen as overtly threatening to Mughal authority. When Guru Hargobind had arrived in the Panjabi hills he was a local squire and was patronised by local kings; Guru Gobind Singh, on the other hand, was no mere squire – he had an estate which rivalled the local kings.

In the late seventeenth century, Sikh public philosophy seems to have been influenced by these political engagements. As a whole the Sikh movement had grown into a powerful religious movement in

the Panjab and the Sikh community had developed a distinct identity. Sikh sectarian divides seem to have hardened as the rival Sikh
Gurus developed different powerbases in Mughal Panjab. Harji and
Ram Rai were everyday 'saints' who ran temples and had a congregation. But Guru Gobind Singh was a regional warlord with a princely
appearance, a well-trained army, a court and growing political influence. The lives of these Gurus altered their perspectives on political
power and changed their image amongst both Sikhs and the Mughal
state. As a result, these Gurus began to discuss sovereignty and social
order in their writings in greater depth than their predecessors. In
early seventeenth century Sikh works, politics had been dealt with
superficially; for instance, Sikh writings had discussed kings with
mystical statements, simply saying, for instance, that saints are 'real'
kings.[40] But by the late seventeenth century, the Sikh community had
the power to discuss politics with the prospect of introducing social
change. In Guru Tegh Bahadur's tenure he developed the notion of
the 'householder-sovereign' and encouraged political and social participation. Harji and Ram Rai critiqued this argument by fostering
the 'householder-ascetic' ideal.[41] Following the demise of Guru Tegh
Bahadur and Dhir Mal, and in conjunction with Guru Gobind Singh's
rising political power, these debates over the 'householder-sovereign'
versus the 'householder-ascetic' evolved into discussion of the politics
of change in Mughal India.

Sikh public philosophy at this time seems to have centred around
two general questions: firstly, is it permissible for Sikhs to get involved
in politics as 'active' agents? Secondly, what is the Sikh political vision?
The answer to these questions can be found in the *Dasam Granth* and
the *Sukhmani Sahasranama* and, significantly, they present two opposing arguments on Sikh political philosophy.

Before I consider late seventeenth century Sikh public philosophy, it is necessary to examine the self-representation of the different Guru lineages. Through the medium of the genealogy the
rival Guru lineages established the claims upon which they could
justify their current lifestyles. These genealogies were important for
the views of the respective Guru lineages on sovereignty and social
order.

Self-Representation: The Guru's Genealogy

During the tempestuous years of great social mobility in medieval South Asia, newly gained socio-political status was frequently legitimised by recourse to genealogy. This has been particularly well studied in the case of the mythic genealogies of the Rajputs which were commissioned in order to show the power and prestige of their respective clans.[42] It must be borne in mind that such genealogies were designed for personal pomp. What is fascinating about Sikh genealogies is that Guru Gobind Singh, Harji and Ram Rai were all family members. So when they discussed genealogies they were talking to each other about their roots and subsequently their ways of life – subjects that were fraught with contestation.

The first issue was the Guru Gobind's spiritual genealogy. The first five Sikh Gurus were considered legitimate (Guru Nanak to Guru Arjan); thereafter, there existed a genealogical difference. Harji stated that Guru Arjan was succeeded by Prithi Chand or as he calls him Sahib Guru, and then by Miharvan:

> Brother, please recite wonderful lord Nanak; True Master Angad; True Master Amar Das; True Master Ram Das; True Master Arjan; True Master Sahib [and] True Master Miharvan. It is they who have described the dalliance of the Lord.[43]

By contrast Guru Gobind Singh responded to Harji by introducing his *var* (martial ballad) on Durga which stated:

> I first meditate on the primordial sword (Durga);
> Thereafter, I meditate on Guru Nanak.
> Then the Gurus Angad and Amar Das;
> Ram Das: they always aide me.
> Then I meditate on Arjan and Hargobind;
> I meditate on Sri Har Rai.
> I meditate on Sri Har Krishan;
> He who sees his sight all pain disappears.
> I meditate on Tegh Bahadur;

As a result, the nine treasures fill the home.
In all places I am aided by them.[44]

Considering the fact that there were several Sikh Gurus to choose from
in seventeenth century Panjab, it is very likely that many Sikhs were
unsure about which lineage was authentic. Sensing this public confusion Guru Gobind Singh and Harji wanted to establish the legitimacy
of their lineage.

While these differences in spiritual genealogy were well established
prior to the late seventeenth century, there were no histories of Guru
Gobind Singh's pedigree. Guru Gobind Singh, Harji and Ram Rai were
all family members who belonged to the Sodhi Khatri clan. The first
Sodhi Guru was Guru Ram Das who succeeded Guru Amar Das in
1574 – prior to his succession there is no information on the Sodhi clan's
history. Because Guru Ram Das was from Amritsar we can assume the
Sodhis mainly resided in central Panjab. They were probably considered
a lower clan group in the Khatri hierarchy and were mostly employed
in local commerce, agriculture and possibly government service. The
Sodhis were nonetheless Khatris and would have held Kshatriya rank.
Guru Ram Das's succession to Guru Amar Das and the subsequent
successions of Sodhi Gurus seem to have transformed the Sodhis from
a low clan group to a powerful clan group. Amongst the Khatris, the
Sodhis became associated with divinity and exalted status.[45]

In Guru Gobind Singh's biographical work, the *Bachitar Natak*
(wonderful drama), he elucidated upon his spiritual and familial
genealogy. In his explanation, the Sodhi clan were descendants of
the *Raghu Bams* (lineage of Raghu) which included illustrious ancestors such as the Vishnu incarnation, Ram. More generally, the Sodhis
were members of the solar dynasty (*ravi bams*). The lineage of Raghu
had its origins in the beginnings of time when the solar and lunar
dynasties were created. After the early kings the most notable incident
that occurred was the *Ramayana*. Following the Valmiki tradition of
the *Ramayana,* Guru Gobind Singh claims that Ram was eventually
confronted by his twin sons, Lava and Kusha,[46] who inherited Ram's
kingdom and founded the celebrated cities of Lahore and Kasur. Their
descendants ruled those cities for a long time, but then war ensued

between them. The king Kalrai was defeated by Kalketu; as a result, Kalrai was expelled from the kingdom and married a neighbouring princess. Kalrai had a son named Sodhi Rai, who was the Sodhis' lineal ancestor and founder of the Sanaud dynasty:

> To that dynasty sons and grandsons were born: in this world
> they were known as Sodhis.
> Across the globe their fame increased: day by day their wealth
> increased. (30)
> They ruled using many methods: far and wide they conquered
> kings.
> They spread *Dharma* in everyplace: upon their heads they
> raised the canopy. (31)
> They performed many times the royal sacrifice: they gained
> victory over foreign kings.
> They performed the horse sacrifice: the sins of the clan were
> destroyed. (32)[47]

Thereafter the dynasty succumbed to their pride and began an epic war which resulted in victory for the Lava descendants, forcing the Kusha descendants to abdicate. The Kusha descendants decided to travel and study at Banaras, where they became experts in Vedas and were known as the Bedis (knower of the Vedas). Guru Nanak was born into the Bedi clan. The Lava dynasty continued to flourish in Panjab and invited the Bedis to perform Vedic recitation. Upon hearing the fourth Veda, the Lava king decided to abdicate and become an ascetic. He offered the Bedis his kingdom as their reward for reading the Vedas with such purity. The Bedis made a prophetic promise to the Sodhi king of the Lava dynasty, telling him that in the Dark Age they would take the form of Guru Nanak and that he, the king, would inherit Nanak's spirit:

> You heard the three Vedas: upon hearing the fourth Veda you
> gave us your land.
> When we have completed our three births: on the fourth birth
> you shall take Guruship. (9)[48]

So after Guru Nanak, Angad and Amar Das, then, Guru Ram Das was destined to take Guruship and the Guruship would remain in the Sodhi household.

Guru Gobind Singh's genealogy justified his temporal lifestyle because he was a descendant of kings. These kings were not all perfect: they were often depicted as being proud and ignorant, but they were warriors. At the same time, Guru Gobind Singh combined this sovereign genealogy with spirituality and piety. This is because his ancestors were not only patrons of Vedic sacrifices, they were students and masters of Vedic literature. The genealogy is interesting because it balances the temporal and spiritual and it supports the 'householder-sovereign' ideal: Sikhs could be warriors and saints like the Sodhis and Bedis, and like the current incumbent, Guru Gobind Singh. This genealogy also attacked Harji and Ram Rai, who as Sodhis themselves, shared the same ancestry. For instance, Harji had criticised Guru Hargobind's 'militancy' but had been unaware of his martial ancestry in which sovereignty was fused with spirituality. Significantly Guru Gobind Singh's genealogy invoked the power of Vishnu because his ancestors included Ram. Ram did not play an isolated role, he was the father of Lava and Kusha, and it was their descendants who started the Sodhi and Bedi lineages. Therefore, the power of Vishnu as the god-king and as a political agent was embedded into the genes of any Sodhi and Bedi.

There were no counter genealogies by rival Sikh Gurus. It is possible they did not disagree with the general narrative and, after all, the genealogy benefited their reputations. But they could counter Guru Gobind Singh's claims by arguing against the legitimacy of 'active' militancy in the seventeenth century. They could argue that many of their ancestors had been householder-ascetics. Importantly they could argue that cosmic time prevented the householder-sovereign ideal and that Guru Gobind Singh had been dwelling too much on previous ages and not on the current age. Another germane point would have been debating the source of spiritual power: they could ask, why were Ram or Vishnu powerful? This debate over the origins of spiritual power seems to have been a major issue in Sikh public philosophy. This debate clearly manifests itself in the versions of the *Ramayana* written by Guru Gobind Singh and Harji respectively, where it focused upon Ram and his life as a 'householder'.

Ram the Householder: Ascetic or Sovereign?

Since its inception the *Ramayana* has been a popular outlet for South Asians to ponder irresolvable ethical and moral dilemmas.[49] The basic story has remained the same: the divine king Ram of Ayodhya has been incarnated as a man and must kill the demon king of Sri Lanka, Ravana.[50] Despite Ram's divinity (he is often seen as a form of Vishnu) he faces numerous obstacles regarding human conduct (*dharma*) and these quagmires have lent themselves to innumerable interpretations.[51] In the late seventeenth century Sikh *Ramayanas,* the particular quagmire which drew attention was Ram's life as a householder-king and as a divine incarnation. The importance of this question was due to its implications for Sikh conduct, and whether it was permissible or forbidden for Sikhs to become political agents. This question related to the 'householder-sovereign' and the 'householder-ascetic' dialectic in Sikh thought.

Harji's *Ramayana* was entitled the *Adi Ramayan* (Primordial Ramayana).[52] The text was written as if Miharvan was narrating the story and it is possible that Harji was simply transcribing Miharvan's narrative. But it seems more likely that he substantially re-wrote the text in order to eulogise Miharvan's saintliness, since in the narrative Miharvan's dialogues are written in the third person, a device which never appears in Miharvan's own writings. Harji's narrative has strong Shaivite elements, but is generally Vaishnavite, with Ram shown as Vishnu. It does not follow Valmiki's classical rendition but represents instead an important medieval Hindi adaptation of the *Ramayana* tradition.[53] The narrative begins by focusing on Shiva and Parvati; for twelve years Shiva performed *tapas* (austerities/penance) and Parvati served him. After finishing his austerities Shiva granted Parvati a boon in lieu of her service and she asked for a home. Shiva agreed and asked Vishwakarma to build them a home in Sri Lanka, but Shiva had an inner conflict: on the one hand, he was an ascetic and on other the hand, he was married to Parvati. Shiva decided he had to get rid of the home Parvarti desired in order to salvage his asceticism. Shiva was aware he had to give a boon to the gods in celebration of his new home so he went to see Brahma and told him that he had to get rid of Sri Lanka. Brahma sent his son to Shiva's home to ask for Sri Lanka as a boon. Shiva happily granted this, but before she left the furious Parvarti cursed the land of Sri Lanka. Shiva and Parvarti then left and performed greater austerities. Eventually the demon king of Sri Lanka, Ravana, was born from the *tapas* of his father, Gosai Paulsatya, who had practised austerities for ten thousand years. Ravana grew into a powerful demon king with ten heads and it was prophesied that he would only gain liberation when he forcefully captured Sita. In Jasrath's house the prince Ram and his brothers were born: Ram was born as a result of *tapas*. Sita's adoptive father, Raja Janak, similarly, gained Sita as a daughter because of his *tapas*. When Ram grew into adulthood he was exiled and went to stay with the sage Valmiki, whose students are known as his Sikhs. Valmiki, like other sages such as Visvamitra, was a master of *tapas* and with this power they could control kings. For example, Visvamitra took Ram as his pupil by coercion so that Ram sought the shelter of Valmiki. After some time, Ram and Sita attracted the attention of Lanka's demons. Ravana desired to capture Sita and used the cunning ruse of the golden deer to do so. Ram and Lakshman went in search of Sita, bringing the brothers into the political strife of the monkeys. Thereafter, Ram, Lakshman and Hanuman engaged Ravana's demons in battle and subsequently defeated them. Ravana was killed by Ram and died reciting 'Ram, Ram'. As a result, the kingdoms of Ayodhya and Sri Lanka became righteous.

In Harji's *Ramayana* the power of *tapas* is constantly reiterated. All the major characters had gained their power through austerities and it was due to *tapas* that both the gods and demons were born. The origins of Ram's and Ravana's strength lay in their austerities; those of gods were greater than those of demons. The poetic mood of the narrative was devotional and it was written with lucid verses but limited poetic creativity. Its ultimate aim was to stress the benefits of Ram worship (*puja*).

Aside from this basic message the narrative also attempted to undermine the householder-sovereign ideal. Throughout, there is little additional commentary by Harji on the ethical and moral issues or even the religious issues raised in the *Ramayana*. However, after Ravana kidnaps Sita the narrative abruptly turns into a discourse between Miharvan and his Sikhs:

A congregant (*sangati*) went to Lord Miharvan and petitioned him.

'Lord, in the three worlds (*tin lok*) it is believed that Ram had the form of the formless and untainted God (*niranjan nirankar ka rup*).

But some foolish men (*agian manukhan*) remark that Ram done deeds which were trapped in illusion's ignorance (*maya ke moh*).

This opinion perplexes our minds.

Could you make us comprehend this opinion?'

Then Lord Miharvan spoke:

'Brother, may fortune (*dhan*) bring you pleasure (*bhog*).

With questions like these, one's love for God grows.

By keeping doubts in the mind one becomes a fool (*bemukh*).

Brother, you've done (*bhala*) well in asking this question;

Listen like a lover (*sangi*) is attached to the object of his affection (*sang karta heh*).

That love is visible from the words they speak.

It is visible when they are sitting down.

People look towards him and laugh.

When he looks at the object of his affection;

Shame overtakes him . . .

For the lover the object of love is inseparable:

So too Ram is God (*ramchand parbraham parmeshur abnasi heh*).

[But in life Ram] was a householder.

[In the life of a householder] what happens is illusion (*adhin*) grows . . .

If you examine your own minds, see how you've become absorbed as householders . . .

The saints know this fear and don't want to become householders.

My mind is also smiling [at the world].

I am attached-detached from the world.

Those who practice loving devotion they remain aloof from the world's deceits.

So Ram lived the life of a householder, but he never became a householder.

He was a man of God (god-man) (*nirankar purkh*)'.

Then the congregant arose and touched Miharvan's feet and said 'truth, truth'.

'Lord you are Ram.

Now you perform the householder's actions and keep us entertained.

Lord, we want to study under your protection.

We want to leave from this householder life.'

Then Lord Miharvan said: 'Brother, before your death the master shall save you.

On you all happiness will fall'.[54]

This is the only Miharvan discourse in the entire narrative and interestingly it is dedicated to the householder-renunciant ideal. Harji identifies the problem of Ram's ethical and moral conduct and how this contradicts his supposed godliness. This issue has confused his Sikhs and we can assume that such intellectual query was shared by others in medieval Hindu pietistic circles. Harji answers these contradictions by arguing that Ram's conduct was flawed not because he was deluded by the world, but rather because his devotion was tainted by the householder lifestyle. Householders were susceptible to illusion's snares and that is why saints became ascetics in order to avoid such distractions. Miharvan, like Ram, lived as a householder-ascetic and Sikhs should aim to become ascetics. The congregant's desire was to leave the householder path. This was clearly an attack on the householder-sovereign ideal by suggesting that no such balance was possible, because if Ram could become somewhat deluded by the householder and sovereign lifestyle, what chance did ordinary Sikh have in balancing these ideals? The answer was plain to see: Sikhs must become householder-ascetics. And, as ascetics, they should practice austerities and devotion to become powerful. Through successful practice Sikhs would develop 'inactive' militancy like the gods and demons. Furthermore, in medieval Tantric and Shakti circles the practice of austerities was cardinal to developing 'power' and immortality, that is to say, austerities were necessary to become god-men.[55]

Harji was arguing that it was impermissible for Sikhs to become political agents because it burdened the meaning of life. The householder, like the sovereign, had to focus upon frivolous necessities such as wealth (*artha*), family (*dharma*) and pleasure (*kama*) and consequently they lost their focus on liberation (*moksha*). At the same time, Harji acknowledged the need to be a householder because even Miharvan was a householder. Yet the life of a householder like Miharvan had to be dedicated towards achieving renunciation, and only through renunciation could he gain liberation. Harji was not oblivious to the issue of power and politics, and that is why he discussed the importance of austerities (*tapas*). These 'austerities' could have been occult rituals and possibly refer to yogic/mystical practices: Harji was the leader of the *Divanas* (the possessed) and it is probable that they practised mystical rituals. His argument was that it was impermissible for Sikhs to engage with politics in a specific way: by becoming spiritually powerful one became the real power on earth, but by becoming powerful on earth one was unlikely to be spiritually powerful, and thus one actually had no power at all. Ram's power lay in his austerities and not his kingly power. So if Sikhs wanted to be powerful they should shun conventional politics and aim to become householder-ascetics.

By comparison Guru Gobind Singh's *Ramayana,* titled *Ram Avatar* (the incarnation Ram), placed emphasis on Ram as the householder-sovereign. Guru Gobind Singh did not alter Valmiki's basic story. The narrative was written in elegant Braj poetry as found amongst poets of the seventeenth century 'mannerist' (*riti*) tradition.[56] The poetic mood combined devotionalism, ornate mannerism and heroism. Guru Gobind Singh's narrative focused attention on Ram as the warrior-king and his heroic deeds on the battlefield. As in his other works, Guru Gobind Singh spent considerable time crafting vivid battle scenes with a quick and lively metre. The timbre of the battle verses was designed to create realistic heroism: the warriors were beautiful athletes engaged in a noble and brutal profession. These chivalric elements were probably based on Guru Gobind Singh's own first-hand knowledge of warfare and may reflect how highly-skilled medieval warriors saw their bloody occupation. For example, Guru Gobind Singh described a battle between Ram and some demon warriors:

> They [demons] saw Ram on the battlefield; fluttering Dharma's standard; they rushed from all sides; their mouths shrieking 'die'. (69)
> Instruments thumping frightful sounds; the thunder clouds felt shame; fixing their standards; challenging each other to fight. (70)
> Bows crunched; swords trembled; striking shields banged; they struck with endearment. (71)
> Warriors absorbed in blood; minds focused like wrestlers; tides of arrows showered; twang of bows sounded. (72)
> Raining arrows; they heard the resounding ding of victory; the demons Subahu and Marich; set out closing their eyes to death. (73)
> They attacked together; they discharged like hawks; encircling Ram; like cupid besieged the moon. (74)
> Surrounded by the demon host; like Rudra caught by cupid; Ram unstill in battle; his mind like the Ganges merging with the ocean. (75)
> Ram roared in battle; the thunder clouds felt shame; with rolled moustaches; warriors dropped dead. (76)[57]

This aggressive and heroic Ram was never discussed by Harji. Of course, Harji spoke of Ram going to war but this was not a crucial element in his imagery. Yet Guru Gobind Singh never discussed a Ram of *tapas,* instead seeing Ram's strength in his weaponry and his martial arts. Ram was a warrior who fought against the demons by using his knowledge of war.

Guru Gobind Singh not only depicted Ram as the warrior, but also Ram as the family man and lover. The household does not burden

Ram's life, but gives fulfilment. For instance, Guru Gobind Singh composed many verses on Sita's beauty and her love for Ram:

> Sita beheld Ram; pierced by cupid's arrow; falling to the
> ground; like a drunkard. (106)
> She arose thoughtfully; like fallen warriors arise; she continued
> to look; like the partridge gazes at the moon. (107)
> They both beheld each other with longing; neither stepped
> aside; they stood opposed; like warriors on the field of battle.
> (108)[58]

This Ram was not fearful of matrimony and pleasure (*kama*). Instead, his greatest joys and pains came with Sita.

The other image Guru Gobind Singh provides of Ram is the glory of his kingship and the benefits of his rule. Ram's life was shown not simply as a self-journey but his actions had benefits for society. After defeating Ravana and establishing himself as the king of Ayodhya, Ram is described as:

> Many varieties of gifts were given to all: the people verily saw
> the Lord, the conqueror of Ravana.
> The Lord was known as the destroyer of evil which opposed
> Vishnu; the four corners knew he was Sita's master and the
> princes. (689)
> They all hailed the Lord as Vishnu's incarnation: the people
> recognised him as the great giver.
> His splendour spread four directions; the knowledge of his
> might was accepted: Ram, killer of Ravana, became the
> Universal Monarch. (690)
> Amongst the master Yogis he was the master Yogi: the God of
> gods, the king of kings.
> Enemy of the evil, saint amongst the saints: the ultimate form
> and remover of evil. (691)[59]

Ram was celebrated as a king who established 'perfect' rule through his 'active' militancy. Guru Gobind Singh's Ram embodied the householder-sovereign: Ram was a man who overcame evil by actively confronting and removing it. There are no suggestions in Guru Gobind Singh's *Ramayana* that Ram was sullied by being a householder; in actual fact he was even more glorious because he was a householder *and* a sovereign.

This seems to reject Harji's argument that it was impermissible for Sikhs to be political agents. Instead Guru Gobind Singh is arguing that Sikhs are allowed to be to be political agents because only they can remove evil and establish justice. Countering Harji's insistence that it was important for Sikhs to cultivate austerities, Guru Gobind Singh seems to directly respond to this point when concluding his legends on Krishna:

> I am the son of a Kshatriya and not of a Brahman: when have I ever known the practice of *tapas?*
> Why should I assume separation from you and become fettered by the household?
> Now if you are delighted, then give me this petition I beg with clasped hands:
> When the time of my death arrives at that instance, may I die fighting on the battlefield.[60]

Guru Gobind Singh takes an opposite stance from Harji: he does not practice austerities nor is it in his nature and duty (*dharma*) to do so. Guru Gobind Singh does not wish to retire as an ascetic, but he yearns to die in battle. These were battles against evil and for the sake of justice. Unlike Harji who argued for a Tantric-orientated 'militancy', Guru Gobind Singh argued that 'real' power came from the sword and martial arts. It also included taking an active interest in political affairs to benefit society as a whole rather than establishing a mystical clique with gnostic activities. In his unfinished work, *Gian Parbodh* (The Illumination of Knowledge), Guru Gobind began a discourse in which the soul asks God to explain the *caturvarga* (the four aims in life).[61] It is possible that Guru Gobind Singh was arguing that the aim of life was to fulfil the four aims and this meant being politically active. Like Ram, Sikhs could balance the life of the householder and sovereign.

These debates over the permissibility of Sikh political participation firmly divided Guru Gobind Singh and Harji. But these positions were developed upon bigger discourses over the politics of change and whether or not society could be changed for the better. Both believed in the Dark Age and its dynamics which asserted that morality would continue to degenerate until the end of time. Yet, even in the Dark Age, humanity was capable of changing their circumstances for the better. This required that the Sikh literati should examine their contemporary political circumstances.

The Politics of Change: Righteousness and Tyranny

The 'householder-sovereign' and the 'householder-ascetic' were grounded upon discourses over power (*Shakti*) and the capacity to harness that power for political change. If Sikhs are allowed to change the world how do they acquire the power to implement this change? As we have seen, Guru Gobind Singh and Harji both believed it was permissible for Sikhs to be political agents in different ways. These doctrinal positions were constructed on a metaphysical and empirical understanding of righteousness and tyranny in the world.

Metaphysically, Guru Gobind Singh and Harji both examined Shaktism (power essence), a ubiquitous concept in classical Hindu thought. "Briefly Saktism is the worship of *sakti,* the primordial power underlying the universe, personified as a female deity who is the supreme being, the totality of existence. As such, it stresses the dynamic quality of the deity as both deluding and saving power".[62] The goddess has many forms, benign and horrific, and there is no singular method for her worship. Shakti philosophy has been integrated into numerous traditions such as Vaishnavism, but it also exists independently with the goddess as the sole object of worship. The purpose of Shaktism was to affirm the power of the goddess in the material world. Shaktism at its core embraced the material world as real and the goddess was often seen as a 'redemptive' and 'temporal' figure. As Coburn notes: "when we ignore the eternal and focus on the temporal, ignore power as a religious phenomenon and focus on it as a secular one, the Goddess has to be shown to be the ultimate agent".[63]

Nevertheless, the goddess was philosophised by numerous theological schools, and for some she was an illusionary (*maya*) force. Shakti's centrality to classical Hinduism has resulted in numerous interpretations of Shakti and its influence in the world. In late seventeenth century Sikh public philosophy, Shaktism became clearly tied to the debate for political change.

Harji's householder-ascetic philosophy essentially viewed the world as illusionary. Hence, the aim of liberation was to realise the non-duality of mind and matter. This monistic philosophy was pivotal to Harji's exoteric views and had many similarities to Advaita Vedanta in its rejection of materialism and emphasis on renunciation. But Harji's work also shows his commitment to austerities (*tapas*) as being important for Sikhism. These austerities allowed the practitioner to develop 'heat' or 'power' within themselves and thereby become a 'god-man'. These 'god-men' possessed 'inactive' militancy because they would obtain supernatural powers and be able to curse men.[64] Harji seems to have been adopting a Tantric view of Shaktism in which the goddess was an illusion but could give one power through sexual acts. The relationship between sex and asceticism in South Asia is complicated and while it is often believed that ascetics abstained from sex, this does not seem to have been the reality. For instance, Shaiva ascetics who had an Advaita Vedantic philosophy seem to have engaged in sexual rituals with both goddesses and women in order to gain 'power'.[65] Interestingly, Harji's ascetic order the *Divanas* were largely composed of married men who lived as householder-ascetics. While it is not clear whether they participated in sexual rituals, it is clear that abstinence was discouraged. Irrespective of why precisely they rejected celibacy, it must in part be related to Shaktism. Because from the householder-ascetic angle, sex had to been seen as an illusion (*maya*) created by the goddess and this illusion had to be overcome to realise non-duality. As a result, Harji's Shaktism did not see the possibility for change because it was an intangible and inaccessible force; the goddess had to be realised as illusion. It is possible that Harji also believed that one could gain 'power' from the goddess.

This Shakti element in Harji's thought related to his Vaishnavite ideas. He had argued that Vishnu was an 'inactive' agent in the Dark

Age and only resided in the devotion of his saints. So Vishnu had no violent redemptive qualities in the current age. Harji's view on Shakti would deny the goddess those violent redemptive qualities in, for instance, the manifestation of Durga. Therefore, in Harji's opinion the politics of change was static because one could not intervene to prevent or to foster either righteousness or tyranny. Only the saints possessed righteousness and 'true' saints like Ram were householder-ascetics.

Unlike Harji, Guru Gobind Singh composed several Shakti (power essence) works dedicated to the myths of the goddess Durga. These compositions included: *Var Sri Bhagauti* (The Ballad of the Sword/Durga); *Chandi Charitra* (Chandi's Episodes), *Chandi Charitra Utki Bilas* (Episodes of Chandi's Radiant Story), and *Bhagauti ji ke Chhand* (popularly known as *Ugardanti* – the goddess with the terrifying tooth). These compositions did not differ in their basic mythical narrative but only in terms of their descriptive detail and their prosodic qualities. The myths recounted by Guru Gobind Singh originated from the crystallised goddess text, the *Devi-Mahatmya* (The Specific Greatness of the Goddess).[66] The *Devi-Mahatmya* narrated Durga's battles with great demon warriors which had conquered the kingdom of the gods. Guru Gobind Singh re-narrated these battles between Durga and the demons without any major changes. The episodes were framed in a similar way: certain demons became powerful and attacked the kingdom of the gods; conquering the three worlds the demons exiled the gods; the gods in turn went to see Durga to seek her protection; Durga, who resides in an occult state, agreed to help the gods; seated on her lion she engaged the demons in battle and annihilated them with furious anger; finally, Durga gave the gods back their kingdom and returned to her occult state. Importantly, Durga remains always in service of the gods whenever they need her protection from demonic forces.[67]

Guru Gobind Singh's Shaktism focused upon the goddess's fierce forms of Durga, Chandi and Kali.[68] His work exclusively dealt with the goddess and her battles with the demons and she is not seen as the universe in its totality. Instead, she is made subordinate to Guru Gobind Singh's supreme God, represented by death. Yet she is portrayed as a redemptive agent who operates in the material world. Specifically the goddess is shown as the divine protectress of humanity: Durga was a manifested and tangible form of Vishnu on earth and she resided in weaponry. Guru Gobind Singh opened his ballad on Chandi:

> In the beginning the Lord created the double-edged sword (Shakti):
> With this he gave birth to the universe.
> He placed Brahma, Vishnu and Mahesh in power:
> With this he set in motion the game of nature.
> The ocean, mountains and earth were formed:
> Without pillars the sky remained in place.
> He created the demons and gods:
> Amidst them he created animosity.
> You alone Lord created Durga:
> You through Durga ordered the annihilation of the demons.
> From you Ram took his strength:
> With his bow he killed Ravana.
> From you Krishna took his strength:
> He seized Kans' hair and threw him down.
> Mighty seers and gods:
> For many ages have practiced austerities in order to please you.
> But no one has ever realised your true extent. (2)[69]

Guru Gobind Singh argued that Shakti underlined the material universe so that in order to create the world God first needed to create Shakti. Yet God resided beyond creation, beyond Shakti and the power of the gods. In the material world Durga was an agent whose objective was to protect the righteous and destroy all forms of tyranny. Durga's strength lay in her capabilities as a warrior: she was unbeatable in war and no agent could destroy her. Only God could eliminate Durga because God was the supreme warrior, God was death and no-one, human or divine, could escape from the power of death. Guru Gobind Singh wrote:

Death placed his power in Vishnu and that is why Vishnu had
the skill to turn the wheel of creation.
Death placed his power in Brahma, Shiva and the seers.
Death placed his power in the gods, demons, celestial
musicians, divine guards; the serpents were sent to all realms.
Alas, all those benefactors of death reside in death; only death
is immortal. (84)[70]

The noun 'death' (*kal*) can also be translated as 'time'. So in Guru
Gobind Singh's thought death was the giver of 'power' but this was
illusionary because 'death' would consume all agents of power including Vishnu. Therefore, there are three levels of God: an unknowable
God, a subtle God like Vishnu and a material God like the form of
the martial Durga. The power of martial Durga was stressed because
in the material world, violence or death was used by God to remove
agents, be they good or bad. But God particularly protected the righteous, and dispersed tyranny. Thus righteous agents like Durga were
far more powerful than unrighteous agents because they could not be
defeated. Guru Gobind Singh opened his eulogy on God as death:

The sword breaks the evil; it eradicates the vile host; chief in
battle; beyond any harm.
Mighty punishing arms wield the sword; the sword's unending
effulgence; burning brightly; glorious as the sun.
It gives peace to the righteous; destroys the evil; remover of
sins; I seek the sword's sanctuary.
Victory, to he who controls the world; to he who eradicates
temporal evil; the one who nurtures me; victory to the sword. (2)[71]

Weapons and warfare were tangible and accessible forms of Durga for
Guru Gobind Singh. But for warriors to gain Durga's strength they
had to fight for righteousness against tyranny because Durga only
fought for justice.

Guru Gobind Singh's Shaktism fundamentally differed from Harji
and other Shakti theological schools, such as the famous Srividya
school, because he saw Shakti as a political entity.[72] In his view of

Shaktism, the goddess was neither a Supreme Being nor an illusion. Instead the goddess was seen as a material power of righteousness which was embedded in the fabric of the universe. Her power dwelt in weaponry and those warriors who fought for righteousness against tyranny were blessed. Guru Gobind Singh was not advocating violence: life and death were not seen in isolation from the transmigration of the soul. Killing 'evil' agents did not, ultimately, cause their soul to die. Humanity, whether they knew it or not, was locked into God's game and God's power lay in his ability to create, maintain and most of all to destroy. The power of death was the real Shakti in the universe and agents like Vishnu and Durga were given the power of violence. Guru Gobind Singh's Shaktism saw political change as possible because one need not escape from the world. This is because in Guru Gobind Singh's thought the material and immaterial were distinct; so too were Shakti (power) and Bhakti (devotion). It was possible to be a 'householder-sovereign' or 'warrior-saint' because one could live as an attached-detached agent like Ram had done. Durga and her horrific forms epitomised this attached-detached agent because she was a fierce warrior queen and was devoted to her duty as God's agent of death. In order to bring political change, Guru Gobind Singh argued one did not need the rewards obtained from occult austerities; one needed to gain the power of violence by getting the goddess' blessings which meant gaining martial skills and submitting to God's will.

The politics of change was related to their empirical views on sovereignty. Harji seems to have little time to comment on temporal authorities. It may be that this lack of interest was borne out of his views on asceticism or his desire to avoid political conflicts. I assume Harji would have supported any political regime that was in power because temporal agents were products of Shakti's illusion.

By contrast, Guru Gobind Singh's conception of sovereignty rested upon Durga's temporal agency. The monarch had to abide by Durga's righteousness, otherwise Durga would eliminate unrighteous elements in society. Sikhs could call upon Durga's protection by grasping the sword and protecting themselves from tyranny. Yet Guru Gobind Singh did not advocate the formation of a new monarchy, there were no suggestions in his work that kingship was beneficial. A persistent theme in Guru Gobind Singh's writings is hatred for kings and their tyranny: kings tended to fall victim to the vice that Durga always avoided, that of pride.

Guru Gobind Singh saw the value and importance of political power but it seems he felt that it, like all forms of power, had a corrupting influence. For instance, he commented upon the pride of kings:

> Some owned mighty elephants adorned with gold; huge in size and decorated colourfully.
> Some owned innumerable horses, leaping like deer, out running the wind, with manifold varieties.
> Some were kings of strong armed men, who prostrated in many ways, the headcount was uncountable.
> In this way they lived and this fact is known: in the end these kings departed barefooted. (22)
> They pervade across many lands for the sake of conquest: triumphantly playing many instruments.
> Beautiful elephants trumpeted loudly: in the king's stable thousands of horses neighed.
> There have been many kings in the past, present and future, they cannot be fully recalled.
> Without worshipping the Lord, in the end, these kings depart to the realm of death. (23)[73]

Later Guru Gobind Singh remarked on the transience of kings and all possessors of power:

> There was one Shiva, he was removed, and then another emerged.
> There have been many incarnations like Ram and Krishna.
> There have been innumerable Brahmas and Vishnus; many Vedas and Puranas have been composed.
> Many Smirtis have been authored; those authors lived and died.
> Many Mondi Madars and many Asuni Kumars.

The progeny of the incarnations is also great: in the end they
all dwell in death.
There have been vast quantities of saints and prophets.
Composed of earth and born on earth, they all become
earth. (77)

There have been many powerful seers, ascetics, celibates, as
well as great emperors.
Kings under the shade of the canopy travel great distances.
They travel many lands with royal authority.
Conquering kingdoms they strip kings of their pride.
Kings like Mandhata who were mighty sovereigns.
He took great pride from the might of his arms.
Kings such as Darius were proud like Duryodhana.
They lived in pleasure on earth, in the end, they returned to
the earth. (78)[74]

Guru Gobind Singh's Shaktism is apparent in these compositions: he
sees no power greater than God and feels that powerful individuals
forget the inevitability of death. Durga was always able to operate as
a perfect agent because she never developed pride. Moreover, Durga
was a unique political agent, more unique even than Vishnu. While
Vishnu took on external forms like Ram and Krishna, Durga took on
forms which dwelt inside her, such as Kali. Also, Vishnu was an actual
king whom Sikh texts often criticised for being arrogant and forgetting
God.[75] Durga was never accused of arrogance and she never claimed
worldly kingship. For example, Vishnu's legends show him living a
full-life as an agent from birth to death, where he often became a
powerful temporal agent like Ram. Durga's legends show her being
incarnated as she is, never living a full-life, nor becoming a powerful temporal figure. Instead, after gaining victory, Durga dutifully
gives power back to the gods: she never takes advantage of her own
strength. Durga's sovereignty was attached and detached and balanced
the householder-sovereign ideal. It is possible to suggest that Guru
Gobind Singh felt kings should live within the boundaries of Durga's
righteousness and any agent who stepped outside these boundaries was

tyrannical and would be subjected to Durga's wrath. But what was this righteous social order?

Harji's work does not yield any information on his understanding of utopia other than the dominating role saints and ascetics would play in it. Given that Harji believed in the value of the 'four stages of life' he arguably believed in a utopia in which society followed the Vedic regimen of rank and duty.[76] In this utopian society the four ranks would follow their duties without fail and without dissent. But Guru Gobind Singh did not endorse a Vedic system of rank. Indeed, in Guru Gobind Singh's writings there are references to 'social chaos' as found in Vedic theories of society. His formulations were less elitist and showed a broader appreciation of the diversity in medieval Indian society. In his unfinished work, *Gian Parbodh,* he discussed how a king in earlier times had visited a Brahmin's home in the kingdom of Tilak. This Brahmin is identified as a member of the Sanaud dynasty which, as we have seen was the Sodhis' ancestral dynasty, and hence the Brahmin represented Guru Gobind Singh's family. It is not entirely clear if Guru Gobind Singh was discussing the idealism of the Brahmin's home or of the entire kingdom, but either way the home or kingdom was distinctly Sodhi. Guru Gobind Singh spoke of this kingdom in the past tense and, given the fact that Islam is discussed, it is worth speculating whether this utopia was also a blueprint for the world he wanted:

At some places people discussed Brahma's words and
discoursed the Vedas;
At other places Brahmins sat and performed Brahma's worship.
There was a Sanaudh Brahman with distinct characteristics: he
wore only bark raiment and ate nothing. (272)
At some places they recited and sung the hymns of the
Samaveda;
At other places the people gained honour by studying the
Yajurveda.
At some place the Rigveda's teachings and exegesis was sought;
At other places they discussed Brahma's teachings and Vishnu's
mysteries. (273)

At some places they discussed the ten incarnations;
The fourteen knowledges were revealed.
There was highly skilful Brahman; he always remained beyond hope and disappointment. (274)
At some places they studied the erotic arts and political science;
At other places they studied the treatises of justice and the duties of kings.
At some places they studied philosophy and astronomy;
At other places they lovingly recited Durga's compositions. (275)
At some places they spoke the vernaculars and serpent language;
At other places studies on the Veda were conducted in Sanskrit.
At some places music was performed in the classical style;
At other places the knowledge of the celestial musicians and guards was discussed. (276)
At some places Indian philosophy was analysed;
At other places the knowledge of engineering and warfare was studied.
At some places the Vedas and Patanjali was studied;
The fourteen knowledges were also examined. (277)
At some places they studied scriptures and the Kaumudi;
At other places they studied the Chandrikas found in Siddha philosophy.
At some places the rules of grammar and the Kashika were studied. (278)
At some places they sat and discoursed on the books of philosophy.
At other places they sang in modes and danced.
At some places they discussed all the knowledge in the treatises;
At some places they studied weaponry and removed fear. (279)
At some places they showed how to use the mace;
At other places warriors gained respect by showing their swordsmanship;
At some places they examined the details of syntax;

At other places they discussed marine knowledge. (280)
At some places they sat and spoke of ending snake poisoning;
At other places they spoke of the Tantric arts;
At some places they studied Greek, Turkish and martial arts;
At other places they studied Persian and the art of armoury. (281)
At some places they studied how to heal weapon wounds;
At other places how to stop a missile;
At some places they studied the four-fold knowledge of defence;
At other places money was given to philosophers. (282)
At some places the art of dance and music were discussed;
At some places the important Puranas and Qur'an were
discussed;
Knowledges were discussed in many scripts and languages;
Throughout the kingdom all forms of worship were given
prominence. (283)[77]

Guru Gobind Singh's righteous society seems to have been a society in
which individuals were free agents, where people were free from fear
and injustice. In this society the worship of God was central to human
life and people thoughtfully engaged in the study of the world. Here
there were only equals so the vice of pride was subdued. Significantly,
this social tranquillity was only possible because the government in
power was righteous and was able to foster peace. Guru Gobind Singh
believed in the power of politics to shape society and in a world where
the powerful shunned their pride for the sake of civil society.

By the 1690s, Guru Gobind Singh had developed a coherent political philosophy in which militancy was not seen as a reactionary force.
Instead it was tied to a political vision of righteousness which contrasted with a view of tyranny. Sikh public philosophy had developed
a clear political thought which moved beyond the parochialism of earlier Sikh Gurus to one which examined the entire Mughal Empire. As
Harji increasingly moved away from politics and mainstream Sikh society, Guru Gobind Singh's ideas became more concerned with Mughal
politics. In Guru Gobind Singh's early reign he did not attempt to
reform Sikh society to reflect these broader political concerns; rather
he continued that early parochialism by maintaining his own court

in the Panjabi hills. However, in the late 1690s, Guru Gobind Singh created an overtly political organisation known as the Khalsa Panth (way of the pure).

Creating the Khalsa Panth: An Army of Righteousness

In 1699 Guru Gobind Singh created the Khalsa Panth. This event marked the most important innovation in the Sikh community since it had been formed under Guru Nanak. Despite its importance in Sikh history there is a dearth of early sources which illuminate this event, the vast majority being from the late eighteenth century when the Khalsa tradition was well-developed.[78] Nevertheless, it is generally agreed by historians that Guru Gobind Singh created the Khalsa in April 1699, at Anandpur.

Sikh tradition says that Guru Gobind Singh encouraged Sikhs to come to his annual Baisakhi festival.[79] The festival marked the beginning of the Panjabi spring and it was the time when all of Guru Gobind Singh's missionaries (*masands*) would gather and bring their offerings from across India. When the festivities were in full swing Guru Gobind Singh appeared before the large congregation. Unexpectedly, he did not appear in a jovial mood and his face was seething with rage. He compounded the congregation's confusion by asking for the head of a Sikh. He made this bizarre request with a gleaming sword in his hand. The congregation shuddered at the prospect that Guru Gobind Singh had gone insane with power but, after repeated requests, a Sikh named Daya Singh arose and offered his head. The Guru took Daya Singh into his tent and returned alone, his sword dripping with blood. The congregation feared Guru Gobind Singh had decapitated Daya Singh, but this killing spree had only just begun as Guru Gobind Singh demanded another head. Four more Sikh men offered their lives and each was taken into the tent, after which Guru Gobind Singh returned with an increasingly bloody sword. As the faithful looked on in despair, they began to fear the Guru would kill them all. But as the last thud was heard Guru Gobind Singh re-emerged with the five men, who were now dressed in strange, martial attire. Guru Gobind Singh declared these men were his 'five beloved ones' and proceeded

to baptise them by offering a drink of sugary water mixed by a double-edged sword. They drank this nectar (*amrit*) and then the five
Sikhs baptised Guru Gobind Singh into his new fold of the Khalsa.
Thereafter, Guru Gobind Singh declared the formation of the Khalsa
and encouraged the Sikh men in the audience to join them by taking
baptism. But what was Khalsa all about?

The earliest source we have on the Khalsa is from the early eighteenth century, by Guru Gobind Singh's court poet, Sainapati, who
composed the *Sri Gur Sobha* (Glory of the Guru).[80] It is the earliest
account of the Khalsa's creation, but the dating of the text and the
identity of the author has proved contentious. While the *Sri Gur Sobha*
appears to be written in the style of an early eighteenth century Sikh
text, some scholars have suggested that the date of composition was
actually 1748, rather than 1711, due to a misspelling of the date in the
manuscript tradition.[81] Recently Mann has suggested that 1701 may be
a more accurate date, after conducting original research on several extant
manuscripts.[82] Mann also noted that the presumption that 1711 is the
actual date is based on weak textual evidence.[83] However, I will place
the text in the early eighteenth century, composed sometime between
1700 and 1711. The authorship has also proved problematic, with some
scholars suggesting that Sainapati was a Mann Jat who served Guru
Gobind Singh's court as a litterateur.[84] In the *Sri Gur Sobha* Sainapati
clearly identifies himself as a Khalsa Sikh and his Braj poetic style is
strikingly similar to Guru Gobind Singh's works in the *Dasam Granth*.
I have used a published version of the text edited by Ganda Singh, who
unfortunately does not identify the manuscript he has used.

In the *Sri Gur Sobha* Sainapati contextualises the metaphysical role
of the Khalsa as the warriors of righteousness (*dharma*). He sees the
Khalsa's formation as a new chapter in the narrative of good and evil
which has enveloped humanity from creation:

Creation and destruction: growth and exhaustion.
The Lord of Actions (*karanhar kartar*) makes us forget our cycle
of births.
There have been scores of warriors (*jodha*) that have been made
mighty by you [God].

In this world their lineages (*sarbans*) have been bestowed with honour (*an*). (22)

The rise and set [of kingdoms]; taking on rule (*raj*); proclaiming yourself as 'king' (*raja*).
Applying focus on nothing other than you; proclaiming yourself as existent.
[Becoming] great demons (*rachhsan*) [with] strong-armed (*jor*) warriors [as servants].
Invading, attacking and looting for your own [political] ends. (23)

Never acknowledging the One [Lord]; indulging your own ego (*garbkari*).
For the destruction [of the unrighteous] Chandi was assigned: thereby re-establishing goodness (*sudhari*).
The ash that covered the earth was replaced by splendour.
They then said 'this is it [God] and there is no other'. (24)

There have been many powerful kings with large canopies [over their heads].
They became lost in illusion [like] many strong warriors.
For the destruction [of the unrighteous] Vishnu was assigned to remove (*hakare*) them.
All the incarnations (*aoutar*) establish goodness (*an*) in the world. (25)[85]

Sainapati believed that humankind was locked in a game of good and evil played by God. In this game, all human beings have access to power of one sort or another: this power is the capacity to do either good or evil actions. Kings and other political agents have far greater power than ordinary individuals because their actions have far greater repercussions for society. For Sainapati power could corrupt. The history of humanity had been a narrative of power and corruption: there will always be structures of power, but Sainapati would question whether the structure was corrupt or incorrupt. What Sainapati meant by corruption is somewhat ambiguous, but it was clearly situated in morality and ethics. Arguably Sainapati had a common sense perspective on virtue and vice, which for him were discernible at all levels of feeling and intelligence. When immoral and unethical agents possessed political power society was sure to descend into chaos. Because God favoured good over evil he assigned saviour gods such as Vishnu and Chandi to re-establish righteousness, for the moment, at least, whenever evil reached intolerable levels. But Sainapati's God was neither benevolent nor malevolent in his ultimate form; he was simply playing a game.

Sainapati was without any doubt that Guru Gobind Singh was an *avatar* (incarnation) sent by God to restore righteousness. This opinion was not unusual since in pre-colonial Sikh literature this image of the Guru as an *avatar* was widely accepted.[86] Sainapati related how God had called Guru Gobind Singh into his court prior to the Guru's birth and specifically assigned the Guru to form a *panth* (spiritual way) dedicated to spreading goodness (*sumatt*).[87] In a later verse Sainapati says: "The Guru is Gobind [i.e. God] and Gobind is the Guru: the Lord of Action; The Guru has come to this world to save it and the entire world knows this truth".[88] When discussing the creation of the Khalsa Sainapati tells us that the Guru told his Sikhs: "Cleanse the senses (*man*), speak (*bach*) truthfully and act (*karm*) justly, then the goddess (*Bhavani*) will protect you and you will reside in an ocean of happiness (*sukh sar*)".[89] This is interesting because Sainapati states that the goddess will protect Khalsa Sikhs and the goddess is, after all, a saviour deity. In Sainapati's view the Khalsa had a mandate from heaven to rule because they were protected by God and had a divine mission to establish order in a chaotic world.

Sainapati informs us that the Khalsa's distinct code of conduct was stipulated by Guru Gobind Singh.[90] This code was not negotiable and could not be broken once accepted. Sainapati states that a Khalsa Sikh had to: 1) keep unshorn hair and beard; 2) never associate with people who shave their hair (*sir-gum*); 3) never associate with five reprobate groups, although Sainapati does not clarify these groups; 4) no longer give offerings to the *masands* (Sikh officers tasked with collecting donations from Sikh communities); 5) not smoke tobacco (*hukka*); and 6) not perform the tonsure rites (*bhaddar*) at times of death.[91] In addition, the Khalsa Sikh was a warrior, but Sainapati does not explain how such a warrior behaves on the battlefield. Sainapati does, however, see the practice of warfare as consistent with religious devotion because Khalsa Sikhs continued to follow practices such as meditation (*nam jap*).[92]

Sainapati gives particular emphasis to two injunctions, namely the *hukka* and *bhaddar*. He makes a passionate plea to Sikhs to give up these customs:

> Abandon smoking tobacco (*hakka*), instead sing God's virtues.
> The food of desire the Lord will bestow that taste (*ras*).
> Hey brother! Abandon the tonsure rites (*bhaddar*).
> This lesson was taught to the Sikhs. (21)

> Whosoever's parents die.
> Don't perform the tonsure rites.
> God is your mother and father.
> These worldly ties are covered with falsehood. (22)

> Please don't forget this injunction on tonsure rites.
> Please sincerely accept this teaching.
> The tonsure rites are delusion (*bharam*), there's no righteousness (*dharm*) in it.
> Know this as the faith that exists in a pious man (*sant*) (23)[93]

The stress placed on these customs is telling. Sainapati was well aware that certain sections of the Sikh community were strongly attached to such customs and they would not abandon them easily, if at all. This is fascinating, because Sainapati did not make the same effort to convince his audience of the other injunctions – because, presumably, he felt they would be accepted without any fuss.

Sainapati continues his narrative of events by explaining why exactly the *hukka* and *bhaddar* proved so controversial to Sikh society. He explains how Delhi's Sikh community began a public discourse on the formation of the Khalsa and its implications on their everyday lives.

Sikh Public Philosophy: Early Eighteenth Century Delhi (c.1700)

When the Khalsa was created the heterogeneous Sikh community was faced with a crucial decision: should they join or reject the Khalsa? This decision was not only based on faith: by accepting the

Khalsa's code of conduct (*rahit maryada*) it would dramatically change their lifestyle. Sikhs would have to physically alter their appearance by keeping unshorn hair and spiritually change their beliefs to accept the power of righteous violence. The Khalsa's conduct was also more specific than Nanakpanthi Sikh traditions, which seem to have had a lenient attitude towards caste practices such as tonsure rites; the Khalsa tradition, by contrast, was inflexible on issues such as hair and weaponry. These changes in lifestyle would undoubtedly impact upon their livelihoods and could bring them into violent conflict with the Mughal state.

In the late 1690s, Sikh public philosophy became engrossed over the legitimacy of the Khalsa. Significantly this debate over legitimacy was conducted by ordinary Sikhs rather than the Sikh literati. Guru Gobind Singh had made his reforms without any consultation and it seems no-one had been aware that he was going to create the Khalsa. On that Baisakhi day, Guru Gobind Singh made his announcement and Sikhs were given the option of accepting or rejecting the new institution and its tenets: they were neither able to reverse the decision nor negotiate the Khalsa's code of conduct. They could not remain undecided, but must choose which type of Sikhism they wanted to follow. After Guru Gobind Singh's declaration, Guru Gobind Singh's representatives spread the message across Panjab and nearby regions like Delhi that the Khalsa had been formed and encouraged Sikhs to join. But local Sikh communities did not immediately accept this innovation; instead, within their local communities, they discussed how joining the Khalsa would impact on their lives.

It seems that in general rural Panjabi communities reacted positively to the Khalsa. These communities mostly comprised Panjabi Jats – in the early eighteenth century the vast majority of Khalsa Sikhs were from Jat backgrounds and other lower-caste groups.[94] It is possible that these lower-caste groups saw in the Khalsa a movement which could provide them with social mobility: by joining the Khalsa they would come under Guru Gobind Singh's protection and might gain service with the Guru. As seen in the last chapter, Guru Tegh Bahadur had proved a popular figure amongst refractory groups and it is possible that Guru Gobind Singh continued to have this appeal. The Khalsa, then, gave lower-caste groups a community which fused religion, politics and social mobility. Since many of these lower-caste groups were outside elite society with limited direct benefits from the Mughals, they seem to have had few issues with challenging both caste and Mughal authorities. Also, the Khalsa identity was a Kshatriya one, and for many Jat and other lower-caste groups, martial civility was a key to social mobility. By joining the Khalsa they could keep their communal identities and become Kshatriya warriors.

In the major cities where Sikhs resided, such as Lahore, Amritsar, Patna, Dacca and Banaras, the temples and bazaars would have been buzzing with discussions on this surprising turn of events. Sainapati only discusses how Delhi's large congregation reacted to the news, which suggests that he lived there for a time at least in the early eighteenth century. He describes how Delhi's Sikhs had mixed feelings about the Khalsa:

When the congregation came for the Guru's sight [i.e. went to the temple];
They made their private concerns public;
They spoke of wisdom in the temple;
All the Sikhs listened to this wisdom and accepted it. (4)

The entire congregation drank the drink of the double-edged sword;
Five Sikhs followed five Sikhs, in this fashion they were baptised;
But both Khatris and Brahmans remained separated;
In their minds they discussed this situation. (5)

'How does one remain a Brahman if they don't perform the tonsure rite (*bhaddar*)?
In this world our honour will be taken away';
In this manner they got lost in delusion (*Bharam bharmane*);
They forgot the teachings of the creator. (6)

Many heard the wisdom put to them and thought in their hearts;
'If we abolish our ancestral traditions (*kula karm*) then we won't
remain'. (7)

Many said this order is unpalatable;
The nitty-gritty of this order means abolishing our ancestral
traditions;
Other said this order lacks wisdom;
Guru did not give this order. (8)

Many said if there is a written order (*hukum*);
Then we'll accept the command as correct;
Some heard the command and were endeared to it;
This was the condition of the congregation. (9)

Many heard the command and abandoned their families (*kutamb*);
Those who felt the order was invaluable;
Know this, those ones are attached to God with body and soul
(*ang sang*);
Recognise them as God's followers (*sangi*). (10)[95]

What is intriguing about this account is firstly the dynamism of the
dialogue. Sainapati describes a discourse occurring amongst ordinary
Sikhs instead of the Sikh literati. Moreover, the concerns of the Sikhs
are not only confined to their Sikh identities but also to their caste
identities. Sainapati describes how Khatri and Brahman Sikhs were
not excited about this innovation and voiced doubts about the origins
of the command. They wanted written evidence directly from Guru
Gobind Singh's court detailing the creation of the Khalsa and the
restructuring of Sikh society. Sainapati explains that their concerns
stemmed from their ancestral traditions (*kula karm*) and how abandoning the tonsure rites would cause them social and spiritual dishonour.
While Sainapati does not inform us about the social backgrounds of
those Sikhs willing to accept the Khalsa, we can assume they were
largely from non-Khatri and non-Brahman backgrounds. But he does
say that many Sikhs left their families (*kutamb*) to join the Khalsa,
which indicates that the situation was not clear-cut as some Sikhs were
choosing faith over family.

The conflict had only just begun, as Delhi's congregation made an initial split between pro-Khalsa and anti-Khalsa factions. Sainapati describes how, in ensuing meetings in the Sikh temples, the atmosphere became more heated and even violent. For instance, he narrated how a prominent Khatri Sikh was forcefully removed from a temple and verbally abused by Khalsa Sikhs:

> From the Khatri community, there was a man of eminence (*prathme*).
> In the congregation he aired his wisdom (*bibek*).
> They seized him by the arm and threw him out.
> They told him 'go back home'. (16)

> They called him a 'shaven head' (*sirganm*).
> The Sikhs raised that Khatri man (*prithme*) to his feet.
> In that man's mind he became enraged.
> He started muttering about class and courtesy (*ouch nich*). (17)

> Then he met up with another [Khalsa Sikh].
> He explained to him the intricacies of the issue.
> [He remarked] 'Take the current situation, I never seen it before'.
> This was a new issue that he had witnessed. (18)[96]

What is striking about this conflict is that the Khatri man appeared bemused at the disharmony in the congregation. It was the first time in his life he had seen the Sikh community so disjointed, their hatred such that they were willing to assault each other. Sainapati further elaborates that this Khatri man was invited for a meal by the Khalsa Sikh.[97] As they ate together the Khalsa Sikh convinced the Khatri man about the glory of the Khalsa so that by the end of the meal he was an ardent supporter of the Khalsa.

It would be reasonable to assume that the pro-Khalsa faction would have been happy at the Khatri man's conversion, but that was not the case. Rather Sainapati informs us that the pro-Khalsa faction was angered at the Khalsa Sikh for eating with the Khatri man, who was a 'shaven head' (*sir-gum*). The pro-Khalsa faction was upset because

the Khalsa Sikh had broken his code of conduct by socialising with a
sir-gum:

> Then that other Sikh came to meet the Sikh congregation.
> That Sikh told the Sikhs what had happened (*bhed*).
> Then the Sikhs began asking him questions.
> They asked 'did you give him [the Khatri man] food?' (28)

> 'He was a shaven head (*sir-gunm*) and we threw him out.
> How did you allow that man to sit in your home?'
> Clasping his hands the Sikh man petitioned.

> 'Forgive me for this transgression'. (29)
> All the Sikhs gathered and came to a consensus.
> Then they met with that man and discussed with him.
> They did not show him any mercy (*prit*).
> If you make a pledge then sincerely abide by it. (30)[98]

The Khalsa group were clearly staunch in their beliefs and unwilling
to make any concessions.

The conflict did not end there; Sainapati tells us that a few days
later another meeting of Sikhs in the temple convened:

> Several days passed [before this meeting].
> Half the congregation was in agreement [with the Khalsa].
> The Sikhs then heard the public issues (*pragat bat*).
> Many heard the issues with interest (*mundi dhuni*). (32)

> Then one Sikh was given the opportunity to address the
> congregation.
> Then he entered into discussions with the other Sikhs.
> Then all the Sikhs disclosed their views (*sikh*).
> They seized the arm of the speaker and threw him out. (33)

> Many of the congregants got up and left.
> Angrily they returned home.
> The anger they felt was great.
> They decided to convene a meeting (*sabha*) for further
> discussions. (34)

They were all in agreement that no policy (*rahi*) had been decided.
'They don't conduct intelligent discussions, they only throw people out'. (35)[99]

The conflict between the pro- and anti-Khalsa factions seems to have reached a stalemate. But it appears the pro-Khalsa faction was particularly zealous in their views, with little patience for anti-Khalsa rhetoric. Perhaps their frustration was due to the arguments presented by the anti-Khalsa faction rather than enthusiam, while the anti-Khalsa faction argued their views were not being considered; perhaps both groups were being stubborn. Unfortunately Sainapati does not provide us with a detailed account of the exchanges between the opposing groups.

The group of congregants that had been outraged at the last meeting decided the issue had to be resolved. They felt the best way would be to call another meeting at Darapur market where the entire congregation would gather. But this time, the anti-Khalsa faction would lead the discussion and present an ultimatum to the pro-Khalsa Sikhs. It is interesting that the anti-Khalsa faction chose to hold the forum at a marketplace instead of a Sikh temple. It is also interesting that the anti-Khalsa faction was led by two wealthy Khatris. Sainapati described the meeting:

Many attended the gathering at Dara market.
Two wealthy Khatris (*darbvant duei khatri*) told their views. (41)

'You lot [pro-Khalsa Sikhs] the injunctions you're trying to impose on us.
Show us the written evidence that has come to you ordering those commands.
That says we can't smoke tobacco (*hukka*) nor perform the tonsure rite (*sis mundaei*).
Brother, whatever comes to your mind you express it. (42)

Our opinion follows this logic.
If you lot offer us written evidence for everything.

For all the things that you lot call sinful.
Until you lot don't meet this demand, then everyone can meet
with us.' (43)

After hearing this everyone was silent.
This discourse concluded with agreement that meeting for
work (*milan kaj*) was appropriate.
They arose saying 'wonderful, wonderful'.
Everyone in the world felt this discourse had concluded well.
(44)[100]

The conclusion of the meeting was amicable: the anti-Khalsa faction
wanted further evidence about the Khalsa's code of conduct. But it
seems that neither faction wanted to abandon their established social
and material relations. Furthermore, it is interesting that the Khatris
in particular raised their objections regarding the *hukka* and *bhaddar.*
The meeting at Darapur market had not resolved the issue.
Moreover, the participants had not agreed upon a process to get the
evidence they sought regarding the Khalsa's etiquette. What followed
was another private meeting held by the anti-Khalsa faction:

On the eleventh month when there was another meeting.
To everyone that came they gave this teaching.
'The lessons we have been given by our ancestors and elders
(*pita purkhi*).
We should follow their examples'. (47)

Those that sat and heard this advice contemplated it.
'Brother, it is an excellent policy'.
Many of them said the 'Khalsa code of conduct (*rahit*) is
nothing.
We don't believe their views'. (48)[101]

As Sainapati comments, these Sikhs had rejected the Khalsa and become
khulasa (empiricists).[102] It seems at this point a firm line had been
drawn between the two factions and the previous demand for a written
order from Guru Gobind Singh's court was no longer required.

However the animosity between both factions had only started as the implications of the Khalsa's creation moved from being largely theoretical to practical. The previous meetings had only centred upon the adoption of the Khalsa's code of conduct. But once both factions had made clear their respective positions the conflict became rooted in their everyday lives. This is because the factions were not conveniently divided along caste lines, with certain individuals choosing to betray their caste loyalties. Sainapati narrates how the death of a Khatri Sikh sparked a campaign of persecution against Delhi's Khalsa Sikhs by certain elements of the Khatri community:

> There was a Sikh with a pure soul.
> In his heart he loved the Guru.
> The order came from God and he died.
> Even in his final moments he loved the Guru. (4)

> His family said 'brothers we won't perform the tonsure rites (*bhaddar*)'.
> Their fellow Khatri caste brothers (*jati lok*) were angered.
> Then what followed was a debate (*charcha*) over the family's conduct.
> The entire Khatri community gathered in the city (*nagar*). (5)

> They decided 'we won't trade (*banju*) with these lot [Khalsa Sikhs].
> They've ruined all the family traditions (*kul ki chal*)'.
> Then the local council (*panchan*) met and wrote this law (*likht*).
> They wrote it in the presence of the Vedas. (6)[103]

In this instance, the death of a Khatri Sikh who wished to follow the new Khalsa practices caused uproar amongst Delhi's Khatri community. The Khatris decided to hit the Khalsa Sikhs financially by severing all trading ties and even stopping the Khalsa Sikhs from operating in Delhi's markets. What is fascinating about this financial assault on the Khalsa is the sheer power the Khatri *panchayat* had in Delhi's economy. The Khatris could make or break trading groups. Furthermore, this assault also reveals that the vast majority of Delhi's Khalsa Sikhs were traders and businessmen who depended on Khatri cooperation. It seems pre-Khalsa Sikhism helped build business bonds, but Khalsa Sikhism had now seriously undermined these working relationships.

Sainapati continues his narrative by telling us the Khatri *panchayat* overwhelmingly supported the policy. The Khatris "closed all the markets" (*sab bajar band kari dina*) to Khalsa Sikhs.[104] The Khalsa Sikhs were helpless in reversing this policy and Sainapati says that some Sikhs kept faith in God, others engaged in criticising the Khatris, and some prayed at the temple. But there was also a group of Sikhs that went to the home of the local commander (*hakam*) of Delhi to protest against the Khatris. These Khalsa Sikhs simply tried to persuade the *hakam* to re-open the marketplace to them[105] but the Khatri *panchayat* became aware of this lobbying activity and became even more determined to end the Khalsa by convincing the *hakam* of the dangers that Khalsa Sikhism posed to the Mughals:

The city council met to form a plan of action.
'We've closed down all the markets'.
Many of them gathered in the city council.
They debated on what way to end the Khalsa. (20)

[They said] 'Look, right now how can we complete our plan?
How will we end the Khalsa's splendour?
Right now we'll follow this approach.
Then no one shall speak of this Khalsa'. (21)

They met the local administrator (*hakam*) and discussed with him.
'These Khalsa lot have started a new path (*rah*).
They've left the path (*marg*) of family traditions (*kula karm*).
They follow a new way and have new beliefs. (22)

When they meet together they say the Khalsa belongs to God (*wahguru ka Khalsa*).
Go and ask them the questions that arise in your mind. (23)

The Emperor of Delhi (*patshah Dilli*) is the lord (*pati*).
It is he who is *Khalsa* (pure).

Think about it, who else can be called Khalsa?
This is all we have to say, contemplate it. (24)

Those Sikhs they say:
That the Guru (*satigur*) is the giver of bliss (*sukhdaei*).
Before we [the Sikh community] used have these officers (*naieb*).
They were called *masand* but they are all gone now'. (25)[106]

The Khatri *panchayat* tactfully suggested to the *hakam* that Khalsa Sikhism was essentially anti-Mughal in thought and practice, since Khalsa Sikhs now accepted the authority of the Sikh Guru before the sovereignty of the Mughal Emperor. Indeed, the Khalsa Sikhs were so audacious in their opposition to the Mughal Emperor they even called themselves Khalsa (pure), which could be interpreted as a play on words on the Mughal administrative term *khalisa* (crown lands reserved for the imperial treasury). In addition, the Khatris remarked they preferred the structure of pre-Khalsa Sikhism with its system of *masands* (officers).

The conflict had not ceased and the Khatris were unconvinced of the effectiveness of their intervention. Sainapati says that, to make sure the local authorities enforced the ban on the Khalsa Sikhs, the Khatris decided to bribe the *hakam*. He writes the Khatris literally gave the local authorities their "expenses" (*kharch*).[107] The local authorities gladly accepted the bribe and began physically and verbally harassing the Khalsa Sikh population.[108] The Khatri *panchayat* did not stop here, they held a further meeting and declared: "On one side there is the Khalsa, on the other side there is world (*sansar*)".[109] What they meant by this was: on one side there is the Khalsa, without any regard for worldly realities, and on the other side there is us, the Khatris, with all our worldly duties. The Khatris became so incensed by the Khalsa Sikhs that they hired factionalists (*dharie*), highwaymen (*bat parie*) and local people (*nagar ko apar log*) to harass and bully them.[110]

The conflict ended after eventually because the *hakam* had a change of mind and re-opened the marketplace to Khalsa Sikhs, probably for economic reasons. Possibly the fiscal loss being incurred and the overall disruption to local businesses were too great for the ban to be sustained. It appears the Khatri community did not have the means to successfully put down the Khalsa community in Delhi. Neither the ban on trading nor the gangs of toughs were enough to quell the Khalsa Sikhs. Indeed, it seems that this period of conflict helped to strengthen the resolve of the Khalsa Sikhs and Sainapati does not report any defections in the community. For Sainapati this change in circumstances was due to the grace of God.

After this lengthy period of public debate within Delhi's Sikh community the key issues seem to have been settled. The dispute between the pro-Khalsa and anti-Khalsa factions could not be solved through arbitration or force. Both sides simply had to accept each other's position as legitimate. It is likely that professional and social relationships between both sides significantly declined in the early eighteenth century. But this is not necessarily the case because both sides would have well-established family, social and professional ties which would probably have survived the stormy weather of recent conflicts. Moreover, the two sides were not easily divided by caste – for instance, many Khatris were willing to accept the Khalsa's code of conduct. In addition, there would have been those Sikhs who would have been sympathetic to the opinions of their counterparts, like the Khalsa Sikh man willing to dine with the 'shaven head' Khatri man. That being said, there was still a clear social boundary between the two sides. The anti-Khalsa faction was mainly composed of literate and mercantile Khatri Sikhs and a smaller Brahman contingent. By contrast, the pro-Khalsa faction mainly consisted of non-Khatri Sikhs, who were either merchants or employed in Delhi's markets. These pro-Khalsa Sikhs were possibly Jat and other lower-caste Sikhs who had migrated from the Panjab region.

An important question is why such a sharp social division occurred in the early eighteenth century Delhi Sikh community? In order to answer this we must understand the social composition of this community and explore the extent to which the Mughal system impinged upon the lives and aspirations of Delhi's Sikhs.

Sikh Society in Early Eighteenth Century Delhi

Sainapati identifies two main caste groups in Delhi's Sikh community – the Khatris and the 'others'. We can also infer from Sainapati's account that the vast majority of Delhi's Sikhs were working in the bazaars as either independent merchants or employees for various businesses.

The Khatri community is portrayed by Sainapati as wealthy, well organised, well connected and having political clout. Moreover the Khatris have a strong attachment to their ancestral traditions such as the tonsure rites, and an attachment to cultural tastes such as the *hukka*. By contrast, the 'other' Sikhs seem to consist of lower-caste groups which lacked wealth and political connections. These other Sikhs were virtually helpless in overcoming the ban imposed by the Khatris and the local Mughal authorities. They were also willing to accept the Khalsa's code of conduct with relative ease and they had a strong presence in Delhi's Sikh temples. It is fair to suggest that these other Sikhs were a cluster of various caste groups, but it is possible that the main group was the Jats of the Punjab. However, it is more probable that these 'other' Sikhs consisted of mercantile castes such as the Aroras and possibly the Ahluwalias. Yet further ethnographic research into Delhi's Sikh community would be required in order verify the precise make-up of the 'other' Sikhs.

What is interesting about these caste groups is they collectively formed a Sikh commercial society.[111] While in the Panjabi countryside the contrast between the Jat agriculturalist and Khatri administrator might seem great in certain contexts, for example, ritual status,[112] in Delhi's urban markets and financial districts the contrast between the Khatri and Jat may have been significantly diminished. Undoubtedly the Khatri had greater caste prestige compared to these 'other' Sikhs, but the bonds of religion would have helped to create a moral community. From Sainapati we learn that the Sikh temple was a lively arena for discussion and fellowship for all Sikhs. It is reasonable to assume that the Sikh temple also facilitated business transactions and offered Sikhs an opportunity to network with other professionals. The creation of the Khalsa caused a severe rupture to these existing commercial relationships. But why did this Sikh commercial society choose to disintegrate instead of remaining together and protecting their commercial interests? An important reason must have been due to their differing economic priorities and cultural associations.

The 'other' Sikhs of Delhi were a minor economic group in the city's markets. Unfortunately, Sainapati does not describe in any detail their backgrounds, occupations or other relevant facts. All we know is they were pious Sikhs; sincerely devoted to the Khalsa, well-represented in Delhi's Sikh institutions and unable to resist the power of the Khatri *panchayat*. It is difficult to determine their exact caste identity, but I assume these Sikhs were from Panjabi backgrounds and possibly Jats, Aroras, Alhuwalias or other merchant/artisan castes. This is because in the Panjab region the main converts to Khalsa Sikhism were from Jat *zamindars* and the Jat peasantry, as well as other lower-caste groups amenable to military service such as Tarkhans (carpenters). In the context of rural Panjab it seems clear that the Jat community joined the Khalsa for a mixture of reasons including religious faith, social mobility and the belief that the Khalsa would offer them a *zamindari* confederation.[113] But the Khalsa did not prove as popular amongst Punjab's urbanites and revenue farmers (*ijaradars*). It is unsurprising to find that Punjab's urban trade and revenue farming was largely controlled by the Khatri community.[114] But why would Delhi's 'other' Sikhs want to join the Khalsa? After all, the Khalsa offered few material advantages to urban Sikhs in the early eighteenth century. In fact joining the Khalsa could have negative consequences for one's material circumstances as the Mughal state became more suspicious of Khalsa Sikhs.[115] This suggests that Delhi's pro-Khalsa Sikhs had strong cultural and/or economic connections to rural Panjab. These cultural and economic relationships must have been immensely strong to sustain them through the period of persecution they endured. Furthermore, we can assume the remit of their trading network was limited: they may not have been trading far beyond Delhi and Panjab.

There may be another reason why Delhi's pro-Khalsa Sikhs felt so attached to the Khalsa. These pro-Khalsa Sikhs may had a dependency on Sikh institutions for education. Sikhism's egalitarian principles and written culture had cultivated Sikh schools across Mughal India. These schools were known as *taksal* (treasury) and *dharamasala* (Sikh temples).[116] Similar to *madrasahs* of that era, Sikh boys would have been sent to the *dharamasala* to study Sikh scriptures. It is unlikely that Persian language and literature would have been taught: instead medieval Hindi and Panjabi would have been the languages of communication. The teachers at these Sikh schools would have ranged from volunteers to professional Sikh orders such as the *masands* (Sikh officers). The *masands* were local officers who principally collected donations and travelled back and forth from their local congregation to the Guru's court. They were individuals of considerable importance to the functioning of early Sikh society. Due to their financial duties it is more than likely that in order to be appointed a *masand* one needed to have strong numeracy skills. As a result, it is likely that in Sikh schools basic numeracy was also taught.[117]

These Sikh schools would have been a vital lifeline for socially mobile Sikhs. While we have little information on these schools, we do know something very significant about the *masands*. In the mid-sixteenth century when the *masand* system began under Guru Amar Das (r.1552–1574) the vast majority of the *masands* were probably from Khatri and Brahman backgrounds. But by the mid-seventeenth century the vast majority came from Jat backgrounds. This information is provided to us by Mobad in the *Dabistan-i Mazahib* who comments: "they have made Khatris subordinate to the Jatts, who are the lowest caste of the *Bais* [Vaishyas]. Thus most of the leading *masands* (commanders/officers) of the Guru are Jatts, and the Brahmans and Khatris (comprise the) . . . disciples and followers of the Guru".[118] From this we can infer that many Jat Sikhs became literate and numerate through education received at Sikh schools. Indeed, some commentators have said Sainapati was a Jat and he became an accomplished Braj litterateur. In Ganda Singh's brief biography on Sainapati, he informs us that he was originally from Lahore and was given a literary education because his father, Bal Chand Mann, had an enthusiasm for academic study.[119] This suggests that many Jats, and perhaps especially those living in urban areas, had access to primary and higher education. It seems that Sainapati was trained by Devi Das Chandan who sent the young Sainapati to complete his apprenticeship at Guru Gobind Singh's court. It is likely that urban Sikhs needed the religious authorities in some way, shape or form to aid their education.

Delhi's Khalsa Sikhs probably were dependent on these Sikh schools, where their children probably did not study alongside Khatri and Brahman children, for free education. While Sikh schools did not offer a Persian education, they did offer one in the local vernaculars and basic numeracy and such linguistic and mathematical skills would have been important to their daily lives. It is possible that many of these Sikh schools became pro-Khalsa because their teachers were from low-caste backgrounds.

In addition, if these pro-Khalsa Sikhs were a relatively poor Panjabi diaspora in Delhi, it is likely they required each other for matrimonial and kinship alliances. The Khatris had no kinship ties with these groups and their mode of marriage was radically different.[120] Therefore, even in Delhi's urban setting, joining the Khalsa was a necessity for these groups in order to survive despite the persecution they suffered for their beliefs.

In comparison, the Khatri community were economically and culturally embedded into the Mughal system. Khatri Sikhs claimed to be natives of the Panjab and from the sixteenth to eighteenth centuries their merchant families had established a vast trading network stretching from the Russian Caspian port of Astrakhan down to southern India.[121] In particular, the Khatris had a mercantile presence in the Panjab and the Ganges valley.[122] In Delhi they were a major commercial bloc.[123] Their success was due to their clearly defined caste structure and their fluency in Persian, which was the lingua-franca of the Indo-Islamic world. The widespread adoption of Persian by a caste group could be very advantageous for their commercial success.[124] Moreover, the Khatris were not simply interested in trade and commerce, they were also widely employed as scribes, writers, statesmen and accountants in the Mughal government.[125] The Khatris seem to have started to learn Persian from the fourteenth century as Persianate regimes began to replace earlier Sanskrit regimes.

The Khatris had clearly benefited from Mughal rule and were a prominent caste in medieval India. But an essential part of Khatri culture in Delhi was Sikhism.[126] So why did the Khatris of Delhi reject the Khalsa so vehemently? After all, many Khatris had supported the temporality of Sikh Gurus since Guru Hargobind and they had supported Guru Gobind Singh prior to the creation of the Khalsa. The obvious reason is that the Khalsa threatened their social status. But how exactly did it do this? The Khatris raised three major objections to the Khalsa: 1) the permanent suspension of the tonsure rite; 2) the permanent ban on tobacco consumption; 3) the inherent challenge to Mughal authority. Let us explore these three issues in more depth.

First, the Khatris wanted to keep the practice of *bhaddar* (tonsure rites) at times of death. The reason put forth in Sainapati's narrative was due to the centrality of the tonsure rites to the ancestral traditions of Khatri society. As Olivelle remarks, the shaving of hair is the most widespread practice found in Hindu rituals with respect to hair.[127] And, as such, the meaning of the ritual shaving of hair is manifold and in certain instances contradictory. But with respect to *bhaddar* the ritual represents a temporary separation from society and is considered an act of re-birth. By shaving the hair one temporally separates and as the hair grows back one re-unites with society. The performance of the act purifies the self and avoids pollution. Usually, in the Panjab region, before a cremation all the sons and grandsons of the deceased got shaved.[128] But in the Panjab the tonsure rites are not confined to times of death, the first tonsure of a young boy is also an important rite.[129] The tonsure rites for a young boy were variously practised in late nineteenth century Panjab, but generally speaking the date of the act was set by a Brahman and either performed at home or at a sacred location.[130] Ibbetson explained that the act of tonsure was an opportunity "to swear lasting friendships" with kinsmen and friends: it was an act of re-enforcing real kinship and forming fictive kinship.[131] Hence the tonsure rites were not simply about pollution, they were about kinship and social ties.

For Khatri society the tonsure rites would have had two main purposes: 1) maintaining a connection to Brahmanical society; 2) maintaining a sense of Khatri homogeneity. The tonsure rites were similar to other Brahmanical rites practised by the Khatris such as taking the 'sacred thread' (*jeneu*).[132] The Khatri community would have sincerely believed in these rituals and Sikhism never dissuaded Khatris from the power of the rites. If the Khatris abandoned the tonsure rites they would have been abandoning Brahmanical society and would be ineligible for every other ritual. Furthermore, the Khatri community's commercial success was dependent upon the co-operation and fellowship of other Khatris across their vast trading network. These trading networks would have operated on trust.[133] But trust could only be maintained if Khatri society possessed a homogenous culture of kinship. If Delhi's Khatris abandoned the tonsure rites they might have been ostracised from the Khatri trading network which could be disastrous for their businesses. Therefore, from the Khatri perspective the permanent suspension of the tonsure rites could potentially destroy their caste structure and it was a risk they could not take.

Recently Deol has suggested that the Khatris also rejected the injunction on the tonsure rites because of the existence of a 'death tax'.[134] Deol cites the fact that in 1728 Emperor Muhammad Shah abolished in perpetuity a tax on *bhaddar* due to a petition from Jai Singh of Amber. While he has found no evidence to determine when the tax was first imposed, he suggests they might have been imposed under Aurangzeb's rule because the Mughal state also abolished the *jizya* in 1722, and the pilgrim tax in 1732, and both these taxes had been introduced under Aurangzeb. So perhaps Guru Gobind Singh's aim of abolishing *bhaddar* was a shrewd move to undermine the Mughal fiscal system. Delhi's Khatris, fully aware of this, did not want to upset the Mughals by forfeiting their tax obligations, especially since they lived in the imperial capital. The argument is interesting, but questionable. Firstly, it needs to be established how effective was the administration and collection of the *bhaddar* tax. Secondly, what was the aim of the *bhaddar* tax – for example, the aim of the *jizya* was to apparently encourage conversions to Islam. Lastly, the Khatris were a highly-skilled commercial community in many respects who would always have been eager to reduce costs. If they rejected *bhaddar* they might have been able to significantly reduce their burden of tax and it is unlikely the Mughal state could object to savvy accounting. Thus the Khalsa, from the 'death tax' angle, was commercially appealing because it could develop a series of tax efficient injunctions. Despite these questions, it seems more likely that the Khatris rejected the permanent ban on the tonsure rites for kinship and social reasons.

The second objection raised by the Khatris was on the permanent ban of tobacco consumption. Though tobacco is undeniably addictive, it seems unlikely the Khatri community was simply too addicted to give up. Also the consumption of tobacco was not a requirement of any kinship or social ritual. The objection towards a ban tobacco cannot be narrowly construed but instead must be seen as symbolic of wider cultural norms of behaviour associated with Mughal courtly culture. The development of a distinct Mughal *adab* (civility) has been well-documented,[135] but as O'Hanlon points out, in late seventeenth century Delhi and other north Indian centres there was "a complexly stratified urban elite, of greater and lesser amirs, lower ranking mansabdars and merchant households".[136] The great households of Delhi were the main consumers of luxury commodities and building projects in the area. But the elites of Mughal India would have abided – or at least appeared to abide – by certain norms of comportment. It is unlikely that the great and the good of Mughal society would have wandered through Delhi's bazaars searching for bargains. Rather they would have had personal relationships with merchant houses and directly bought goods from merchants. And of course, merchant houses would have fiercely competed for clients from Delhi's upper echelons. The merchant could not appear uncouth in the presence of an elite customer and would have to adopt the etiquette of their client by whom, perhaps, the smoking of tobacco was considered refined. For Khatri merchants the ban on tobacco might have appeared as the stepping stone for other injunctions which could threaten the stability of their client relationships.

Moreover, the Khatri community needed to ensure the stability of their financial services sector. Certain members of the Khatri community would have worked as accountants, bankers and consultants. These services would largely be consumed by Delhi's rich households, which needed these services to stay solvent. These service professionals would have been dependent on Mughal high society for business and could not risk alienating clients.

The last reason why the Khatris objected to the Khalsa was due to its inherent threat to Mughal authority. Political change and warfare is not necessarily negative for commercial enterprise. For instance, weapons and ammunition suppliers would see a short-term increase in sales.[137] More thoughtfully, political change could result in safer commercial conditions as law and order becomes more secure and business friendly. Khalsa Sikhism, however, did not look business friendly and the chances for Khalsa political success were limited. In the early eighteenth century, the Mughal Empire was far from dead and buried and few traders would have taken a gamble on the Khalsa succeeding. By contrast, many Khatri families had invested heavily in the Mughal Empire by establishing client and courtly relationships over many decades. They had hustled in the marketplaces and sent their children to learn Persian and the etiquette of a Mughal gentleman. Now suddenly the Khalsa Sikhs began criticising their Mughal dispositions. As Alam and Subrahmanyam inform us, after 1700 there was a "veritable explosion" in the ranks of Khatris and other high-caste Hindu scribalists in the Mughal administrative system.[138] Thus, at the turn of the eighteenth century the Khatri community would have been composed of many parents witnessing the start of their boys' professional careers; and many young men eager to start their careers.[139] All this Khalsa talk would have undermined both parental and communal aspirations.

Against these contrasting social backgrounds, it is not surprising that Delhi's Sikh society were so divided following the Khalsa's formation. The main adherents of the Khalsa movement came from lower-caste backgrounds with a narrow regional view of the Mughal Empire. In stark contrast, the Khatris had a comprehensive view of the Mughal Empire. The Khatri Sikhs could not afford to make calculations based on faith or their immediate surroundings, but had to consider how their actions might affect their vast trading and services network. They could not forget that their most significant clientele came from elite Mughal society. Khalsa Sikhs, on the other hand, often had a dependency on Sikh institutions for economic and social support. They could clearly see the benefits of a Sikh kingdom in the Panjab, and even in the Delhi region.

The Reaction of Rival Gurus

The rival Sikh Guru lineages seem to have supported the Khatri view of 'tradition' versus 'innovation'. The Miharvan Sikhs were ideologically opposed to the creation of the Khalsa because it violated devotion. I have already discussed how Harji was opposed to Guru Gobind Singh's ideas of Shaktism and militancy. While Harji died in 1696, the

Miharvan school of thought (*sampraday*) did not disappear into oblivion but continued to cultivate their religious philosophy, although the circulation of their ideas grew increasingly narrow as Khalsa Sikhism became the main expression of 'true' Sikhism. At the time of Harji's demise, his sons inherited Amritsar from their father. Harji had three sons: the eldest son was Har Narayan (also known as Niranjan Rai); the middle son was Hargopal and the youngest was Kavalnain (1639–1717). As the eldest, Har Narayan inherited his father's position as Guru and took control of Amritsar's Harmandir temple. But his tenure was cut short when, in 1698, Guru Gobind Singh sent his votary, Bhai Mani Singh, to take charge of the Harmandir temple. Apparently the local residents of Amritsar had become disgruntled with Har Narayan and had requested Guru Gobind Singh to take command. When Bhai Mani Singh arrived in Amritsar it seems Har Narayan and his supporters did not challenge this hostile takeover; instead they seem to have fled to safer climes in the Malwa (southern Panjab) region.[140] Malwa had become a safe region for the Miharvan *sampraday* ever since Prithi Chand had established the village of Kotha Guru there, and this property remained in the possession of his sons and grandsons. Furthermore, the *Divanas* (the possessed) seem to have been based in Malwa. Interestingly, sources from the Khalsa Sikh tradition claim that when Guru Gobind Singh travelled to southern Panjab a member of the *Divanas* attempted to meet him but was killed by the guards of the Guru before the ascetic could reach him.[141]

The three brothers continued to uphold their father's philosophy, but they established their own headquarters. Har Narayan and Kavalnain established separate bases in Malwa, near the city of Faridkot; Hargopal took over Miharvan's old headquarters in Muhammadipur, near Lahore.[142]

Kavalnain was a particularly interesting character and his successors established a popular Sant tradition in the Malwa region. He established his headquarters in the village of Dhilva, where he continued to preach and educate his flock. When Guru Gobind Singh was travelling through the Malwa region, he occasionally met his cousins and their supporters. While there was a natural hostility between these rival Gurus and Sikhs, there was also cordiality between cousins meeting each other for the first time. Guru Gobind Singh met Kavalnain at either Dhilva or Kotha Guru. It is likely the two cousins spent time discoursing with one another and Guru Gobind Singh encouraged his cousin to join the Khalsa. It appears that Kavalnain and his clique did join the Khalsa in the sense they performed the initiation ceremony. According to the early nineteenth century chronicler, Rattan Singh Bhangu, Guru Gobind Singh met with his cousin, Kaul Sodhi (Kavalnain), and Kavalnain's grandson, Abhai Ram (r.1717–1761) in Kotha Guru.[143] Bhangu comments that both Kavalnain and Abhai Ram joined the Khalsa:

[The Guru, i.e. Guru Gobind Singh] called Sodhi Kaul
[Kavalnain] to meet him at Kotha Guru.
[Kavalnain] brought his grandson, Abhai Ram, as his
companion.
The True Guru (*satgur*) showed mercy to both of them.
[He instructed them] to keep the tenets of the Khalsa (*kahdai
pahul*) with them. (21)

In this manner the Guru advised them.
"This bowl [i.e. the bowl of *amrit*] has been filled fully".
Sodhi Kaul was brought to the Guru's presence.
He was told to do homage (*darshan*) to this ideal every
morning. (22)[144]

These verses are somewhat unclear and Bhangu does not describe the scene with any more detail. We can infer that Kavalnain and Abhai Ram performed the Khalsa's initiation rites, but a more complex question is why they did this? What makes answering this question even more difficult is the fact that neither Kavalnain nor Abhai Ram abandoned the Miharvan tradition. Perhaps they were compelled to join the Khalsa as a tactical move in order to create a more harmonious relationship with the Khalsa Sikhs. After all, the Khalsa Sikhs had only recently evicted Kavalnain and his brothers from Amritsar, so he may have felt he had no option for resistance. Then again, Kavalnain and Abhai Ram may have been sincere in their motivations.

After Guru Gobind Singh's brief stay in Kotha Guru, Kavalnain continued to foster his community. Like his predecessors he was devoted to religious worship and academic study. It appears that at the centre of Kavalnain's temple was a college dedicated to the study of Sikh and devotional literature.[145] Kavalnain was probably trying to rear the next generation of Miharvan savants from his supporters' children, as well as his own family members. Towards the end of his reign he moved to Kotha Guru. Kavalnain's only son, Harnand, died unexpectedly and as a result Kavalnain bequeathed his Guruship to his grandson, Abhai Ram, in 1717.

Abhai Ram shared his grandfather's enthusiasm for rigorous academic study and religious devotion. He continued to cultivate Miharvan savants during his forty-four year reign as Guru and encouraged his students to produce literary and philosophic works that expressed the Miharvan tradition's ideals. Abhai Ram's most well-known student was Darbari Das (1723?–1803?).[146] There is scant information on Darbari Das' life and the circulation of his literary works was confined largely to the Malwa region. That being said, we know that Darbari Das was probably a Khatri belonging to the 'Ghei' clan (*gotra*). Darbari's father was known as Daya Ram and he was Abhai Ram's votary. According to legend, Darbari had been named Darbari (court) because Daya Ram had begged Abhai Ram to bless him and his wife with a child; Abhai Ram asked his entire court to pray for this blessing and so Darbari was born due to the prays of the *darbar*. At the age of five Darbari was enrolled into the service of Abhai Ram's court where he was personally tutored by Abhai Ram. Darbari's works indicate he was tutored in Sikh literature, Hindi devotional literature, Sanskrit classics and poetics. He developed into a highly-skilled Panjabi litterateur and ascetic. When Abhai Ram passed away in 1761, his son Nirbhau and then grandson Didar Das, inherited the seat of authority (*gaddi*). Darbari, however, decided to leave Kotha Guru soon after Abhai Ram's demise and established his own base (*dera*) in his sister's village of Vairoke, near to Kotha Guru. He did not leave Kotha Guru out of hostility and continued to believe in the leadership of Abhai Ram's successors. In Vairoke Darbari Das became a local saint with a strong following, but his fame was confined to the Malwa region.

Darbari Das's poetic works shine a light on the intellectual position of the eighteenth century Miharvan *sampraday* and especially reflect Kavalnain's ideas. Darbari composed a series of works dedicated to singing God's praises and eulogising the great devotees of God throughout the ages, as well as composing exegetical works. His complete works were compiled in an anthology titled *Harjas* (God's praise). In his works he identifies himself as a *Nanakpanthi* and a sincere believer in the Miharvan *sampraday*. In his eyes, the Guru Hargobind tradition was lacking spirituality (*bhakti*), having become too temporally focused. Darbari remarked upon how the Khalsa tradition had distorted the practice of *bhakti:*

> There are no Sikhs left in the Kaliyug: everyone calls himself "Guru".
> Who will give water to another [when they say to each other] "I am Khalsa and you are Khalsa"?
> There is no distinction between great and small, and no one bows his head to another.
> Darbari, when they are reluctant to touch another's feet
> Who will follow the nine-fold [path of] *bhakti?*[147]

The Khalsa's egalitarian ethos had wiped away the distinctions between master and student. For Darbari, *bhakti* clearly was undemocratic in the sense that one needed to accept the authority of a teacher who was a superior in all ways. Darbari wanted a society in which rank and class was fully acknowledged and respected. This criticism was unduly harsh towards the Khalsa because while they had an egalitarian culture in many ways, for instance, with to respect to membership, they also had new structures and hierarchies to abide by and amongst the Khalsa Sikhs there were leaders and followers. There were also new saints to be revered, such as the martyrs who fell in battle.

Darbari's critique of the Guru Hargobind tradition was not solely directed at the Khalsa. Rather Darbari attempted to explain the divergence between Prithi Chand and Guru Hargobind. This is intriguing because, as we have seen, neither Miharvan nor Harji overtly discussed the existence of a rival Guru tradition. But Darbari is not shy about raising this issue which perhaps reflects a milieu in which the Guru Hargobind tradition had now cemented itself as the mainstream tradition. Darbari explained the split as a difference in blessing:

> [Guru Arjan] gave the book (*pothi*) [i.e. Adi Granth] and rosary (*mala*) [to Prithi Chand].
> On his head [Prithi Chand] he [Guru Arjan] tied his own turban (*pag*). (6)

> To Guru Hargobind was bestowed the book (*giranth*).
> The sword (*teg*) was fastened [on him] and [he was] instructed to form a way (*panth*).
> To Guru Sahib [Prithi Chand] the word (*shabad thapna*) was given.
> The entire congregation touches his feet.[148]

The distinction between Guru Hargobind and Prithi Chand was clear: Guru Hargobind was a powerful warrior, but he did not have the 'word'. In Harji's hagiography of Miharvan he asserted that the possession of the 'sacred word' (*bani*) was the hallmark of a 'real' Guru.[149] Darbari follows this logic and concludes that the Miharvan tradition was the chosen one because they had the word. Just as Harji had done before him, Darbari stresses the possession of the 'foundation of the sacred word' (*shabad thapna*) as the cardinal quality of a Guru.[150] He also states that Prithi Chand was given the symbols of Guruship including turban, book and rosary. But, unlike previous Miharvan savants, Darbari feels it is necessary to recognise Guru Hargobind as a saint, thereby recognising Hargobind's successors as legitimate saints. Of course, for Darbari this did not mean that Guru Hargobind or his successors were the 'real' heirs to Nanak's throne. It is possible that this recognition of Guru Hargobind was influenced by Abhai Ram, who had allegedly met Guru Gobind Singh and performed the Khalsa's initiation rites. Abhai Ram would have no doubt related this anecdote to his gifted student.

In another work Darbari fully elaborates upon the divergence between Guru Hargobind and Prithi Chand. Darbari wrote:

When Guru Arjan began performing his *bhakti* [i.e. he started
his reign as the Guru].
He showed the road of knowledge leading to detachment.
All the words of the saints he bound together in a book.
He who recognises the book as the Guru, then all the pain of
death disappears.
He called Prithi Mal [Prithi Chand].
He gave him the title 'Sahib Guru' (Lord Guru).
On his head he tied his own turban.
He placed in his hands the book (*pothi*) and the rosary (*mala*).
On Hargobind's forehead he applied the sectarian mark (*tika*).
He gave him the *Adi Granth*.[151]

In these verses Darbari continues to acknowledge that Guru
Hargobind had been blessed by Guru Arjan but it was not the blessing of Guruship – that honour went to Prithi Chand who had been
given the title of 'Sahib Guru' by Guru Arjan and received the para-
phernalia of Guruship including a turban, book and rosary. In his own
mind, Darbari had complete faith in this narrative despite the fact that
in eighteenth century Panjab it would been strongly refuted by the
majority of Sikhs. Yet Darbari and his Gurus do manage to establish
enclaves of support, especially from local residents, and this suggests
that local communities were always willing to accept the authority of
local saints, regardless of their theological beliefs, if they reflected the
community.

Darbari Das's writings articulated the position of the eighteenth
century Miharvan tradition.[152] It is likely that when the Khalsa was
formed this is how the rival Gurus reacted, but without the retrospective calm that Darbari Das had.

At the turn of the eighteenth century the Sikh community was more
fractured than ever before. Yet at the same time the Khalsa Sikh community were poised to discourse the legitimacy of Mughal sovereignty
and the political future of the Sikh community. By contrast, the rival
Sikh Gurus and sections of the Khatri community were still reeling from
the Khalsa's formation. These opposition groups had to decide where
they stood on the Khalsa's political ambitions: were they supporters or

were they enemies? These questions would be at the forefront of early eighteenth century Sikh public philosophy.

Conclusion

In this chapter I have attempted to show how Sikh public philosophy developed after Guru Tegh Bahadur's execution. While historical narratives have seen this period as an era in which the Sikh community was subjected to Mughal persecution, I have tried to show the dialectical engagement between the Sikh literati and the Sikh public. At the beginning of the period the issue of the 'householder-sovereign' opposed to the 'householder-ascetic' had not been fully resolved. The end of this period, however, saw the triumph of the 'householder-sovereign' ideal, and those Sikhs who accepted this ideal subsequently became the mainstream Sikh community. The 'householder-ascetic' did continue to have supporters but these Sikhs gradually became marginalised and descended into enclosed mystical communities.

In this era, Sikh public philosophy was driven by Guru Gobind Singh and Harji. The two Gurus spent a lot of time and effort debating Shaktism and the material world. Guru Gobind Singh's Shaktism embraced a goddess who maintained righteousness through the power of violence. Using the goddess' material agency, Guru Gobind Singh developed a political philosophy which allowed for change and encouraged Sikhs to become political agents. This was in marked contrast to Harji's Shaktism which saw the goddess as an illusion to be overcome in order to achieve liberation. Harji's ideas denied Sikhs political agency beyond an 'inactive' militancy which was may have been associated with Tantric philosophy. Significantly, in the late seventeenth century, the Sikh community had a distinct political philosophy from which they could analyse the world around them and it was from this perspective that they judged the activities of the Mughal state. This Sikh perspective had its own subtleties in comparison to other military groups at the time, such as the Marathas.

Guru Gobind Singh's political philosophy led to the formation of the Khalsa. This transformed Sikh public philosophy and caused intense debate amongst the heterogeneous Sikh community. The adoption of the Khalsa code of conduct was not straightforward for communities which had been Sikhs for many generations. While rural Panjabi groups, especially lower-caste groups, were largely willing to join the Khalsa, Khatri and Brahman groups were very reluctant. They felt the Khalsa's code of conduct violated their caste duties and could conflict with their livelihoods, which were tied to Mughal power. It was the Sikh public in Delhi which found it most difficult to adopt Khalsa Sikhism and this fractured the Sikh community. These conflicts radically shaped Sikh community formation and Sikh public philosophy. The Khalsa was clearly intended to be a political organisation, but it was still unclear what its political ambitions would be or how they would change the wider world. But it was obvious to the Sikh community that it was a significant change.

Guru Gobind Singh's Khalsa embodied the 'householder-sovereign' ideal which was intellectually steeped in classical Kshatriya notions of sovereignty and social order. In particular the Khalsa had a belief in the divine agency of Durga as a righteous agent. Moreover, the Khalsa were composed of Panjabi caste groups which had not abandoned their caste traditions and local ambitions: by joining the Khalsa they had been transformed, but not fully re-invented. In the early eighteenth century we will see how the Khalsa became an organisation which attracted members from a broad spectrum. These members ranged from staunch Sikhs to local gentry groups which saw the Khalsa as a platform for social mobility. But the Khalsa Sikh community had developed a distinct mentality with which they saw Mughal India. The Mughal Emperor, Aurangzeb, was critiqued by this Khalsa Sikh political philosophy: he was not only a 'bigot', but a 'bad' king.

5

CRITIQUING MUGHAL POWER 1700–1708

At the turn of the eighteenth century, the Sikh community were more divided and more politically active than ever before. The creation of the Khalsa marked a turning point in Sikh community formation and had a significant impact upon Sikh–Mughal relations. The Khalsa Sikh community had a distinct political philosophy regarding sovereignty and social order; in addition they sought to enlarge their military capabilities, offering a direct challenge to local Mughal authority. Although at this time it was still unclear how the Khalsa's militancy would influence politics in Mughal Panjab, there was little doubt that their political coherence gave them the intellectual platform to essay a challenge to their primary competitors in the Panjab region: the Khalsa theories of justice were articulating a specific political judgement on the nature of Mughal rule. The Sikh community were no longer simply facing Mughal 'persecution' led by Aurangzeb; they were now interpreting Mughal actions through Sikh parameters of justice. And yet, within the Sikh community, the debates regarding its new philosophic orientation had not ceased and the community was still deeply divided over the political activism inherent in the ideas that formed the Khalsa. It was beginning to be increasingly futile to criticise the legitimacy of the Khalsa because it had proved too popular and coherent in its socio-religious vision, but passionate debates could still shape the its political policies and limit the spread of its power. As these debates progressed, Sikh public philosophy also became embroiled in debates over Mughal 'legitimacy' – whether the Mughals were fulfilling their duties as rulers. Placing them as the 'others' to the Khalsa detracted from the ability of the Miharvan and other lineages to speak for the Sikh community. In that context, the more the Mughals were seen as failures the more politically legitimate the Khalsa became.

The early eighteenth century has often been depicted as the start of Mughal decline because the empire imploded with insurrections.[1] However, the Mughal Empire was not facing a unified rebellion; these rebels were embedded in specific localities and each protagonist had their own vision of Mughal power.[2] In the early eighteenth century the Mughal state's legitimacy was being discussed by various sections of Mughal society. In the previous decades Sikh public philosophy had never engaged with this issue because the community lacked a coherent alternative political system and the resources to implement political change. In the late seventeenth century, the Sikh community developed an alternative political utopia and acquired the resources for implementing political change. These processes had been ongoing throughout the seventeenth century, and by the start of the eighteenth century, Sikh–Mughal relations were tenuous. Sikh public philosophy abandoned the dialectic over the 'householder-sovereign' versus the 'householder-ascetic'. For the more pressing issue of Sikh power against Mughal power: the formation of the Khalsa had divided the Sikh community along caste and social lines and Sikhs were acutely divided over their relationship to Mughal power. Different sections of the heterogeneous Sikh community had complex relationships with the Mughal state. Hence, for some Sikhs, the Khalsa's political ambitions were dangerous to their livelihoods, while for others the Khalsa's ambitions offered them social mobility.

In early eighteenth century Sikh literature, the issue of Sikh–Mughal relations becomes prominent. My major source is the *Dasam Granth* though I have also examined some courtly literature produced by Guru Gobind Singh's poets.[3] Unfortunately, this courtly literature is very scarce because much of it was destroyed in the early eighteenth century.[4] Some Persian sources provide interesting insights into Sikh

society during this period, but they are at best only glimpses and lack
details.

In this chapter I will examine how the Khalsa Sikh movement led
by Guru Gobind Singh critiqued Mughal power in the early eighteenth century. Using Guru Gobind Singh's personal writings and the
compositions of his poets, I will try to show how the Sikhs perceived
Mughal power. Furthermore, I will attempt to contextualise these
Sikh Braj poetic writings by comparing them with the Braj poetry
produced in other courts which were challenging Mughal power, such
as the Marathas. I will try to explain how the Khalsa Sikh movement became virulently anti-Mughal and how the Khalsa believed
the Mughals had violated universal laws of righteousness. Despite this
anti-Mughal bias, Guru Gobind Singh was willing to negotiate peace
with the Mughal state, but their inability to broker peace resulted in
an all-out Sikh uprising. Finally, I will examine how the heterogeneous Sikh community reacted to these developments in Khalsa thought.
After the demise of Aurangzeb and Guru Gobind Singh respectively,
the dynamics of Mughal political power and Sikh society radically
changed. The rise of Banda Bahadur (d.1716) as the Khalsa's guerrilla leader against the Mughals in Panjab transformed the Sikh community: the political uncertainty of early eighteenth century Panjab
forced Sikhs to choose between either the Khalsa or Mughal rule.

Sikh–Mughal Conflict (1700–1708)

In 1700, Guru Gobind Singh was the most powerful and popular
claimant to Sikh Guruship. With the death of Ram Rai in 1687 and
Harji in 1696, their movements became largely peripheral Sikh mystical orders. Harji's son Har Narayan did continue to administer the
Golden Temple but his tenure was eventually cut short by Amritsar's
Sikhs who grew weary of the Miharvan tradition.[5] While in the eighteenth century the Miharvan and Ram Rai traditions continued to exist
– and they produced popular saints and intellectuals – their claims to
Guruship dwindled.[6] Guru Gobind Singh's prohibition on associating with these 'unlawful' groups seems to have pushed them outside
mainstream Sikh society, which rejected their Guru lineages. As a

result, while their charisma still attracted Sikh veneration, post-1700 they would never mount a serious challenge against Guru Gobind Singh's authority and lineage. Only in nineteenth century Sikh society would non-mystical Sikh movements emerge which had alternative Guru lineages.[7]

The formation of the Khalsa in 1699 did not foster peace between Guru Gobind Singh and local Mughal officials and the hill chieftains. It is possible that Guru Gobind Singh was fully aware that the Khalsa's creation could only prove antagonistic, but perhaps he feared that his court would have been subjected to further Mughal hostility with or without the Khalsa's creation. In the early eighteenth century the Mughal state was facing a precarious situation as they engaged with several insurgency movements, which stretched troops and depleted the treasury.[8] Notably, the Deccan wars against the Marathas and other local groups had forced Aurangzeb to leave North India in 1685 and he remained in the Deccan until his death in 1707.[9] While Aurangzeb's energies were geared towards bringing the Deccan under Mughal control he continued to direct military and political operations in North India. The formation of the Khalsa alarmed local Mughal agents who were worried about the Khalsa's political ambitions. It seems that from 1700, Aurangzeb took a greater interest in chastising the Khalsa and he delegated Wazir Khan, the *faujdar* of Sirhind, to take responsibility for this campaign.[10] Wazir Khan was the natural choice to lead this campaign against the Sikhs because the Panjabi hill region of Kahlur-Bilaspur came under the jurisdiction of Sirhind district.[11] It seems clear that Wazir Khan was not trying to integrate Guru Gobind Singh as a *mansabdar* (Mughal officer) because the Guru was never invited to any meetings by Mughal agents. Either Wazir Khan was trying to make Guru Gobind Singh submit to Mughal power or he was trying to kill the Guru. What does seem clear is that Aurangzeb had given Wazir Khan the right to use deadly force and the right to eliminate the Khalsa Sikhs. In the *Ibratnama* (1734) Muhammad Qasim clarified Wazir Khan's orders:

Honoured orders were issued from the Imperial Court to Wazir Khan, *faujdar* [commandant] of *chakla* Sirhind, that if *Guru*

Gobind lives like other recluses, and his own ancestors, and shuns and avoids [unsuitable] words such as his followers used by giving him title of king (*padshah*), as well as imitating the ways and practices of sovereigns, such as showing one's face in the *jharoka* and receiving the *sijda* from the people, this would be better. But if he insists on actions that are against the regulations and does not shun them or act on this reprimand, then he [Wazir Khan] should exert himself to the utmost to devastate the places [under his control] and expel him [Guru Gobind] from those territories of his.[12]

If this order is accurate it seems Aurangzeb opted for a dual strategy of conciliation and force. Interestingly, he was willing to allow Guru Gobind Singh his status as a 'saint' but he felt his militarism was inappropriate and had to be curbed. Yet it seems unlikely that Guru Gobind Singh would have ever agreed to such conditions if offered to him by Mughal officials, and this illustrates Aurangzeb's weak diplomatic skills; Aurangzeb was blind to Khalsa concerns in the Panjabi hills and he was willing to resort to warfare. But Guru Gobind Singh had heavily fortified Anandpur and the bulk of his army were with him inside his fortress city.

Guru Gobind Singh had previously engaged with Mughal forces in the late 1690s. Sikh sources say that Aurangzeb was directly involved in these discussions between Guru Gobind Singh and Mughal officials but it is somewhat unclear whether this was indeed the case. Perhaps the Sikh view reflected a belief that all Mughal actions were directed by Aurangzeb and not by the initiative of local agents. In Guru Gobind Singh's biographical work, the *Bachitar Natak,* he discussed Aurangzeb's role in the conflict between hill chieftains and Mughal officials in 1696–1697. This conflict was mainly due to the principality of Kangra and its complaints against the Guru. Guru Gobind Singh mentions three major Mughal agents in this conflict: Husain Khan, Jujhar Singh and Prince Muazzam (later Emperor Bahadur Shah, r.1707–12).[13] Guru Gobind Singh says Aurangzeb sent an enforcer to his territory named Mirza Beg:

Then in the core of Aurangzeb's heart he became angered; he sent an enforcer to us.

Those fools that deserted us their homes were torn down by Mughal forces. (4)

Mirza Beg was the enforcer's name; he was the one who tore the fools' homes.

Those who looked directly at the Guru were saved; to them no injuries happened. (16)

Aurangzeb's heart became further enraged; he sent four more enforcers.

Those fools which had remained unscathed; these four proceeded to tear their homes. (17)[14]

It is possible that Aurangzeb had taken an interest in Sikh activities prior to 1700, but after the formation of the Khalsa he seems to have given the Sikh situation greater attention especially since Mughal worries were echoed by local hill chieftains.

Wazir Khan does not seem to have approached Guru Gobind Singh diplomatically.[15] There does not seem to have been any Mughal attempt to persuade the Guru to abandon his temporal ways. This may be because Wazir Khan gave the king of Bilaspur, Bhim Chand, the opportunity to remove Guru Gobind Singh without Mughal help. Bhim Chand had desired to undermine Guru Gobind Singh's power since the 1680s. In 1702, Bhim Chand, along with Mughal contingents, fought a battle with the Khalsa at Nirmoh; this short battle saw the Khalsa take heavy causalities. Guru Gobind Singh safely returned the Khalsa to Anandpur where he continued to fortify his city. In April 1702, Guru Gobind Singh attacked Bhim Chand and inflicted causalities on him at the battle of Basoli. In the period 1701–1704, Anandpur was attacked several times by Bhim Chand and other hill chieftains but they could not make the Khalsa relent. In 1704, the hill chieftains asked for Wazir Khan's help in overcoming Anandpur and Wazir Khan agreed to send a large contingent. Anandpur was besieged for approximately three months from September to December. Inside Anandpur starvation and disease had begun to take hold of the Khalsa. Guru Gobind Singh was uninterested in surrendering Anandpur but there was growing unrest amongst his soldiers. Significantly, Sikh tradition argues that Guru Gobind Singh was sent a letter from Aurangzeb in which he asked the Guru to surrender and assured him that neither he nor his army would be attacked once they had surrendered. Later Sikh tradition recalled that Aurangzeb had made this oath on the Qur'an.[16] Guru Gobind Singh was sceptical about Aurangzeb's piety and promise but, given the deterioration of his army, he chose to surrender. However, he believed the moment he surrendered and stepped out of his fort, he and his men would be attacked, so he decided to prepare his men for one last stand just in case his fears were justified. On 20 December 1704, Guru Gobind Singh stepped out of Anandpur on a bitterly cold night and, just as he had predicted, he was attacked. The Khalsa valiantly fought the Mughal forces and suffered high causalities, but Guru Gobind Singh and a handful of Sikhs crossed the Sarsa River and fled to Chamkaur in the Sirhind district. But Guru Gobind Singh's mother and two young sons were captured by Mughal forces and brought to Sirhind.

Guru Gobind Singh saw Aurangzeb's betrayal as an example of his unjust and impious conduct. He and forty other Sikhs, including his two elder sons, were trapped in the fort of Chamkaur. On 22 December 1704, those forty Sikhs engaged in a battle against besieging Mughal forces. The Sikhs decided to ensure that Guru Gobind Singh was able to flee from the battlefield even at the cost of their own lives. Guru Gobind Singh fled further into southern Panjab to Machhiwara Jungle where he was able to contact his Khalsa. Through the help of his Khalsa and other Sikhs he eventually re-grouped his forces in the Dina-Bhatinda area. The news had emerged that Wazir Khan had executed his two young sons and his mother had also died in Mughal custody. Wazir Khan was determined to catch Guru Gobind Singh and in 1705 in Khidrana (Muktsar) the Khalsa repulsed Wazir Khan's attack. Guru Gobind Singh was determined to meet Aurangzeb and he wrote him a letter titled *Zafarnama* (epistle of victory) in 1705.[17] But Guru Gobind Singh desired a face-to-face audience with Aurangzeb and he and his court were determined to travel to the Deccan. In the *Akham-i Alamgiri* it was noted that Guru Gobind Singh made an official petition to meet Aurangzeb in the Deccan and a receipt was sent to Wazir

Khan to halt his campaign against the Guru because the Guru had been granted an audience with Aurangzeb.[18]

In late 1706, Guru Gobind Singh and his court left Panjab and began their journey to Ahmadnagar.[19] Guru Gobind Singh entered Rajasthan and the kingdom of Amber where he discoursed with Dadupanthi leaders. From Amber he travelled to Udaipur and it was in Udaipur that news reached him of Aurangzeb's death on 3 March 1707, in Ahmadnagar. Aurangzeb's death did not come as a shock to imperial officers; in the last few years of his life he had been suffering from infirmity and his sons were waiting in the wings. Immediately a war of succession broke out. Guru Gobind Singh had halted his trip to the Deccan in March 1707 and decided instead to visit Delhi. In June 1707, after hearing of Bahadur Shah's victory at Jajau, Guru Gobind Singh decided to meet the new Emperor at Agra. The meeting took place on 4 August 1707, and an official report by Sawai Jai Singh's *vakil* (agent) confirms this meeting:

Gobind the Nanaki came armed, in accordance with orders, and presented himself, making an offering of 100 *ashrafis* [gold coins]. A robe of honour and *padak* [medallion], set with precious stones, was given to him, and he was permitted to leave.[20]

The famous Mughal courtier Bhimsen Saxsena also mentioned this meeting:

When His Majesty Emperor Bahadur Shah, after his victory [over Prince A'zam] occupied the throne at Akbarabad [Agra], he [Guru Gobind] obtained good fortune of presenting himself before him. [This writer] heard that he does not follow the ways of religious men and dervishes, but is proud of his soldierly profession (*sipahgari*).[21]

It is unclear what talks occurred between Guru Gobind Singh and Bahadur Shah; it is possible that Bahadur Shah was trying to foster peace with the Sikhs. It does seem that these discussions were amicable, so much so that Guru Gobind Singh accompanied Bahadur Shah's court for the following few months into Rajasthan and then into the Deccan. Bahadur Shah had first to quell a Rajput revolt and then deal with a revolt by his brother in Hyderabad. During this period, however, Guru Gobind Singh did not aid the Mughals militarily or politically. When Bahadur Shah travelled to Hyderabad, Guru Gobind Singh parted company with him at Hingoli and travelled to Nander. He arrived in Nander by the beginning of August 1708 and established a court. This court lasted only a few months and in October 1708 a botched assassination attempt was made against the Guru. The two assassins were identified as Pathans and may have been dispatched by Wazir Khan. They entered Guru Gobind Singh's room while he was sleeping and stabbed him, but the Guru instantly awoke and decapitated one assailant while the other was killed by his guards. The wound did not instantly prove fatal, yet after several days, on the 18 October 1708, Guru Gobind Singh passed away due to his injuries at the age of forty-two.

Guru Gobind Singh's relationship with the Mughals in the last few years of his life did not end the Khalsa's political ambitions. Instead he had renewed the Khalsa's campaign with greater vigour than ever before. Prior to his death he had declared that his Guru lineage would no longer have a 'living' Guru, but that the Sikh scriptures would be his successor. In other words, the Guru's word was now the living Guru.[22] He also sent from the Deccan to Panjab a contingent of six Khalsa Sikhs led by Banda Bahadur to re-organise and restart the Khalsa's political campaign with the overt goal of dislodging Mughal power in the region. Banda Bahadur would become a painful thorn in Bahadur Shah's side because he was a formidable guerrilla commander with a reputation for necromancy.[23] After 1708 the Khalsa would begin a long and bitter war against the Mughals and other rivals over the control of the Panjab.[24]

Despite Guru Gobind Singh's cordial relations with Bahadur Shah he did not accept Mughal authority. The reason why Guru Gobind Singh did not accept Mughal suzerainty was because he felt there was a fundamental difference between Sikh power and Mughal power. The Mughal state had failed to appease Guru Gobind Singh and his writings portray a vision of the Mughals as unrighteous rulers.

Judging Mughal Power

The Khalsa had a unique relationship with Mughal power in early eighteenth century Panjab. Unlike other rebellious groups such as the Rajputs, Marathas and Mughal agents, the Khalsa Sikhs were not enrolled in Mughal service.[25] In fact the Khalsa, composed, as it was, of Panjabi peasantry groups, had limited ties with Mughal court and courtesy.[26] Guru Gobind Singh had, however, developed a distinctly Braj-Persianate culture in his court, but this sophisticated culture would not have resonated with much of the Khalsa. In the late eighteenth century the Khalsa's head, Jassa Singh Ahluwalia, explained to the British agent, Major John Browne that he and the Sikhs had been willing to work with the Mughals, but the Mughal nobility were untrustworthy.[27] Indeed, Guru Gobind Singh was willing to negotiate with Aurangzeb and Bahadur Shah on Sikh–Mughal relations but the Sikhs felt that Mughal political culture reeked of disloyalty, selfishness and pride. In the early eighteenth century, Guru Gobind Singh and his Khalsa had a marked distaste for Mughal politics.

In Guru Gobind Singh's biographical work on his battles against Mughal forces in 1696–1697 he makes clear the distinction between Sikh and Mughal power:

If one turns their face from the master, here and there their homes will be razed.
In this world they'll be ridiculed and in the heavens they find no dwelling;
in all matters they remain hopeless. (5)
Continually pain and hunger afflicts them; those which have abandoned service to the saints.
In this world no desire adorns their lives; finally, they're trapped in hell's bowels. (6)
In this life they are the source of laughter, in the end they live in hell's pit.
If that fool flees from the Guru's feet; here and there their faces will be blackened. (7)
They won't see their sons and grandsons flourish; giving their parents suffering they watch them die.

The Guru watches them die a dog's death; thrown into hell's
recesses filled with repentance. (8)
Baba Nanak and Babur are separate: but both were given
power by the Lord.
Recognise Nanak as the King of Spirituality (*Din Shah*); value
Babur's descendants as Kings of Temporality. (9)
Those who don't bestow wealth on Baba Nanak (Spirituality);
then that wealth is seized by lords like Babur.
They receive hefty fines and their homes are properly
looted. (10)
When that fool becomes impoverished, then they come to beg
from Sikhs.
Those Sikhs which give them wealth; then those barbarians
will loot you too. (11)
When their wealth is exhausted, then, they tie their hopes to
the Guru.
When they come for the Guru's sight; the Guru doesn't turn
his face to them. (12)
Leaving without permission and then going home; their works
will remained unfulfilled.
Neither do they gain shelter at the door of the Guru's refuge
nor in God's city;
In both worlds they remain destitute. (13)
Those who remain at God's feet, they neither see nor feel any
troubles.
In their homes dwell metaphysical powers; sins and austerities
don't affect them. (14)[28]

Guru Gobind Singh divides Nanak and Babur in terms of their power:
Nanak is the king of spirituality and Babur the king of temporality.
Both these kings have been given authority by God and have a mandate to rule their respective realms. Though Guru Nanak's power is
greater than Babur's power, Guru Gobind Singh did not disregard
material power as insignificant; Nanak and Babur had different func-
tions in society. The differences in their powers and functional roles
altered their actions and the benefits they gave to humanity. Guru

Nanak provided society with wisdom and spiritual liberation, but Babur gave society law and order. Yet Guru Gobind Singh remarked that those people who do not give their wealth and service to saints like Guru Nanak are then robbed by men like Babur and his descendants. Mughal kings are shown as being selfish and hoarders of wealth, but Guru Nanak is shown as selfless and as a re-distributor of wealth. This is because Guru Gobind Singh says that those who remain with the spiritual kings are forever safe, but those who go with temporal kings ultimately become impoverished. And when they have nothing left they turn to God, saints and Sikhs to beg for wealth, but they will receive nothing for crocodile tears. On closer inspection the distinction between Guru Nanak and Babur is over their virtue and duties: Guru Nanak fulfils his role for humanity but Babur's descendants have forgotten their duties. Guru Gobind Singh's point might have been that Aurangzeb was more willing to kill him and his supporters for the sake of Mughal power and he was less willing to investigate the problem with prudence and diplomacy. While Aurangzeb was willing to shed innocent blood for the glory of his empire, the Khalsa were asking: how do ordinary people get justice in Mughal India?

It seems clear that Guru Gobind Singh and the Khalsa were cynical about Mughal political culture and their concept of justice. Since the late 1690s, the Sikhs had suffered badly from hostility generated by hill chieftains and supported by Mughal agents. In Sikh literature from that era there are no discussions about unfair land policy or taxation or religious persecution, but the arrogance of Mughal power is often discussed.[29] In Khalsa thought the Mughals were decadent to the point where they neglected the duties of sovereignty.

Khalsa dislike for Mughal sovereignty was epitomised in Guru Gobind Singh's letter to Aurangzeb, presumed to have been sent in 1705. This letter was known as the *Zafarnama* (epistle of victory) and it was written in Persian in the *masnavi* form. The historicity of this letter is tricky: while there is a general consensus that Guru Gobind did write the *Zafarnama*, it is less clear whether Aurangzeb ever received it, or whether the extant version is the original one.[30] The letter must have been written when Guru Gobind Singh was in southern Panjab after the sieges at Anandpur and Chamkaur.

The *Zafarnama* was a dissection of Aurangzeb's sovereignty and his policies against the Khalsa in the last three years. Guru Gobind Singh wrote the letter in a Perso-Islamic style in order to appeal to Aurangzeb's Persianate and Islamic sentiments. Its central motif was borrowed from Persian wisdom literature and Sufism; it borrowed allegories from Sadi's *Gulistan* (Rose Garden) and in particular from Firdausi's *Shahnama* (Book of Kings).[31] It was intended to shame Aurangzeb by making him realise he had violated the tenets of Islam and kingship. In the text Guru Gobind Singh directly attacked Aurangzeb's image as the pious Muslim king doing God's work and cleverly reminded him of his Timurid ancestry.[32] Guru Gobind Singh ferociously attacked Aurangzeb's honesty and godliness by pointing out that he had lied on the Qur'an when he offered the Guru and the Khalsa safe passage from Anandpur:

> I have no consideration for this pledge
> Saying that God is my witness and the Lord is One
> I do not have an ounce [lit: a drop] of consideration for him
> For the *Bakhshi* and *Divan* are all liars.[33]

> Whoever worships faith
> But turns his pledge upside down
> I have no consideration for this man:
> What kind of a swearer by the Koran is he? God is One.[34]
> Do not raise your sword and spill anyone's blood without regret
> Heaven too will spill your blood with its sword.[35]

> If someone respectfully presents himself with all his heart and soul
> The Lord grants him safe conduct
> When the enemy devises ruses against the latter
> The Lord himself devises stratagems against him
> If ten thousand and ten come to confront one man,
> The Creator becomes his Protector.[36]

In another section Guru Gobind Singh states the power of the *homa* (phoenix) which protects kings:

If someone becomes the shadow under the Homa
It is it that controls him, not some valiant crow
If someone falls behind a male lion
Neither goat nor ewe nor even gazelle passes between them.[37]

Guru Gobind Singh justifies his usage of violence because it is the last resort when facing intolerable forces like Aurangzeb. This shows Guru Gobind Singh's distinction between 'good' and 'bad' violence and ultimately 'just war'. In this case, he does not use Hindu classic imagery to describe righteous violence, but refers to 'good' violence as *halal*:

I could not help charging in
I came determined to shoot arrows from my bow
When things are past any stratagem
It is religiously licit [*halal*] to draw one's sword
To what kind of a swearer by the Koran am I to give credit?
And if not, you tell me: what am I to do with him?[38]

Guru Gobind Singh argues that Aurangzeb does not understand that he, Guru Gobind, was the real idol-breaker of the hill chieftains:

Aurangzeb, King of Kings
Who is the sovereign of the age and who has faith
I am the one who killed rebellious mountain dwellers
They are the idol-worshippers and I am the idol-breaker
Consider the revolution of time devoid of loyalty
When it turns upside down it causes harm.[39]

Finally Guru Gobind Singh reminds Aurangzeb of his need to repent because death will consume him:

Where are King Keykhosrow (sic) and the cup of Jam[shid]
Where is King Adam? He has been given away to annihilation.
Fereydun! Where are Bahman and Esfandiyar?
The count ended with Dara [?]
Where are Shah Eskandar and Shir Shah

Not one of whom remains alive on his throne.[40]
Where is Shah Teymur? And Babur, where is he?
Where is Homayun? Shah Akbar, where is he?[41]

The *Zafarnama* directed piercing venom towards subjects and people
that challenged Guru Gobind Singh's ideas on Shaktism and righteousness. It also exhibited Guru Gobind Singh's poetic craft and his
ability to transform his Sanskritic-Braj style into Persian.

The *Zafarnama* shows exactly what the Khalsa felt about Mughal
political culture. The Mughal nobility had forgotten the etiquette of
kings and had been overcome with pride. Mughal political culture violated Perso-Islamic traditions of kingship, but more importantly the
Mughals violated Sikh traditions of kingship. The Khalsa had a profound distrust of Mughal power and this distrust ruined any chances
of Sikh–Mughal peace in the early eighteenth century. While Bahadur
Shah might have appeared friendly in his attitude towards Guru
Gobind Singh, he was weaker than his predecessors and did not inspire
confidence with his pledges. This was a crucial issue: the Khalsa would
always voice their doubt about Mughal promises of friendship. They
kept alive the memory of Aurangzeb's betrayal of Guru Gobind Singh;
just like Guru Gobind Singh, Khalsa Sikhs should remember that
even a promise made on the Qur'an was not solemn for a Mughal.

The *Zafarnama* is often seen as a clear example of how Guru
Gobind Singh felt that Aurangzeb had violated the tenets of Islam and
kingship. And, of course, this is self-evident, as demonstrated by the
quoted passages. But there is also another important thing to discuss
with respect to the Mughal Empire in the early eighteenth century,
and that is the need of Guru Gobind Singh to communicate his feelings to Aurangzeb. Guru Gobind Singh was finding it very difficult
to sit and discuss with Mughal officials the hostility he was facing in
the Panjabi hills, as well as his general grievances. This inability to
talk with the state reveals a major failure of the local Mughal system in
this period. Aurangzeb had left for the Deccan in 1685 and the Deccan
Wars consumed the rest of his reign. But, as historians have pointed
out, the Deccan campaign was not a planned military campaign: the
expansion into the Deccan became necessary due to the menacing

threat of the Marathas and the inability of Mughal agents to quell the Marathas with force and/or diplomacy.[42] The Deccan Wars expanded the empire to its farthest reaches and put new strains on the Mughal system as their resources became increasingly drained and officer morale fell.[43] The Deccan highlighted how Akbar's *mansabdari* system and its dependency on officer recruitment and assimilation had its limits. As Richards explained, a key part of forming bonds of loyalty between Emperor and imperial officer came via "personal encounters" and a mutual culture of civility.[44] Guru Gobind Singh undoubtedly possessed the refinement of a Mughal officer, but he never was given any opportunities to meet with the Emperor. Moreover, the *Zafarnama* informs us that when Aurangzeb made promises he had no qualms about changing his mind. Guru Gobind Singh's frustration with Aurangzeb should not be seen in a narrow communal sense, but rather as a more endemic problem of communication and imperial assimilation in Aurangzeb's reign. In the early 1700s, even the Emperor's fiercest loyalists were beginning to lose heart and were planning their own exit strategies.[45] Someone like Guru Gobind Singh represents a local warrior chief who was being ignored by the empire, but if the empire had been listening perhaps things would have been different.

This Sikh distrust and critique of Mughal power had been developing throughout the late seventeenth and early eighteenth centuries. Courtly literature produced by Guru Gobind Singh and his courtiers began insulting and mocking the Mughal system. These musings on Mughal culture were not just confined to the Sikh court, but others such as the Maratha court also produced this type of literature.[46] Interestingly, all these poets were writing in Braj as opposed to Persian.[47]

The Poet in the 'Rebel' Court: Mocking the Mughals

In medieval India the professional poet was a staple member of any court. These poets formed a unique professional group in South Asia; they were highly-educated, cultured, adaptable and always in need of a royal patron.[48] Often poets would be employed as writers, translators and private tutors. In seventeenth century India there was considerable

demand for Persian and Braj poets. The poet was given artistic freedom to develop his prosodic and literary devices, but the contingen-
cies of service often touched the subject-matter of his poetry. Most
patrons were aesthetes and appreciated the art of poetry but verse was
produced not only for beauty, but also to entertain and magnify the
glory of the court.

The historical value of courtly poetry is cultural and not factual.
In Busch's recent work on the revolutionary Braj poet, Keshavdas,
who served the Rajput court of Orcha, she has attempted to re-ignite
the debate over poetry as history.[49] In the early seventeenth century
Keshavdas wrote several works on Orcha–Mughal relations in which
the poetry alters in accordance to changing political circumstances.
So in his earlier works Keshavdas depicted the Mughals as enemies of
Orcha and in his later works the Mughals are shown as Orcha's sav-
iours; this reflected how Orcha initially resisted, but then eventually
accepted, Mughal authority. While Busch calls this genre of literature
'historical Brajbhasa kavya' there is still a profound difference between
history and poetry in their methodology and purpose.[50] Similarly,
in Marwari bardic poetry, Akbar's initial raids into Rajasthan were
depicted with hatred while later he is deified.[51] In Ziegler's study of
Rajasthani bardic poetry he clarifies the purpose of the minstrel: "it
must be remembered that the role of Caran [bard] is not that of an
'objective' historian, but that of a seer, a guardian of legend and a
conserver of tradition. As a seer, he is not a conscious manipulator of
'truth' and historical fact, but a preserver of the truth of what he sees.
This truth lies less in the realm of objective fact than in religious values and social ideals, the means of attaining life and happiness."[52] The
court poet is not completely identical to a bard, but the basic purpose
is the same: the poet must write works which please the court by
presenting the universe in a particular way. This vision of the world is
idealised and vainglorious; the poet's work does not show the political
realities because the court wanted the poet to entertain them and not
to give them political counsel.

The vision of the world presented in courtly poetry reflects the
court's self-image and allows us to see how the court viewed the outside world. These courtly attitudes do help us understand medieval

political history because we can better understand the prejudices and policies of regional courts.[53] In late seventeenth century India when 'rebel' regional courts emerged against the ecumenical Mughal court, rebel courts borrowed Mughal notions of civility at the same time as they began mocking the Mughals. These jibes against Mughal authority reflected how rebel courts both hated and admired the Mughals, yet most of all they illustrated their want to be independent from the label of 'Mughal'.

Guru Gobind Singh's court frequently created an opposition between Sikh power and Mughal power. The Mughal Emperors were shown as buffoons and as unfit for sovereignty. The Mughals were proud, lustful and short of wisdom. For example, in his composition *Var Sri Guru Gobind Singh Ji Ki* (the ballad of Guru Gobind Singh) also known as *Jangnama Bhangani* (the battle account of Bhangani), an anonymous poet in Guru Gobind Singh's retinue depicted Aurangzeb as an arrogant king when he tried negotiating with Guru Gobind Singh over his surrender. According to the poet, Aurangzeb's arrogance and fanaticism caused the battle of Bhangani (1688) between Guru Gobind Singh and the local rulers of the Panjabi hills.[54] It is unlikely this was the case and most historians have attributed the cause of Bhangani as primarily a local conflict without the involvement of Aurangzeb or Mughal forces. Also, the poet seems to make several factual errors, the most blatant being that Guru Gobind Singh's eldest son, Ajit Singh (1686–1704), participated in this battle, despite being a young child. The poet's retrospective account and hatred for Aurangzeb suggests this work was composed sometime between 1700 to 1708: it seems likely it was written after the Khalsa's creation and during Guru Gobind Singh's lifetime. There is only one known manuscript of this work in a private collection, but fortunately Shamsher Singh 'Ashok' published the poem in a collection of Sikh ballad literature in 1947. 'Ashok', an eminent scholar of pre-modern Sikh literature, felt the poem was composed around 1700.[55] The point of the poem was to demonise Aurangzeb's sovereignty:

Aurangzeb wrote this honest order:
'You Guru Gobind Lord and doughty warrior;

My commands are obeyed in Kandahar, Kabul and
Khurasan;
All the kings in the Deccan and mountains come to me and
offer salutations;
I am with you, I offer an oath on the Qur'an;
Seeing this order may it bring you haste, don't remain battle-
ready;
After all, I shall forcefully seize [your forces] and play the drum
of victory;
Then I shall apply double *jiziya* on you as obligated by the
Qur'an;
Those who are willing to abandon their faith and take on the
true faith;
They shall read my *Khutba* in both worlds;
Those who shall rebel against me, their homes will be like the
Pundits of Kashmir;
Listen to the realities of Kashmir, the tale of those Pundits;
I need only send one hawk to you and you shall be a bunch of
frightened sparrows. (1)
The True Emperor read this order;
He wrote and sent this reply which was the true order;
He only wrote realities: 'You idiot understand this;
That deceitful oath you gave me, I know your heart;
What you speak brims with pride, your tongue is dishonest;
Satan spoke arrogance, his words cursed him to hell;
Ravana that ten-headed demon died due to his pride;
If the Lord gives the ant the strength then the elephant
becomes his food;
I clutch onto God's crutch, I know no other, my wrist is tied
with the marriage bracelet;
I shall make my path of the Khalsa known in the two worlds;
I shall be rebellious to your lords;
There will be uproar in the land, what'll become of your
lieutenants?
We'll fire untainted bullets that kill Mughals and Pathans;
Offering this petition to God to slash the ignorant one's face;

I shall move the *Sharia* away and hold the true *Sunnat;*
The sparrows shall kill the hawk, the lords will be frightened'.
(2)[56]

According to the poet, after hearing this reply Aurangzeb began a
war against Guru Gobind Singh. Aurangzeb received positive advice
from his ministers about his campaign, but his daughter, Zebunissa,
attempted to dissuade Aurangzeb from war against the Guru.
Aurangzeb attempted to dispel Zebunissa's fears by arguing that he
embodied justice, yet Zebunissa replied:

Zebunissa holding her hands made this speech:
'Since that day you sat on the throne, what justice have you
done?
You imprisoned Shah Jahan! You killed Dara!
With Guru Tegh Bahadur you committed injustice;
You've sowed poisonous seeds and now it's time to eat your
fruits;
Ahead of you the orders come, the weight slowly mounting;
That king who doesn't do justice, he gets sent to hell!' [57]

There is a clear image in the Sikh court that Aurangzeb was an 'unjust'
king because his actions were dressed in piety while in reality he was
an evil man. History is invoked in a telling condemnation of the
Emperor's actions.

In another Sikh court poem titled *Jangnama Sri Guru Gobind Singh*
(battle account of Guru Gobind Singh) by Ani Rai, Aurangzeb is shown
as being so evil that God sent Guru Gobind Singh specially to destroy
his power. As in the previous poem, Ani Rai depicts Aurangzeb as a
bigot with an obsessive desire to turn his empire into an Islamic theocracy. While the previous poem's author was anonymous, Ani Rai has
been identified as a key court poet who served Guru Gobind Singh's
court extensively.[58] A manuscript of the poem is preserved in a private collection, but has also been published by 'Ashok' in his collection of Sikh ballad literature. This poem was definitely produced after
the Khalsa's creation and during Guru Gobind Singh's lifetime. Even

a brief snippet of the poem clearly gives the reader an understanding of the patriotic mood Ani Rai was trying to evoke from his Sikh audience:

> When he [Aurangzeb] sat on the throne to do injustice,
> He neither listened nor thought and he became agitated;
> From that day the Lord gave him no fruits. (6)
> Trying to turn Hindus into Muslims;
> On a daily basis he razed Hindu temples and objects;
> In the court the complaint was heard:
> God acted without any need for thought. (7)
> The command was given to Gobind: 'Arise and get ready to depart;
> Aurangzeb is acting wickedly, thus you must take bodily form'. (8)
> He grasped the bow, quoits and double-edged sword;
> He is the *Pat Sultan* of the Hindus;
> He is the incarnation of the Sodhi family; the Valiant Gobind Singh. (9)
> The Lord told him and sent him: 'Liberate everyone in society;
> Someday you'll form the Khalsa,
> They'll be given the throne and crown. (10)[59]

This Sikh courtly poetry showed a world in which the Mughals, specifically Aurangzeb, were so wicked that it was legitimate to rebel against their authority. Guru Gobind Singh and the Khalsa were shown as righteous and as the bringers of a newer and better political system. In Sikh courtly poetry the Mughal Empire was approaching its end-game; it was only a matter of time.

The Sikh court not only produced heroic poetry belittling the Mughals, they also produced comic poetry directed at the Mughals. The largest section of the *Dasam Granth* is occupied by the *Chritropakhyan* (tales of deceit): the *Chritropakhyan* contains 404 pithy tales on bawdy themes. The style, language and stories in the *Chritropakhyan* are sexually explicit and have caused much controversy in Sikh circles regarding its authorship; many Sikhs believe Guru Gobind Singh could not have possibly penned such racy literature.[60] Elsewhere I have argued that the *Chritropakhyan* was a form of Sikh didactic literature and that the text's sexuality was a trick in itself: the *Chritropakhyan*, like medieval French Fabliaux literature, wanted to arouse the reader.[61] Not only did the *Chritropakhyan* want to arouse the reader, the stories also wanted to entertain with bawdy comedy. Several tales in the text revolved around Mughal protagonists and even Mughal Emperors. For instance, the following story was about Akbar and his lust for a beautiful woman:

In the middle of Akbarabad [Agra] there was a beautiful woman. When the gods and demons look at this girl, Ran Rang Kumari, they felt lust. (1) King Akbar went out hunting and when he saw her beauty he was tamed. He sent a courtesan to deliver an arrow (message); telling the girl he'd like to meet with her face-to-face. (2) Then the courtesan went to her home and there she let it be known what Akbar desired. Yet Ran Rang Kumari refused to go to Akbar's mansion and she instead invited Akbar over to her house. (3) When Akbar arrived at her home that delicate woman lay in her bed. Then the woman spoke this: 'Listen my Lord and beloved' (4) 'If you allow me to take leave so I can urinate, then, I shall return immediately to bed'. Saying this she got up and left, behind her she locked the door of the house. (5) She went to her husband and told him the truth. Then she came back home with the company of her husband. He arrived in great anger and he took off his shoes and firmly held his shoes. (6) He then proceeded to pummel Akbar's head with his shoes. The ashamed Akbar just kept silent. After beating him with his shoes he threw Akbar into his cellar and shut the door behind him. (7) When morning arrived the husband went and called the local officials; he brought home the local Qazi and Mufti. (8) He said: 'He could be a thief, holy man, banker or a king'; Qazi go inside and see. (9) After saying this, the husband and wife left the officials. The rest looked dumbfounded at Akbar. The humiliated Akbar remained silent and hung his head and kept his eyes closed. (10) If anyone goes to another's house for such a liaison, why won't they get their just desserts? If anyone tries to seduce another man's wife they'll be beaten by shoes in this life and the next life. (11) After this happened to Akbar, he never went to another man's house for such an affair. What you sow is what you reap. From then on he removed improper conduct from his mind. (12)[62]

This story poked fun at Akbar and his carnal desires. In many ways the story shows Akbar in a positive light, after all, he learnt from his mistakes. But such laughter at Akbar's expense also makes the monarch fallible and nullifies the image of him as a mighty king. After hearing this story the audience would no longer view Akbar with the same reverence because he is victim, like any other, to ordinary human frailties. This fallibility extends to his descendants and shows the Mughals as individuals whose conduct was open to interrogation. If one takes a Freudian perspective on the reading of this comic tale, then jokes, which are signs of 'suppressed anger', transform this story into a tabloid satire.[63] By contrast the virtuous Khalsa can take the high moral ground, and the Mughals look depraved and unfit for kingship on moral leadership.

In the late seventeenth century when the court poet wrote about the real world he wanted to lampoon the Mughals. The Sikh court wanted to hear the absurdities of Mughal politics and culture. But the Sikh poets did not attack Mughal politics in the sense that they attacked specific elements like Mughal land policies or the political system. Sikh poets attacked the whole Mughal way of life: the Mughals were arrogant, carnal and corrupt, and their ethos reproduced their malaise.

The Sikh critique of the Mughal system was an overtly moral and ethical criticism. However, other rebel courts critiqued bad political policies and, in particular, policies over land. In Marwari court chronicles, Aurangzeb was seen as a 'bad' ruler because he threatened traditional land control.[64] When ownership was threatened and the Rajputs were tossed from their traditional territories they saw it as a period of 'distress' (*vikhau*). In the Maratha rebel court the late seventeenth century poet, Bhushan, composed the *Shivrajbhushan* (the ornament of Shivaji's rule) from 1673 onwards. Bhushan's critique of the Mughals was mainly political and his work can be seen as supporting the establishment of a Maratha *svarajya* in which the administration of land was paramount.[65] For example, Bhushan continually attacked the *suba* (provincial) system; in the following verses he likens the province to a prostitute and Aurangzeb as its pimp:

> A governorship under Delhi rule is like a prostitute.
> Seeing her beauty, who doesn't long to possess her,
> She who has the power to conquer the world with her
> capricious ways?
> As soon as she comes into a man's possession, she renders him penniless.
> Bhushan says, keeping companying with her brings no reward
> But Shivaji is under the sole sway of a woman called "fame."
> So that loose woman who entraps all – but is faithful to none –
> Is powerless to entice him.[66]

> Bhushan says, the noble came home from court all anxious and in tears
> And everybody asked what had happened.
> His heart was racing, his body had broken out into sweat,
> He was pale, and he stared absentmindedly.
> And then they guessed the cause of his grief –
> The Emperor Aurangzeb had assigned him a governorship
> Near the invincible Shivaji's territory.[67]

Bhushan's poetry differed to that produced in Sikh courts because the Marathas had a very different relationship to the Mughal state from the Sikhs. It seems that the Marathas wanted to hear about how much the Mughal state feared Shivaji's ferocity and about the administrative challenges of dealing with him. Another verse from of Bhushan's poetry dwelled on Aurangzeb's fear of Shivaji:

> Once Alamgir went out on a hunting party with his companions.
> Suddenly somebody issued a warning, "Watch out! A lion has come!"

Aurangzeb mistakenly took this to refer to the Bhonsla king
Shivaji.
Then his companions ran to revive the emperor from his
fainting fit,
Reassuring him that they had only meant a lion.[68]

In Maratha court poetry, Aurangzeb is shown as being frightened of
the Marathas but in Sikh court poetry, Aurangzeb is always shown as
eager for war. The Sikh poets wanted to show Aurangzeb's pride, the
Marathas wanted to show his lack of mettle. Maratha court poetry also
seems to place emphasis on its 'Hinduness' and revivalism:

The poet Bhushan says, first of all we're in the *Kaliyug*
To make matters worse, Aurangzeb has befouled the Hindu
paths.
But now all the Turks are crossing the ocean in fear of Shahuji
son of Shivaji.
The recitation of the Vedas and the Puranas is back in full
swing.
Restored is the worship of the Brahmans and gods.[69]

Sikh court poetry does not share the Maratha vision of Hinduism in
Mughal India. Instead, it embeds the Khalsa into a narrative of righteousness which intertwines with Sikh theology.

In the early eighteenth century the Khalsa had two options: either
they could disband or they could revolt. They chose revolution because
Guru Gobind Singh's powerful thought enthused Khalsa Sikhs to
dream of empire and to reject the Mughals as sovereigns. But the
Khalsa's ethical stance caused discord within in the Sikh community
because the condemnatory reading of the Mughals was not universally shared. Khatri and Brahman Sikhs had expressed anger over the
Khalsa's creation but, in the early eighteenth century, Sikhs had to
deal with a Khalsa which had a clear political objective. In 1708, when
Guru Gobind Singh sent Banda Bahadur to the Panjab he gave him
several letters to distribute to Khalsa Sikhs; these letters confirmed
Banda Bahadur's leadership and finalised an unending campaign of

war against any rivals. The Khalsa would rule and they would not sacrifice their ambitions for Mughal service. In Sikh public philosophy it was now pointless to argue against the Khalsa's existence; there was only one question left: do you support or reject the Khalsa's political ambitions?

The Dawn of a Khalsa Era (Post-1708)

After Guru Gobind Singh's demise in 1708, the heterogeneous Sikh community faced another significant situation. It no longer had any notable 'living' Sikh Gurus; Guru Gobind Singh had declared that the Sikh scriptures of the Gurus would possess ultimate authority as the leaders of the Khalsa. The creation of this 'authoritative' textual tradition coterminous with one spiritual genealogy ignored and further undermined the Miharvan tradition. And yet, inside the Sikh community there was no centralised organisation apart from the precocious presence of the Khalsa. The Nanakpanth Sikh community had Sikh temples, Sikh scriptures, Sikh thought and specific Sikh social markers, but the 'community' still lacked any uniformity in its organisation and administration. By comparison the nascent Khalsa Sikh community had a bold identity and the community possessed a more centralised organisation. By the early eighteenth century one could distinguish between the Nanakpanthi and the Khalsa Sikhs by their differing relationship to the Mughal state. Khalsa Sikhs inherited a socio-religious culture which hated the Mughals and wanted to create their own kingdom. But Nanakpanthi Sikhs continued to place an emphasis on Sikh devotionalism and living under Mughal power. Sikhs knew that Guru Gobind Singh had reproached Aurangzeb's conduct as a king and had criticised Mughal power. They also knew that Guru Gobind Singh had created the Khalsa and had given it an organisation that focused on its military skill and political principles. But during Guru Gobind Singh's lifetime the Khalsa's activities had a narrow sphere of influence; it had not mobilised sufficiently to take on the Mughals and the control of the Panjab region. From June 1705 to October 1708 the Khalsa did not engage in any warfare against the Mughals. On the contrary, there were opportune moments for

Sikh–Mughal peace talks between Guru Gobind Singh and Bahadur Shah. But these talks proved fruitless because Guru Gobind Singh and the Khalsa had a deep distrust of the Mughals and their political culture.

In November 1708 there were two leaders of the Khalsa: the military leader was Banda Bahadur and the spiritual leader was Guru Gobind Singh's widow, Mata Sundari. The appointment of Banda Bahadur to lead the Khalsa's post-1708 campaigns against the Mughals was a curious choice by Guru Gobind Singh. Banda Bahadur had only met Guru Gobind Singh in the Deccan in 1707 and prior to that point he had no connections to Sikhism.[70] There is great mystery surrounding Banda Bahadur's life; he seems to have been a Panjabi Rajput who became an ascetic and wandered down into the Deccan. In the Deccan he was a charismatic local ascetic famed for his skill as a conjurer. When Guru Gobind Singh arrived, Banda Bahadur became a convert and a sincere believer. Despite his obvious skills as a military commander, there is no evidence to suggest that Banda Bahadur had any prior military experience. Banda Bahadur was sent to Panjab where he proved to be a talented guerrilla commander and used his ascetic powers to intimidate his opponents. He rallied the existing Khalsa troops in the Panjab and recruited many new followers. He brought a fervent millenarianism to his style of leadership which seems to have added to his appeal. In Panjab there existed a hardcore of Khalsa warriors who had served Guru Gobind Singh and some, even, Guru Tegh Bahadur; this Khalsa core formed the basis of Banda's army. It was battle hardened and had learnt guerrilla warfare from Guru Gobind Singh, a strategy which they called 'two-and-half strikes' (*dhai phat*).[71] This Khalsa core was less sure of Banda's leadership and gave greater respect and credence to their other leader, Mata Sundari. Mata Sundari lived in Delhi but kept in regular contact with the Khalsa especially through agents such as Bhai Mani Singh, who was a staunch votary of Guru Gobind Singh. Despite this, in the early years of Banda's leadership the Khalsa seems to have supported him without dissent.

There is very little information on Banda's thought but in one letter, dated 1710, he attempted to recruit supporters from Jaunpur:

This is the command of the True Lord. The entire Khalsa congregation of Jaunpur the Guru shall keep you safe; always recite Guru and your life shall be adorned. You are the Immortal Lord's Khalsa. Tie five weapons to your person, seeing this command then come and join us; adhere to the Khalsa's code of conduct: don't consume cannabis, tobacco, opium, poppy seeds, alcohol or any other intoxicants; don't eat meat, fish or onions; don't commit theft or have improper sexual relations. We have created the Age of Truth (*Sat Yug*) and fondly keep my order in your heart. As a result, your code of conduct shall remain intact because the Guru shall assist you.[72]

Banda says "we have created the Age of Truth", a reference to the millenarian sentiments that were an intrinsic part of his rhetoric. He created a substantial support base for the Khalsa which believed it was time for profound social and political change. In addition, Banda, like the eighteenth century Khalsa in general, detailed the proper conduct of a Khalsa warrior.[73] Khalsa Sikhs spent much of their time debating their conduct and, in their normative literature, they often referred to their *adab* (Persianate civility) and their *adhikara* (Hindu social rights).[74] This continuous discussion of Khalsa conduct reflected the ways in which the Khalsa wished to displace existing Mughal notions of civility and desired to establish an independent identity.[75] This identity had its moorings in Kshatriya martial endeavour where the Khalsa were imagined as members of Durga's army – re-creating a chivalric civility associated with the primordial Vedic warriors. The Khalsa's attempt to create new identity also involved the making of distinctly Sikh notions of masculinity.[76] While many parvenu Khalsa Sikhs might have been attracted by the prospect of adopting the new chivalric code of conduct, others, especially many Khatri groups and Nanakpanthi Sikhs who were entrenched in the Mughal order, still saw Mughal civility as epitomising the conduct of an aristocrat.

The development of eighteenth century Sikhism goes beyond the remit of this study. But even a glance at the Khalsa's code of conduct literature from the eighteenth century reveals how Khalsa Sikhism sought to undermine the Mughal system and punish its adherents.

While there were attacks on Islam, perhaps most poignantly there were assaults against the Persian language and Persian speakers. Persian was attacked because it represented Mughal civility.[77] In the *Daya Singh Rahitnama* of the eighteenth century,[78] the author tells Khalsa Sikhs to avoid Persian-speaking Sikhs:

> Those I have named above do not eat their food; do not offer them any patronage (*dhan*); he who smokes tobacco, he who is learned in Persian, he is not mine nor am I his, never drink water from that Sikh's hands. Never trust one learned in Persian, never eat any grain (*ann*) off him, he who gets married by Brahmanical rites. Fine him who does not follows the Guru's customs. Fine him who learns Persian.[79]

The author was clearly attacking the Khatris and other Persianate elites. The author reiterated this point by stating "only hire Khalsa Sikhs for the positions of warrior (*fauj*), clerk (*musaddi*), minster (*wazir*) and treasurer (*diwan*), it will increase the faith (*dharm*)".[80] The religious bias advocated by the author would have significantly crippled the social status of the Khatris and other *munshi* groups. The order is clearly not meant to be taken literally because the Sikh Gurus were literate in Persian and many prominent Khalsa Sikhs had excellent Persian. But the injunction wanted to make it clear that the Khalsa were not Mughals and they had no trust in Mughal refinement.

In the *Chaupa Singh Rahitnama* the author also relates to the Khalsa an interesting tale about a Persian-speaking Khatri. The text was composed in the 1740s and interestingly the putative author, Chaupa Singh, was a Chhibbar Brahman.[81] While Chaupa Singh was from a learned Brahman family, he and his family had long served the Sikh Gurus and had joined the Khalsa when it was created.[82] The author narrates an anecdote between a Khatri Sikh and Guru Gobind Singh:

> In Sambat 1759 [1702 C.E.] the festival of Vaisakhi (Punjabi spring) had finished, the commander (*nakib*) was ordered to – "tell all the congregants it is time to return home". So the commander

loudly commanded, "The order as come from the Guru that it is now time for all the congregants to go home".

Hearing this all the congregations began on their journeys home. The commander gave the order and all the congregations left. But one Rai Singh [a Khatri] remained from the departed congregations, he was told: "Hey Sikh, if you want to keep your Sikhi [i.e. religion] then go home". He [Rai Singh] then spoke, "True Lord (*Sache Patshah*), I have taken all my household hopes (*asan*) [i.e. left his household duties] to come and remain here. How will my Sikhi then remain if I go home?" The Guru replied: "Your Sikhi can only remain at home and not here. You are fluent in Persian (*pariaa hoya farsi*) and we are going to war (*judhdh*). People like you need advice (*salah*) and plans (*mansube*), we only have commotion (*roula*). You will see this commotion and ask due to your learning (*tatvijan*), notice all the things we are doing wrong, saying 'here the Lord (*sahib*) was mistaken'. You will sit down, conduct discourses and meticulously count the details. But we are solely causing commotion. Because there is commotion in the community (*panth*) that is why war is occurring, but if there was not any commotion, then right now we would return home and get engrossed in our children, property and wealth. Because right now it is a period of commotion there is no attachment (*moh*) in our minds".[83]

The Khatri Sikh was considered inadequate for military service principally because he was literate in Persian. Being of a Persianate disposition he was familiar with analysing and debating ideas, but he did not have the carefree disposition of a warrior. The Khalsa Sikhs did not have time for the leisurely exchange of ideas, they needed men with the ability to follow commands and efficiently kill their enemies. The Khalsa warrior had no time to worry about the financial or political repercussions of defying the Mughals. But for Persianate Sikhs life involved taking calculated risks because they had an interest in the existing social structure.

'Militancy' was only one of the adjustments that the Khalsa demanded of the Sikhs and the debates that centred on its ideas had a long, already familiar genealogy. More than militancy, it was the organisation of the Khalsa that introduced new debates and conflicts over possible options amongst the larger fraternity of the Nanakpanthis. Many of these were caused by the potential foreclosure of options demanded by the formation of the Khalsa. Disaggregating the complex changes that occurred through the seventeenth century allows us to better appreciate the context of the formation of the Khalsa, the debates and conflicts endogenous to the history of the community that propelled differing reactions from its constituents to Mughal intervention in the Panjab.

Conclusion

Why did Sikhism emerge and evolve in the manner it did? What factors and figures significantly influenced this development? And how do we explain the history of the early Sikh community?

The historian is tasked with answering these overlapping questions. But history is not a redundant sphere that occupies the faculties of the historian alone. Every individual and every community has an understanding of the past. Each individual and each community needs history in order to establish a connection between the self in the present and the unchangeable actions of those that came before us. That historical memory shapes us in profound ways; it drives human beings to feel a plethora of emotions ranging from compassion to hatred. Visions of the past can liberate, alienate and confine us. The study of history can always be apparently undermined by those that regard the historian's pursuit for 'truth' as naïve but rather, true naïvety lies in dismissing the power of history and the ways in which common sense conceptions of the past can be shown to influence the actions and identities of communities.

For the Sikh community the historical narrative of Sikhism in the seventeenth century remains and will continue to be most significant for their self-identity. That turbulent century was packed with tragedy and innovation, starting with Guru Arjan's execution and ending with the creation of the Khalsa. Since the eighteenth century the events of that preceding period have occupied the thoughts of the Sikh literati and public. Important questions include: why did the Mughal state execute Guru Arjan and Guru Tegh Bahadur? Why did Guru Gobind Singh create the Khalsa? And what does that development towards political sovereignty mean for us in our contemporary circumstances? Pre-colonial Sikhs saw the developments in the context of early modern South Asian society in which sovereignty was devoid of nationalist boundaries and the community was capable of forming Sikh kingdoms. For Sikhs in the colonial and the post-colonial eras these questions have become more complicated as Sikh kingdoms have disappeared and sovereignty solely rests in the hands of the nation state. If seventeenth century Sikhism was, for instance, a narrative of freedom from tyranny, then how do nation-less Sikhs come to terms with their past? Contemporary Sikh ethno-nationalists will vigorously argue that the Sikhs need a nation. Others, however, would view the past as a tale that reflects the need for a secular state because the Khalsa's creation reflects the need to overcome narrow theocratic aims. These living historical discourses rage on, but there is always the tendency to see the past with convenience and rose-tinted lenses. Historical agents can become homogenous, rigid and bereft of thought. They can become models that are sculpted into images that perpetuate our opinions. As a result, the past becomes a desolate realm that cannot inform us about why change happens, making it impossible for us to shine a light on the dark and dangerous dreams that motivate people to improve humanity.

I was drawn to re-examine this period because of the near unanimity in opinion that Sikh militancy was 'natural' and 'inevitable' given the supposed 'oppressive' milieu. It is reasonable to find that this narrative has been recycled time and again by scholars and communities because of the provocative nature of the era. For many Sikhs a selective trawl of the seventeenth century only identifies the suffering the community was forced to endure, such as the executions of their beloved Gurus. Those iconoclastic events, when recreated in each generation, can only result in feelings of utter disdain for the perpetrators and empathic feelings for the need for survival in the face of persecution. When pushed to the brink, violence no longer seems so horrible; instead, it seems justified and necessary. The view from afar makes the brutality of war less frightening and morally fraught because we do not have to see the blood and pain, but only to imagine it. Moreover, when the violence of the past is so distant that the scars are no longer visible, we can forgive those conflicts and view them as being separate from our own realities. The violence of the past reflects the despotism of earlier societies: we can declare that in Mughal India violence was the *only* option for protest. These perceptions are well-intentioned but fail to appreciate the way human societies in all eras must make sense of their actions, especially their violence. Violence on a large scale, such as religious violence, is not simply spasmodic, it is rationalised. But the predominant reading of Sikh violence in the Mughal period has been depicted as being commonsensical and reactive. How long could the 'peaceful' Sikhs turn the other cheek in the face of an 'oppressive' Mughal state that was gradually moving to a position of 'fanatical' Islamic 'orthodoxy'? This narrative has provided historians with convenient avenues for detailed historical research, none of which have gone on to disturb the consensually determined metanarrative of early Sikh history. For example, in recent years historical studies have explored the militant aspects of Sikh society by embedding the community within the military labour market, theories of Mughal decline and medieval codes of civility. While these studies have inflected our awareness of the socio-economic contexts of Mughal Panjab, the dependent, causal relationship between the Empire and its province which determined the character of Sikhism has remained unaltered.

At a very basic level, in the reading of Sikh history it was quite apparent that scholars had not contextualised the concepts of 'peace' and 'militancy' within medieval South Asian theology and society. Historians assumed that post-Enlightenment definitions of religious violence were applicable to medieval Sikh society. However, it was apparent that a post-Enlightenment distinction between 'peace' and 'militancy' or 'violence' seems inappropriate in our context because in medieval South Asian theology, the distinctions were far more subtle. Hence I have argued that Sikh society never shifted from 'peace' to 'militancy' but rather Sikh society changed the *type* of religious violence it possessed. This distinction was clearly captured by the opposing views on Sikhism held by Guru Hargobind and Miharvan. Not only were there alternative visions of Sikhism presented by eloquent thinkers, there were also alternative forms of religious militancy. On occasion in this book I have made a distinction between Guru Hargobind's 'active' militancy as opposed to Guru Miharvan's 'inactive' militancy. In the following decades these binaries developed into the 'householder-sovereign' ideal and 'householder-ascetic' ideal. Therefore, the issue at hand, when examining the development of seventeenth century Sikh militancy is why did the householder-sovereign ideal appear more alluring to the majority of the Sikhs than alternative visions? The contest between Hargobind and Miharvan was tied to a sophisticated intellectual debate over the lifestyle of the householder as enunciated in Guru Nanak's thought. These intellectual debates divided the Sikh literati and gradually influenced the Sikh public. It is necessary when investigating South Asian, and non Western history, that we conceptualise the intellectual and cultural histories of our historical agents without universally accepting Euro-American definitions.

As I have said, pre-modern Sikh society has been usually characterised in terms of doxa and, as a result, the contribution of 'unorthodox' Sikh groups has been underappreciated. In particular, the Miharvan School made an important contribution to early Sikh society as leaders, intellectuals and mystics. I have used Miharvan School sources to show the intellectual challenge they posed to the 'orthodox' Guru lineage. The retrospective and teleological readings of why Sikh 'militancy' emerged have been unable to show how the early Sikh community engaged with Sikhism. While, on occasion, some literary texts discussed how Guru Hargobind and Guru Gobind Singh created discord within the community because of their reforms, historians could not qualify this discord because historical agents could only be 'Sikhs' if they adhered to the 'orthodox' lineage. By removing the boundaries of doxa, I have been able to show how medieval Sikhs did not share the same vision of Sikhism as found in modernity; Sikhs could discourse on Sikhism beyond the confines of anything approaching a universally determined 'correct' reading of Sikhism.

I also sought to show how medieval Sikhs were embedded into wider social processes and possessed communal identities beyond a homogenous Sikh identity. This supports the need to remove doxa from early Sikh history because groups such as Jats and Khatris were joined to larger social worlds which already had well-developed identities. Reconfiguring local identities in the Panjab region also led to a further interrogation of the aristocratic depiction of caste – indeed, even racial in its implication – present in the epistemologies of so many scholars working on Sikh history, where caste groups were defined by their intrinsic 'nature'. Instead I have attempted to show the internal complexities of caste groups and how their social positions provided alternative cultural notions regarding violence. This interpretive shift has allowed for a closer analysis of the role of social mobility in influencing the actions of caste groups. As I have argued, Sikh 'militancy' did not occur outside the pale of these ethnographic and parochial identities; instead, the evolution of the community was intrinsically connected to its locality. For example, the processes of gentrification and social mobility in medieval Panjab are cardinal in the understanding of how Sikh 'militancy' developed. I have provided some insights into these processes such as suggesting the emergence of a common medieval Panjabi culture and reasons behind Guru Hargobind's gentrification.

In the last quarter of the seventeenth century, the Sikh community developed a coherent critique of the Mughal Empire and in particular the reign of Aurangzeb. While the historiography has almost always shown Aurangzeb as a 'bigot' with megalomaniacal ambitions to rid his empire of all non-Muslims, thus forcing the Sikhs and others to react with rebellion, I have shown that the Sikh community did not simply react because they felt anger at the actions of the Mughal state. Of course, it is common sense to expect that when a community is forced to endure persecution, they will respond with violent resistance because there is only so much that can be endured. And there is some truth in this perspective because all revolutions have a narrative of toleration: the revolutionaries could no longer tolerate the burden of the yoke. But this view fails to consider so many other questions, such as why did the revolution happen at that particular moment? What was the oppression they endured? How did the revolutionaries develop an alternative vision of political power? In this book, I have attempted to show how Guru Gobind Singh's Khalsa was not a mere reactive force, but that instead the community had an alternative vision of sovereignty and just war that was constructed in opposition to the Mughal Empire. It was within these Sikh parameters of sovereignty and justice that the Mughal state was judged and deemed to be a failure. The Khalsa critique was virtue ethical in its substance and saw human emotions such as greed at the root of moral corruption. It appears it was the less the case that the Mughals were dogmatic puritans, but more the fact they were avaricious and this bred in them a propensity to be cruel. The Khalsa critique of Mughal power was uniquely Sikh in its understanding of morality, but the specific critique of Mughal corruption was reflected in the ideas of other rebellious groups in the period. The wars in the Deccan and the need to expand the state bureaucracy and crucially integrate new *mansabdars* put an incredible weight on the Mughal system. The Sikhs, like other groups, were victims of a state that had outgrown its resources, making it unable to deal with local challenges, rather than a state that had become ideologically intolerant of non-Muslims. Aurangzeb's folly, perhaps, was not in his faith but in his empire's corruption.

In sum, the development of Sikh 'militancy' in the seventeenth century was far from a simple process of militarisation, but instead a process of intellectual dialogue amongst the Sikh literati and a gradually enlarging Sikh public, a process of mobilising people and minds, of restructuring local society and imparting meaning and organisation to a community, initially the Nanakpanthis and, at the end of the seventeenth century, the Khalsa. There was no inevitability in the triumph of Guru Hargobind's lineage; distinct social and cultural conditions created a community which was largely receptive to 'militant' discourses. By contrast, Miharvan's lineage, like other Sikh orders, gradually lost ground as it was unable to mobilise mass support and eventually retained only niche popularity. The Sikh community was the target of these dialectics and contemplated these views in the context of their individual communal identities. For some Sikhs, a more politically active Sikhism was empowering, while others were clearly more inclined to the existing power structures and status quo. The development of the Mughal state significantly impinged upon these Sikh dialectics, yet the image of a centralist Mughal leviathan has undermined the importance of local–Mughal relations. For example, Guru Hargobind, Guru Har Rai, Guru Har Krishan, Guru Tegh Bahadur and Guru Gobind Singh, all seem to have attracted Mughal attention at Agra and Delhi because of their relationships with local power networks. In addition, long-term socio-economic processes such as gentrification benefited the development of Sikh 'militancy' and, without these conditions, it is probable the early history of Sikhism would have been different. Importantly, the role of Mughal religious 'persecution' in causing spasmodic reactions towards Sikh 'militancy' has been undermined when we view the development of Sikh 'militancy' as a dialogical process. The Sikh community discussed the political policies and structures which surrounded them rather than being passively at the mercy of the Mughal state. These ranged from early discussions on the vanity of kings to sophisticated Khalsa critiques of Mughal sovereignty. These discussions of political power became enveloped within Sikh dialogues about militancy and led eventually to rebellion against the Mughals spearheaded by the Khalsa. Yet even in the last years of Guru Gobind Singh's reign, Sikh–Mughal relations were not irreconcilable; there was always the possibility the Khalsa would accept Mughal service or create pragmatic political alliances with other groups. Indeed, in the eighteenth century the Khalsa, like other military entrepreneurs of the time, would re-work Mughal political culture rather than abolish it. It was these processes within the community that shaped the development of seventeenth century Sikh 'militancy'. This supple dialogue allows us to see a heterogeneous Sikh community trying to fathom Sikhism; and undermines the coherent grand narratives of a homogenous community suffering at the whims of despotic kings.

NOTES

1 The Early History of the Sikh Community

1. There have been many studies on Guru Nanak and his life and teachings. W.H. McLeod's analysis on Nanak's life, despite its limitation, perhaps ranks as the best introduction in English, see W.H. McLeod, *Guru Nanak and Sikh Religion*, Oxford, 1968. For a collection of translations of Guru Nanak's poetry and the poetry of the other Sikh Gurus, see Christopher Shackle and Arvind-pal Singh Mandair, trans., *Teachings of the Sikh Gurus: Selections from Sikh Scriptures*, London, 2005. For a collection of translations of Sikh scriptures and other related medieval Indian literature, see Ainslie T. Embree, ed., *Sources of Indian Tradition*, vol.1, New York, 1988. There is also a range of introductory guides on Sikhism with varying degrees of detail and academic rigour. A good starting point for exploring the Sikh tradition is, Gurinder Singh Mann, *Sikhism*, New Jersey, 2004.

2. For an introduction into the Sant tradition see Karine Schomer and W.H. McLeod, eds., *Sants: Studies in a Devotional Tradition of India*, New Delhi, 1987. Also see John Stratton Hawley and Mark Juergensmeyer, trans., *Songs of the Saints in India*, New York, 1988, for examples of Sant poetry.

3. The term Nanakpanth is widely used by scholars to refer to Guru Nanak's original community, but it appears the term emerged fully in the early seventeenth century. Mann has noted that the designation of Nanakpanth was not used by Guru Nanak, his mainstream successors or their supporters. See Gurinder Singh Mann, 'Guru Nanak's Life and Legacy: An Appraisal', *Journal of Punjab Studies*, 17/1, 2010, p.23.

4. These successors were: Guru Angad (r.1539–52); Guru Amar Das (r.1552–74); Guru Ram Das (r.1574–81) and Guru Arjan Dev (r.1581–1606).

5. The reason why Guru Arjan's execution has often been attributed to Jahangir's bigotry is because of a reference to it in Jahangir's memoirs. However, it is disputable what Jahangir meant and I feel the execution needs to be more carefully examined within the context of religious dissent and Mughal power. For an overview of Guru Arjan's amazing life and his execution, see Pashaura Singh, *Life and Work of Guru Arjan*, New Delhi, 2006. For a translation of Jahangir's comments on Guru Arjan see one of the following: Jahangir, *Tuzuk-i Jahangiri*, vol. 1, trans., Alexander Rogers, London, 1909–14, pp.72–73; Shireen Moosvi in J.S. Grewal and Irfan Habib, eds., *Sikh History from Persian Sources*, Lahore, 1998, pp.56–57; Jahangir, *The Jahangirnama*, trans., Wheeler M. Thackston, New York, 1999, p. 59.

6. This evolution of Mughal history in terms of the religious sentiments of its rulers was common in pre-colonial histories; for an overview of these developments see Muzaffar Alam and Sanjay Subrahmanyam, eds., *The Mughal State 1526–1750*, Delhi, 2000. For a well-known example of this type of Mughal history see Sri Ram Sharma, *The Religious Policy of the Mughal Emperors*, London, 1962. For a bird's eye perspective on general developments in Indian history, including communally orientated Mughal histories, see Vinay Lal, *The History of History: Politics and Scholarship in Modern India*, New Delhi, 2003.

7. In recent years scholarly studies have examined how Guru Arjan's execution was perceived by early seventeenth-century Sikh society: was it seen as martyrdom or something else? This relates to the development of modern Sikh martyrdom culture: see Louis Fenech, *Martyrdom in the Sikh Tradition*, Delhi, 2000; Louis Fenech, 'Martyrdom and Execution of Guru Arjan in Early Sikh Sources', *JAOS*, 121/1, 2001, pp.20–31; and Pashaura Singh, *Life and Work of Guru Arjan*, New Delhi, 2006.

8. For background on this execution see Fauja Singh and G.S. Talib, *Guru Tegh Bahadur: Martyr and Teacher*, Patiala, 1975.

9. The reign of Aurangzeb has always proved difficult to analyse because of his apparent bigotry and modern South Asian communalism. For an introduction to these debates see Satish Chandra, 'Reassessing Aurangzeb', in Satish Chandra, *Historiography, Religion, and State in Medieval India*, New Delhi, 1996.

10. Aurangzeb's religious policies have often been blamed for Mughal decline, yet in recent decades this was challenged by some historians. For an overview of these developments see Muzaffar Alam and Sanjay Subrahmanyam, eds., *The Mughal State 1526–1750*, pp.1–77.

11. Early modern Sikh kingdoms still require more research, but for a detailed, though somewhat outdated, introduction see Hari Ram Gupta, *History of the Sikhs:* vols 2–5, New Delhi, 2000–2001.

12. Bayly briefly discusses the growing influence of Ranjit Singh's kingdom in the general context of early nineteenth-century India, see C.A. Bayly, *Rulers, Townsmen and Bazaars*, New Delhi, 1983, pp.202–204.

13. The involvement of the Sikhs in the 1857 rebellion/mutiny needs more work; this is because thus far scholars have not fully assessed the cultural variations in Sikh Panjabis and Sikh state formation in the Panjab which contributed to different attitudes in 1857. See Dolores Domin, *India: A Study in the Role of the Sikhs in 1857–59*, Berlin, 1977; Salahuddin Malik, 'The Punjab and the Indian 'Mutiny': A Reassessment', *Islamic Studies*, 15, 1976.

14. The categorisation of the Sikhs as a 'martial race' and their role in the British army has been well documented; for an insight into the history of the British army in India see David Omissi, *The Sepoy and the Raj*, Basingstoke, 1994.

15. For background on this theory and its practice see Heather Streets, *Martial Races*, Manchester, 2004.

16. The anthropologist, R.G. Fox, has argued that the colonial state fostered an entirely new Sikh or 'Singh' identity for their own political interests. That 'Singh' identity foreshadowed the Sikh/Singh identity propounded by the reformist Sikh movement, the Singh Sabha. In essence, Fox argues that the colonial state fundamentally reinvented the Sikh identity; and that modified Sikh identity became the basis for Sikh revivalist movements of the late nineteenth and early twentieth centuries. While it is true that colonial rule must have had a profound impact on the Sikh community of the Punjab because pre-colonial Sikh identity was heavily tied to notions of Sikh sovereignty and warfare, Fox fails to address how reformist Sikh intellectuals directly engaged with pre-colonial Sikh dialectics on conduct and faith in the Punjabi/Hindi vernacular. Moreover, Fox presents the colonial vision of Sikhism as homogenous, and does not show how various colonial officials had different views of Sikhism. See R.G. Fox, *Lions of the Punjab*, Berkeley, 1985.

17. For an accessible look at this British bias on Khalsa recruitment see Amardeep Singh Madra and Parmjit Singh, *Warrior Saints*, London, 1999.

18. The idea of being Sikh and being a non-Khalsa has caused problems in Sikhism since the eighteenth century. However, in colonial India, Sikhism, like other religions, became more narrowly defined and the distinction between Khalsa and non-Khalsa became more prominent. For these historical developments see Harjot Oberoi, *Construction of Religious Boundaries*, Delhi, 1994; for a more general insight into these problems of Sikh identity see W.H. McLeod, *Who is a Sikh?*, Delhi, 1989.

19. See Balbinder Singh Bhogal, 'Text as Sword: Sikh Religious Violence taken for Wonder', in John R. Hinnells and Richard King, eds., *Religion and Violence in South Asia*, New York, 2007; Navdeep Singh Mandair, 'Virtual Corpus: Solicitous Mutilation and the Body of Tradition', in Phillip Goodchild, ed., *Difference in Philosophy of Religion*, Aldershot, 2003.

20. In the colonial period the British ruthlessly eliminated the Sikh war machine; this history has not been told yet. As Richards explains British rule is still shown as 'benign and bloodless' and the tale of colonial conquest and indigenous resistance has still many significant gaps that can only be filled with careful historical research on the process of colonial demilitarisation in India. See John F. Richards, 'Warriors and the State in Early Modern India', *JESHO*, 47/3, 2004, pp.390–400.

21. There were numerous Sikh reform movements and, notably, the Singh Sabha movement; see Harjot Oberoi, *Construction of Religious Boundaries*, 1994, for a history of Sikh reformation movements. For a general overview of reformist movements across India, see K.W. Jones, *Socio-Religious Reform Movements in British India*, Cambridge, 1989. For an interesting insight into South Asian debates in colonial India, see K.W. Jones, ed., *Religious Controversy in British India: Dialogues in South Asian Languages*, Albany, 1992.

22. For these cultural developments in Sikh Panjabi culture see Rajit K. Mazumder, *The Indian Army and the Making of the Punjab*, Delhi, 2003.

23. For a lucid history of Panjabi literature which culminated in the novel, see Swinder Singh Uppal, *Panjabi Short Story: Its Origin and Development*, Delhi, 1966; for an insight into Vir Singh's literary genius, see Gurbachan Singh Talib and Attar Singh, eds., *Bhai Vir Singh: Life, Times & Works*, Chandigarh, 1973.

24. Vir Singh's novels essentially focused on Sikh men and women fighting evil Muslims. For example, his first novel, *Sundari* (1898), was about a Sikh woman and her Khalsa brother fighting against the Mughals. Bhai Vir Singh explained his motive for writing *Sundari* as an attempt "to educate the Sikhs about their history and inspire them to become true adherents of their religion", quoted and translated by S.S. Kohli, 'Bhai Vir Singh's Novels' in Gurbachan Singh Talib and Attar Singh, eds., *Bhai Vir Singh: Life, Times & Works*, 1973, p.148.

25. See Christine M. Fair, 'The Historical Novels of Bhai Vir Singh: Narratives of Sikh Nationhood', Unpublished PhD, University of Chicago, 2004.

26. See Harjot Oberoi, 'From Punjab to "Khalistan": Territoriality and Metacommentary', *Pacific Affairs*, 60/1, 1987; Joyce Pettigrew, 'In Search of a New Kingdom of Lahore', *Pacific Affairs*, 60/1, 1987.

27. I say this because there is a distinction between Sikh minority issues and Sikh fundamentalism; few Sikhs have advocated the establishment of a Sikh

war against 'hostile' forces; see Harjot Oberoi, 'Sikh Fundamentalism', in Sudipta Kaviraj, ed., *Politics in India*, Oxford, 2003.

28. Contemporary views regarding Sikh ethno-nationalism and Khalistan are wide-ranging. See issues 6/2, 2010, and 7/1, 2011 of *Sikh Formations* for a two-part special on a range of articles focusing on the legacy and impact of Operation Blue Star 1984 on the global Sikh community.

29. To my knowledge there has never been any Sikh history which has questioned the need for a *violent* reaction to the Mughal state.

30. Khushwant Singh, *A History of the Sikhs*, vol.1, Delhi, 1963, p.62.

31. W.H. McLeod, *Evolution of the Sikh Community*, Delhi, 1976, pp.12–13.

32. J.S. Grewal, *The Sikhs of the Punjab*, Cambridge, 2000, p.64.

33. Hari Ram Gupta, *History of the Sikhs*, vol.1, Delhi, 2000, pp.218–19.

34. Ibid., p.266.

35. W.H. McLeod, *Evolution of the Sikh Community*, 1976, p.13.

36. Bhagat Singh, *Sikh Polity in the Eighteenth and Nineteenth Centuries*, Delhi, 1978, pp.100–101.

37. See Jeevan Singh Deol, 'Eighteenth Century Khalsa Identity: Discourse, Praxis and Narrative' in Christopher Shackle et al., eds., *Sikh Religion, Culture and Ethnicity*, Richmond, 2000.

38. Jeevan Singh Deol, *Sikh Discourses of Community and Sovereignty in the Seventeenth and Eighteenth Centuries*, unpublished PhD, University of Cambridge, 2000, p.349.

39. See Purnima Dhavan, 'The Warrior's Way: The Making of the Eighteenth-Century 'Khalsa Panth', unpublished PhD, University of Virginia, 2003.

40. Orthodoxy is a retrospective term referring to the beliefs and practices of the dominant contemporary community. When I use this term in relation to Sikhism, I refer to the mainstream Sikh community which emerged as the dominant one in early twentieth-century Panjab. The emergence of this dominant Sikh community resulted in the historiographical marginalisation of other Sikh groups and their practices as 'unorthodox'.

41. For better understanding of the Christian and Islamic traditions of 'just war', see James Turner Johnson and John Kelsay, eds., *Cross, Crescent, and Sword: The Justification and Limitation of War in Western and Islamic Tradition*, Westport, 1990.

42. For various understandings of violence in history see Phillip P. Weiner and John Fisher, eds., *Violence and Aggression in the History of Ideas*, New Jersey, 1974; Bruce B. Lawrence and Aisha Khan, eds., *On Violence: A Reader*, Durham and London, 2007.

43. Richard W. Kaeuper's work represents a good example of how a history of violence and social order could be written and its importance to history

writing, see Richard W. Kaeuper, *Chivalry and Violence in Medieval Europe*, New York, 1999.

44. The study of violence seems universal, however, there are cultural differences in how societies view and perform violence. Riches, for example, identifies a particular Anglo-Saxon culture of violence which allows us to engage in cross-cultural studies of violence, see David Riches, ed., *The Anthropology of Violence*, Oxford, 1986.

45. For a concise history of Western Christianity see John Bossy, *Christianity in the West, 1400–1700*, New York, 1985.

46. For example, see Paul Hershman, *Punjabi Kinship and Marriage*, New Delhi, 1981; Indera P. Singh, 'A Sikh Village', in Milton Singer, ed., *Traditional India Structures and Change*, Philadelphia, 1959; Ravinder Kaur, 'Jat Sikhs: A Question of Identity', *Contributions to Indian Sociology*, 2/2, July–December, 1986.

47. The obsession with Sikh thinkers such as Bhai Vir Singh is evident in the recent work of scholars such as Oberoi and Mandair; they fail to consider the debates occurring among 'everyday' Sikhs, who have no literature or mode of communication to audiences outside of their communities, and it would be patronising to assume an absence of intellectual discourse amongst them. These debates can only be sought by examining Sikh communal identities, field work and popular literature. There is a dire need to enrich Sikh intellectual histories by creating space for their everyday theorists, their 'organic intellectuals' as it were.

48. See Georges Duby, *The Chivalrous Society*, trans., Cynthia Postan, Edward Arnold, 1977; Georges Duby, *The Three Orders: Feudal Society Imagined*, trans., Arthur Goldhammer, Chicago and London, 1980; Maurice Keen, *Chivalry*, New Haven and London, 1984.

49. Benjamin J. Kaplan, *Divided by Faith*, Cambridge and London, 2007, pp.172–97.

50. Western 'tolerance' is not entirely false because many Western countries can illustrate their tolerance for all peoples and, crucially, highlight the ability of Western democracies to eventually comprehend the injustices they have committed and right the wrongs of history. It would be false, though, for Western democracies to ignore how cruel and inhuman they can be. The great tragedies of modernity include the Jewish holocaust in Nazi Germany and American suppression of African-American civil rights. But there are the bitter blows of racism and discrimination that affect people on a daily basis. To suggest that the Enlightenment civilised human beings to the extent that they overcame their most horrid prejudices is a step too far.

51. Benjamin J. Kaplan, *Divided by Faith*, 2007, p.344.

52. James Turner Johnson and John Kelsay, eds., *Cross, Crescent, and Sword*, 1990, pp. xi–xviii.

53. See John Kelsay, *Arguing the Just War in Islam*, Cambridge, MA, and London, 2007.

54. Ibid., pp.220–24.

55. See Jan E.M. Houben and Karel R. Van Kooij, eds., *Violence Denied: Violence, Non-Violence and the Rationalization of Violence in South Asian Cultural History*, Leiden, 1999, for an interesting array of articles on violence in the South Asian, mainly 'Hindu', milieu.

56. Indeed, many of Gandhi's methods of social protest had their origins in Jain social protest, as found in his native Kathiawad. Moreover, Gandhi often described himself a warrior, and belonging to the warrior caste, despite his non-violence. See Howard Spodek, 'On the Origins of Gandhi's Political Methodology: The Heritage of Kathiawad and Gujarat', *JAS*, 30/2, 1971, pp.361–72.

57. See Vinay Lal, *The History of History: Politics and Scholarship in Modern India*, 2003.

58. There are many studies on this subject and a pertinent array of essays can be found in David Gilmartin and Bruce B. Lawrence, eds., *Beyond Hindu and Turk*, Tallahassee, 2000.

59. See Richard M. Eaton, 'Temple Desecration in Indo-Islamic States' in David Gilmartin and Bruce B. Lawrence, eds., *Beyond Hindu and Turk*, 2000.

60. See, for instance, Sunil Kumar, *The Emergence of the Delhi Sultanate, 1192–1286*, Delhi, 2007. Kumar shows how a monolithic understanding of Islam in the early medieval period is flawed.

61. William R. Pinch, *Warrior Ascetics and Indian Empires*, 2006, pp.1–27.

62. For more information on these ascetic warriors, see Pinch, *Warrior Ascetics and Indian Empires*, 2006; David N. Lorenzen, 'Warrior Ascetics in Indian History', *JAOS*, 98/1, 1978, pp.61–75.

63. For background on *hatha-yoga* see David Gordon White, *The Alchemical Body*, Chicago, 1996.

64. See Simon Digby, 'Qalandars and Related Groups: Elements of Social Deviance in the Religious Life of the Delhi Sultanate in the Thirteenth and Fourteenth Centuries', in Yohanan Friedmann, ed., *Islam in Asia*, vol.1, Jerusalem, 1984, pp.60–108.

65. See James Turner Johnson and John Kelsay, eds., *Just War and Jihad: Historical and Theoretical on War and Peace in Western and Islamic Traditions*, New York, 1991.

66. For example, interesting studies include: Jos Gommans, *Mughal Warfare*, London, 2002; Rosalind O'Hanlon, 'Kingdom, Household, and Body

History, Gender and Imperial Service under Akbar', *MAS*, 41/5, 2007, pp.889–923; Kumkum Chatterjee, *The Cultures of History in Early Modern India: Persianization and Mughal Culture in Bengal*, Delhi, 2009.

67. See Karine Schomer and W.H. McLeod, eds., *Sants: Studies in a Devotional Tradition of India*, 1987.

68. For a background to the Satnami rebellion see Irfan Habib, *The Agrarian System of Mughal India*, Delhi, 1963; for the Dadupanth see James M. Hastings, 'Poets, Saints, and Warriors: The Dadu Panth, religious change, and Identity formation in Jaipur state, c.1562–1860 C.E.', unpublished PhD, University of Wisconsin-Madison, 2002.

69. See, for example, Simon Digby, 'Encounters with Jogis in Indian Sufi Hagiography', unpublished paper delivered at SOAS, London, 1970.

70. Pinch, *Warrior Ascetics and Indian Empires*, p.212.

71. For background on these encounters between Guru Nanak and the *yogis* see W.H. McLeod, *Early Sikh Tradition*, Delhi, 1980, pp.66–70.

72. See Patrick Olivelle, *Renunciation in Hinduism: A Medieval Debate*, 2 vols, Vienna, 1986–87; Patrick Olivelle, *Samnyasa Upanishads*, New York, 1992; J.C. Heesterman, 'Brahman, Ritual, and Renouncer' in J.C. Heesterman, *The Conflict of the Inner Tradition*, Chicago, 1985, pp.26–44; J.C. Heesterman, 'India and the Inner Conflict of Tradition' in J.C. Heesterman, *The Conflict of the Inner Tradition*, 1985, pp.10–25.

73. See Patrick Olivelle, *The Ashrama System*, New York, 1993.

74. *AG*, p.26.)

75. Ibid., p. 29.

76. Ibid., p.496.

77. The importance of immortality in Indic religious traditions and the personal metamorphosis this causes is eruditely explained in David Gordon White, *The Alchemical Body*, 1996, pp.1–14.

78. *AS*, pp.75–76.

79. For examples of this metaphor in Bhakti poetry see Monika Thiel-Horstmann, *Crossing the Ocean of Existence*, Wiesbaden, 1983.

80. McLeod discusses this image of Nanak as a figure who can cause terror in those who disrespect his power, see W.H. McLeod, *Early Sikh Tradition*, 1986, pp.82–105.

81. Norman Peter Ziegler, 'Action, Power, and Service in Rajasthani Culture: A Social History of the Rajputs of Middle Period Rajasthan', unpublished PhD, University of Chicago, 1973, pp.132–33.

82. *AG*, p.199.

83. See David Riches, ed., *The Anthropology of Violence*, 1986; and Bruce B. Lawrence and Aisha Khan, eds., *On Violence: A Reader*, 2007.

84. W.H. McLeod, *Evolution of the Sikh Community*, 1976, pp. 9–11.

85. Ibid., pp.12–13.

86. J.S. Grewal, *The Sikhs of the Punjab*, 2000, p.46.

87. Ibid., p.64.

88. In a recent essay Mann has made an interesting suggestion that Guru Nanak's original community at Kartarpur had a broad social spectrum of Khatris and lower caste groups mainly made up of Jats. If this was the case, then the received wisdom advanced by McLeod and Grewal that the Jat community arrived later than the Khatri community in significant numbers would be altered. But Mann's argument does still accept that the Khatri and Jat communities formed the main caste groups of the Sikh community since the times of Guru Nanak. Also Mann's argument does not change the fact that Khatri and Jat societies had important cultural and socio-economic differences. In fact, Mann argues that the Jat community perhaps joined the Sikh fold in order to "construct ties with the society around them". It is unlikely that the Khatri community used Sikhism as means for social mobility. See Gurinder Singh Mann, 'Guru Nanak's Life and Legacy: An Appraisal', *Journal of Punjab Studies*, 17/1, 2010, pp.17–21.

89. Paul Hershman, *Punjabi Kinship and Marriage*, New Delhi, 1981, p.155.

90. Pnina Werbner, 'The Ranking of Brotherhoods: The Dialectics of Muslim Caste among Overseas Pakistanis', *Contributions to Indian Sociology*, 23/285, 1989, p.298.

91. *AG*, p.55.

92. *VG*, p.431.

93. See M. Leaf, 'The Punjabi Kinship Terminology as a Semantic System', *American Anthropologist*, 73, 1971, pp.545–54.

94. See Paul Hershman, *Punjabi Kinship and Marriage*, 1981, pp.214–215.

95. *VG*, p.544.

96. Ibid., p.617.

97. Ibid., p.618.

98. *Miharvan*, p.29.

99. See Karen Isaksen Leonard, *Social History of an Indian Caste: The Kayasths of Hyderabad*, London, 1978.

100. See Stephen Frederick Dale, *Indian Merchants and Eurasian Trade, 1600–1750*, Cambridge, 1994.

101. See C.A. Bayly, *Rulers, Townsmen, and Bazaars*, 1983, p.140.

102. See C.A. Bayly, 'Patrons and Politics in Northern India', *MAS*, 7/3, 1973.

103. Moti Lal Seth, *A Brief Ethnological Survey of the Khattris*, 1905, pp.xvii–xviii.

104. Kashi Nath, 'Khatris', *Indian Antiquary*, 1873, p.26.

105. Ibid., p.27.

106. Moti Lal Seth, *A Brief Ethnological Survey of the Khattris*, 1905, pp.170–78.

107. Muzaffar Alam and Sanjay Subrahmanyam, 'Discovering the Familiar: Notes on the Travel Account of Anand Ram Mukhlis', *SAR, 16/2*, 1996, p. 148.

108. See H.A. Rose, *A Glossary of the Tribes and Castes of the Punjab and North West Frontier Provinces*, vol.2, Lahore, 1919, pp.508–514.

109. Ibbetson comments that while the term *Sarin* is often given as the derivation of *sharia-i ain*, it is probably false. Instead *Sarin* is probably a corruption of *sreni* (guild). Ibid., p.513.

110. *VG*, p.132.

111. *B40*, p.238.

112. *BN*, p.63.

113. See Muzaffar Alam and Sanjay Subrahmanyam, 'The Making of a Munshi', *Comparative Studies of South Asia, Africa, and Middle East*, 24/2, 2004, pp.61–72.

114. H.A. Rose, *A Glossary of the Tribes and Castes of the Punjab and North West Frontier Provinces*, vol.2, 1919, pp.501–26.

115. Ibid., p.515.

116. Muzaffar Alam, 'Trade, State Policy, and Regional Change: Aspects of Mughal-Uzbek Commercial Relations, c.1550–1750', *JESHO*, 37, p.211.

117. Later in this chapter I discuss with greater detail Guru Nanak's family and education.

118. For background into the history of the Gurmukhi script see G.B. Singh, *Gurmukhi Lippi da Janam te Vikas*, Simla, 1950.

119. For an example of this type of linguistic analysis see Christopher Shackle, 'Approaches to the Persian loans in the Adi Granth', *BSOAS*, XL, 1, 1977, pp.36–50. Shackle highlights how Guru Nanak employed more Persian loanwords than his immediate successors.

120. See below for Bhai Gurdas' composition on the Rajputs.

121. See Irfan Habib, 'Jatts in Medieval Punjab' in Reeta Grewal and Sheena Pall, eds. *Precolonial and Colonial Punjab*, New Delhi, 2005.

122. Chetan Singh, 'Conformity and Conflict: Tribes and the "agrarian system" of Mughal India', *IESHR*, vol. xxv, 3, 1988.

123. H.A. Rose, *A Glossary of the Tribes and Castes of the Punjab and North West Frontier Provinces*, vol.2, Lahore, 1919, pp.364–366.

124. *VG*, p.133.

125. Ibid., p.133.

126. See Jeevan Singh Deol, 'Sikh Discourses on Community and Sovereignty in the Seventeenth and Eighteenth Centuries', unpublished PhD, University

of Cambridge, 2000; Purnima Dhavan, 'The Warrior's Way: The Making of the Eighteenth-Century "Khalsa Panth"', unpublished PhD, University of Virginia, 2003; J.S. Grewal and Veena Sachdeva, *Kinship and State Formation*, Chandigarh, 2007.

127. See Joginder Kaur, ed., *Ram Sukh Rao's Sri Fateh Singh Pratap Prabhakar*, Patiala, 1980.

128. Norman Peter Ziegler, 'Action, Power, and Service in Rajasthani Culture: A Social History of the Rajputs of Middle Period Rajasthan', unpublished PhD, University of Chicago, 1973, pp.107–35.

129. See Chetan Singh, 'Conformity and Conflict: Tribes and the "agrarian system" of Mughal India', *IESHR*, vol. xxv, 3, 1988.

130. See J. Hutchinson and J. Ph. Vogel, *History of the Panjab Hill States*, vol.2, Lahore, 1933; Norman Peter Ziegler, 'Action, Power, and Service in Rajasthani Culture', unpublished PhD, University of Chicago, 1973.

131. Richard M. Eaton, 'The Political and Religious Authority of the Shrine of Baba Farid', in Richard M. Eaton, *Essays on Islam and Indian History*, New Delhi, 2000, pp. 203–27.

132. Ibid., p. 219.

133. W.H. McLeod, *Evolution of the Sikh Community*, 1976, p.11.

134. Gurinder Singh Mann, 'Guru Nanak's Life and Legacy: An Appraisal', *Journal of Punjab Studies*, 17/1, 2010, pp.17–21.

135. Ibid., pp.17–21.

136. Ibid., pp.17–20.

137. Christopher Shackle in David Gilmartin and Bruce Lawrence, eds., *Beyond Turk and Hindu: Rethinking Identities in Islamicate South Asia*, 2000, p.59.

138. See Jeevan Deol, 'Love and Mysticism in the Punjabi Qissas of the seventeenth and eighteenth centuries', unpublished MPhil dissertation, School of Oriental and African Studies, London, 1996.

139. See Farina Mir, 'The Social Space of Language: Punjabi Popular Narrative in Colonial India, c.1850–1900', unpublished PhD, Columbia University, 2002.

140. H.A. Rose, *A Glossary of the Tribes and Castes of the Punjab and North West Frontier Provinces*, vol.2, 1919, pp.101–106.

141. See Richard M. Eaton, 'The Political and Religious Authority of the Shrine of Baba Farid', in Richard M. Eaton, *Essays on Islam and Indian History*, 2000, for an understanding on the process of Islamisation in West Panjab and the significant role played by Sufis.

142. For better understanding of these Jat tales, see Jeevan Deol, 'To die in the hands of Love' in Francesca Orsini, ed. *Love in South Asia: A Cultural History*, Cambridge, 2006; Jeevan Deol, 'Sex, Social Critique and the

Female Figure in Premodern Punjabi Poetry: Varis Shah's "Hir"', *MAS*, 36/1, 2002, pp.141–171.

143. See Daniel Gold, 'What the Merchant-Guru Sold: Social and Literary Types in Hindi Devotional Verse', *JAOS*, 112/1, 1992, pp.22–35.

144. For background on Guru Nanak's life see W.H. McLeod, *Guru Nanak and the Sikh Religion*, 1968.

145. *Miharvan*, p.12.

146. Ibid., p.15.

147. I infer Guru Nanak had mastered these subjects, especially Persian and Sanskrit, because his hymns indicate this fluency. In addition, Guru Nanak worked briefly as an administrator in Sultanpur, Panjab. For background on the language used by Guru Nanak in his compositions see Christopher Shackle, *A Guru Nanak Glossary*, New Delhi, 1981; Christopher Shackle, '"South-Western" Elements in the language of the Adi Granth', *BSOAS*, XL, 1, 1977, pp.36–50; Christopher Shackle, 'Approaches to the Persian Loans in the Adi Granth', *BSOAS*, XLI, 1, 1978, pp.73–96; and Christopher Shackle, 'The Sahaskriti poetic idiom in the Adi Granth', *BSOAS*, XLI, 2, 1978, pp.297–313.

148. *AS*, pp.10–11.

149. For background into this anecdote see W.H. McLeod, *Early Sikh Tradition*, 1980, pp.120–22.

150. *AS*, pp.76–78.

2   The Emergence of the Sikh Militancy, 1606–1644

1. See Max Arthur Macauliffe, *The Sikh Religion: Its Gurus, Sacred Writings, and Authors*, vol.4, New Delhi, 1963 [1909], pp.1–7. Macauliffe has paraphrased his narrative of Guru Hargobind's succession by using nineteenth-century Sikh chronicles.

2. Pre-modern Sikh chroniclers embedded Guru Hargobind's reforms inside a narrative of Sikh righteousness, see Kavi Santokh Singh, *Sri Gur Pratap Suraj Granth*, 10 vols, ed., Vir Singh, Amritsar, 1961–64; Bhagat Singh, *Gurbilas Patshahi Chhevin*, ed., Gurmukh Singh, Patiala, 1997; Rattan Singh Bhangu, *Sri Gur Panth Prakash*, ed., Jit Singh Sital, Amritsar, 1984; Giani Gian Singh, *Panth Prakash*, Patiala, 1987; Surjit Hans, *A Reconstruction of Sikh History from Sikh Literature*, Jalandhar, 1988. Early European histories argued Guru Hargobind took a very manly choice in order to avenge Guru Arjan, see: J.D. Cunningham, *History of the Sikhs*, Amritsar, 2002 [1849], pp.50–51. Modern histories have combined these ideas of righteousness, vengeance and socio-economic factors, see: W.H. McLeod, *The Evolution of*

the Sikh Community, 1976, pp.1–19; J.S. Grewal, *The Sikhs of the Punjab*, 1998, pp.62–69.

3. In most Sikh histories Prithi Chand is either ignored or deemed 'unorthodox' and so unimportant. For example, in Grewal's concise history of early Sikh society he only mentions Prithi Chand as 'rival' of Guru Hargobind, but he is described as just some upstart who cannot appreciate 'truth': J.S. Grewal, *The Sikhs of the Punjab*, 1998, p.65.

4. So far no Sikh history has attempted to show the contest between these 'orthodox' and 'unorthodox' lineages. This is surprising because these 'unorthodox' produced a lot of literature, see Gurmohan Singh Ahluwalia, 'Miharvan Sampradae di Panjabi Vartak nu Dehn' in Rattan Singh Jaggi, ed., *Khoj Patrika*, Patiala, 1988, pp.345–59; Jeevan Deol, 'The Minas and their Literature', *JAOS*, 118/2, 1998, pp. 172–84.

5. This is a very specific insult and while it carries negative connotations, it is largely unused in modern Sikhism because today no proper *mina* groups exist.

6. See Pritam Singh and Joginder Singh Ahluwalia, *Sikhan da Chhota Mel*, California, 2009. By contrast, the Sodhis of Anandpur, who are the descendants of Suraj Mal, Guru Hargobind's son, are called the *bare mel ke Sodhi* (the Sodhis that were joined with the Guru for a great time).

7. The *Dabistan* states that the Prithi Chand sect called themselves the *Bhagats*, see *Dabistan*, p.67–68. But in Miharvan literature the group usually referred to themselves as the *Nanakpanthis* or *Sikhs* and by implication the 'true' Sikhs.

8. For a biography of Prithi Chand's life and times see Joginder Singh Ahluwalia, ed., *Sodhi Prithi Chand di Rachna*, California, 2010.

9. For a summary of this orthodox narrative see 'Guru Arjan' and 'Prithi Chand' in Harbans Singh, ed., *The Encyclopaedia of Sikhism*, Patiala, 1992–1998.

10. For a biography of 'Sulahi Khan' and 'Chandu Shah' in Harbans Singh, ed., *The Encyclopaedia of Sikhism*, Patiala, 1992–1998.

11. For a study of Prithi Chand's poetry see Joginder Singh Ahluwalia, ed., *Sodhi Prithi Chand di Rachna*, 2010.

12. Ibid., pp.18–21.

13. For an overview of Miharvan's life and works see Pritam Singh and Joginder Singh Ahluwalia, *Sikhan da Chhota Mel*, 2009, pp.70–97.

14. Kesar Singh Chhibbar discusses Miharvan's education see *BN*, pp.80–81.

15. For Miharvan's biography see Kirpal Singh, *Manohar Das, Miharban: Jivan ate Rachnava*, Patiala, 1974. For background on his style of exegesis see Pashaura Singh, *The Guru Granth Sahib*, New Delhi, 2000, pp.247–49.

16. Original titles: *Goshtan Kabir Ji dian; Masle Hazrat Rasul ke, Piran Fakiran dian Goshtan; Bhagatan dian Goshtan; Nathan Jogian dian Goshtan; Sach Khand Pothi; Goshtan Guru Amar Das.*

17. For these debates see Gurmohan Singh Ahluwalia, 'Miharvan Sampradae di Panjabi Vartak nu Dehn' in Rattan Singh Jaggi, ed., *Khoj Patrika*, Patiala, 1988, pp.345–59; Jeevan Deol, 'The Minas and their Literature', *JAOS*, 118/2, 1998, pp. 172–84; and Pritam Singh and Joginder Singh Ahluwalia, *Sikhan da Chhota Mel*, 2009, pp.70–97.

18. For these debates over Guru Hargobind's detention in Gwalior fort see Hari Ram Gupta, *History of the Sikhs*, vol.1, pp.159–62.

19. For a biographical background of Bhai Gurdas and a study of his works see Rahuldeep Singh Gill, *Growing the Banyan Tree: Early Sikh Tradition in the Works of Bhai Gurdas Bhalla*, unpublished PhD, University of California, Santa Barbara, 2009.

20. The published text I will be using is *VG*.

21. Rahuldeep Singh Gill, *Growing the Banyan Tree: Early Sikh Tradition in the Works of Bhai Gurdas Bhalla*, unpublished PhD, University of California, Santa Barbara, 2009, pp.53–79.

22. There are several characteristics of early seventeenth-century Sikh literature that are distinctive. For example, linguistically writers tend to use a mixture of medieval Panjabi and Hindi, whether writing in prose or verse. The writers of the period describe a developed Sikh community with specific practices, ideas and caste communities. They also have a profound knowledge of canonised Sikh scripture and similar anecdotes about Guru Nanak's life. And unlike late seventeenth-century and early eighteenth-century writers they do not have explicit references to Mughal power nor a sense of ease with the temporal power of Guru Hargobind's lineage as continued by Hargobind's successors. Instead early seventeenth-century writers have a clearer connection with the conduct of the early Sikh Gurus. In order to gain a good understanding of pre-modern Sikh literary styles from the sixteenth to the nineteenth centuries see Surjit Hans, *A Reconstruction of Sikh History from Sikh Literature*, 1988.

23. See Gurmohan Singh Ahluwalia, 'Miharvan Sampradae di Panjabi Vartak nu Dehn' in Rattan Singh Jaggi, ed., *Khoj Patrika*, 1988, pp.345–59, for a discussion of Harji's writings.

24. The published text I will be using is *Harji*.

25. *VG*, pp.417–418.

26. *Harji*, pp.179–80.

27. For more information on the civility of the court and the roles of patron and servant, see Daud Ali, *Courtly Culture and Political Life in Early Medieval India*, Cambridge, 2004, pp.103–40.

28. For a detailed insight into Sikh music see Gobind Singh Mansukhani, *Indian Classical Music and Sikh Kirtan*, Delhi, 1982.

29. Classical and folk forms of dancing play an important role for many devotional traditions in South Asia. For instance, the Vallabha tradition has a long history of devotional dancing such as *kathak* (story) dancing. The Chishti Sufi tradition of South Asia has a long history of devotional dancing and music (*sama*) as well.

30. *Harji*, p.160.

31. For background on the Adi Granth see Pashaura Singh, *The Guru Granth Sahib*, 2000; Gurinder Singh Mann, *The Making of Sikh Scripture*, 2001.

32. See Joginder Singh Ahluwalia, ed., *Sodhi Prithi Chand di Rachna*, 2010.

33. Both Bhai Gurdas and Miharvan are regarded as significant exegetes of the Adi Granth; for an understanding of their ideas on Sikh theology see Taran Singh, *Gurubani Dian Viakhia Pranalian*, Patiala, 1980.

34. See *Harji*, pp.179–80.

35. See Jodh Singh, *Sri Kartarpuri Bir de Darshan*, Patiala, 1968.

36. This thorny issue has a large and complicated bibliography, for an introduction see Piar Singh, *Gatha Sri Adi Granth and the Controversy*, 1996; Pashaura Singh, *The Guru Granth Sahib*, 2000; Gurinder Singh Mann, *The Making of Sikh Scripture*, 2001; Jeevan Singh Deol, 'Text and lineage in early Sikh history: issues in the study of the Adi Granth', *BSOAS, 64/1*, 2001.

37. *VG*, pp.187–96.

38. *HN*, pp.61–67.

39. See Chetan Singh, *Region and Empire: Panjab in the Seventeenth Century*, New Delhi, 1991, for a history the growth of commercialisation and monetisation in seventeenth-century Panjab.

40. W.H. McLeod, *Early Sikh Tradition*, 1980, pp.256–65. This opinion has been recently contended by Gurinder Singh Mann and his view that the Jats formed an important part of Guru Nanak's community at Talwandi. But I feel that Mann's idea still does not fully undermine the premise that the Khatris played a more significant role in early Sikh society than any other caste group; see Gurinder Singh Mann, 'Guru Nanak's Life and Legacy: An Appraisal', *Journal of Panjab Studies*, 17/1, 2010, pp.17–21.

41. For a background on Jat history in medieval Panjab see Irfan Habib, 'Jatts in Medieval Punjab' in Reeta Grewal and Sheena Pall, eds. *Precolonial and Colonial Punjab*, 2005. Habib discusses the migration of early Jat communities into Panjab and their socio-economic development. In particular, Habib is interested in the Jats' conversion from pastoralism to sedentarisation; and in turn how this development fits into the general economic history of medieval India. Habib is also interested in exploring the role of the Persian-wheel in fostering the sedentarisation of the Jats.

42. For background on medieval Panjabi Jat society see Richard M. Eaton, 'The Political and Religious Authority of the Shrine of Baba Farid', in Richard M. Eaton, *Essays on Islam and Indian History*, 2000. In contrast to Habib, Eaton examines settled Jat communities in Western Panjab and specifically the role of Islam in the evolution of these communities. Eaton explores how Islamic conversion occurred amongst the community, as well as the role of Sufi saints within the community.

43. See Surjit Hans, *A Reconstruction of Sikh History from Sikh Literature*, 1988, pp.178–220.

44. For an in-depth analysis of the Janamsakhis see W.H. McLeod, *Early Sikh Tradition*, 1980; and Kirpal Singh, *Janamsakhi Tradition: An Analytical Study*, Amritsar, 2004.

45. For a particularly Weberian explanation for Jat support for Guru Hargobind see W.H. McLeod, *The Evolution of the Sikh Community*, 1976, pp.1–19.

46. Large support from lower social groups is clearly visible in late seventeenth century sources on Sikh revolt. Chetan Singh analyses the appeal of Sikhism for the masses, see Chetan Singh, *Region and Empire: Panjab in the Seventeenth Century*, 1991, pp.256–85.

47. The early Janamsakhis have many anecdotes on rich Khatris such as Mula (foolish) Khatri whose arrogance causes him to disrespect Guru Nanak. There is another anecdote on poor Khatri man asking Guru Nanak's help to pay for his daughter's wedding. Guru Nanak sends his servant, Bhagirath, to Lahore's market on the condition he gets everything that is required and returns in one day or his liberation will be denied. For summaries of these anecdotes see W.H. McLeod, *Guru Nanak and the Sikh Religion*, 1968, pp.46, for Bhagirath's anecdote. For Mula's anecdote see W.H. McLeod, *The Early Sikh Tradition*, 1980, pp.120–122.

48. The nineteenth-century Sikh chronicler, Giani Gian Singh, briefly discusses this relationship; see Giani Gian Singh, *Panth Prakash*, 1987, pp.120–21. For an English narrative account of Sikh chronicles on Guru Hargobind's life and Miharvan's involvement with Khatri elites see Max Arthur Macauliffe, *The Sikh Religion: Its Gurus, Sacred Writings, and Authors*, vol.4, 1963 [1909].

49. The Khatris from the early medieval period onwards developed into a caste community which saw commerce and government administration as their chosen professions. Prior to this period they claimed to have been warriors. See H.A. Rose, *A Glossary of the Tribes and Castes of the Punjab and North West Frontier Provinces*, vol.2, 1919, pp.501–526.

50. For a discussion on Sikhism and caste see W.H. McLeod, *The Evolution of the Sikh Community*, 1976, pp.83–104.

51. See Frank Perlin, 'Of White Whale and Countrymen in the Eighteenth-century Martha Deccan. Extended Class Relations, Rights, and the Problem of Rural Autonomy under the Old Regime', *The Journal of Peasant Studies*, 5/2, 1978.

52. In medieval Indian history the most detailed analysis of this clash of authority has been done on Sufi communities; see Simon Digby, 'The Sufi Shaikh as a Source of Authority in Medieval India', *Purusartha*, vol.9, 1986, pp. 57–77; Simon Digby, 'The Sufi Shaykh and the Sultan: A Conflict of Claims to Authority in Medieval India', *Iran*, 28, 1990; Sunil Kumar, 'Assertions of Authority: A Study of the Discursive Statements of Two Sultans in Delhi' in Muzaffar Alam, et al., eds. *The Making of Indo-Persian Culture*, New Delhi, 2000.

53. See Richard M Eaton, 'The Political and Religious Authority of the Shrine of Baba Farid', in Richard M Eaton, *Essays on Islam and Indian History*, 2000.

54. See Louis Fenech, *The Darbar of the Sikh Gurus: The Court of God in the World of Men*, New Delhi, 2008.

55. Bhai Gurdas's compositions most eloquently articulate these various titles and images of the early Sikh Gurus. For examples of these titles and images see the following compositions in *VG: Var* 5 p.91, p.96; *Var* 6 p.134; *Var* 20 p.326; *Var* 24 p.372; *Var* 30 p.469.

56. *AG*, p.141.

57. Ibid., p.63.

58. Ibid., p.61.

59. Ibid., p.1012.

60. I have presented these opinions by examining the theology of Miharvan and Hargobind as found in the *Adi Granth*, Bhai Gurdas' works, Miharvan works, and Harji's works.

61. In this chapter I will introduce the role of Vishnu in Bhai Gurdas' works, and in the later chapters the role of Vishnu in early Sikh thought will be obvious. In Chapter 4 I discuss the importance of Shakti traditions in early Sikh thought.

62. For background on the Janamsakhis see Surjit Hans, *A Reconstruction of Sikh History from Sikh Literature*, 1988, pp.178–220; W.H. McLeod, *Early Sikh Tradition*, 1980; Kirpal Singh, *Janamsakhi Parampara*, Patiala, 1969

63. W.H. McLeod, *Early Sikh Tradition*, 1980, pp.106–116.

64. Gurinder Singh Mann, 'Guru Nanak's Life and Legacy: An Appraisal', *Journal of Punjab Studies*, 17/1, 2010, p.7.

65. W.H. McLeod, *Early Sikh Tradition*, 1980, pp.263–264.

66. Mann has made the very important point that *Janamsakhi* manuscripts need to be re-examined. Indeed, he offers us his opinions on how the *Janamsakhi*

tradition developed, but his views are brief and do not fully explore the various source traditions: it is to be hoped that in the near future he will develop his ideas into a more substantial textual history. In brief Mann feels the *Puratan* tradition is the earliest (but he does not clarify if he is referring to the Colebrooke and/or Hafizabad manuscripts) source tradition (pre-1600) followed by the Miharvan (pre-1620) and then the Bala (1648–1658). See Gurinder Singh Mann, 'Guru Nanak's Life and Legacy: An Appraisal', *Journal of Punjab Studies*, 17/1, 2010, pp.3–44. For McLeod's opinions of all these source traditions see W.H. McLeod, *Early Sikh Tradition*, 1980, pp.15–48.

67. For a brief biography of Baba Hindal see the reference 'Hindal (Handal), Bhai' in *The Sikh Encyclopaedia*, vol.3, ed., Harbans Singh, Patiala, 1995, p.272.

68. McLeod identifies this anecdote as an early one, a part of his textual category 'Narrative I' see W.H. McLeod, *Early Sikh Tradition*, Oxford, 1980, pp.174–234.

69. *AG*, p.360, pp.417–18.

70. See W.H. McLeod, *Guru Nanak and the Sikh Religion*, Oxford, 1968, pp.132–38.

71. A good example is the history by the nineteenth-century Sikh chronicler Rattan Singh Bhangu, see Rattan Singh Bhangu, *Sri Gur Panth Prakash*, ed., Jit Singh Sital, 1984, p.366.

72. See Richard Barz, *The Bhakti Sect of Vallabhacarya*, New Delhi, 1992, pp.120–22; John Stratton Hawley, *Sur Das: Poet, Singer, Saint*, Seattle and London, 1984; Winand M Callewaert, ed., *The Hindi Biography of Dadu Dyal*, New Delhi, 1988, pp.98–103.

73. *Miharvan*, p. 469.

74. The Puratan Janamsakhi has two manuscripts and the earlier Colebrooke manuscript, unlike the Hafizabad manuscript, does not have a discourse between Guru Nanak and Babur.

75. *VG*, p.415.

76. *AS*, pp.54–57.

77. See Max Arthur Macauliffe, *The Sikh Religion: Its Gurus, Sacred Writings, and Authors*, vol.4, 1963 [1909].

78. For a discussion of the Bala source tradition see W.H. McLeod, *The Early Sikh Tradition*, 1980, pp.15–22.

79. *Bala*, p.313.

80. Surjit Hans offers a lucid explanation of early Sikh notions of identity in the seventeenth century; see Surjit Hans, *A Reconstruction of Sikh History from Sikh Literature*, 1988, pp.178–220.

81. *Miharvan*, pp.1–11.
82. For a brief background on Raja Janak in Indian mythology see John Dowson, *A Classical Dictionary of Hindu Mythology*, London, 1914, pp.132–133.
83. *Miharvan*, p.8.
84. *Dabistan*, pp.65–66.
85. *VG*, p.18.
86. *VG*, p.201.
87. For a discussion of Vishnu's unassuming forms see Sheldon Pollock, 'The Divine King in the Indian Epic', *JAOS*, 104/3, 1984, pp.505–28
88. See Irfan Habib's brief background on the *Dabistan* in J.S. Grewal and Irfan Habib, eds., *Sikh History from Persian Sources*, Lahore, 2004, pp. 59–61.
89. *Dabistan*, pp.67–68.
90. Ibid., p.66.
91. Ibid., p.78.
92. These distinctions in audiences are disputable but probable, see W.H. McLeod, *Early Sikh Tradition*, 1980, pp.256–67.
93. *Dabistan*, pp.67–68.
94. I made this discovery through observing in my sources how Sikh Gurus ascended to the Sikh throne and how rules of inheritance operated in Panjabi society. The fact that Sikh Gurus always moved from the base of their predecessor immediately after ascending the throne; and the fact that new Sikh Gurus always received hostility from the predecessors' sons about residing in their hometowns, led me to realise how inheritance must have worked. As a result, I understood that Guru Hargobind was in a unique position regarding the inheritance of property. I then considered the large amount of property Guru Arjan owned and the wealth these pilgrimage towns must have generated. I next considered the lifestyle Guru Hargobind adopted and the reforms he introduced and contextualised these circumstances with other socially mobile groups in seventeenth-century India; thus I believe Guru Hargobind experienced a process of gentrification.
95. *VG*, p.425.
96. See Brendan P. Larocque, 'Trade, State, and Religion in Early Modern India: Devotionalism and the Market Economy in the Mughal Empire', unpublished PhD, University of Wisconsin-Madison, 2004.
97. Chetan Singh, *Region and Empire: Panjab in the Seventeenth Century*, New Delhi, 1991.
98. The development of *naukari* (service) in medieval India as a secular term reflects how early Islamic states became assimilated into the South Asian milieu, see Dirk Kolff, *Naukar, Rajput, and Sepoy*, Cambridge, 1990, p. 20.

99. Macauliffe discusses the story behind Painda Khan as recalled in early modern Sikh works; see Max Arthur Macauliffe, *The Sikh Religion: Its Gurus, Sacred Writings, and Authors*, vol.4, pp.52–53.

100. *Dabistan*, pp.74–75; For background on the medieval horse trade see Jos Gommans, *Mughal Warfare*, London, 2002.

101. In particular see Bhagat Singh, *Gurbilas Patshahi Chhevin*, ed., Gurmukh Singh, Patiala, 1997.

102. *Dabistan*, p.69.

103. Bards singing in the heroic style (*dhadhi*) were closely attached to Guru Hargobind's court; see Giani Gurdit Singh, 'Adi Granth vich 'Dhunan'', *Panjabi Dunian*, September, 1954. For a contemporary understanding of this musical tradition see Michael Nijhawan, *Dhadi Darbar: Religion, Violence, and the Performance of Sikh History*, Delhi, 2006.

104. In Bayly's analysis of early modern India's market economy and society he demonstrates the importance of military expenditure on the development of local markets; see, C.A. Bayly, *Rulers, Townsmen and Bazaars*, 1983, pp.35–73.

105. The development and composition of aristocratic demand in India has been largely unexplored, but demand for luxury goods reveals both the history of taste and the history of economic production. Bayly makes this point in C.A. Bayly, *Rulers, Townsmen and Bazaars*, 1983, pp.57–63. O'Hanlon also discusses the luxury goods market in Mughal India, see Rosalind O'Hanlon, 'Manliness and Imperial Service in Mughal North India', *JESHO*, 42/1, 1999, p. 72.

106. *HN*, p.65.

107. For Miharvan's biography see Kirpal Singh, *Manohar Das, Miharban: Jivan ate Rachnava*, 1974.

108. For a summary of his travels see Pritam Singh and Joginder Singh Ahluwalia, *Sikhan da Chhota Mel*, 2009, pp.71–73.

109. See Kirpal Singh, *Manohar Das, Miharban: Jivan ate Rachnava*, 1974.

110. Jahangir vigorously attempted to conquer Kangra and in his memoirs there are frequent references to those campaigns. He recorded the news of victory in 1621 with delight; see Jahangir, *The Jahangirnama*, trans. Wheeler M. Thackston, 1999, pp.351–53.

111. J. Hutchinson and J. Ph. Vogel, *History of the Panjab Hill States, vols1*, 1933, p.173.

112. Ibid., pp.172–173.

113. Raja Chander Bhan Chand attempted to remove Mughal influence from his territory, see J. Hutchinson and J. Ph. Vogel, *History of the Panjab Hill States, vols2*, 1933.

114. J. Hutchinson and J. Ph. Vogel, *History of the Panjab Hill States*, vol.1, 1933, p.735.

115. The reason why exactly Guru Arjan was executed is complicated. Pre-colonial Sikh chroniclers who had no access to Persian sources blamed Prithi Chand and Chandu Shah for the execution. But colonial scholars had access to Persian sources and these widen the possible reasons for the execution to include the roles that Jahangir and Shaykh Ahmad Sirhindi may have played. See Hari Ram Gupta, *History of the Sikhs*, vol.1, 1984, pp.144–153, for a comprehensive summary of the main protagonists.

116. Giani Gian Singh, *Panth Prakash*, Patiala, 1987, pp.120–121.

117. Max Arthur Macauliffe, *The Sikh Religion: Its Gurus, Sacred Writings, and Authors*, vol.4, 1963 [1909], p.36.

118. Giani Gian Singh, *Tawarikh Guru Khalsa*, vol.1, Patiala, 1999, p.434.

119. *Dabistan*, p.68.

120. For a detailed overview of all these battles see Hari Ram Gupta, *History of the Sikhs*, vol.1, New Delhi, 1984, pp.166–71.

121. The town of Kiratpur was constructed in 1624 by Guru Hargobind's eldest son, Baba Gurditta, and the Guru simply moved to that base in 1635.

122. *Dabistan*, p.69.

123. See Muzaffar Alam, *The Crisis of Empire in Mughal North India*, New Delhi, 1986, pp.92–133; Andre Wink, *Land and Sovereignty in India*, Cambridge, 1986, pp.34–155; Dirk Kolff, *Naukar, Rajput, and Sepoy*, 1990, pp.1–31.

124. *VG*, p.335.

125. Ibid., pp.423–424.

126. For examples of Gurdas' criticisms against worldly kings see the following compositions in *VG: Var* 5, p.95; *Var* 15, p.242; *Var* 18, p.301; *Var* 38, p.591.

127. Pashaura Singh, *The Guru Granth Sahib*, 2000, pp.206–212.

128. J.S. Grewal, 'The Sikh Movement During the Reign of Akbar' in Irfan Habib, ed., *Akbar and His India*, Delhi, 1997, pp.243–244.

3   Debating the Householder's Path, 1644–1675

1. The period (1644–75) is often seen as uneventful and unimportant by Sikh historians; these sentiments are usually expressed during the reign of Guru Har Rai. The main reasons why this period has been forgotten is because most early Sikh histories ignore the intellectual contest between differing Sikh Guru lineages; and also because there is a dearth of sources. So far no historical study has adequately considered the writings of Guru Harji in this period because he is seen as 'unorthodox' and insignificant. For these

opinions see especially J.S. Grewal, *The Sikhs of the Punjab*, 2000, pp.67–73; and W.H. McLeod, *The Evolution of the Sikh Community*, 1973, pp.1–19.

2. The personality of Aurangzeb is notoriously difficult to untangle due to the complexities of South Asian nationalism. For a concise narrative of Aurangzeb's reign, see John F. Richards, *The Mughal Empire*, Cambridge, 1993, pp.151–252. For an insight into the nationalist and post-nationalist debates surrounding Aurangzeb see Romila Thapar, et al., *Communalism and the Writing of Indian History*, Delhi, 1969; Satish Chandra, 'Reassessing Aurangzeb' in Satish Chandra, *Historiography, Religion and State in Medieval India*, 1997; Harbans Mukhia, *The Mughals of India*, Delhi, 2004; Muzaffar Alam and Sanjay Subrahmanyam, eds., *The Mughal State*, 2000, pp.1–77 and Katherine Butler Brown, 'Did Aurangzeb Ban Music? Questions for the Historiography of His Reign', *MAS*, 41/1, 2007, pp.77–120.

3. There are many examples of this historical narrative, see for instance, Khushwant Singh, *A History of the Sikhs*, vol.1, 1963. This narrative of Sikh history is not only found in specialist Sikh histories but is popularly held in Mughal studies as well; a classic example is S.R. Sharma, *The Religious Policy of the Mughal Emperors*, Delhi, 1940.

4. Guru Nanak's philosophy has been analysed by a diverse range of scholars in a variety of languages and each study offers us a unique view on Guru Nanak as a thinker. For background on Guru Nanak's teachings in English see W.H. McLeod, *Guru Nanak and the Sikh Religion*, 1968; Susan Elizabeth Prill, 'The Sant tradition and community formation in the works of Guru Nanak and Dadu Dayal', unpublished PhD, SOAS, London, 2005.

5. See Chapter 1.

6. As detailed below, Guru Hargobind was succeeded by his grandson, Guru Har Rai and Miharvan was succeeded by his eldest son, Harji.

7. For a brief biography of 'Dhir Mal' see Harbans Singh, ed., *The Sikh Encyclopaedia:* vol.1, Patiala, 1992, pp.579–80.

8. See Jeevan Singh Deol, 'Non-Canonical Compositions Attributed to the Seventh and Ninth Sikh Gurus', *JAOS*, 121/2, 2001, pp.193–203.

9. It is not known when Harji was born, but Ahluwalia has estimated his year of birth as 1605, see Gurmohan Singh Ahluwalia, *Sodhi Harji Jiwan te Rachna*, Patiala, 1985.

10. For a summary of Harji's works see Pritam Singh and Joginder Singh Ahluwalia, *Sikhan da Chhota Mel*, 2009, pp.98–114.

11. It possible that Guru Har Rai did not engage in hunting personally, but it is unlikely he rejected the practice. For a brief discussion of Guru Har Rai's relationship to hunting, see Louis Fenech, *The Darbar of the Sikh of the Sikh Gurus*, 2008, pp.98–100.

12. There is scant information on Guru Har Rai's life; however, the *Dabistan's* author Mobad claims to have been a close companion of Guru Har Rai and records that the Guru continued the lifestyle established by Guru Hargobind: see *Dabistan*, p.72.

13. The Golden Temple officially came into existence in the nineteenth century when Ranjit Singh decorated the temple with gold. Underneath the gold is white marble; the temple was constructed by Guru Arjan and is known as *Harmandir Sahib* (temple of God); see Madanjit Kaur, *The Golden Temple: Past and Present*, Amritsar, 1983.

14. Temple towns and cities such as Amritsar were economically flourishing in the seventeenth century; for detailed study of these developments see Brendan P. Laroque, 'Trade, State, and Religion in Early Modern India: Devotionalism and the Market Economy in Mughal India', unpublished PhD, University of Wisconsin-Madison, 2004.

15. *Dabistan*, p.66.

16. *Dabistan*, pp.72–74.

17. Harbans Singh, ed., *The Sikh Encyclopaedia:* vol.1, Patiala, 1992, pp.579–80.

18. The dating of the *Goshti Guru Miharivanu*, like other Miharvan texts, is somewhat dubious. This text was definitely composed by Harji sometime in the mid-to-late seventeenth century. See Gurmohan Singh Ahluwalia, 'Miharvan Sampradaei di Panjabi Vartak nun Den' in Rattan Singh Jaggi, ed., *Khoj Patrika*, Patiala, 1988, pp.345–59 and the introduction in *Harji* by Govindnath Rajguru, pp.9–166.

19. Though of course Miharvan had written about the life and times of Guru Nanak and Guru Amar Das, no Guru had written about the career of their immediate predecessor.

20. Muhammadipur was the town where Miharvan spent most of his reign and it is the town where he passed away. But throughout his life Miharvan travelled across the Panjab region. The Miharvan lineage evidently continued to own property in Muhammadipur because, in the early eighteenth century, Miharvan's grandson, Hargopal, established his headquarters there.

21. Unfortunately the *Goshti Guru Miharivanu*, like other *Mina* texts has not yet been adequately analysed as an early Sikh exegetical work. An academic history of early Sikh exegesis with any sophistication has yet to be written. For background on Sikh exegetical traditions see Pashaura Singh, *The Guru Granth Sahib*, 2000.

22. *Harji*, p.169.

23. *Shabad* and *Bani* are synonymous.

24. *Harji*, p.169.

25. Ibid., p.170.

26. Ibid., p.172.
27. For an example of Guru Nanak's birth as described in the *Janamsakhis* see *B40*, pp.3–5.
28. *Harji*, pp.172–73.
29. Ibid., p.174.
30. Ibid., p.174.
31. Ibid., pp.175–181.
32. Ibid., p.177.
33. *VG*, p.425.
34. *Harji*, p.181.
35. Ibid., p.173.
36. See Winand M. Callewaert and Rupert Snell, eds., *According to tradition: Hagiographical writing in India*, Wiesbaden, 1994.
37. *Harji*, pp.181–82.
38. For a history of these bodily signs see Daud Ali, *Courtly Culture and Political Life in Early Medieval India*, 2004, pp.144–48.
39. *Harji*, p.183.
40. Ibid., p.188.
41. Ibid., p.190.
42. Ibid., p.350.
43. *Harji*, pp.231–32.
44. The concept of 'time' has been pivotal to most Indic philosophies and has been variously understood by different philosophers. For an introduction to this analysis of 'time', see Randy Kloetzli and Alf Hiltebeitel, 'Kala' in Sushil Mittal and Gene Thursby, eds., *The Hindu World*, New York, 2004.
45. *Harji*, pp.248–49.
46. Sikhism challenged the authority of Vedic rituals such as wearing the 'sacred thread' (*jeneu/yajnopavita*). An individual needed this sacred thread in order to correctly follow the four stages of life but it was not given to low-caste groups, only to high-caste groups like the Khatris. Early Sikh society seems to dismiss the importance of taking the sacred thread from the times of Guru Nanak. For more information on the origins of the sacred thread see A.L. Basham, *The Sacred Cow*, London, 1989, p.39.
47. J.S. Grewal and Irfan Habib, eds., *Sikh History from Persian Sources*, 2001, p.94.
48. Chetan Singh, *Region and Empire*, 1991, p.272.
49. Aurangzeb's alleged growing interest in Sikh society is easily found in the historiography, for example see J.S. Grewal, *The Sikhs of the Punjab*, 2000, pp.67–81.

50. Guru Har Rai's legends as recorded in Sikh chronicles and in particular for this legend involving Aurangzeb, see Max Arthur Macauliffe, *The Sikh Religion: Its Gurus, Sacred Writings, and Authors*, vol.4, 1963.

51. For a biography of Ram Rai and his land grants see Harbans Singh, ed., *The Sikh Encyclopaedia*, vol.3, 1997, pp.461–62.

52. The land grant possessed by Dhir Mal's ancestors is dated 30 November 1643, yet the document has several peculiarities, see Jeevan Singh Deol, 'Sikh Discourses on Community and Sovereignty in the Seventeenth and Eighteenth Centuries', unpublished PhD, University of Cambridge, 2000, p.38.

53. Harbans Singh, ed., *The Sikh Encyclopaedia:* vol.1, 1994, p.580.

54. Unfortunately there have been no detailed studies on Guru Har Krishan's reign. Nevertheless, there is a considerable amount of anecdotal and architectural evidence on his travels around Delhi. For an anecdotal account see J.S. Grewal, *The Sikhs of the Punjab*, 2000, pp.67–81. For a history of the Sikh temples associated with Guru Har Krishan in Delhi see Amrik Singh, *Sikh Shrines in Delhi*, New Delhi, 2003.

55. Most Sikh histories depict Aurangzeb as having a vendetta against Guru Hargobind's Sikh tradition. It seems the Miharvan tradition does not share this opinion. For an account of Aurangzeb's anti-Sikh policies see Hari Ram Gupta, *History of the Sikhs*, vol.1, 2000, pp.178–282.

56. The Panjabi hills remained perpetually semi-independent from Mughal rule; the region was more like a Mughal feudatory. See Chetan Singh, *Region and Empire*, 1991, pp.137–42; J. Hutchinson and J. Ph. Vogel, *History of the Panjab Hill States*, vols2, 1933.

57. The Lahore province and in particular the city of Lahore had both symbolic and actual significance to Mughal authority, and the region was heavily fortified. See Chetan Singh, *Region and Empire*, 1991, pp.30–88.

58. For a biography on Guru Tegh Bahadur's life see Fauja Singh and Gurbachan Singh Talib, *Guru Tegh Bahadur: Martyr and Teacher*, 1975.

59. Ibid., pp.30–31.

60. It is unclear whether Guru Tegh Bahadur did have an armed contingent with him while he was travelling. But it is likely that Guru Har Rai's army still existed and was probably stationary, residing in Makhowal. However, he did seem to have a treasury with him and a growing number of scribes; it is possible he also hired some court poets. See Louis Fenech, *The Darbar of the Sikh Gurus: The Court of God in the World of Men*, 2008, pp.100–105.

61. Ibid., pp.50–52.

62. *HN*, p.87.

63. John F. Richards, *The Mughal Empire*, 1995, p.178.

64. Fauja Singh and Gurbachan Singh Talib, *Guru Tegh Bahadur: Martyr and Teacher*, 1975, pp.90–104.

65. This miracle is repeated below in Suri's account. The origin of this tradition comes directly from Guru Gobind Singh who mentions this when discussing Guru Tegh Bahadur's demise, see Chapter 4.

66. Muzaffar Alam, *The Crisis of Empire in Mughal North India*, 1986, p.136.

67. See J.S. Grewal, *Guru Tegh Bahadur and The Persian Chroniclers*, Amritsar, 1976.

68. Ibid., pp.35–42.

69. Ibid., pp.36–39.

70. See *HN*, pp.74–119.

71. For an understanding of the *Hukumnama* style see Hardip Singh Syan, 'Hukumnama' in *Encyclopaedia of Indian Religions*, ed., Arvind Sharma, (forthcoming June 2013).

72. *HN*, p.65.

73. Ibid., p.67.

74. Ibid., p.73.

75. Ibid., p.77.

76. Ibid., p.87.

77. Ibid., p.119.

78. Ibid., p.93.

79. *AG*, p.633.

80. Jadunath Sarkar, trans. *Maasir-I Alamgiri: A History of the Emperor Aurangzib*, Calcutta, 1947, p.94. The *Maasir-I Alamgiri* was completed in 1710 after Aurangzeb's death and after the creation of the Khalsa in 1699. This is probably the reason why the chronicle says Guru Tegh 'Singh' and not Bahadur.

81. Fauja Singh and Gurbachan Singh Talib, *Guru Tegh Bahadur: Martyr and Teacher*, 1975, p.98.

82. Unfortunately there is not a great deal of information on the *Divanas*. See H.A. Rose, *A Glossary of the Tribes and Castes of the Punjab and North West Frontier Provinces*, vol.2, 1919, p.243; Jeevan Deol, 'The Minas and their Literature', *JAOS*, 118/2, 1998, pp. 172–84.

83. This information has been derived from: H.A. Rose, *A Glossary of the Tribes and Castes of the Punjab and North West Frontier Provinces*, vol.2, Lahore, 1919, p.243; Jeevan Deol, 'The Minas and their Literature', *JAOS*, 118/2, 1998, pp. 172–84.

84. Renunciation always carried a social danger to Brahmanical society and in many respects the four stages of life attempted to accommodate renunciation without causing a social crisis. See Patrick Olivelle, *Samnyasa Upanishads: Hindu Scriptures on Asceticism and Renunciation*, 1992, pp.1–112.

85. Ram Rai's fraternity was said to be an order belonging to the *Udasis* (detached ones): the *Udasis* were a Sikh order of missionaries established by Guru Nanak's son, Baba Sri Chand. The *Udasis* had several orders, some more prominent than others; it is possible that many Sikh mystical traditions became *Udasis* in order to keep their individual mystical traditions while remaining Sikhs. For background on Ram Rai's followers see Harbans Singh, ed., *The Sikh Encyclopaedia*, vol.3, 1995, p.462; and for background on the *Udasis* see Sulakhan Singh, *Heterodoxy in the Sikh Tradition*, Jalandhar, 1999.

86. The Khatris were a prominent mercantile community in Benares; see C.A. Bayly, 'Patrons and Politics in Northern India', *MAS*, 7/3, 1973.

87. These Brahmin votaries were Bhai Mati Das and Bhai Sati Das. Mati Das and Sati Das were brothers and members of the Chhibbar family; the Chhibbar would become a renowned family of Sikh intellectuals in the eighteenth and nineteenth centuries. For background on the lives of Mati Das and Sati Das see Fauja Singh and Gurbachan Singh Talib, *Guru Tegh Bahadur: Martyr and Teacher*, 1975; for background on the Chhibbar family see Jeevan Singh Deol, 'Sikh Discourses on Community and Sovereignty in the Seventeenth and Eighteenth Centuries', unpublished PhD, University of Cambridge, 2000, pp.246–317.

88. J. Hutchinson and J. Ph. Vogel, *History of the Panjab Hill States*, vol.1, 1933, p.735.

4 Sovereignty and Social Order, 1675–1699

1. For example, see the following studies on the Rajputs, Marathas and Sikhs: Robert C. Hallissey, *The Rajput Rebellion against Aurangzeb*, Columbia and London, 1977; Andre Wink, *Land and Sovereignty in India*, Cambridge, 1986; Jeevan Singh Deol, 'Eighteenth Century Khalsa Identity: Discourse, Praxis and Narrative' in Christopher Shackle et al., eds., *Sikh Religion, Culture and Ethnicity*, 2000.

2. For background on the distinctions between 'Hindu' and 'Turk' see David Gilmartin and Bruce B. Lawrence, eds., *Beyond Hindu and Turk*, 2000.

3. See James M. Hastings, 'Poets, Saints and Warriors: The Dadu Panth, Religious Change and Identity Formation in Jaipur State, c.1562–1860CE', unpublished PhD, University of Wisconsin-Madison, 2002.

4. The relationship between Sikhism and Islam has often been seen in hostile terms after the Khalsa was formed. This is because early Sikhism has often been seen as an eclectic movement comparable to 'moderate' Sufi orders and later, 'militant', Sikhism was less eclectic and more hostile to Islam. An

example of this opinion can be found in Raziuddin Aquil, *Sufism, Culture and Politics*, New Delhi, 2007; Aziz Ahmad, *Studies in Islamic Culture in the Indian Environment*, New Delhi, 1999.

5. For a comprehensive background on Oriental Despotism see Brendan O'Leary, *The Asiatic Mode of Production: Oriental Despotism, Historical Materialism and Indian History*, Oxford, 1989. For an understanding of how Oriental Despotism shaped debates over 'individuality' see Gyan Prakash, *Bonded Histories: Genealogies of Labor Servitude in colonial India*, Cambridge, 1990.

6. See Louis Fenech, *Martyrdom in the Sikh Tradition*, 2000.

7. *DG*, vol.1, p.73.

8. See Chapter 3.

9. The *Dasam Granth* has a long and complicated textual history and position in modern Sikhism. The text has been called the *Dasam Granth* since the turn of the twentieth century. Most standard versions of the *Dasam Granth* include: *Jap Sahib* (meditation); *Akal Ustat* (Panegyric of the Immortal); *Bachitar Natak* (Wonderful Drama); *Chandi Charitra* (Chandi's Episodes, Parts One and Two); *Chandi Charitra Ukti Bilas* (Chandi's Radiant Story); *Var Sri Bhagauti* (Chandi's Ballad); *Ugardanti* (Terrifying Tooth Goddess); *Gian Parbodh* (Illumination of Knowledge); *Chaubis Avatar* (Twenty-Four Incarnations of Vishnu); *Chritropakhyan* (Tales of Deceit); *Shastar Nam Mala* (Garland of Weapons); *Hikayat* (Tales); *Zafarnama* (Epistle of Victory) and several quatrains and compositions by Guru Gobind Singh. For background on the Dasam Granth see Robin Rinehart, *Debating the Dasam Granth*, New York, 2011; C.H. Loehlin, *The Granth of Guru Gobind Singh and the Khalsa Brotherhood*, Lucknow, 1971; Dharam Pal Ashta, *The Poetry of the Dasam Granth*, Delhi, 1959.

10. Simplistically put, this debate on Sikh identity was over whether Sikhs are Hindus or whether Sikhism was distinct from Hinduism. See Harjot Oberoi, *The Construction of Religious Boundaries*, 1994; Kenneth W. Jones, 'Ham Hindu Nahin: Arya-Sikh Relations, 1877–1905', *JAS*, 32/3, May 1973, pp.457–75.

11. For an understanding of these debates see Robin Rinehart, *Debating the Dasam Granth*, 2011. For an overview of these debates in Sikh historiography see J.S. Grewal, *Contesting Interpretations of the Sikh Tradition*, Delhi, 1998, pp.238–67. In Panjabi many high-quality monographs have been produced on the subject: see Rattan Singh Jaggi, *Dasam Granth da Kartritav*, Delhi, 1966 and Piara Singh 'Padam', *Dasam Granth Darshan*, Patiala, 1982.

12. As already touched upon, even saying the *Dasam Granth* was fully accepted as the works of Guru Gobind Singh in pre-colonial Sikh society is very

controversial, because certain Sikhs are vehemently opposed to the *Dasam Granth*. But such an entrenched position is based on rigid faith instead of empirical evidence. Even a cursory glance at pre-modern Sikh literature from the late seventeenth century onwards illustrates how the literary style and thematic interests of the Sikh literati were shaped by the works of the *Dasam Granth*. That does not mean that further textual studies on the *Dasam Granth* are not required, but it is imperative, I feel, that this issue is treated with greater historical context. The ideas expressed in the *Dasam Granth* might not sit comfortably with the beliefs of certain contemporary Sikhs. This discomfort does not mean that pre-modern Sikhs shared those feelings. In the context of early modern South Asian thought and literature the *Dasam Granth* was not an unusual text: it clearly displays the intellectual milieu of the period. It is necessary to contextualise the *Dasam Granth* in Sikh history, instead of debating the text as if it exists in a vacuum. For some of these ideas, see Gurinder Singh Mann, 'Sources for the Study of Guru Gobind Singh's Life and Times', *Journal of Punjab Studies*, 15/1&2, 2010, pp.229–280.

13. Few studies have been done on Harji's work, but for an exception see Krishna Kumari Bansal, 'Sukhmani Sahasranam Parmarth' in Rattan Singh Jaggi, ed., *Khoj Patrika*, 1988.

14. Some examples include Louis Fenech, *The Darbar of the Sikh Gurus: The Court of God in the World of Men*, 2008; Anne Murphy, 'Sikh History in the Past', *History and Theory*, 46/3, 2007, pp.345–65; Purnima Dhavan, 'The Warrior's Way: The Making of the Eighteenth-Century 'Khalsa Panth', unpublished PhD, University of Virginia, 2003.

15. The subject of courtly civility has received much attention in recent medieval history: see John F. Richards, 'Norms of Comportment among Imperial Mughal Officers' in Barbara Metcalf, ed., *Moral Conduct and Authority*, Berkeley, 1984; Rosalind O'Hanlon, 'Manliness and Imperial Service in Mughal North India', *JESHO*, 42/1, 1999, pp.47–93.

16. See Jeevan Singh Deol, *Sikh Discourses of Community and Sovereignty in the Seventeenth and Eighteenth Centuries*, Unpublished PhD, University of Cambridge, 2000.

17. Ibid., pp.49–145.

18. See Norman Peter Ziegler, 'Action, Power and Service in Rajasthani Culture: A Social History of the Rajputs in Middle Period Rajasthan', unpublished PhD, University of Chicago, 1973; Norman Peter Ziegler, 'Some Notes on Rajput Loyalties During the Mughal Period' in John F. Richards, ed., *Kingship and Authority in South Asia*, Wisconsin-Madison, 1978; Dirk Kolff, *Naukar, Rajput, and Sepoy*, 1990. A visible difference between Ziegler and

Kolff are their readings of Rajputs as respectively, kin and kindred based groups and their flexibility/inflexibility on questions concerning 'tradition'.

19. Dirk Kolff, *Naukar, Rajput, and Sepoy*, 1990, pp.73–74. As Kolff's critics have pointed out his notion of the 'great' and 'spurious' traditions lack critical explanation. It is not clear why genealogical orthodoxy emerged in the Mughal period and not earlier or later. Ziegler's work contradicts Kolff's ideas of 'orthodoxy'. Deol, however, accepts Kolff without identifying the weaknesses in his argument and Ziegler's alternative ideas.

20. Jeevan Singh Deol, *Sikh Discourses of Community and Sovereignty in the Seventeenth and Eighteenth Centuries*, unpublished PhD, University of Cambridge, 2000, pp.56–57.

21. Ibid., pp.143–44.

22. Andre Wink, *Land and Sovereignty in India*, 1986, p.31.

23. Ibid., pp.34–38.

24. Ibid., pp.43–44.

25. Ibid., pp.46–47.

26. Rosalind O'Hanlon, 'The social worth of scribes: Brahmins, Kayasths and the social order in early modern India', *IESHR*, 47/4, 2010, pp.563–595.

27. For a better understanding of these lively Pundit networks, see Rosalind O'Hanlon and Christopher Minkowski, 'What makes people who they are? Pandit Networks and the Problem Livelihoods in Early Modern Western India', *IESHR*, 45/3, 2008, pp.318–416.

28. For a concise biography on Guru Gobind Singh see J.S. Grewal and S.S. Bal, *Guru Gobind Singh (A Biographical Study)*, Chandigarh, 1967. Guru Gobind Singh's life and times are central to the history of Sikhism and especially early modern Sikh history. However there is a need to re-examine his life in light of the important developments in scholarly research since the 1970s. There have not only been major changes in our knowledge of the early modern era, but there are many sources that have not been fully utilised. Mann has recently made a case for writing a new biography on Guru Gobind Singh's life and times, see Gurinder Singh Mann, 'Sources for the Study of Guru Gobind Singh's Life and Times', *Journal of Punjab Studies*, 15/1&2, 2010, pp.229–280.

29. There has been limited work on Guru Gobind Singh's court poets partly because there is a dearth of information and partly because scholars of Hindi/Braj have not given Sikh writers adequate attention. The seminal work on these court poets is Piara Singh 'Padam', *Sri Guru Gobind Singh ji de Darbari Ratan*, Patiala, 1976; recently Fenech has touched upon these court poets, see Louis Fenech, *The Darbar of the Sikh Gurus*, 2008; and Mann also discusses Guru Gobind Singh's court poetry, see Gurinder Singh Mann,

'Sources for the Study of Guru Gobind Singh's Life and Times', *Journal of Punjab Studies*, 15/1&2, 2010, pp.229–280.

30. Braj courtly culture bloomed in the seventeenth century; see Allison Busch, 'The Courtly Vernacular: The Transformation of Brajbhasa Literary Culture (1590–1690)', unpublished PhD, University of Chicago, 2003. Also see Rupert Snell, *The Hindi Classical Tradition*, London, 1991; K.P. Bahadur, trans., *The Rasikapriya of Keshavadasa*, Delhi, 1972.

31. For Guru Gobind Singh's anecdotes as told by early modern Sikh chroniclers see Max Arthur Macauliffe, *The Sikh Religion: Its Gurus, Sacred Writings, and Authors*, vol.5, 1963.

32. For Guru Gobind Singh's travels see Fauja Singh, ed., *Travels of Guru Gobind Singh*, Patiala, 2002.

33. For a history of Guru Gobind Singh's court and its evolution see Piara Singh 'Padam', *Sri Guru Gobind Singh ji de Darbari Ratan*, 1976; Louis Fenech, *The Darbar of the Sikh Gurus*, 2008.

34. Jeevan Deol, 'The Minas and their Literature', *JAOS*, 118/2, 1998, p.177.

35. For a history of Amritsar and the Golden Temple see Madanjit Kaur, *The Golden Temple: Past and Present*, 1983.

36. Jeevan Deol, 'The Minas and their Literature', *JAOS*, 118/2, 1998, p.177.

37. The following narrative is dependent upon the detailed studies of Guru Gobind Singh's life, see J.S. Grewal and S.S. Bal, *Guru Gobind Singh (A Biographical Study)*, 1967; Dalbir Singh Dhillon and Shangana Singh Bhullar, *Battles of Guru Gobind Singh*, Delhi, 1990.

38. For the history of the Panjabi hills and Mughal state see Chetan Singh, *Region and Empire*, 1991, pp.137–42; J. Hutchinson and J. PH. Vogel, *History of the Panjab Hill States*, vols2, 1933.

39. J.S. Grewal and Irfan Habib, eds., *Sikh History from Persian Sources*, 2001, p.113.

40. For examples of early Sikh visions of kingship, see Chapter 1 and the compositions of the *Adi Granth* and Bhai Gurdas regarding worldly kings.

41. For a detailed discussion of this contest over the householder-sovereign and the householder-ascetic see Chapter 3.

42. See Brajadulal Chattopadhyaya, *The Making of Early Medieval India*, Delhi, 1994; Norman Peter Ziegler, 'Action, Power and Service in Rajasthani Culture: A Social History of the Rajputs in Middle Period Rajasthan', unpublished PhD, University of Chicago, 1973.

43. *Harji*, p.169.

44. *DG*, vol.1, p.158.

45. See H.A. Rose, *A Glossary of the Tribes and Castes of the Punjab and North West Frontier Provinces*, vol.2, 1919, p.512.

46. *DG*, vol.1, p.65.

47. For a discussion of this Valmiki tradition see Robert P. Goldman and Sally J. Sutherland Goldman, 'Ramayana' in Sushil Mittal and Gene Thursby, eds., *The Hindu World*, 2004, pp.75–96; John Brockington, *Righteous Rama*, Delhi, 1985.

48. *DG*, vol.1, p.71.

49. See Paula Richman, ed., *Questioning Ramayanas: A South Asian Tradition*, Berkeley, 2001; Sheldon Pollock, 'Ramayana and the Political Imagination in India', *JAS*, 52/2, 1993, pp.261–297; Monika Thiel-Horstmann, ed., *Ramayana and Ramayanas*, Wiesbaden, 1991.

50. For this story see Robert P. Goldman and Sally J. Sutherland Goldman, 'Ramayana' in Sushil Mittal and Gene Thursby, eds., *The Hindu World*, 2004.

51. See Paula Richman, ed., *Many Ramayanas: The Diversity of a Narrative Tradition in South Asia*, Berkeley, 1991.

52. See *AR*.

53. Unfortunately it seems most Hindi and South Asian scholars of the Ramayana tradition are completely unaware that the Sikhs produced Ramayanas because in every major work there is no mention of these Sikh texts. But in order to contextualise these Sikh texts in the medieval vernacular adaptations, see John Brockington, *Righteous Rama*, 1985, pp.260–306.

54. *AR*, pp.99–100.

55. See William R. Pinch, *Warrior Ascetics and Indian Empires*, 2006, pp.194–230.

56. For an introduction into the mannerist tradition see the introduction in K.P. Bahadur, trans., *The Rasikapriya of Keshavadasa*, 1972.

57. *SDG*, p.108.

58. Ibid., p.114.

59. Ibid., p.240.

60. *DG*, vol.2, p.792.

61. The four aims of life are duty (*Dharma*); pleasure (*Kama*); wealth (*Artha*); and liberation (*Moksha*).

62. Kathleen M. Erndl, 'Sakta', in Sushil Mittal and Gene Thursby, eds., *The Hindu World*, 2004, p.141.

63. Thomas B. Coburn, *Devi-Mahatmya: The Crystallization of the Goddess Tradition*, Delhi, 1984, p.229.

64. See Chapter 1.

65. For this relationship between sexuality and asceticism see William R. Pinch, *Warrior Ascetics and Indian Empires*, 2006, pp.194–230; David Gordon White, *Kiss of the Yogini: 'Tantric Sex' in South Asian Contexts*, Chicago, 2003.

66. See Thomas B. Coburn, trans., *Encountering the Goddess: A Translation of the Devi-Mahatmya and a Study of its Interpretation*, Albany, 1991.

67. Ibid., pp.13–28.

68. The distinction between the goddess' benign and fierce forms is significant; while all worshippers of the goddess accept her multiple forms they usually accept a specific form to worship. So it is important that Guru Gobind Singh chooses to discuss the fierce forms rather than the benign forms. For background on these forms and their worship see Kathleen M. Erndl, 'Sakta', in Sushil Mittal and Gene Thursby, eds., *The Hindu World*, 2004. For an understanding of the goddess and her relationship to kings and royal authority see Sanjukta Gupta and Richard Gombrich, 'Kings, Power and the Goddess', *SAR*, 6/2, November 1986, pp.123–138.

69. *DG*, vol.1, p.158.

70. Ibid., p.60.

71. Ibid., p.53.

72. See Kathleen M. Erndl, 'Sakta', in Sushil Mittal and Gene Thursby, eds., *The Hindu World*, 2004.

73. *DG*, vol.1, pp.19–20.

74. Ibid., p.25.

75. See Chapter 1.

76. Vedic social order was inherently caste-based. In medieval India and within Bhakti philosophy the *Bhagavad-Gita* represents a text which re-interpreted Vedic social order inside devotionalism; the *Bhagavad-Gita* limited the power of the Vedas for the power of Krishna worship, but maintained a staunch belief in caste and rank. Perhaps Harji also believed in this school of thought, his works do have strong allusions to the *Gita*. See R.C. Zaehner, trans., *The Bhagavad-Gita*, Oxford, 1969, pp.1–41.

77. *DG*, vol.1, p.199.

78. For a range of essays on the history and evolution of the Khalsa see the following anthologies: Gurnam Kaur, ed., *Khalsa: a Thematic Perspective*, Patiala, 2001; J.S. Grewal, ed., *The Khalsa: Sikh and non-Sikh Perspectives*, Delhi, 2004; Himadri Banerjee, ed., *The Khalsa and the Punjab*, Delhi, 2002.

79. Of course this narrative is a 'living' one that has been modified by different authors and Sikh communities since the eighteenth century and will continue to change in accordance to the author and audience. What I mean by this 'above narrative' is that central narrative of creation: that Guru Gobind Singh created this distinctive order known as the Khalsa. And that the Khalsa's creation was something radical. My own brief narrative is an amalgamation of earlier ones, but without any interesting details, only an

attempt at producing a literary narrative for the purpose of this chapter. For a comprehensive discussion of the various narratives of the Khalsa's creation see the above citations and W.H. McLeod, *Sikhs of the Khalsa: A History of the Khalsa Rahit*, Delhi, 2003.

80. For thematic essays on the *Sri Gur Sobha*, see Anne Murphy, 'History in the Sikh Past', *History and Theory*, 46/3, 2007, pp.345–65; Raijasbir Singh, 'Creation of Khalsa and Sri Gur Sobha', *Journal of Sikh Studies*, 22/2, 1998; and Jeevan Singh Deol, '18th century Khalsa Identity: Discourse, Praxis and Narrative' in C. Shackle et al., eds., *Sikh Religion, Culture and Ethnicity*, Curzon , 2000, pp.25–46.

81. The textual history of the *Sri Gur Sobha* has been discussed with further depth in W.H. McLeod, *Sikhs of the Khalsa*, pp.59–61. McLeod feels that 1711 is the more likely date. In order to further understand these textual debates see the introductions to the three published versions of the text by Akali Kaur Singh (1935); Ganda Singh (1967); and Shamsher Singh 'Ashok' (1967).

82. Gurinder Singh Mann, 'Sources for the Study of Guru Gobind Singh's Life and Times', *Journal of Punjab Studies*, 15/1&2, 2010, p.248.

83. Ibid., p.248.

84. See Ganda Singh's essay on Sainapati's background, Sainapati, *Kavi Sainapati rachit Sri Gur Sobha*, ed., Ganda Singh, Patiala, 1996, pp.1–4.

85. *Sainapati*, p. 66.

86. See, Surjit Hans, *A Reconstruction of Sikh History from Sikh Literature*, 1988, for an understanding of pre-colonial Sikh views on Sikhism.

87. *Sainapati*, p.65.

88. Ibid., p.78.

89. Ibid., p.78.

90. For a comprehensive discussion of Sikh code of conduct literature, see W.H. McLeod, *Sikhs of the Khalsa*, 2003.

91. *Sainapati*, pp.78–101.

92. Ibid., p.87.

93. Ibid., p.80.

94. Lower social groups seem to have readily embraced the Khalsa; many of these groups would have been Sikhs before the Khalsa was formed. This is because newly converted Khalsa Sikhs often had conflicts with other rural groups, such as Gujars, due to their new militancy. These non-Sikh rural groups did not convert to the Khalsa possibly because they had no earlier attachment or interest in Sikhism. For detailed analysis of how the Khalsa's creation caused rural conflicts between Sikhs and non-Sikhs, see Chetan Singh, *Region and Empire*, 1991, pp.271–85.

95. *Sainapati*, pp.88–89.
96. Ibid., p.90.
97. Ibid., pp.90–91.
98. Ibid., p.91.
99. Ibid., p.92.
100. Ibid., p.93.
101. Ibid., pp.93–94.
102. Ibid., p.94.
103. Ibid., p.97.
104. Ibid., p.98.
105. Ibid., pp.98–99.
106. Ibid., pp.99–100.
107. Ibid., p.100.
108. Ibid., p.100.
109. Ibid., p.100.
110. Ibid., p.100.
111. Some have argued that Bhakti religions were particularly conducive for capitalist enterprises see, Brendan P. Larocque, *Trade, State, and Religion in Early Modern India: Devotionalism and the Market Economy in the Mughal Empire*, unpublished PhD, University of Wisconsin-Madison, 2004.
112. For this contrast between the Jats and Khatris in medieval Punjab see W.H. McLeod, *Evolution of the Sikh Community*, 1976, pp. 9–11 and J.S. Grewal, *The Sikhs of the Punjab*, 2000, p.46. For an important counter-argument to this dominant narrative, see Gurinder Singh Mann, 'Guru Nanak's Life and Legacy: An Appraisal', *Journal of Punjab Studies*, 17/1, 2010, pp.17–21.
113. See Chetan Singh, *Region and Empire: Panjab in the Seventeenth Century*, 1991, pp.271–85.
114. Muzaffar Alam, *The Crisis of Empire in Mughal North India*, pp.39–42.
115. For example, in 1715 the Emperor Bahadur Shah made all Khatri courtiers shave their beards because he felt that Khatris with beards were pro-Khalsa. See, Muzaffar Alam, *The Crisis of Empire in Mughal North India*, pp.164–166.
116. To the best of my knowledge there have not been any studies on the history of Sikh schools in the modern or pre-modern periods. There is a big difference between run-of-the-mill schools in Sikh temples and Sikh schools with a spiritual genealogy and tradition (*parampara*). Schools with a *parampara* were founded by an apotheosised Sikh and they usually have an exegetical tradition. These *parampara* schools are usually called *taksal* or *akhara*. In 1781, the British orientalist Charles Wilkins visited a

Sikh college in Patna; for his account see Ganda Singh ed., *Early European Accounts of the Sikhs*, New Delhi, 1974, pp.71–73. This account has been reprinted in Amardeep Singh Madra and Parmjit Singh, eds., *Sicques, Tiger or Thieves: Eyewitness accounts of the Sikhs, 1606–1809*, Basingstoke, 2005.

117. It would be necessary to have skills in basic numeracy in order to effectively read Sikh literature, let alone perform more complicated numerical tasks such as accountancy. So it seems reasonable that students would be taught how to count at least in order to develop proficiency in reading. But I cannot be absolutely certain.

118. *Dabistan*, p. 66.

119. *Sainapati*, pp.2–3.

120. The Khatris had a highly refined matrimonial system. For a detailed background on colonial Khatri kinship practices see, H.A. Rose, *A Glossary of the Tribes and Castes of the Punjab and North West Frontier Provinces*, vol.2, 1919, pp.501–526. For a modern account of Khatri marriage practices in Delhi and the Panjab, see Saroj Kapoor, 'Family and Kinship Groups Among the Khatris in Delhi', *Sociological Bulletin*, 14, 1965, pp. 54–63; Veena Das, 'Masks and Faces: an Essay on Punjabi Kinship' in Patricia Uberoi, ed., *Family, Kinship, and Marriage in India*, New Delhi, 1993.

121. See Stephen Frederick Dale, *Indian Merchants and Eurasian Trade, 1600–1750*, 1994.

122. See C.A. Bayly, *Rulers, Townsmen and Bazaars*, 1983.

123. See Stephen P. Blake, *Shahjahanabad: The Sovereign City in Mughal India, 1639–1739*, Cambridge, 1991.

124. For a history on the importance of Persian to Mughal society, see Muzaffar Alam, 'The Pursuit of Persian: Language in Mughal Politics', *Modern Asian Studies*, 32/2, 1998, pp.317–49.

125. See Muzaffar Alam and Sanjay Subrahmanyam, 'The Making of a Munshi', *Comparative Studies of South Asia, Africa, and Middle East*, 24/2, 2004, pp.61–72.

126. For example, in Kashi Nath's 1873 essay on the Khatris he states Guru Nanak was the patron saint of the Khatris, Kashi Nath, 'Khatris', *Indian Antiquary*, 1873, p.26.

127. Patrick Olivelle, 'Hair and Society: Social Significance of Hair in South Asian Traditions' in *Hair: Its Power and Meaning in Asian Cultures*, eds., Alf Hiltebeitel and Barbara D. Miller, New York, pp.11–49.

128. H.A. Rose, *A Glossary of the Tribes and Castes of the Punjab and North West Frontier Provinces*, vol.1, 1919, p. 843.

129. Ibid., pp.755–56.

130. Ibid., pp.755–56.

131. Ibid., pp.904–905.
132. For further details on the ritual of the sacred thread in the Panjab see, ibid., pp.756–58.
133. Trust was an important virtue for the early modern merchant family see, C.A. Bayly, *Rulers, Townsmen and Baazars*,1983, pp.369–426.
134. Jeevan Singh Deol, '18th century Khalsa Identity: Discourse, Praxis and Narrative' in C. Shackle et al., eds., *Sikh Religion, Culture and Ethnicity*, 2000, pp.25–46.
135. See John F. Richards, 'Norms of Comportment among Imperial Mughal Officers' in Barbara Daly Metcalf, ed., *Moral Conduct and Authority: The Place of Adab in South Asian Islam*, 1984; Rosalind O'Hanlon, 'Kingdom, Household and Body History, Gender and Imperial Service under Akbar', *MAS*, 41/5, 2007, pp.889–923 and Muzaffar Alam, 'Akhlaqi Norms and Mughal Governance' in Muzaffar Alam et al., eds., *The Making of Indo-Persian Culture*, 2000.
136. Rosalind O'Hanlon, 'Manliness and Imperial Service in Mughal North India', *JESHO*, 42/1, 1999, p. 72.
137. Military expenditure was an important part of early modern India's political economy, see C.A. Bayly, *Rulers, Townsmen and Bazaars*, 1983, pp.35–73.
138. Muzaffar Alam and Sanjay Subrahmanyam, 'The Making of a Munshi', *Comparative Studies of South Asia, Africa, and Middle East*, 24/2, 2004, p. 64.
139. A prominent eighteenth-century Khatri intellectual and administrator was Anand Ram 'Mukhlis' (1699–1751), see Muzaffar Alam and Sanjay Subrahmanyam, 'Discovering the Familiar: Notes on the Travel Account of Anand Ram Mukhlis', *SAR*, 16/2, 1996, pp.131–154.
140. For a summary of Har Narayan's life see Pritam Singh and Joginder Singh Ahluwalia, *Sikhan da Chhota Mel*, 2009, pp.115–38.
141. Ibid., pp. 165–72.
142. Ibid., pp.115–38.
143. Rattan Singh Bhangu, *Sri Gur Panth Prakash*, ed., Jit Singh Sital, 1984, p.115.
144. Ibid., p.115.
145. See Gurcharan Singh Sek, ed., *Bhai Darbari Das rachit Parchian Bhagtan Kian*, 1991, pp.vii–x, for background on Kavalnain's and Abhai Ram's community.
146. For a biography of Darbari Das see Gurcharan Singh Sek, ed., *Bhai Darbari Das rachit Parchian Bhagtan Kian*, 1991; and Pritam Singh and Joginder Singh Ahluwalia, *Sikhan da Chhota Mel*, 2009, pp.151–64.
147. Quoted in Jeevan Deol, 'The Minas and their Literature', *JAOS*, 118/2, 1998, p.173, f.n.

148. Gurcharan Singh Sek, ed., *Bhai Darbari Das rachit Parchian Bhagtan Kian*, 1991, p.vii.
149. See Chapter 3.
150. Gurcharan Singh Sek, ed., *Bhai Darbari Das rachit Parchian Bhagtan Kian*, 1991, p.617.
151. Ibid., p.617.
152. Darbari Das was not the only great Miharvan intellectual of the eighteenth century – others include Haria, who produced the *Granth Haria ji ka,* and Baba Ram Das (also known as Bava Ram Das), another prolific writer. For information on the lives and works of Haria and Ram Das see Pritam Singh and Joginder Singh Ahluwalia, *Sikhan da Chhota Mel,* 2009, pp.165–89.

5   Critiquing Mughal Power, 1700–1708

1. Many historians have argued that Mughal decline set in towards the end of Aurangzeb's reign due to the growing opposition to Mughal power by various groups such as the Marathas, Rajputs, Sikhs, Jats and Mughal officers. Often in pre-independence histories these insurrections against Mughal power were attributed to Aurangzeb's religious policies. However, in many post-independence Marxist histories, Mughal decline was attributed to structural weaknesses in their agrarian policies and the Mughal administrative system. In recent decades many historians have attempted to inject a greater processual understanding on Mughal state formation and decline; this processual endeavour has been influenced by eighteenth- and early nineteenth-century Persian histories which have undermined the view that Mughal decline resulted in a 'dark age'. For an overview of these developments, see Muzaffar Alam and Sanjay Subrahmanyam, eds., *The Mughal State*, 1998. For more specific studies see: Jadunath Sarkar, *Fall of the Mughal Empire,* 4 vols, Calcutta, 1932–50; Irfan Habib, *The Agrarian System of Mughal India,* New Delhi, 1963; Satish Chandra, *Parties and Politics at the Mughal Court,* New Delhi, 1959; M. Athar Ali, *The Mughal Nobility under Aurangzeb,* Bombay, 1970; John F. Richards, *Mughal Administration in Golconda,* Oxford, 1975; C.A. Bayly, *Rulers, Townsmen and Bazaars,* 1983; Muzaffar Alam, *The Crisis of Empire in Mughal North India,* 1986; Sanjay Subrahmanyam, 'The Mughal State – Structure or Process? Reflections on recent Western Historiography', *IESHR, 29/3,* 1992, pp.291–321; and Andrea Hintze, *The Mughal Empire and Its Decline,* Aldershot, 1997.

2. The 'localised' historiographical approach is a part of the processual endeavour. Amongst recent works see Muzaffar Alam, *The Crisis of Empire in*

Mughal North India, 1986; Andre Wink, *Land and Sovereignty in India*, 1986; Chetan Singh, *Region and Empire*, 1991; and Farhat Hasan, *State and Locality in Mughal India*, Cambridge, 2004.

3. For a comprehensive background on Guru Gobind Singh's court poets and their works, see Piara Singh 'Padam', *Sri Guru Gobind Singh ji de Darbari Ratan*, 1976.

4. Guru Gobind Singh's poets did produce a large volume of works which were compiled in an anthology known as *Vidiya Sagar* (Ocean of Knowledge). This anthology apparently contained original Braj poetry and Braj translations of the Upanishads, Mahabharata and classical treatises on political philosophy, as well as other texts. Unfortunately, in 1705, when the Khalsa were fleeing from the siege of Anandpur, this anthology fell into the River Sarsa. The anthology was lost forever and Guru Gobind Singh was unable to commission any replacement works. Thus we only have fragments from Guru Gobind Singh's court poets. For more information see Piara Singh 'Padam', *Sri Guru Gobind Singh ji de Darbari Ratan*, 1976, pp.56–61.

5. See Chapter 4.

6. In the eighteenth and following centuries the rival Guru lineages did not become completely ostracised from mainstream Sikh society. Many of these rival Guru lineages produced popular saints and intellectuals in the Panjab, such as the eighteenth-century 'saint' Bhai Darbari Das. This is because Guru Gobind Singh outlawed these groups as 'un-Sikh', but he prohibited any coercive measures against any of his family members. Consequently Khalsa Sikhs did not attack these rival Gurus; they often patronised and protected them, though they usually did not accept their views. But as is often the case many patrons had little or no knowledge of what the intellectuals they patronised actually thought. For example, when Gurcharan Singh 'Sek' conducted research on the popularity of the Miharvan intellectual, Bhai Darbari Das, he discovered that local residents were impressed by his charisma, but had no idea about his writings and philosophical school. See Gurcharan Singh Sek, ed., *Bhai Darbari Das rachit Parchian Bhagtan Kian*, 1991.

7. In the eighteenth century there seems to have been very few rival Guru lineage movements comparable to the types of rival Guru movements found in the sixteenth and seventeenth centuries. That is not say they did not exist, but rather they seem to have had limited social and political appeal. Arguably the most significant example of a rival Guru movement came in the early eighteenth century when the Khalsa leader, Banda Singh Bahadur (1670–1716), spawned a Khalsa sect known as the *Bandai Khalsa* (Banda's Khalsa). The *Bandai* sect accepted Banda Bahadur as Guru Gobind Singh's

successor as Guru and adopted a new code of conduct. The Khalsa members that rejected this innovation accepted the leadership of Guru Gobind Singh's widow, Mata Sundari, and called themselves the *Tat Khalsa* (True Khalsa). Banda's execution by the Mughal state in 1716 resulted in the end of *Bandai Khalsa* and led to the triumph of the *Tat Khalsa* as the dominant expression of Khalsa Sikhism. Nevertheless, in the eighteenth century there seems to have been a growth in saint leaders in all segments of Sikh society. These saints were found in the Khalsa tradition, as well as in popular Sikh orders such as the *Udasis*, *Nirmalas*, and *Sewa Panthis*. In the nineteenth century, several saint leaders created rival Guru lineages that claimed direct inheritance from Guru Gobind Singh. Prominent examples include the *Namdharis*, *Radha Swamis* and *Niranakris*. For an overview of this nineteenth-century Sikh development see Harjot Oberoi, *The Construction of Religious Boundaries*, 1994.

8. For an overview of these developments in late seventeenth century Mughal India see John F. Richards, *The Mughal Empire*, 1993, pp.165–260.

9. See John F. Richards, 'The Imperial Crisis in the Deccan', *JAS*, 35/2, February, 1976, pp.237–56; M.N. Pearson, 'Shivaji and the Decline of the Mughal Empire', *JAS*, 35/2, February, 1976, pp.221–35.

10. Chetan Singh, *Region and Empire*, 1991, p.274.

11. For detailed understanding of how Panjab was administratively organised see Abul Fazl, *The Ain-i-Akbari*, vol. 2, trans., H.S. Jarrett, New Delhi, 2008 [1927 and 1949], pp.315–33. Sirhind was officially joined to the Delhi province, see pp.283–314. An important secondary study is P. Saran, *The Provincial Government of the Mughals, 1526–1658*, Allahabad, 1941.

12. J.S. Grewal and Irfan Habib, eds., *Sikh History from Persian Sources*, 2001, pp.113–114.

13. *DG*, vol. 1, pp.92–96.

14. Ibid., pp.94–95.

15. For a general narrative of this era see Hari Ram Gupta, *The History of the Sikhs*, vol. 1, 2000, pp.248–338.

16. There is no Mughal evidence to suggest Aurangzeb made such an oath, but in the Sikh tradition it is staunchly believed that he did. In Guru Gobind Singh's writings there is no doubt he believed he was given an oath by Aurangzeb.

17. See below.

18. J.S. Grewal and Irfan Habib, eds., *Sikh History from Persian Sources*, 2001, pp.98–99.

19. For detailed examination of Guru Gobind Singh's travels see Fauja Singh, ed., *Travels of Guru Gobind Singh*, 2001.

20. J.S. Grewal and Irfan Habib, eds., *Sikh History from Persian Sources*, 2001, p.106

21. Ibid., p.105.

22. In Sikhism, Sikh scriptures are literally the 'Guru'. Each word of the text is considered to be the Guru's limb and the entire text forms his body. For background on the position of the canon in Sikhism see Pashaura Singh, *The Guru Granth Sahib*, 2000. Sikh understandings of scripture and the sacred 'word' is not unique to the Sikhs in South Asian religious traditions – numerous other religious traditions gave the 'word' special reverence see Thomas B. Coburn, '"Scripture" in India: Towards a Typology of the Word in Hindu Life', *Journal of the American Academy of Religion*, 52, 1984, pp.435–59; Cheever Mackenzie Brown, 'Purana as Scripture: From Sound to Image of the Holy Word in the Hindu Tradition', *History of Religions*, 26/1, August 1986, pp.68–86.

23. For background on Banda Bahadur's life and military campaigns see: Ganda Singh, *Life of Banda Singh Bahadur*, Amritsar, 1935; Muzaffar Alam, *The Crisis of Empire in Mughal North India*, 1986, pp.134–75.

24. For general histories of the eighteenth century Khalsa, see Hari Ram Gupta, *History of the Sikhs*, vol.2, 2000; Bhagat Singh, *History of the Sikh Misals*, Patiala, 1993.

25. There were no Khalsa Sikhs in Mughal military service in the late seventeenth and eighteenth centuries. While non-Khalsa Sikhs were enrolled in Mughal service such as the Khatris they rarely held military posts. In comparison, Rajput and Marathas were enrolled in Mughal service and seem to have no issues with becoming Mughal men. See M. Athar Ali, *The Mughal Nobility under Aurangzeb*, 1970.

26. The Khalsa was largely made up of Jats and other Panjabi peasantry groups which had formed the early Sikh community. For general background of the social composition of seventeenth-century Sikhism see W.H. McLeod, *Early Sikh Tradition*, 1980, pp.256–65; for an analysis of early eighteenth century Jat Sikhs see Purnima Dhavan, 'The Warrior's Way: The Making of the Eighteenth-Century "Khalsa Panth"', unpublished PhD, University of Virginia, 2003, pp.87–150.

27. Purnima Dhavan, 'Redemptive Pasts and Imperilled Futures: The Writing of a Sikh History', *Sikh Formations*, 3/2, December 2007, p.117.

28. *DG*, vol. 1, p.94.

29. Irfan Habib's seminal argument that the Mughal economy was facing an agrarian crisis due to a structural flaw in *jagirs* is not borne out in Sikh sources. In Sikh texts from that era and even in the early modern period the Mughals are not criticised for their management of the economy and

the distribution of resources. Sikh sources tend to discuss the lack of social justice in the Mughal Empire; examples of important Sikh works which express these views include the *Dasam Granth* and *Gurbilas* (Splendour of the Guru) literature. *Gurbilas* literature was unique to eighteenth and nineteenth century Sikh litterateurs who borrowed their literary style from the heroic timbre of the *Dasam Granth*. *Gurbilas* texts often explored the historical conditions resulting in the Khalsa's creation and usually they blamed Aurangzeb's religious policies. For an introduction to *Gurbilas* literature see Surjit Hans, *A Reconstruction of Sikh History from Sikh Literature*, 1988, pp.266–294. For Habib's argument about an agrarian crisis, see Irfan Habib, *The Agrarian System of Mughal India*, New Delhi, 1963.

30. The *Zafarnama* has been generally accepted by Sikh scholars as Guru Gobind Singh's work. But it is a matter of contention whether Aurangzeb ever received and read this letter. It is also unclear whether or not the letter is exactly in the form written by Guru Gobind Singh; currently there are at least two variant versions of the letter. For a general overview of these debates see Louis Fenech, *The Darbar of the Sikh Gurus: The Court of God in the World of Men*, 2008, pp.196–97.

31. See Assadullah Souren Melikian-Chirvani, 'The *Shah-Name* Echoes in Sikh Poetry and the Origins of the Nihangs' Name', *Bulletin of the Asia Institute*, 16, 2002, pp.1–22; Fenech notes the connection between the *Zafarnama* and the *Gulistan*; see Louis Fenech, *The Darbar of the Sikh Gurus: The Court of God in the World of Men*, 2008, p.288. The prominent Persian poet, Bhai Nand Lal, was present in Guru Gobind Singh's court; see Louis Fenech, 'Persian Sikh Scripture: the Ghazals of Bhai Nand Lal Goya', *International Journal of Punjab Studies*, 1/1, 1994, pp.49–70.

32. Aurangzeb's great ancestor Timur commissioned a famous chronicle on his life titled the *Zafarnama* by Sharafuddin Yazdi. For a background on the Timurids see Maria E. Subtelny, *Timurids in Transition: Turko-Persian Politics and Acculturation in Medieval Iran*, Leiden, 2007; Beatrice Forbes Manz, *Power, Politics and Religion in Timurid Iran*, Cambridge, 2007.

33. Assadullah Souren Melikian-Chirvani, 'The *Shah-Name* Echoes in Sikh Poetry and the Origins of the Nihangs' Name', *Bulletin of the Asia Institute*, 16, 2002, p.4: the following translations have all been taken from Melikian-Chirvani. They have been taken selectively and do not show the letter in its complete form. Another good translation of the *Zafarnama* has been done by Christopher Shackle in Christopher Shackle and Arvind-pal Singh Mandair, trans., *Teachings of the Sikh Gurus: Selections from Sikh Scriptures*, 2005, pp.137–44. However, Shackle's translation lacks the same verve as Melikian-Chirvani's translation which successfully captures the poetic and

mystic qualities of the *Zafarnama*. Yet another good translation into English from a Panjabi version of the text is that of Joginder Singh; see Giani Ishar Singh Nara, *Safarnama and Zafarnama*, Delhi, 1985, pp.129–136.

34. Ibid., p.6.
35. Ibid., p.7.
36. Ibid., p.7.
37. Ibid., p.6.
38. Ibid., p.7.
39. Ibid., p.5.
40. Ibid., p.9.
41. Ibid., p.10.
42. For this argument see M.N. Pearson, 'Shivaji and the Decline of the Mughal Empire', *JAS*, 35/2, February, 1976, pp.221–35.
43. John F. Richards, 'The Imperial Crisis in the Deccan', *JAS*, 35/2, February, 1976, pp.237–56.
44. Ibid., p.243.
45. See John F. Richards, 'The Imperial Crisis in the Deccan', *JAS*, 35/2, February, 1976, pp.237–56; Muzaffar Alam, *The Crisis of Empire in Mughal North India*, 1986.
46. For instance, the Maratha poet, Bhushan, composed *Shivrajbhushan* (1673). This work has been published see Kavi Bhushan, *Shiva-Bhushan*, ed., Shivanatha Prasada Mishra, Benares, 1953. For background into Bhushan's life and other rebel poets see Allison Busch, 'The Courtly Vernacular: The Transformation of Brajbhasa Literary Culture (1590–1690)', unpublished PhD, University of Chicago, 2003, pp.200–256.
47. In recent years Busch has brought this Braj poetic world to the fore; see Allison Busch, 'The Courtly Vernacular: The Transformation of Brajbhasa Literary Culture (1590–1690)', unpublished PhD, University of Chicago, 2003.
48. The study of courtly culture in medieval South Asia inevitably results in the study of poetry. Poets were always tied to the court under patrons of all backgrounds. For brief overview of this poetic world, see Daud Ali, *Courtly Culture and Political Life in Early Medieval India*, 2004; Aziz Ahmad, 'Safavid Poets in India', *Iran*, 14, pp.17–32; Muzaffar Alam, 'Pursuit of Persian: Language in Mughal Politics', *MAS*, 32/2, pp.317–49; Rupert Snell, *The Hindi Classical Tradition*, 1991; K.P. Bahadur, trans., *The Rasikapriya of Keshavadasa*, 1972.
49. Allison Busch, 'Literary Responses to the Mughal Imperium: The Historical Poems of Keshavdas', *SAR*, 25/1, 2005, pp.31–54. Sanjay Subrahmanyam also briefly notes the importance of Keshavdas's poetry in understanding

Mughal India beyond the monopoly of Persian sources. Yet Subrahmanyam wishes to contextualise this poetry as a cultural source rather than suggesting that poetry is history; see Sanjay Subrahmanyam, 'The Mughal State – Structure or Process? Reflections on recent Western Historiography', *IESHR, 29/3*, 1992, p.319.

50. Allison Busch, 'The Courtly Vernacular: The Transformation of Brajbhasa Literary Culture (1590–1690)', unpublished PhD, University of Chicago, 2003, pp.200–56.

51. Norman Peter Ziegler, 'Marvari Historical Chronicles: Sources for the Social and Cultural History of Rajasthan', *IESHR*, 13, 1976, p.241.

52. Ibid., pp.225–26.

53. For an analysis of political folktales and jokes which are similar to courtly poetry, see C.M. Naim, 'Popular Jokes and Political History: The Case of Akbar, Birbal and Mulla Do-Piyaza' in C.M. Naim, *Selected Essays of C.M. Naim*, Delhi, 2004.

54. For more information of the battle of Bhangani see Hari Ram Gupta, *History of the Sikhs*, vol.1, Delhi, pp.234–38.

55. *JN*, p.3.

56. Ibid., pp.4–5.

57. Ibid., pp.5–6.

58. See Piara Singh 'Padam', *Sri Guru Gobind Singh ji de Darbari Ratan*, 1976.

59. Ibid., p.18.

60. For example, see Surinder Singh Kohli's translation of the *Dasam Granth* and his refusal to translate the *Chritropakhyan* because it is not Sikh scripture; Surinder Singh Kohli, trans., *Sri Dasam Granth Sahib*, vol.1, Birmingham, 2003, pp.xxxii–xxxiv. For a general background on the text see C.H. Loehlin, *The Granth of Guru Gobind Singh and the Khalsa Brotherhood*, Lucknow, 1971, pp.48–51.

61. See Hardip Singh Syan, 'An Analysis of the Chritropakhyaan as Sikh Didactic Literature', unpublished MA Dissertation, School of Oriental and African Studies, University of London, 2007. See also Lee Siegel, *Sacred and Profane Dimensions of Love in Indian Traditions: As Exemplified in the Gitagovinda of Jayadeva*, Delhi, 1990; Catherine Benton, *God of Desire: Tales of Kamadeva in Sanskrit Story Literature*, Albany, 2006; Wendy Doniger, 'Sexual Masquerades in Hindu Myths: Aspects of the Transmission of Knowledge in Ancient India', in Nigel Crook, ed., *The Transmission of Knowledge in South Asia*, Delhi, 2001.

62. *DG*, vol. 4, pp.725–26.

63. This Freudian reading was suggested by C.M. Naim in C.M. Naim, 'Popular Jokes and Political History: The Case of Akbar, Birbal and Mulla Do-Piyaza'

in C.M. Naim, *Selected Essays of C.M. Naim*, 2004. Naim partially agrees with Freud while also attempting to refute him.

64. Norman Peter Ziegler, 'Marvari Historical Chronicles: Sources for the Social and Cultural History of Rajasthan', *IESHR*, 13, 1976, p.241.

65. See Andre Wink, *Land and Sovereignty in India*, 1986.

66. Allison Busch, 'The Courtly Vernacular: The Transformation of Brajbhasa Literary Culture (1590–1690)', unpublished PhD, University of Chicago, 2003, pp.236–37. All the following translations of Bhushan's work are directly taken from Busch's thesis.

67. Ibid., p.237.

68. Ibid., p.237.

69. Ibid., p.240.

70. For biography on Banda Bahadur see Ganda Singh, *Life of Banda Singh Bahadur*, Amritsar, 1935. For an analysis of Banda Bahadur's political and military impact on early eighteenth-century Mughal Panjab, see Muzaffar Alam, *The Crisis of Empire in Mughal North India*, 1986, pp.134–75; Muzaffar Alam, 'Sikh Uprisings under Banda Bahadur, 1708–1715', *Studies in History*, XLI/2, 1979.

71. The early Khalsa army never engaged in pitch battled warfare, they only used guerrilla tactics in order to overcome much larger Mughal forces. For an understanding of Mughal warfare see Jos Gommans, *Mughal Warfare*, 2002 and for Sikh warfare see Arjan Dass Malik, *The Sword of the Khalsa: the Sikh peoples' war, 1699–1768*, New Delhi, 1999.

72. *HN*, p.195.

73. See W.H. McLeod, *Sikhs of the Khalsa: History of the Khalsa Rahit*, New Delhi, 2003; W.H. McLeod, ed., *The Chaupa-Singh Rahitnamah*, Dunedin, 1987; Purnima Dhavan, 'The Warrior's Way: The Making of the Eighteenth-Century 'Khalsa Panth', unpublished PhD, University of Virginia, 2003, pp.198–244.

74. See the various Rahitnama texts in original in Piara Singh 'Padam', *Rahitnameh*, Amritsar, 1974.

75. In Mughal India the subject of conduct was important for political society; see Rosalind O'Hanlon, 'Kingdom, Household, and Body History, Gender and Imperial Service under Akbar', *MAS*, 41/5, 2007, pp.889–923; Muzaffar Alam, 'Akhlaqi norms and Mughal Governance' in Muzaffar Alam, et al., eds., *The Making of Indo-Persian Culture*, 2000; Sajida Sultana Alvi, ed. and trans., *Advice on the Art of Governance*, Albany, 1989.

76. Eighteenth-century warrior aristocracies such as the Sikhs developed new ideas of masculinity; for this view see Rosalind O'Hanlon, 'Issues of Masculinity in North Indian History: The Bangsh Nawabs of Furrukhabad', *Indian Journal of Gender Studies*, 4/1, 1997, pp.61–78.

77. See Muzaffar Alam, 'The Pursuit of Persian: Language in Mughal Politics', *MAS*, 32/2, 1998, pp.317–349.

78. The dating of the *Daya Singh Rahitnama* is not entirely certain, see W.H. McLeod, *Sikhs of the Khalsa: A History of the Khalsa Rahit*, pp.122–33.

79. Piara Singh Padam, ed., *Rahitname*, Amritsar, 2000, p.74.

80. Ibid., p.75.

81. The dating of the *Chaupa Singh Rahitnama* is also uncertain see, W.H. McLeod, *Sikhs of the Khalsa: A History of the Khalsa Rahit*, pp.93–113.

82. For background on the Chhibbar family see Jeevan Singh Deol, 'Sikh Discourses on Community and Sovereignty in the Seventeenth and Eighteenth centuries', unpublished PhD, University of Cambridge, 2000, pp.246–317.

83. Piara Singh Padam, ed., *Rahitname*, p.109.

BIBLIOGRAPHY

Abbreviations

BSOAS – *Bulletin of the School of Oriental and African Studies.*
CSSH – *Comparative Study of Society and History.*
IESHR – *Indian Economic and Social History Review.*
JAOS – *Journal of American Oriental Society.*
JAS – *Journal of Asian Studies.*
JESHO – *Journal of the Economic and Social History of the Orient.*
MAS – *Modern Asian Studies.*
SAR – *South Asia Research.*

Unpublished Manuscripts

Adi Granth, ms.Panj.C5, British Library, India Office, London.
B40 *Janamsakhi*, ms.Panj.B40, British Library, India Office, London.
Bala Janamsakhi, ms.Panj.B41, British Library, India Office, London.
Colebrooke Janamsakhi, ms.Panj.B6, British Library, India Office, London.
Dasam Granth, ms.Or.6298, British Library, London.
Harji Adi Ramayana, ms.Hindi.44468, School of Oriental and African Studies, University of London.

Published Primary Sources

Abul Fazl, *Ain-i-Akbari*, 3 vols, trans., H. Blochmann (vol.1) and H.S. Jarrett (vols 2/3) (Low Price Publications, New Delhi, 2008 [1867–77]).
Abrol, Daya Ram, *The B40 Janam-Sakhi*, ed. and trans., W.H. McLeod (Guru Nanak Dev University, Amritsar, 1980).

Adi Granth, *Sri Guru Granth Sahib Ji* (Bhai Javahar Singh Kirpal Singh, Amritsar, n.d).

Adi Granth, *Adi Sri Guru Granth Sahib ji Satik (Faridkot Vala Teeka)*. (http://www.ik13.com/online_library.html#fridkot).

Ahluwalia, Joginder Singh ed., *Sodhi Prithi Chand di Rachna* (Punjabi Educational and Cultural Foundation, California, 2010).

'Ashok', Shamsher Singh, ed., *Prachin Vara te Jangname* (Shiromani Gurdwara Prabandak Committee, Amritsar, 1971).

Babur, *Baburnama*, trans., Wheeler M. Thackston (Oxford University Press, New York, 1996).

Bala, Bhai, *Bhai Bale Vali Janamsakhi* (Bhai Javahar Singh Kirpal Singh, Amritsar, n.d.).

Bhagat Singh, *Gurbilas Patshahi Chhevin*, ed., Gurmukh Singh (Punjabi University, Patiala, 1997).

Bindra, Pritpal Singh, trans., *Chritropakhyaan: Tales of Male-Female Tricky deceptions from Sri Dasam Granth*, 2 vols (Bhai Chattar Singh Jiwan Singh, Amritsar, 2002).

Callewaert, Winand M., ed., *The Hindi Biography of Dadu Dyal* (Motilal Banarsidass, New Delhi, 1988).

Chhibbar, Kesar Singh, *Bhai Kesar Singh Chhibbar krit Bansavalinama dasa patashahia ka*, ed., Piara Singh Padam (Singh Brothers, Amritsar, 1995).

Coburn, Thomas B., trans., *Encountering the Goddess: A Translation of the Devi-Mahatmya and a Study of its Interpretation* (State University of New York Press, Albany, 1991).

Dasam Granth, *Sri Dasam Granth Sahib: Path-Sampadan ate Wiakhia*, 5 vols, eds., Rattan Singh Jaggi and Gursharan Kaur Jaggi (Gobind Sadan, New Delhi, 1999).

Dasam Granth, *Sri Dasam Granth Sahib: Text and Translation*, 2 vols, ed. and trans., Jodh Singh and Dharam Singh (Heritage Publications, Patiala, 1999).

Dasam Granth, *Sri Dasam Granth Sahib Steek*, 9 vols, ed., Pundit Narain Singh (Bhai Javahar Singh Kirpal Singh, Amritsar, 2006).

Ganda Singh, ed., *Hukumname: Guru Sahiban, Mata Sahiban, Banda Singh ate Khalsa ji de* (Punjabi University, Patiala, 1999).

Grewal, J.S., *Guru Tegh Bahadur and the Persian Chroniclers* (Guru Nanak Dev University, Amritsar, 1976).

Grewal, J.S. and Irfan Habib, eds., *Sikh History from Persian Sources* (Fiction House, Lahore, 2004).

Goswamy, B.N. and J.S. Grewal, *The Mughals and the Jogis of Jakhbar* (Indian Institute of Advanced Study, Simla, 1967).

Gurdas Bhalla (Bhai Gurdas)., *Varan Bhai Gurdas*, eds., Hazara Singh and Vir Singh (Bhai Vir Singh Sahit Sadan, New Delhi, 2005).

Harji Sodhi, *Goshti Guru Miharivanu*, ed., Govindnath Rajguru (Panjab University, Publication Bureau, Chandigarh, 1974).

Husaini, Khwaja Kamgar, *Ma'asir-i-Jahangiri: A Contemporary Account of Jahangir*, ed., Azra Alavi (Asia Publishing House, New Delhi, 1978).

Jahangir, *Tuzuk-i Jahangiri or the Memoirs of Jahangir*, 2 vols, trans., Alexander Rogers, ed., Henry Beveridge (Royal Asiatic Society, London, 1909–14).

—— *Jahangirnama: Tuzuk-i Jahangiri*, ed., Muhammad Hashim (Intisharat-i Bunyad-i Farhang-i Iran, Tehran, 1980).

—— *The Jahangirnama*, trans., Wheeler M. Thackston (Oxford University Press, New York, 1999).

Khan, Saqi Mustaid, *Maasir-i-Alamgiri: A History of the Emperor Aurangzih-Alamgir, Reign 1658–1707 a.d.*, trans., Jadunath Sarkar (Royal Asiatic Society of Bengal, Calcutta, 1947).

Khafi Khan, *Khafi Khan's History of Alamgiri (Muntakhab al-Lubab).*, trans., Moinul Haq (Pakistan Historical Society, Karachi, 1975).

Kirpal Singh, ed., *Janamsakhi Parampara* (Punjabi University Patiala, Patiala, 1969).

McLeod, W.H., ed., *The Chaupa Singh Rahit-Nama* (University of Otago Press, Dunedin, 1987).

McLeod, W.H, trans., *Prem Sumarag: The Testimony of a Sanatan Sikh* (Oxford University Press, New Delhi, 2006).

Miharban Ji Sodhi, *Janamsakhi Sri Guru Nanak Dev Ji*, vol.1, ed., Kirpal Singh (Sikh History Research Department, Khalsa College, Amritsar, 1962).

Miharban Sodhi, *Miharban vali Janamsakhi Bhagat Kabir Ji ki*, ed., Narinder Kaur Bhatia (Guru Nanak Dev University, Amritsar, 1995).

Miharvanu Sodhi, *Adi Ramayana*, ed., Prem Sagar Shastri (Bhasha Vibag, Patiala, 1989).

Nath, Kashi, 'Khatris', *Indian Antiquary*, January 1873.

'Padam', Piara Singh, *Sri Guru Gobind Singh ji de Darbari Ratan* (Kalam Mandir, Patiala, 1976).

'Padam', Piara Singh, ed., *Rahitname* (Singh Brothers, Amritsar, 2000).

Piar Singh, ed., *Shanbhu Nath Vali Janam Patri Babe Nanak ji ki: Prasidh nan Adi Sakhian* (Loeir Mal, Patiala, 1969).

Rose, H.A., *A Glossary of the Tribes and Castes of the Punjab and North-West Frontier Province*, 3 vols (Language Department Punjab, Patiala, 1990).

Sainapati, *Kavi Sainapati rachit Sri Gur Sobha*, ed., Ganda Singh (Publication Bureau, Punjabi University, Patiala, 1996).

Sek, Gurcharan Singh, ed., *Bhai Darbari Das rachit Parchian Bhagtan Kian* (Publication Bureau, Punjabi University, Patiala, 1991).

Seth, Moti Lal, *A Brief Ethnological Survey of the Khattris* (Khattri Hitkari Association, Agra, 1905).

Vidiarathi, Devinder Singh, ed., *Sri Guru Gobind Singh Abinandan* (Guru Nanak Dev University, Amritsar, Amritsar, 1983).

Secondary Sources (Panjabi)

Ahluwalia, Gurmohan Singh, 'Miharvan Sampradae di Panjabi Vartak nu Dehn' in Rattan Singh Jaggi, ed., *Khoj Patrika* (Publication Bureau, Punjabi University, Patiala, 1988).

Bansal, Krishna Kumari, 'Sukhmani Saliasranam Parmarth' in Rattan Singh Jaggi, ed., *Khoj Patrika* (Publication Bureau, Punjabi University, Patiala, 1988).

Giani Gian Singh, *Panth Prakash* (Bhasha Vibag, Patiala, 1987).

Giani Gurdit Singh, 'Adi Granth vich 'Dhunan'', *Panjabi Dunian*, September, 1954.

Jaggi, Rattan Singh, *Dasam Granth da Paraunik Adhiain* (New Book Company, Jalandar, 1965).

—— *Dasam Granth da Kartritav* (Punjabi Sahit Sabha, New Delhi, 1966).

Kirpal Singh, *Manohar Das, Miharban: Jivan ate Rachnava* (Punjabi University, Patiala, 1974).

'Padam', Piara Singh, *Dasam Granth Darshan* (Kalam Mandir, Loeir Mal, Patiala, 1982).

Singh, Pritam and Joginder Singh Ahluwalia, *Sikhan da Chhota Mel: Itihas te Sarvekhn* (Punjabi Educational and Cultural Foundation, California, 2009).

Secondary Sources (English)

Ahmad, Aziz, *Studies in Islamic Culture in the Indian Environment* (Oxford University Press, New Delhi, 1999).

—— 'Safavid Poets in India', *Iran*, 14, 1976, pp.17–32.

Alam, Muzaffar, 'Sikh Uprisings under Banda Bahadur, 1708–1715', *Studies in History*, vol. XLI/2, 1979.

—— *The Crisis of Empire in Mughal North India: Awadh and the Punjab, 1707–48* (Oxford University Press, New Delhi, 1986).

—— 'Trade, State Policy and Regional Change: Aspects of Mughal-Uzbek Commercial Relations, c.1550–1750', *JESHO*, 37/2, pp.202–27.

—— 'The Pursuit of Persian: Language in Mughal Politics', *MAS*, 32/2, 1998, pp.317–49.

—— 'Akhlaqi Norms and Mughal Governance' in Muzaffar Alam, et al., eds. *The Making of Indo-Persian Culture* (Centre de Sciences Humaines, New Delhi, 2000).

—— 'The Culture and Politics of Persian in Pre-colonial Hindustan' in Sheldon Pollock, ed. *Literary Cultures in History: Reconstructions from South Asia* (University of California Press, Berkeley, 2003).

—— 'The Mughals, the Sufi Shaikhs and the Formation of the Akbari Dispensation', *MAS*, 43/1, 2009, pp.135–74.

Alam, Muzaffar and Sanjay Subrahmanyam, eds., *The Mughal State 1526–1750* (Oxford University Press, Delhi, 2000).

Alam, Muzaffar and Sanjay Subrahmanyam, 'Discovering the Familiar: Notes on the Travel Account of Anand Ram Mukhlis', *SAR*, 16/2, 1996, pp.131–54.

Alam, Muzaffar and Sanjay Subrahmanyam, 'The Making of a Munshi', *Comparative Studies of South Asia, Africa and the Middle East*, 24/2, 2004, pp.61–72.

Ali, M. Athar, *The Mughal Nobility Under Aurangzeb* (Oxford University Press, New Delhi, 1997).

Ali, Daud, *Courtly Culture and Political Life in Medieval India* (Cambridge University Press, Cambridge, 2004).

Anooshahr, Ali, *The Ghazi Sultans and the Frontiers of Islam: A comparative study of the late medieval and early modern periods* (Routledge, New York, 2009).

—— 'Mughal Historians and the Memory of the Islamic Conquest of India', *IESHR*, 43/3, 2006, pp.275–300.

Aquil, Raziuddin, *Sufism, Culture, and Politics: Afghans and Islam in Medieval North India* (Oxford University Press, New Delhi, 2007).

Ashta, Dharam Pal, *The Poetry of the Dasam Granth* (Arun Prakashan, New Delhi, 1959).

Bahadur, K.P, trans., *The Rasikapriya of Keshavadasa* (Manohar, Delhi, 1972).

Balabanlilar, Lisa, 'Lords of the Auspicious Conjunction: Turco-Mongol Imperial Identity on the Subcontinent', *Journal of World History*, 18/1, 2007, pp.1–39.

Banerjee, Himadri, ed., *The Khalsa and the Punjab: studies in Sikh history, to the Nineteenth century* (Tulika, Delhi, 2002).

Banga, Indu, *Agrarian System of the Sikhs: Late Eighteenth and Early Nineteenth Century* (Manohar, New Delhi, 1978).

Barz, Richard, *The Bhakti Sect of Vallabhacarya* (Munishram Manoharlal, New Delhi, 1992).

Bayly, C.A, *Rulers, Townsmen and Bazaars: North Indian Society in the Age of British Expansion, 1770–1870* (Oxford University Press, New Delhi, 1983).

—— *Empire and Information: Intelligence gathering and Social communication in India, 1780–1870* (Cambridge University Press, Cambridge, 1996).

—— 'Patrons and Politics in Northern India', *MAS*, 7/3, 1973, pp.349–88.

Benton, Catherine, *God of Desire: Tales of Kamadeva in Sanskrit Story Literature* (State University of New York Press, Albany, 2006).

Bhagat Singh, *Sikh Polity in the Eighteenth and Nineteenth Centuries* (Oriental Publishers and Distributors, New Delhi, 1978).

—— *A History of the Sikh Misals* (Punjabi University, Publication Bureau, Patiala, 1993).

Bhogal, Balbinder Singh, 'Text as Sword: Sikh Religious Violence taken for Wonder', in John R. Hinnells and Richard King, eds., *Religion and Violence in South Asia* (Routledge, New York, 2007).

Blake, Stephen P., *Shahjahanabad: The Sovereign City in Mughal India, 1639–1739* (Cambridge University Press, Cambridge, 1991).

—— 'The Patrimonial-Bureaucratic Empire of the Mughals', *JAS*, 39, 1979, pp.77–94.

Bossy, John, *Christianity in the West, 1400–1700* (Oxford University Press, New York, 1985).

Busch, Allison, 'Literary Responses to the Mughal Imperium: The Historical Poems of Keshavdas', *SAR*, 25/1, 2005.

Brockington, John, *Righteous Rama: The Evolution of an Epic*, Oxford University Press, Delhi, 1985.

Brown, Cheever Mackenzie, 'Purana as Scripture: From Sound to Image of the Holy Word in the Hindu Tradition', *History of Religions*, 26/1, August 1986, pp.68–86.

Brown, Katherine Butler, 'Did Aurangzeb Ban Music? Questions for the Historiography of his Reign', *MAS*, 41/1, 2007, pp.77–120.

Callewart, Winand M., 'Dadu and the Dadu-Panth: The Sources' in Katherine Schomer and W.H. McLeod, eds. *The Sants* (California University Press, Berkeley, 1987).

Chandra, Satish, *Mughal Religious Policies: The Rajputs and the Deccan* (Vikas Publishing House, New Delhi, 1993).

——— *Historiography, Religion and State in Medieval India* (Ashok Gosain: Har-Anand Publications, New Delhi, 1996).

——— *Parties and Politics at the Mughal Court, 1707–1740* (Oxford University Press, New Delhi, 2002).

——— 'The Eighteenth Century in India – Its Economy and the Role of the Marathas, the Jats, the Sikhs, and the Afghans' in Satish Chandra, *Essays on Medieval Indian History* (Oxford University Press, New Delhi, 2003).

Chatterjee, Kumkum, *The Cultures of Early Modern India: Persianization and Mughal Culture in Bengal* (Oxford University Press, New Delhi, 2008).

——— 'The Persianization of *Itihasa*: Performance Narratives and Mughal Political Culture in Eighteenth-Century Bengal', *JAS*, 67/2, 2008, pp.513–43.

Chattopadhyaya, Brajadulal, *The Making of Early Medieval India* (Oxford University Press, New Delhi, 1999).

Coburn, Thomas B., *Devi-Mahatmya: The Crystallization of the Goddess Tradition* (Motilal Banarsidass, New Delhi, 1984).

——— '"Scripture" in India: Towards a Typology of the Word in Hindu Life', *Journal of the American Academy of Religion*, 52, 1984, pp.435–59.

Cohn, Bernard S, 'Political Systems in Eighteenth Century India: The Banaras Region', *JAOS*, 82/3, 1962.

Clooney, Francis X and Tony K. Stewart, 'Vaisnava', in Sushil Mittal and Gene Thursby, eds., *The Hindu World* (Routledge, New York, 2004).

Dale, Stephen Frederick, *Indian Merchants and Eurasian Trade, 1600–1750* (Cambridge University Press, Cambridge, 1994).

Das, Veena, 'Masks and Faces: an Essay on Punjabi Kinship' in Patricia Uberoi, ed., *Family, Kinship, and Marriage in India* (Oxford University Press, New Delhi, 1993).

Datta, Nonica, *Forming an Identity: A Social History of the Jats* (Oxford University Press, New Delhi, 1999).

Deol, Jeevan Singh, '18th century Khalsa Identity: Discourse, Praxis and Narrative' in C. Shackle et al., eds., *Sikh Religion, Culture and Ethnicity* (Curzon, Richmond, 2000).

—— 'To die in the hands of Love' in Francesca Orsini, ed., *Love in South Asia: A Cultural History* (Cambridge University Press, Cambridge, 2006).

—— 'The Minas and their Literature', *JAOS*, 118/2, 1998, pp. 172–84.

—— 'Text and Lineage in Early Sikh History: Issues in the Study of the Adi Granth', *BSOAS*, 64/1, 2001, pp.34–58.

—— 'Sex, Social Critique and the Female Figure in Premodern Punjabi Poetry: Varis Shah's 'Hir'', *MAS*, 36/1, 2002, pp.141–171.

Dhavan, Purnima, 'Redemptive Pasts and Imperilled Futures: The Writing of a Sikh History', *Sikh Formations*, 3/2, December 2007, pp.111–24.

Dhillon, Dalbir Singh and Shangana Singh Bhullar, *Battles of Guru Gobind Singh* (Deep & Deep Publications, New Delhi, 1990).

Digby, Simon, 'Qalandars and Related Groups: Elements of Social Deviance in the Religious Life of the Delhi Sultanate in the Thirteenth and Fourteenth Centuries', in Yohanan Friedmann, ed., *Islam in Asia*, vol.1 (Magnes Press, Jerusalem, 1984, pp.60–108).

—— 'The Sufi Shaikh as a Source of Authority in Medieval India', *Purusartha*, vol.9, Paris, 1986, pp. 57–77.

—— 'The Sufi Shaykh and the Sultan: A Conflict of Claims to Authority in Medieval India', *Iran*, 28, 1990, pp. 71–81.

—— 'Encounters with Jogis in Indian Sufi Hagiography', unpublished paper delivered at SOAS, London, 1970.

Domin, Dolores, *India: A Study in the Role of the Sikhs in 1857–59* (Akademie-Verlag, Berlin, 1977).

Doniger, Wendy, 'Sexual Masquerades in Hindu Myths: Aspects of the Transmission of Knowledge in Ancient India' in Nigel Crook, ed., *The Transmission of Knowledge in South Asia: Essays on Education, Religion, History and Politics* (Oxford University Press, New Delhi, 2001).

Duby, Georges, *The Chivalrous Society*, trans., Cynthia Postan (Edward Arnold, London, 1977).

—— *The Three Orders: Feudal Society Imagined*, trans., Arthur Goldhammer (Chicago University Press, Chicago and London, 1980).

Eaton, Richard M., 'The Political and Religious Authority of the Shrine of Baba Farid', in Richard M. Eaton, *Essays on Islam and Indian History* (Oxford University Press, New Delhi, 2000).

—— 'Temple Desecration in Indo-Muslim States' in David Gilmartin and Bruce Lawrence, eds., *Beyond Turk and Hindu: Rethinking Identities in Islamicate South Asia* (University of Florida Press, Tallahassee, 2000).

Erndl, Kathleen M., 'Sakta' in Sushil Mittal and Gene Thursby, eds., *The Hindu World* (Routledge, London, 2004).

Ernst, Carl W., *Eternal Garden: Mysticism, History, and Politics at a South Asian Sufi Center* (Oxford University Press, New Delhi, 2004).

Faruqui, Munis D., 'The Forgotten Prince: Mirza Hakim and the Formation of the Mughal Empire in India', *JESHO*, 48/4, 2005, pp. 487–523.

Fauja Singh and Gurbachan Singh Talib, *Guru Tegh Bahadur: Martyr and Teacher* (Punjabi University, Patiala, 1975).

Fenech, Louis, *Martyrdom in the Sikh Tradition: Playing the 'Game of Love'* (Oxford University Press, New Delhi, 2000).

—— *The Darbar of the Sikh Gurus: The Court of God in the World of Men* (Oxford University Press, New Delhi, 2008).

—— 'Persian Sikh Scripture: the Ghazals of Bhai Nand Lal Goya', *International Journal of Punjab Studies*, 1/1, 1994, pp.49–70.

—— 'Martyrdom and Execution of Guru Arjan in Early Sikh Sources', *JAOS*, 121/1, 2001, pp.20–31.

Fox, Richard G., *Lions of the Punjab: Culture in the Making* (University of California Press, Berkeley, 1985).

Ganda Singh, *Life of Banda Singh Bahadur* (Sikh History Research Department, Khalsa College, Amritsar, 1935).

Ganda Singh, ed., *Early European Accounts of the Sikhs and History of the Origin and Progress of the Sikhs* (Today & Tomorrow Printers and Publishers, New Delhi, 1974).

Gold, Daniel, 'What the Merchant-Guru Sold: Social and Literary Types in Hindi Devotional Verse', *JAOS*, 112/1, 1992, pp.22–35.

Goldman, Robert P. and Sally J. Sutherland Goldman, 'Ramayana' in Sushil Mittal and Gene Thursby, eds., *The Hindu World* (Routledge, New York, 2004).

Gommans, Jos, *Mughal Warfare* (Routledge, London, 2002).

Gordon, Stewart, 'Legitimacy and Loyalty in Some Successor States of the Eighteenth Century' in John F. Richards, ed., *Kingship and Authority in South Asia* (University of Wisconsin-Madison, Wisconsin-Madison, 1978).

Grewal, J.S., *From Guru Nanak to Maharaja Ranjit Singh: Essays in Sikh History* (Punjab University, Chandigarh, 1970).

—— *Miscellaneous Articles* (Guru Nanak Dev University, Amritsar, 1976).

—— *Historical Perspectives on Sikh Identity* (Publication Bureau Punjabi University, Patiala, Patiala, 1997).

—— *Contesting interpretations of the Sikh Traditions* (Manohar, New Delhi, 1998).

—— *The Sikhs of the Punjab: Revised Edition* (Cambridge University Press, Cambridge, 2000).

—— ed., *The Khalsa: Sikh and non-Sikh Perspectives* (Manohar, Delhi, 2004).

—— 'The Sikh Movement During the Reign of Akbar' in Irfan Habib, ed., *Akbar and His India* (Oxford University Press, Delhi, 1997).

Grewal, J.S. and S.S. Bal, *Guru Gobind Singh (A Biographical Study).* (Punjab University, Chandigarh, 1967).

Grewal, J.S. and Veena Sachdeva, *Kinship and State Formation: The Gills of Nabha* (Manohar, Chandigarh, 2007).

Grewal, J.S. and Indu Banga, eds., *History and Ideology: the Khalsa over 300 years* (Tulika, New Delhi, 1999).

Gupta, Hari Ram, *History of the Sikhs*, vol.1, *The Sikh Gurus, 1469–1708* (Munshiram Manoharlal Publishers, New Delhi, 2000).

Gupta, Sanjukta and Richard Gombrich, 'Kings, Power and the Goddess', *SAR*, 6/2, November 1986, pp.123–38.

Habib, Irfan, *The Agrarian System of Mughal India* (Oxford University Press, New Delhi, 1999).

Habib, Irfan, 'The Peasant in Indian History' [1983] in Irfan Habib, *Essays in Indian History: Towards a Marxist Perception* (Anthem Press, London, 2002).

—— 'Potentialities of Capitalistic Development in the Economy of Mughal India' [1968] in Irfan Habib, *Essays in Indian History: Towards a Marxist Perception* (Anthem Press, London, 2002).

—— 'Forms of Class Struggle in Mughal India' [1980] in Irfan Habib, *Essays in Indian History: Towards a Marxist Perception* (Anthem Press, London, 2002).

—— 'Jatts in Medieval Punjab' in Reeta Grewal and Sheena Pall, eds. *Precolonial and Colonial Punjab* (Manohar, New Delhi, 2005).

Hallissey, Robert C., *The Rajput Rebellion Against Aurangzeb: A Study of the Mughal Empire in Seventeenth-century India* (University of Missouri Press, Columbia and London, 1977).

Hans, Surjit, *A Reconstruction of Sikh History from Sikh Literature* (ABS Publications, Jalandar, 1988).

Hasan, Farhat, *State and Locality in Mughal India: Power Relations in Western India, c.1572–1730* (Cambridge University Press, Cambridge, 2004).

Hasan, S. Nurul, 'Zamindars Under the Mughals' in Satish Chandra, ed., *Religion, State, and Society in Medieval India: Collected Works of S. Nurul Hasan* (Oxford University Press, 2005).

Hauser, Walter, 'From Peasant Soldiering to Peasant Activism: Reflections of a Martial Tradition in the Flaming Fields of Bihar', *JESHO*, 47/3, 2004, pp.401–34.

Hawley, John Stratton, *Sur Das: Poet, Singer, Saint* (University of Washington Press, Seattle and London, 1984).

Heesterman, J.C., 'India and the Inner Conflict of Tradition' in J.C. Heesterman, *The Inner Conflict of Tradition: Essays in Indian Ritual, Kingship, and Society* (University of Chicago Press, Chicago, 1985).

—— 'Western Expansion, Indian Reaction: Mughal Empire and British Raj' in J.C. Heesterman, *The Inner Conflict of Tradition: Essays in Indian Ritual, Kingship, and Society* (University of Chicago Press, Chicago, 1985).

Hiltebeitel, Alf and Barbara D Miller, eds., *Hair: Its Power and Meaning in Asian Cultures* (State University of New York Press, Albany, 1998).

Hershman, Paul, *Punjabi Kinship and Marriage* (Hindustan Publishing Corporation, Delhi, 1981).

—— 'Hair, Sex and Dirt', *Man*, 9/2, June, 1974, pp.274–98.

Houben, Jan E.M. and Karel R. Van Kooij, eds., *Violence Denied: Violence, Non-Violence and the Rationalization of Violence in South Asian Cultural History* (Brill, Leiden, 1999).

Housley, Norman, *Religious Warfare in Europe, 1400–1536* (Oxford University Press, Oxford, 2002).

Hutchinson, J. and J. Ph. Vogel, *History of the Panjab Hill States*, 2 vols (Government Printing, Lahore, 1933).

Israel, Jonathan P., *Radical Enlightenment: Philosophy and the Making of Modernity, 1650–1750* (Oxford University Press, Oxford, 2001).

Johnson, James Turner and John Kelsay, eds., *Cross, Crescent, and Sword: The Justification and Limitation of War in Western and Islamic Tradition* (Greenwood Press, Westport, 1990).

—— *Just War and Jihad: Historical and Theoretical on War and Peace in Western and Islamic Traditions* (Greenwood Press, New York, 1991).

Jones, Kenneth W., *Socio-Religious Reform Movements in British India* (Cambridge University Press, Cambridge, 1989).

—— 'Ham Hindu Nahin: Arya-Sikh Relations, 1877–1905', *JAS*, 32/3, May 1973, pp.457–75.

Jones, Kenneth W., ed., *Religious Controversy in British India: Dialogues in South Asian Languages* (State University of New York Press, Albany, 1992).

Kaeuper, Richard W, *Chivalry and Violence in Medieval Europe* (Oxford University Press, New York, 1999).

Kaplan, Benjamin J, *Divided by Faith: Religious Conflict and the Practice of Toleration in Early Modern Europe* (Belknap Press, Cambridge, MA, and London, 2007).

Kapoor, Saroj, 'Family and Kinship Groups among the Khatris in Delhi' in Tulsi Patel, ed., *The Family in India* (Sage Publications, New Delhi, 2005).

Kaur, Gurnam, ed., *Khalsa: A Thematic Perspective* (Publication Bureau Punjabi University Patiala, Patiala, 2001).

Kaur, Madanjit, *The Golden Temple: Past and Present* (Guru Nanak Dev University, Amritsar, 1983).

Kaur, Ravinder, 'Jat Sikhs: A Question of Identity', *Contributions to Indian Sociology*, 2/2, July–December, 1986.

Kelsay, John, *Arguing the Just War in Islam* (Belknap Press, Cambridge, MA, and London, 2007).

Kharak Singh, ed., *Current Thoughts on Sikhism* (Institute of Sikh Studies, Chandigarh, 1996).

Khushwant Singh, *A History of the Sikhs*, vol.1: *1469–1839* (Oxford University Press, New Delhi, 2004).

Kolff, Dirk, *Naukar, Rajput and Sepoy: The Ethnohistory of the Military Labour Market in Hindustan, 1450–1850* (Cambridge University Press, Cambridge, 1990).

Kulke, Hermann, ed., *The State in India 1000–1700* (Oxford University Press, New Delhi, 1995).

Kumar, Sunil, 'Assertions of Authority: A Study of the Discursive Statements of Two Sultans in Delhi' in Muzaffar Alam, et al., eds., *The Making of Indo-Persian Culture* (Centre de Sciences Humaines, New Delhi, 2000).

Kumar, Sunil, *The Emergence of the Delhi Sultanate, 1192–1286* (Permanent Black, New Delhi, 2007).

Lal, Vinay, *The History of History: Politics and Scholarship in Modern India* (Oxford University Press, New Delhi, 2003).

Lawrence, Bruce B. and Aisha Khan, eds., *On Violence: A Reader* (Duke University Press, Durham and London, 2007).

Leonard, Karen Isaksen, *Social History of an Indian Caste: The Kayasths of Hyderabad* (Sangam Books, London, 1994).

Loehlin, C.H., *The Granth of Guru Gobind Singh and the Khalsa Brotherhood* (Lucknow Publishing House, Lucknow, 1971).

Lorenzen, David N., 'Warrior Ascetics in Indian History', *JAOS*, 98/1, 1978, pp.61–75.

—— 'Europeans in late Mughal south Asia: The perceptions of Italian missionaries', *IESHR*, 40/1, 2003, pp.1–31.

Macauliffe, M.A., *The Sikh Religion; its Gurus, Sacred Writings, and Authors*, 6 vols (Claredon Press, Oxford, 1964).

Madra, Amardeep Singh and Parmjit Singh, *Warrior Saints: Three Centuries of the Sikh Military Tradition* (I.B.Tauris, London, 1999).

Madra, Amardeep Singh and Parmjit Singh, eds., *"Sicques, tigers, or thieves": Eyewitness accounts of the Sikhs, 1606–1809* (Palgrave Macmillian, Basingstoke, 2005).

Malik, Arjan Dass, *The Sword of the Khalsa: the Sikh peoples war, 1699–1768* (Manohar, New Delhi, 1999).

Malik, Salahuddin, 'The Punjab and the Indian 'Mutiny': A Reassessment', *Islamic Studies*, 15, 1976.

Mandair, Arvind, *Religion and the Specter of the West: Sikhism, India, Postcoloniality, and the Politics of Translation* (University of Columbia Press, New York, 2009).

Mandair, Arvind-Pal Singh, 'The Emergence of Modern 'Sikh Theology': Reassessing the Passage of Ideas from Trumpp to Bhai Vir Singh', *BSOAS*, 68/2, 2005, pp.253–275.

Mandair, Arvind, 'The Politics of Nonduality', *Journal of the American Academy of Religion*, 74/3, 2006, pp.646–73.

Mandair, Navdeep Singh, 'Virtual Corpus: Solicitous Mutilation and the Body of Tradition', in Phillip Goodchild, ed., *Difference in Philosophy of Religion* (Ashgate, Aldershot, 2003).

Mann, Gurinder Singh, *The Making of Sikh Scripture* (Oxford University Press, New Delhi, 2001).

—— 'Sources for the Study of Guru Gobind Singh's Life and Times', *Journal of Punjab Studies*, 15, 1/2, 2010, pp.229–284.

—— 'Guru Nanak's Life and Legacy: An Appraisal', *Journal of Punjab Studies*, 17/1, 2010, pp.3–44.

Mann, Jasbir Singh and Harbans Singh Saraon, eds., *Advanced Studies in Sikhism* (Sikh Community of North America, California, 1988).

Mann, Jasbir Singh and Kharak Singh, eds., *Recent Researches in Sikhism* (Publication Bureau Punjabi University, Patiala, Patiala, 1992).

Manz, Beatrice Forbes, *Power, Politics and Religion in Timurid Iran* (Cambridge University Press, Cambridge, 2007).

Mazumder, Rajit K., *The Indian Army and the Making of the Punjab* (Permanent Black, New Delhi, 2003).

McLeod, W.H., *Guru Nanak and the Sikh Religion* (Clarendon Press, Oxford, 1968).

—— *The Evolution of the Sikh Community* (Oxford University Press, New Delhi, 1974).

—— *The Early Sikh Tradition* (Clarendon Press, Oxford, 1980).

—— *Sikhs of the Khalsa: A History of the Khalsa Rahit* (Oxford University Press, New Delhi, 2003).

—— 'The Development of the Sikh Panth' in Katherine Schomer and W.H. McLeod, eds., *The Sants* (University of California, Berkeley, 1987).

—— 'The Sikh Struggle in the Eighteenth Century and Its Relevance for Today', *History of Religions*, 31/4, May 1992, pp.342–64.

—— 'Sikh Fundamentalism', *JAOS*, 118/1, 1998, pp.15–27.

—— 'Discord in the Sikh Panth', *JAOS*, 119/3, 1999, pp.381–89.

Melikian-Chirvani, Assadullah Souren, 'The *Shah-Name* Echoes in Sikh Poetry and the Origins of the Nihangs' Name', *Bulletin of the Asia Institute*, 16, 2002.

Mir, Farina, 'Genre and Devotion in Punjabi Popular Narratives: Rethinking Cultural and Religious Syncretism', *CSSH*, 2006, pp.727–58.

—— 'Imperial Policy, Provincial Practices: Colonial Language policy in nineteenth-century India', *IESHR*, 43/4, 2006, pp.395–427.

Murphy, Anne, 'History in the Sikh Past', *History and Theory*, 46/3, 2007, pp.345–65.

Naim, C.M., 'Popular Jokes and Political History: The Case of Akbar, Birbal and Mulla Do-Piyaza' in C.M. Naim, *Selected Essays of C.M. Naim* (Permanent Black, Delhi, 2004).

Najm-i Sani, Muhammad Baqir, *Advice on the Art of Governance: Mauizah-i Jahangiri of Muhammad Baqir Najm-i Sani, An Indo-Islamic Mirror for Princes*, trans., Sajida Sultana Alvi (State University of New York Press, Albany, 1989).

Oberoi, Harjot, *The Construction of Religious Boundaries: Culture, Identity and Diversity in the Sikh Tradition* (Oxford University Press, New Delhi, 1994).

—— 'From Punjab to "Khalistan": Territoriality and Metacommentary', *Pacific Affairs*, 60/1, 1987, pp.26–41.

—— 'From Ritual to Counter-Ritual: Rethinking the Hindu-Sikh Question, 1884–1915' in Joseph T. O'Connell et al., eds. *Sikh History and Religion in the Twentieth Century* (Centre for South Asian Studies, University of Toronto, Toronto, 1988).

O'Connell, Joseph T. et al., eds., *Sikh History and Religion in the Twentieth Century* (Centre for South Asian Studies, University of Toronto, Toronto, 1988).

O'Hanlon, Rosalind, 'Issues of Masculinity in North Indian History: The Bangash Nawabs of Farrukhabad', *Indian Journal of Gender Studies*, 4/1, 1997.

—— 'Manliness and Imperial Service in Mughal North India', *JESHO*, 42/1, 1999, pp.47–93.

—— 'Kingdom, Household and Body History, Gender and Imperial Service under Akbar', *MAS*, 41/5, 2007, pp.889–923.

—— 'Military Sports and the History of the Martial Body in India', *JESHO*, 50/4, 2007, pp.490–523.

—— 'The social worth of scribes: Brahmins, Kayasths and the social order in early modern India', *IESHR*, 47/4, 2010, pp.563–95.

O'Hanlon, Rosalind and Christopher Minkowski, 'What makes people who they are? Pandit Networks and the Problem Livelihoods in Early Modern Western India', *IESHR*, 45/3, 2008, pp.318–416.

O'Leary, Brendan, *The Asiatic Mode of Production: Oriental Despotism, Historical Materialism, and Indian History* (Basil Blackwell, Oxford, 1989).

Olivelle, Patrick, *Renunciation in Hinduism: A Medieval Debate*, 2 vols (Institut für Indologie der Universität Wien, Vienna, 1986–87).

—— *Samnyasa Upanishads: Hindu Scriptures on Asceticism and Renunciation* (Oxford University Press, New York, 1992).

—— *The Asrama System: The History and Hermeneutics of a Religious Institution* (Oxford University Press, New York, 1993).

Omissi, David, *The Sepoy and the Raj: The Indian Army, 1860–1940* (Macmillian, Basingstoke, 1994).

Pearson, M.N., 'Shivaji and the Decline of the Mughal Empire', *JAS*, 35/2, 1976, pp.221–35.

Perlin, Frank, 'Of White Whale and Countrymen in the Eighteenth-century Martha Deccan. Extended Class Relations, Rights, and the Problem of Rural Autonomy under the Old Regime', *The Journal of Peasant Studies*, 5/2, 1978.

Pettigrew, Joyce, 'In Search of a New Kingdom of Lahore', *Pacific Affairs*, 60/1, 1987, pp.1–25.

Pinch, William R., *Warrior Ascetics and Indian Empires* (Cambridge University Press, Cambridge, 2006).

Pollock, Sheldon, 'The Divine King in the Indian Epic', *JAOS*, 104/3, 1984, pp.505–28.

—— 'New Intellectuals in Seventeenth-Century India', *IESHR*, 38/1, 2001, pp.3–31.

Prakash, Gyan, *Bonded Histories: Genealogies of Labor Servitude in colonial India* (Cambridge University Press, Cambridge, 1990).

Puri, B.N., *The Khatris – A Socio-Economic Study* (M.N. Publishers and Distributors, New Delhi, 1988).

Rinehart, Robin, *Debating the Dasam Granth* (Oxford University Press, New York, 2011).

Richards, John F., *Mughal Administration in Golconda* (Claredon Press, Oxford, 1975).

—— *The Mughal Empire* (Cambridge University Press, Cambridge, 1999).

—— 'The Formulation of Imperial Authority under Akbar and Jahangir' in John F. Richards, ed., *Kingship and Authority in South Asia* (University of Wisconsin-Madison, Wisconsin-Madison, 1978).

—— 'Norms of Comportment among Imperial Mughal Officers' in Barbara Daly Metcalf, ed., *Moral Conduct and Authority: The Place of Adab in South Asian Islam* (University of California Press, Berkeley, 1984).

—— 'The Imperial Crisis in the Deccan', *JAS*, 35/2, 1976, pp.237–56.

—— 'The Seventeenth-Century Crisis in South Asia', *MAS*, 24/4, 1990, pp.625–38.

—— 'Warriors and the State in Early Modern India', *JESHO*, 47/3, 2004, pp.390–400.

Riches, David, ed., *The Anthropology of Violence* (Blackwell, Oxford, 1986).

Richman, Paula, ed., *Many Ramayanas: The Diversity of a Narrative Tradition in South Asia* (University of California Press, Berkeley, 1991).

—— *Questioning Ramayanas: A South Asian Tradition* (University of California Press, Berkeley, 2001).

Sachdeva, Veena, *Polity and Economy of the Punjab During the Late Eighteenth Century* (Manohar, New Delhi, 1993).

Sahai, Nandita Prasad, *Politics of Patronage and Protest: The State, Society, and Artisans in Early Modern Rajasthan* (Oxford University Press, New Delhi, 2006).

Schomer, Karine and W.H. McLeod, eds., *Sants: Studies in a Devotional Tradition of India* (Motilal Banarsidass, New Delhi, 1987).

Shackle, Christopher, *A Guru Nanak Glossary* (Heritage Publishers, New Delhi, 1995).

—— '"South-Western" Elements in the language of the Adi Granth', *BSOAS*, XL, 1, 1977, pp.36–50.

—— 'Approaches to the Persian Loans in the "Adi Granth"', *BSOAS*, 41/1, 1978, pp.73–96.

—— 'The Sahaskriti poetic idiom in the Adi Granth', *BSOAS*, XLI, 2, 1978, pp.297–313.

—— 'Beyond Hindu and Turk: Crossing the Boundaries in Indo-Muslim Romance', in David Gilmartin and Bruce Lawrence, eds., *Beyond Turk and Hindu: Rethinking Identities in Islamicate South Asia* (University Press of Florida, Tallahassee, 2000).

Siegel, Lee, *Sacred and Profane Dimensions of Love in Indian Traditions: As Exemplified in the Gitagovinda of Jayadeva* (Oxford University Press, New Delhi, 1990).

Singer, Milton and Bernard S. Cohn, eds., *Structure and Change in Indian Society* (Aldine Publishing Company, Chicago, 1968).

Singh, Chetan, *Region and Empire: Panjab in the Seventeenth Century* (Oxford University Press, New Delhi, 1991).

—— 'Centre and Periphery in the Mughal State: The Case of Seventeenth-Century Panjab', *MAS*, 22/2, 1988, pp.299–318.

—— 'Conformity and Conflict: Tribes and the "agrarian system" of Mughal India', *IESHR*, vol. xxv, 3, 1988.

Singh, Harbans, ed., *The Encyclopaedia of Sikhism*, 4 vols (Punjabi University, Patiala, 1995).

Singh, Indera P., 'A Sikh Village', in Milton Singer, ed., *Traditional India Structures and Change* (American Folklore Society, Philadelphia, 1959).

Singh, Pashaura, *The Guru Granth Sahib: Canon, Meaning and Authority* (Oxford University Press, New Delhi, 2000).

—— *Life and Work of Guru Arjan* (Oxford University Press, New Delhi, 2006).

Singh, Piar, *Gatha Sri Adi Granth and the Controversy* (Michigan, 1996).

Singh, Raijasbir, 'Creation of Khalsa and *Sri Gur Sobha*', *Journal of Sikh Studies*, 22/2, 1998.

Snell, Rupert, *The Hindi Classical Tradition: A Braj Bhasa Redaer* (School of Oriental and African Studies, London, 1991).

Spodek, Howard, 'On the Origins of Gandhi's Political Methodology: The Heritage of Kathiawad and Gujarat', *JAS*, 30/2, 1971, pp.361–372.

Streets, Heather, *Martial Races: The Military, Race and Masculinity in British Imperial Culture, 1857–1914* (Manchester University Press, Manchester, 2004).

Subrahmanyam, Sanjay, 'The Mughal State – Structure or Process? Reflections on recent Western historiography', *IESHR*, 29/3, 1992, pp.291–321.

Subtelny, Maria E., *Timurids in Transition: Turko-Persian Politics and Acculturation in Medieval Iran* (Brill, Leiden, 2007).

Talib, Gurbachan Singh and Attar Singh, eds., *Bhai Vir Singh: Life, Times & Works* (Panjab University, Chandigarh, 1973).

Thapar, Romila, Harbans Mukhia, Bipan Chandra, *Communalism and the Writing of Indian History* (People's Publishing House, New Delhi, 1977).

Thiel-Horstmann, Monika, ed., *Ramayana and Ramayanas* (Otto Harrassowitz, Wiesbaden, 1991).

Uppal, Swinder Singh, *Panjabi Short Story: Its Origin and Development* (Pushp Prakashan, New Delhi, 1966).

Weiner, Phillip P. and John Fisher, eds., *Violence and Aggression in the History of Ideas* (Rutgers University Press, New Jersey, 1974).

Werbner, Pninia, 'The Ranking of Brotherhoods: The Dialectics of Muslim Caste among Overseas Pakistanis', *Contributions to Indian Sociology*, 23/285, 1989, pp.285–315.

White, David Gordon, *The Alchemical Body* (Chicago University Press, Chicago, 1996).

—— *Kiss of the Yogini: 'Tantric Sex' in South Asian Contexts* (Chicago University Press, Chicago, 2003).

Wink, Andre, *Land and Sovereignty in India: Agrarian Society and Politics under the Eighteenth-century Maratha Svarajya* (Cambridge University Press, Cambridge, 1986).

Ziegler, Norman Peter, 'Some Notes on Rajput Loyalties During the Mughal Period' in John F Richards, ed., *Kingship and Authority in South Asia* (University of Wisconsin-Madison, Wisconsin-Madison, 1978).

—— 'Marvari Historical Chronicles: Sources for the Social and Cultural History of Rajasthan', *IESHR*, 13, 1976, pp.219–50.

Unpublished Theses

Busch, Allison Renee, 'The Courtly Vernacular: The Transformation of Brajbhasa Literary Culture (1590–1690)., Unpublished PhD thesis, University of Chicago, 2003.

Deol, Jeevan Singh, 'Love and Mysticism in the Punjabi Qissas of the seventeenth and eighteenth centuries', Unpublished MPhil dissertation, School of Oriental and African Studies, London, 1996.

—— 'Sikh Discourses on Community and Sovereignty in the Seventeenth and Eighteenth Centuries', Unpublished PhD, University of Cambridge, 2000.

Dhavan, Purnima, 'The Warrior's Way: The Making of the Eighteenth-Century "Khalsa Panth", Unpublished PhD, University of Virginia, 2003.

Hastings, James M., 'Poets, Saints, and Warriors: The Dadu Panth, Religious Change and Identity Formation in Jaipur state, c.1562–1860 c.e.', Unpublished PhD, University of Wisconsin-Madison, 2002.

Fair, Christine, 'The Historical Novels of Bhai Vir Singh: Narratives of Sikh Nationhood', Unpublished PhD, University of Chicago, 2004.

Larocque, Brendan P., 'Trade, State, and Religion in Early Modern India: Devotionalism and the Market Economy in the Mughal Empire', Unpublished PhD, University of Wisconsin-Madison, 2004.

Mir, Farina, 'The Social Space of Language: Punjabi Popular Narrative in Colonial India, c.1850–1900', Unpublished PhD, Columbia University, 2002.

Phukan, Shantanu, 'Through a Persian Prism: Hindi and Padmavat in the Mughal Imagination', Unpublished PhD, University of Chicago, 2000.

Prill, Elizabeth Susan, 'The Sant tradition and community formation in the works of Guru Nanak and Dadu Dyal', Unpublished PhD, School of Oriental and African Studies, London, 2005.

Syan, Hardip Singh, 'An Analysis of the Chritropakhyaan as Sikh Didactic Literature', Unpublished MA Dissertation, School of Oriental and African Studies, London, 2007.

Ziegler, Norman Peter, 'Action, Power and Service in Rajasthani Culture: A Social History of the Rajputs of Middle Period Rajasthan', Unpublished PhD, University of Chicago, 1973.

INDEX